REFORMED THEOLOGY AND VISUAL CULTURE

The Protestant Imagination from Calvin to Edwards

With the walls of their churches bereft of imagery and color and their worship centered around sermons with carefully constructed outlines (as opposed to movement and drama), Reformed Protestants have often been accused of being dour and unimaginative. Here, William Dyrness explores the roots of Reformed theology in an attempt to counteract these prevailing notions. Studying sixteenth-century Geneva and England, seventeenth-century England and Holland, and seventeenth- and eighteenth-century Puritan New England, Dyrness argues that, though this tradition impeded development of particular visual forms, it encouraged others, especially in areas of popular culture and the ordering of family and community. Exploring the theology of John Calvin, William Ames, John Cotton and Jonathan Edwards, Dyrness shows how this tradition created a new aesthetic of simplicity, inwardness and order to express underlying theological commitments. With over forty illustrations, this book will prove invaluable to those interested in the Reformed tradition.

WILLIAM DYRNESS is Professor of Theology and Culture in the School of Theology at Fuller Theological Seminary, Pasadena, California. He is the author of over a dozen books on theology and culture including *The Earth is God: A Theology of American Culture* (1997) and *Visual Faith: Art, Theology and Worship in Dialogue* (2001).

D1518120

REFORMED THEOLOGY AND VISUAL CULTURE

The Protestant Imagination from Calvin to Edwards

WILLIAM A. DYRNESS

CAMBRIDGE
UNIVERSITY PRESS

PUBLISHED BY THE PRESS SYNDICATE OF THE UNIVERSITY OF CAMBRIDGE
The Pitt Building, Trumpington Street, Cambridge, United Kingdom

CAMBRIDGE UNIVERSITY PRESS
The Edinburgh Building, Cambridge, CB2 2RU, UK
40 West 20th Street, New York, NY 10011-4211, USA
477 Williamstown Road, Port Melbourne, VIC 3207, Australia
Ruiz de Alarcón 13, 28014 Madrid, Spain
Dock House, The Waterfront, Cape Town 8001, South Africa

http://www.cambridge.org

First published 2004

Printed in the United Kingdom at the University Press, Cambridge

Typeface Adobe Garamond 11/12.5 pt   *System* LATEX 2ε   [TB]

A catalogue record for this book is available from the British Library

Library of Congress Cataloguing in Publication data
Dyrness, William A.
Reformed theology and visual culture: the Protestant imagination from Calvin to
Edwards / William A. Dyrness.
p.   cm.
Includes bibliographical references and index.
ISBN 0 521 83323 X – ISBN 0 521 54073 9 (pbk.)
1. Christianity and art – Reformed Church – History.   2. Imagination – Religious aspects –
Reformed Church – History.   3. Popular culture – Religious aspects – Reformed
Church – History.   1. Title.
BX9423.A77D97   2004
230'.42 – dc22   2003055814

ISBN 0 521 83323 X hardback
ISBN 0 521 54073 9 paperback

To the memory of Hans R. Rookmaaker and Anna Marie Rookmaaker-Huitker, mentors, friends and models.

Contents

Figures

Preface

This book seeks to explore a way of thinking about God and the world that developed in Reformed theology between 1500 and 1750. It is not only concerned with theological reflection, but also with the mental habits and cultural practices that resulted – with the imagination that developed. The concerns addressed grow out of very personal and lifelong questions: Why have the walls of my own (Protestant) churches always been bereft of imagery and color when the churches of my friends have frequently been crowded with images and carvings? Why has my worship experience centered around sermons and studies with carefully constructed outlines, while that of my friends has often focused centrally on movement and drama? Of course these questions are too large for anyone to answer and even posing them in this way is misleading. But these are questions I *felt* even before I was able to verbalize them. And I have subsequently learned that many other people, especially those with various artistic gifts, have similar discomfort about their own worship experience.

Given that these questions are general and oversimplified, this study makes no claim to answer them. Indeed in exploring the roots of this tradition more general theological and historical issues arose. But the present work may be considered a series of probes that might illumine the context in which present Protestant and Reformed worship experiences were formed. It is addressed to students of this period and pastors and theological students with an interest or background in this tradition. Addressing such questions at this time may be important for at least two related reasons. First the period that I explore, roughly from 1500 to 1750, against all odds, continues to influence large swaths of the Christian population. It manifests itself not only in the aesthetics of worship, which are a primary concern of this book, but also in the way theology continues to be taught and studied and in attitudes toward contemporary culture. Influences from this period are evident, for example, in dominant Christian attitudes toward the visual arts and visual culture more generally – movies, TV and videos.

To Christians nurtured by attitudes I explore, images in various forms are seen largely as entertainment which may be enjoyed or avoided. They are for better or worse a kind of "distraction" from the serious business – the reading, writing and arithmetic – of life. In any case they are seldom allowed to invade the time and space of worship. One result of our study is to show that these views are not "natural"; they may be contested or at least refined. And they carry with them particular assets and liabilities.

The second reason these probings might be important is that most Christians have no clear sense of what this tradition, for better or worse, has contributed to life and worship today. In the culture at large attitudes toward the Reformed tradition – especially in its Puritan forms – are as uninformed as they are negative. Even those influenced by this tradition are frequently unable to specify either the source or the contours of the values they are supposed to hold. And their children are, if anything, even more indifferent to such institutionalized traditions. The historical soundings presented here might then be considered a work of retrieval. They may provide resources for persons to evaluate their own contemporary worship life and cultural engagement. In the light of the so-called postmodern shift in sensibilities and the so-called visual turn in culture, such retrieval is all the more important.

These excursions are necessarily limited not only in the period studied but in the areas explored. Beginning in sixteenth-century Geneva with Calvin, I trace the Reformed heritage through its influence in Puritan England, in early seventeenth-century Holland, and in Puritan New England up to Jonathan Edwards. Other persons and places could easily have been included – Scotland being the most obvious example. But these constitute a central progression in this tradition, especially for Protestant North America, and may be taken as typical and even constitutive for the developing Reformed imagination.

A project like this accrues many debts that I am happy to acknowledge. Fuller Theological Seminary provided support through its generous sabbatical program, and I am grateful to former Provost Russell Spittler for his support. An earlier version of Chapter Four was given in March 2001 at a conference sponsored by the Institute for Theology, Imagination and the Arts at the University of St. Andrews in Scotland, and I thank Dr. Trevor Hart for his invitation and hospitality on that occasion. The Huntington Library in San Marino, California has proved to be an invaluable research home for work on this project and I would like to thank librarians Christopher Adde, Jill Cogen, Beth Green, Susi Krasnoo, Mona Shulman and Anne Mar for their generous assistance. Additionally I have been greatly helped by colleagues and friends whose patience and generosity saved me from many mistakes. Ena Heller, Henry Luttikhuizen, David Morgan, John Thompson and E. John Walford read part or all of the manuscript and made valuable suggestions. They have my deep gratitude. An additional contribution of Fuller Seminary is their support of research assistants Wilfred Graves, Nelleke Bosshardt, and especially my valued teaching assistant Tim Stanley, who was responsible for securing reproductions. Susan Carlson Wood, in the midst of difficult circumstances, did her usual competent job in preparing the manuscript for publication. Kevin Taylor, Sue Dickinson and Kate Brett of Cambridge University Press were unfailingly friendly and supportive through the long publication process. Finally and more personally, I want to express my love and gratitude to Grace Roberts Dyrness for her love and support over many years; and to the memory of my honored professor who first taught me to reflect on the history of art in the context of the Reformed tradition, to whom, together with his wife Anna Marie, I have dedicated this book.

CHAPTER I

Introduction: imagination, theology and visual culture

This book attempts to describe how a way of thinking about the world and God, an "imagination," that was uniquely Protestant, and in particular Reformed, developed from the Reformation to the eighteenth century. The particular focus will be on the interaction of theology and visual culture, and the way this interaction shaped the world Reformed Christians inhabited. Two problems present themselves immediately for anyone foolish enough to embark on such a project. The first has been invariably raised whenever I have tried to describe my project. Oh, came the usual response, did the Protestants have an imagination? For there is probably no more settled opinion on the part of most people, especially those with any sensitivity to religious traditions, than that the Protestant tradition (especially that part associated with Puritanism) has generally lacked what we think of as imagination. It might seem that our findings might run the risk of resembling the meager chapter that Dr. Samuel Johnson claimed to have seen in a natural history of Iceland. The chapter on snakes consisted of one sentence: "There are no snakes to be found anywhere on the island."[1]

The general feeling that Protestants lack imagination is usually connected with the view that this tradition has, in the main, not been influential in the development of the fine arts. To accept the commonly held view, outside of Protestant Holland one is hard pressed to find a part of the world where Protestant influence has been influential in the development of the fine arts in general and the visual arts in particular. Andrew Greeley has recently presented evidence for the continuing presence of this supposed handicap. Greeley claims his research on American Christians found that the worship environment of Protestant churches seems to impede the development of an artistic imagination. Comparing a sample of Catholic and Protestant churchgoers, he found that frequency of church attendance

---

[1] Quoted in Patrick Collinson, *The Birthpangs of Protestant England: Religion and Cultural Change in the Sixteenth and Seventeenth Century* (London: Macmillan, 1988), p. 95.

correlates dramatically with fine arts involvement among Catholics, but
does not correlate significantly with such activity among Protestants.[2] But
that is not all. Greeley developed what he called a "grace scale," to measure people's sensitivity to religious imagery. Respondents were asked to
describe their view of God – as mother versus father, lover versus judge,
spouse versus master, friend versus king. For Catholics again there was a
high positive correlation between a high score on the grace scale (that is
a preference for the first item of these pairs) and fine arts involvement.
For Protestants, it turns out, the more frequently they went to church, the
lower the score on the grace scale! These findings support the assumption
that Protestants seem to lack a particular kind of imagination that is usually
associated with fine arts production and enjoyment.

In a similar study Peter Marsden uncovered data that provide a somewhat different perspective on these matters – one that is directly relevant
to our study. Using data from the 1998 General Social Survey, Marsden
found that conservative and mainline Protestants were *more* likely to feel
that art brings one closer to God – 75.9 percent and 79 percent of these
Protestant groups as opposed, for example, to 67.6 percent of Catholic
and 62.5 percent of Jewish respondents. Even among those who claim to
have experienced art in worship, Protestants again led Catholic and Jewish
respondents 41.2 percent to 18.1 percent and 35 percent respectively.[3] But
as in Greeley's study the figures are reversed when it comes to visiting art
museums or classical music performances, fewer (especially conservative)
Protestants participate in such events. So it would seem that the problem
is not with art in any general sense but with particular kinds of art. There
may in fact be more interest in the experience of certain arts, perhaps those
that represent what might be called popular arts as opposed to "fine art."

WHAT IS THE IMAGINATION?

Clearly the common assumption that Protestants lack imagination begs
the question this book seeks to address. Is it the case that the Protestant
tradition has not encouraged a creative imagination, or has it encouraged a
different and equally creative way of shaping the world? This immediately

[2] Andrew Greeley, *The Catholic Imagination* (Berkeley: University of California, 2000), p. 42; the grace
scale is discussed on p. 43.
[3] Peter V. Marsden, "Religious Americans and the Arts in the 1990s," in Alberta Arthurs and Glenn
Wallech (eds.), *Crossroads: Art and Religion in American Life* (New York: The New Press, 2001); data
is from the table on p. 76. In the latter comparison conservative respondents even led mainline
Protestants 41.2 percent to 38.8 percent. Is this because these identify "art" with "music"?

raises the second problem this study faces: What is meant by imagination? In an important sense, of course, the modern notion of imagination began only with David Hume and Immanuel Kant, after the period this book explores. For Hume the imagination and memory play the role of guaranteeing uniformity to our experience, by maintaining in our mind images that over time tend to fade.[4] Though his writings coincide with the end of the period examined here, they arguably continue an emphasis that characterizes a Protestant way of thinking about the world and especially the working of the mind. In 1748, writing in a Scotland very much influenced by Presbyterian (Reformed) ways of thinking, he argued that a critical part of science involved discerning the various operations of the mind:

To separate them from each other, to class them under their proper heads, and to correct all that seeming disorder in which they lie involved when made the object of reflection and inquiry . . . And if we can go no further than this *mental geography*, or delineation of the distinct parts and powers of the mind, it is at least a satisfaction to go so far.[5]

Kant went further and proposed the imagination, this mental geography, involved the capacity not only to shape our world, but to discover and, if one were an artist, to create symbols of some finality of form that is pleasurable. "The imagination," says Kant, "is namely very powerful in creating, as it were, another nature, out of the material which the real one gives it. We entertain ourselves with it when experience seems too mundane; we transform the latter."[6] As Mary Warnock describes this process: "What we perceive as sublime in nature, or what we appreciate or create in the highest art, is a symbol of something which is forever beyond it."[7] And it is precisely the imagination that connects the object to feelings of pleasure. As Kant puts it: "In order to decide whether or not something is beautiful, we do not relate the representation by means of understanding to the object or cognition but rather relate it by means of the imagination . . . and its feeling of pleasure or displeasure."[8]

The modern usage of imagination then is inevitably associated with creativity and the ability to appreciate, or shape, images that go beyond what is immediately visible, that give pleasure, and that usually are connected

---

[4] See D. Hume, *Treatise of Human Nature*, ed. L. A. Selby-Bigge (Oxford: Clarendon, 1981), p. 9.
[5] *An Enquiry concerning Human Understanding*, ed. Tom L. Beauchamp (Oxford: Clarendon Press, 2000), p. 10; emphasis added.
[6] Immanuel Kant, *Critique of the Power of Judgment*, ed. Paul Guyer (Cambridge University Press, 2000), 5: 314, p. 192.
[7] Mary Warnock, *Imagination* (Berkeley: University of California Press, 1976), p. 63.
[8] *Critique of the Power of Judgment*, 5: 204, p. 89.

with some deeper reality. Modern people mostly believe this is not only a good thing, but that it is an essential part of the way we find and make human meaning in the world. While this study seeks to avoid imposing these views on the past, such modern assumptions will obviously infect any discussion of this subject; indeed it will become clear that the historical perspective on imagination and current assumptions are related.

The most obvious continuity is in the fundamental understanding of imagination: the ability to shape mental images of things not present to the senses. From the first usage of "imagination" in the Middle Ages to the present this has been the core understanding of the word. The massive change which makes our probing difficult is represented in the fact that this function of the mind has been transformed from something negative and dangerous to a universally praised capacity. Much of this has to do with a change in the understanding of "creativity." In one sense it has always been recognized that the human mind can create images that did not previously exist. It can be creative. But, while, in the sixteenth and seventeenth centuries, such creativity is precisely its problem, this is for us its virtue.

Jonathan Edwards, for example, who did so much to develop (or at least anticipate) the modern notion of imagination, reflects this negative view. Writing in 1746 he seeks to counter some of the excesses of the recent religious awakenings. Clearly the mind can make up powerful and moving images of something that is not present to our senses, as the recent revivals had amply shown, but this, he argues, has no necessary relation to the work of God's Spirit. These "impressions which some have made on their imagination, or the imaginary ideas which they have of God or Christ, or heaven, or anything appertaining to religion have nothing in them that is spiritual or of the nature of true grace."[9] This has largely to do with the "creative" character of these experiences. By contrast the real work of God in affections has nothing to do with the emotionally striking character of such abilities, it rests squarely on the promises of God's Word, for God cannot lie. "If a sinner be once convinced of the veracity of God, and that the Scriptures are His word, he will need no more to convince and satisfy him" (p. 223). Edwards belonged to the stream of Reformed theologians who allowed imagination a role in enhancing or highlighting the work of grace. But the idea that the imagination can create the true experience of grace would have been unthinkable for him.

---

[9] *The Religious Affections*, vol. II of *Works of Jonathan Edwards* (New Haven: Yale University Press, 1959), p. 210. He goes on to say such external ideas are the "lowest sort of ideas," since they are generated from the animal part of human nature (p. 211). Future references given as page numbers in the text.

What is unthinkable for him has become for us indispensable. We universally celebrate the power of the "imagination" to deliver us from the bondage of everyday life and live creatively. To take but one example consider William Wordsworth's lines from the end of *The Prelude*. Never have I fallen, he says, to the perceptions of "mean cares and low pursuits":

But shrunk with apprehensive jealousy
From every combination which might aid
The tendency, so potent in itself,
Of use and custom to bow down the soul
Under a growing weight of vulgar sense.
And substitute a universe of death
For that which moves with light and life informed
Actual divine and true. To fear and love,
To love in prime and chief, for here fear ends,
Be this ascribed; to early intercourse
In presence of sublime and beautiful forms.[10]

Not only are love and fear identified with this power of imagination, they are "actual divine and true." Interestingly though this love must be hallowed by a higher (divine) love, this Spiritual Love cannot act or even exist without imagination

which, in truth,
Is but another name for absolute power
And clearest insight, amplitude of mind
And reason in her exalted mood.

While this study will not be using the imagination with its modern celebration of creativity, even these widely shared cultural assumptions are significant for the developments that we are tracing. For the uniquely modern notion of "imagination" can be traced back through Kant and Hume to John Locke and René Descartes who became influential during our period. As Mary Warnock points out, these all share the assumption that to find meaning one has to turn one's attention inward, and examine the contents of the mind.[11] This assumption, in our view, owed an important debt to the characteristically Protestant way of giving the world its contour. Though it is not our purpose to describe the development of modern notions of the imagination, or to trace lines of descent in any precise way, it

[10] W. Wordsworth, *The Prelude*, ed. J. C. Maxwell (New Haven: Yale University Press, 1971), p. 519. The following lines are from page 521.
[11] *Imagination*, p. 13. It is true that Warnock's concern is more narrowly with epistemology. But it may be that this inward turn of Protestantism may have facilitated the increasing preoccupation with the contents of the mind. In this respect, it may not be accidental that René Descartes was a student of William Ames at the University in Franeker in the 1620s.

will become clear that we are exploring some of the antecedents that were later developed in these familiar ways.

We will use *imagination* then in the general sense of the way people give shape to their world, in particular through the images and practices that express this shape. We will be concerned more with what Germans call a *Weltbild* (world picture) than with a *Weltanschauung* (world view), or perhaps more accurately, with what the Annales historians would call a *mentalité*. In the present work of historical and practical theology we will seek to demonstrate how Reformed Protestants, in ways analogous to other religious traditions, developed an "imagination" that is a characteristic way of laying hold of the world and of God that comes to expression in their material (and especially their visual) culture. We will argue that at the Reformation a major shift in the use of the imagination took place. This was both a reaction to and a further development of various medieval devotional trends. Briefly this involved making a clean break with the visual mediation of faith the reformers inherited. This iconoclasm, however, had a positive and not only a negative influence on the developing culture. In place of previous practices the reformers promoted an internalized faith that privileged the ear over the eye, but that nevertheless embodied structures that were in themselves visual. These tendencies influenced visual culture in various ways. This transformation has often been described in terms of a loss of metaphor and the rise of a literal mindedness.[12] But we will argue with Peter Burke that this did not involve so much an abandonment of metaphor as "a change in the conception of metaphor from objective correspondence to mere subjective 'analogy'."[13] The emerging disposition involved a kind of mental and narrative structuring of the world and life according to theological realities, that resulted in a moral and ethical order which pressed into service the practices and objects of everyday life, and that issued in a unique aesthetic. These structuring principles, however, were often invisible, especially in their influence on the developing culture, and so have been misrepresented or, more often, simply overlooked. This mental orientation, we claim, made certain developments in the arts impossible, but it facilitated others. While we seek to correct misconceptions our goal is critical understanding and explanation, rather than simple approbation.

The imaginative picturing and reflection of God will be central in our discussion; for the people of this study the shaping of the world was through

---

[12] As John Bossy puts this commonly held view, a typographical world replaced a sacramental one (*Christianity in the West 1400–1700* [Oxford University Press, 1985], pp. 97–104).

[13] "Strengths and Weaknesses of the History and Mentalities," in *Varieties of Cultural History* (Ithaca, N.Y.: Cornell University Press, 1997), p. 180.

and through theological. Their lives revolved around their relations with God in ways that modern people find difficult to conceive, a fact which in itself may account for some of the incomprehension associated with modern perspectives on this period. In this work of historical and practical theology we explore ways in which theology became effective in the lives and communities of these believers.

PROTESTANT SUSPICIONS

But surely puzzlement over the association of Protestantism and imagination cannot be eliminated by the simple expedient of changing the definition. For clearly the Protestants inherited (and further articulated) a long-standing suspicion toward "image making" – which must be central to any discussion of imagination. In many ways they did not differ greatly from Plato who believed that making images had to do with shadows rather than reality and therefore was inherently illusory. They further shared his suspicion that the faculty of "imaging" fed and watered passions, which are wild and unruly unless kept in check by reason. In portraying only the image and not the substance of reality, Plato says, "paintings and works of art in general are far removed from reality, and . . . the element in our nature which is accessible to art and responds to its advances is equally far from wisdom."[14]

This tradition of suspicion continued in the original usage of the word "imagination" in English, which antedated the Reformation. The *Oxford English Dictionary* gives this primary definition: "The action of imagining, or forming a mental concept of what is not actually present to the senses." From the beginning its usage was associated with the worry that such activity would distract from or distort what was actually present to the senses. The first usage listed in the *OED* is Hampole in 1340: "Travails my soule in vayn ymagynacion." "Vain" and "imagination" were invariably associated in early usage, which well into the eighteenth century had a generally negative connotation. A related word, which often comes closer to modern ideas of imagination, is "fancy." Though it is often used by Protestants interchangeably with imagination, it more properly meant a surface delight in what is sensible, or in the specters the mind can produce. Richard Hooker in 1594 can speak of "Beasts . . . in action of sense and phancie go beyond them [men]" (*OED*). Like imagination it was associated

---

[14] *The Republic*, ed. Francis M. Cornford (Oxford University Press, 1945), x.602, pp. 334–5.

with the spectral or illusive productions of the mind which often, so it was feared, distracted one from the concrete life of obedience to God's truth.

Richard Sibbes, an influential Puritan professor at Cambridge University, writing in the 1620s describes the typical struggle believers had with the "imagination." In "The Soul's Conflict with itself,"[15] he notes that in our search for a well-ordered soul we often feel we lack the spiritual means to persevere. This is because, he argues, we depend too much on the imagination. This faculty, he argues, is nothing else than "a shallow apprehension of good or evil taken from the senses" (p. 178). Because, in our fallen state, judgment has yielded to imagination, we set too great a price on "sensible good things." These stir our affections and in turn our spirits, so that the life of many is nothing but "fancy." This must be counteracted by laboring to bring these "risings of the soul" into obedience to God's truth and Spirit – which reveal to us realities on which our soul can properly feed: the greatness of God, the joys of heaven and so on. In tones reminiscent of Plato he notes: "Whatever is in the world are but shadows of things in comparison of those true realities which religion affords" (p. 180). The special danger of the imagination is to present shadows as though they were real, for, Sibbes notes, it "shapes things as itself pleaseth" (p. 180.) There is another side to the use of imagination, however. Having once regained this divine perspective on things, Sibbes believes, the imagination can be reclaimed: "[The] putting of lively colours upon common truths hath oft a strong working both upon the fancy and our will and affections"(p. 184). Thus can we make fancy "serviceable to us in spiritual things" (p. 185).

So while we will be interested to discover what the suspicions toward the making of images excluded, we also want to ask what they made possible. Indeed we will inquire into the way in which particular images – the light of God, joys of heaven – did in fact structure their lives, sometimes in highly "imaginative" ways. On the basis of this, one might say it is precisely the serviceability of imagination to spiritual things that we will want to explore, both in ways these theologians intended, and, sometimes, in ways they did not.

THEOLOGY AND VISUAL CULTURE

The particular nature of this study involves theological reflection on the visual and material culture of Reformed Protestants, those particularly

---

[15] *The Complete Works of Richard Sibbes*, ed. Alexander B. Grosart (Edinburgh: James Nichol, 1862), vol. 1, pp. 130–294. Future page references in the text are from this work.

under the influence of John Calvin. Though it is primarily a work of historical theology, it will necessarily transgress onto fields occupied by people not ordinarily consulted by theologians: historians of art and popular culture. The multidisciplinary nature of the study will raise suspicions of its own and therefore calls for some explanation.

The period of history we survey, roughly the late 1400s to 1750, is one of the most important periods of religious history, and it is well plowed by historical theologians. But theologians traditionally have focused their study on texts, too often without regard to their social and cultural contexts.[16] Part of the impetus for this study lies in the need to contextualize the theological texts of this period. We want to ask: what was the effective theology of these people? This inquires not only about the theology written in texts, but the theology that actually shaped and structured believers' lives. It is increasingly recognized that an understanding of the use which is made of theological texts is as important for the study of theology as the exegesis or precise understanding of those texts. Obviously, since we deal with a period in which theological questions dominated people's minds (and imaginations!), and a period in which literacy rates were rising dramatically, theological texts play a critical role. For the culture of this time in fact one could say reading theological texts and listening to sermons made up much of what today we would call popular culture. Any study that seeks to comprehend this period must make careful use of such texts. But it should also ask: how did the people read and understand them? And, more importantly, what practices resulted?

It is typical, for example, that Lady Margaret Hoby, a prominent puritan woman living in Scarborough around 1600, read regularly *Foxe's Book of Martyrs* or theologian William Perkins alongside the Scriptures. But it is equally important to read this entry in her diary on a particular Sabbath: "I went to the Church, then I came home and praied [and] after dined. Then I read in Perkins till I went againe to the Church." Or this description of a typical day: "After privat praier I read of the bible: and . . . after dinner, I continued my ordinarie course of working, reading and disposing of

---

[16] This oversimplifies a very complex field of course. An excellent recent example of a correction in this regard is Sarah Coakley (ed.), *Religion and the Body* (Cambridge University Press, 2000). But see also Pierre Hadot, who argues that it is impossible to properly understand ancient texts outside of the (highly disciplined) communal practices which produced them (*Philosophy as a Way of Life: Spiritual Exercises from Socrates to Foucault*, trans. Michael Chase [University of Chicago Press, 1995]). See also Margaret R. Miles (*Image as Insight: Visual Understanding in Western Christianity and Secular Culture* [Boston, Mass.: Beacon, 1985]), who demonstrates that undue concentration on texts systematically excludes the perspectives of what she calls the nonlanguage users (the illiterate, who for most of the history of Christianity made up the majority of the population).

business in the House, till after 5: at which time I praied, read a sermon and examined myself."[17] Her reading was a constituent of a larger cultural world in which church attendance, sermons, private prayer and self-examination all played critical roles. The reading was a part of the devotional life by which she laid out her life and which shaped her world. Her reading no doubt illumined that world, but the structure of that world in turn influenced the ways that she interpreted what she read.

Our method, then, will be to begin our consideration of each period by listening to the prominent theological voices: John Calvin, William Ames and John Cotton, and Jonathan Edwards. Our study of their writing will seek especially to discover the theological impetus behind their attitudes toward images, the arts and visual culture more generally. A focus throughout will be developing attitudes toward the imagination. Then we will seek to describe the larger cultural practices in which these attitudes were reflected, with special attention to the visual elements of culture, and, where possible, what we today call visual art. In the earlier period at least, visual elements at times anticipated, at other times reflected, theological developments. As Craig Harbison says of the early sixteenth century, "due to [its] very suggestiveness art seems to have been an active agent in the formulation of religious thought and feeling."[18] There is no question of course of playing texts and practices, or the visual and aural, against each other.[19] Rather we will attempt to discover some ways these interacted during our period, and the significance of this for understanding their way of shaping the world. The assumption is that theological propositions were influential, though not always determinative, in the ways people constructed their lives, and that this construction, in turn, influenced the direction that theology developed. For example, the antinomian debate in the 1630s in Massachusetts was the result of some very specific teaching about God's working in individual lives. But this debate itself was to have some impact on the way theology developed and, as a result, on the cultural embodiment of that theology.

---

[17] Dorothy M. Meads (ed.), *Diary of Lady Margaret Hoby (1599–1605)* (London: Routledge & Sons, 1930), pp. 97, 67.

[18] Craig Harbison, "Some Artistic Anticipations of Theological Thought," *Art Quarterly* n.s. 2 (1979), p. 85.

[19] Our argument will seek to nuance Walter Ong's claim that the Reformation replaced an oral with a written culture; see especially Walter J. Ong, *Orality and Literacy: The Technologizing of the Word* (London: Methuen, 1982). It will become clear that putting things in these terms oversimplifies the dynamic way that text and oral practices interact. See above all Ruth H. Finnegan, *Literacy and Orality: Studies in the Technology of Communication* (Oxford: Basil Blackwell, 1988). She wants to question the whole idea that "technologies can be taken as self-standing or regarded as of themselves having consequences" (p. 12).

CULTURAL STUDIES AND THE VISUAL ARTS AS
THEOLOGICAL RESOURCES

A focus on cultural developments and especially the visual arts, it is hoped, will provide a window into the reception of theology by the people who read and listened to these texts. Here the work necessarily depends on recent studies in art history and popular culture. In the field of art history there is fortunately a growing tendency to examine particular works of art in their social and religious contexts.[20] This broadening perspective on art parallels, in many ways, that in theology. Proponents of what is called the new art history describe their approach this way:

Unimpressed by the special claims made for art, they ask what purpose it served for the people who owned it . . . Art's subject matter is scrutinized and questioned as to why the poor, or landscapes, or women look as they do in the "representations" art makes of them. Art's economic and political role in contemporary society is addressed.[21]

During our period, it is clear that no separate understanding of "art" is possible apart from its religious setting. Indeed for most of the period the word *art* (Latin: *ars*) was used generally for any special skill or activity that required some practice. An object would simply never have been made for the purposes of aesthetic contemplation alone. As a result individual works of art made during this period are largely misconstrued when they are examined on their own – as is typically the case in modern museum exhibitions. Often the works that survive, since they have been selected according to standards that developed long after they were made, do not give an accurate picture of the visual culture of a given period. Hans Belting, who has done so much to elaborate the multirelational context of images, has pointed out that "holy images were never the affair of religion alone, but also always of society, which expressed itself in and through religion."[22]

To take two examples at random, exquisitely painted Books of Hours from the fifteenth century, or fine prints of Albrecht Dürer from the following century are often displayed in exhibitions of "The Art of the Late Middle

---

[20] To give only two examples from many others, see Timothy J. Verdon and John Henderson (eds.), *Christianity and the Renaissance: Image and Religious Imagination in the Quattrocento* (Syracuse University Press, 1990); and Neil MacGregor with Erika Langmuir, *Seeing Salvation: Images of Christ in Art* (New Haven: Yale University Press, 2000).

[21] A. L. Rees and Frances Borzello, *The New Art History* (London: Camden Press, 1986), p. 4.

[22] *Image and Likeness: A History of the Image before the Era of Art*, ed. and trans. Edmund Jephcott (University of Chicago Press, 1994), p. 3. After the Reformation images became "art": "Images, which had lost their function in the church, took on a new role in representing art" (p. 458). See also David Freedberg, who describes the diversity of responses to images in *The Power of Images: Studies in the History and Theory of Response* (University of Chicago Press, 1989).

Ages (or Early Renaissance)." But the real significance of these pieces for their historical setting does not lie in the occasional beauty that these genres reached, but in the social and devotional trends that they represent. In the fifteenth century, with the rise of printing and literacy, "Books of Hours" or prayer books proliferated and marked an important change, a kind of democratization of devotional practice, that was of great significance in preparing for the Reformation. The prints of Dürer, similarly, were part of an explosion of printmaking that occurred in the early sixteenth century, which made prints available to even the poorest households, and served as one of the most important media in which Reformation debates were carried out and communicated to the people.

Here we have consulted not only historians of art, but historians who examine popular culture. In England this field has been richly developed based on pioneering studies of Christopher Hill and Peter Burke.[23] These have influenced a generation of scholars who have described the life of non-elites, what Burke has called the "Little Tradition," using folklore, oral tradition, ritual and social anthropology. He has documented the various ways in which this tradition has interacted with elite culture, or the "Great Tradition." In America, this kind of study was begun more recently. But here too a growing light is being shed on the everyday life of Colonial New England.[24]

The thick description that social historians have provided has corrected many misconceptions about the period. For example, sociologists have previously argued that the theology (and theologians) of the period exercised a kind of hegemonic social control over the people. But a closer reading of the popular culture of the people, especially the artifacts and images that would have furnished their homes and public spaces, indicates this is an oversimplification. The traffic of influence was, Peter Burke argues, two-way; there was both a rising and a lowering of ideas.[25] Often in this

---

[23] See Christopher Hill, *Society and Puritanism in Pre-revolutionary England* (London: Secker & Warburg, 1964); and Peter Burke, *Popular Culture in Early Modern Europe* (New York University Press, 1978; rev. edn. Aldershot: Scolar Press, 1994).

[24] Burke notes, in general, "The elite participated in the little tradition, but the common people did not participate in the great tradition," though this decisively changed at the Reformation (*Popular Culture in Early Modern Europe*, p. 28). For too long in America, David D. Hall noted in 1984, the shadow of Perry Miller was large, and the history of Puritanism was largely the history of its ministry: "Somehow the Puritanism of the people has failed to attract the social historian" ("Towards a History of Popular Religion in Early New England," *William and Mary Quarterly* 3rd series, 41 [1984], p. 49). Since this was written Hall himself has done much to correct this, see for example his *Worlds of Wonder, Days of Judgment: Popular Religious Belief in Early New England* (New York: Knopf, 1989). In addition to Hall see, for example, Lisa Wilson, *Ye Heart of a Man: The Domestic Life of Men in Colonial New England* (New Haven: Yale University Press, 1999).

[25] Burke, *Popular Culture in Early Modern Europe*, pp. 58–61.

exchange the semi-educated artisan played an important mediating role: those, for example, who wrote and printed the omnipresent chap books or the ballad singers. These mediated between ideas of the elite and the oral performances of the people. Similarly in 1549 Denis Raguenier began to take down Calvin's sermons in shorthand so they could be immediately and accurately printed and made available to the people.[26] Calvin's sermons, like Luther's tracts before him, were widely distributed. The people took them home and read them aloud; the ballad singer incorporated the themes in his songs. It is better to think of this process as a continuing negotiation between the demands of everyday life and the urgings of the clergy. Perhaps the most illuminating notion is that of Lee Palmer Wandel. She argues that one can search for a "resonance" between the teaching of the Reformers and the response and practices of the people.[27] One asks then about the "resonance" people found in the Reformers' teaching with their own aspirations. More precisely how did they put these "resonances" to work in their world? Clearly they often took what they could and, in a kind of bricolage, used elements from various sources to construct their world. But throughout we argue there was a growing shared understanding that structured their world and found expression in the furnishings of their lives, and that, over time, began to reflect a distinctly Protestant imagination.

Reading texts in the context of the social history of the people provides a way into a more comprehensive understanding of a people's imagination. Social historians have sometimes used the term "mentalities" for what we are calling imagination. Peter Burke defines these in terms of collective attitudes that emphasize unspoken or unconscious assumptions and a concern with the structure of beliefs as well as their content, especially as these take flesh in dominant metaphors and symbols.[28] He notes that in the attempt to bridge the gap between the social and intellectual life of the people something like this must be used (p. 162). While an emphasis on mentalities, or what we are calling imagination, tends to overemphasize homogeneity and thus to reify culture, Burke argues this tendency can be overcome. One can correct such tendencies by inquiring into the interests such ideas

[26] Pamela Ann Moeller, *Calvin's Doxology: Worship in the 1559 Institutes* (Allison Park, Penn.: Pickwick Publications, 1997), p. 70.
[27] Lee Palmer Wandel, *Voracious Idols and Violent Hands: Iconoclasm in Reformation Zurich, Strasbourg, and Basel* (Cambridge University Press, 1995), p. 26. Peter Matheson argues similarly that the "civic reformers filtered out of Luther what suited them" (*The Imaginative World of the Reformation* [Minneapolis: Fortress, 2001], p. 63).
[28] Burke, "Strengths and Weaknesses of the History and Mentalities," in *Varieties of Cultural History* (Ithaca, N.Y.: Cornell University Press, 1997), p. 162. He traces the origin of this notion to Lucien Febvre and Marc Bloch and ultimately to Emile Durkheim's idea of collective representation. Subsequent page numbers in the text are to this article.

serve and using these structures as paradigmatic (in the sense of Kuhn and Gombrich), understood as a combination of internal and external approaches that illumine the period (pp. 175–8).

We believe a focus on a developing world picture can be used heuristically to illumine the texture of devotional practices, and thus paint a richer picture of what we call theology.[29] This is especially true when we can focus on particular "representations" that serve metaphorically, often in ways the leaders and people could not have anticipated. John Calvin, for example, for all his positive evaluation of art and painting, could not have known what the influence would be of his tendency to conflate image and idol, and privilege the word as heard, throughout the *Institutes*. But it was the latter rather than the former that became a building block in the mentality we wish to explore. At the same time this tendency itself must be examined in the social context of Calvin and his fundamental motivation – in view of the social upheaval of late medieval culture – to shape life (and especially human behavior) in a way that would reflect God.

During our period then the full meaning of what we call today works of art can only emerge when they are read in terms of the social, theological and devotional world in which they appeared. Alternatively the full meaning of the theological texts will only emerge when they are placed in the spaces and practices in which they were played out in particular performances. Since these worlds are so alien to the modern person it takes a special effort for us to learn the assumptions that would have been widely shared at the time. Needless to say our accepted aesthetic standards were seldom determining factors in the production or enjoyment of images that were important at the time. Ironically, as we will see, the beauty that has caused certain works to survive, in some cases actually served as an impediment to the devotional purposes for which these pieces were ostensibly made. But in other cases – for example the earliest portraits painted in the American colonies – when the work is examined carefully in the light of the theological values that produced it, an aesthetic quality emerges that would otherwise be invisible.

These historical soundings then have the potential of enlarging our capacity to appreciate even aesthetic qualities to which we have previously been blind – that is it may expand even our vaunted modern imagination. At the very least, it is hoped, the study will serve to enrich our understanding of this faculty and its role not only in art but also in theology and worship.

---

[29] Garrett Green has argued recently that this paradigmatic function is how in fact theology works in structuring the lives of believers; see *Imagining God: Theology and the Religious Imagination* (Grand Rapids, Mich.: Eerdmans, 1989).

A more thickly described and contextualized understanding of theology and theological texts, it is further hoped, will alert us to the way theology continues to function in ways we do not realize and, occasionally, do not intend. Amidst the current rediscovery of visual arts among Protestants, these developments of pastoral theology may serve to provide instruction – both encouragement and caution – about the habits and attitudes Reformed Protestants developed toward their visual environment.

CHAPTER 2

Medieval faith and the ambiguity of sight

Sometime in the last decade of the fifteenth century, William Farel, the future Swiss reformer, accompanied his family on a pilgrimage to a relic of the Holy Cross in a mountain not far from Tallard, in the Diocese of Gap, Farel's hometown. Recounting the experience later, the Reformer Farel shudders to think of this first experience with idolatry:

When I think about what I was then, I am horrified: The Hours, the prayers, the divine services that I made there and was made to perform at the cross, and similar things against the commandment of God. And if Satan was not blinding my eyes, that which I was doing and what I saw should have shown me and made me realize how far I had strayed from the right path.

Farel could not have been more than 10 when this happened ("I was very small, barely able to read"), but thirty years later the details are engraved on his memory – the crowds, the priests' stories of the miracles, even the color and texture of the cross. What is especially painful to him is the faith he had in these things and that of his parents, who, he notes, "believed everything."[1]

When Farel writes this, in the 1520s, all such physical and visible mediations of faith – the pilgrimages, the relics, and the so-called miracles associated with such things – to his mind, belonged to an era that was past. John Calvin similarly recalls with disgust the practice, he watched as a boy, of the people carrying images around his parish on the feast of Stephen. All the images, he recalls, were adorned with garlands and necklaces, even those who were the murderers of Stephen. So the old women seeing these thought they were companions of Stephen.[2] For the Reformers, the very

---

[1] Guillaume Farel, *Du vray usage de la croix* ([1530] Geneva: Imprimerie de Jules-Guillaume Fick, new edn, 1865), pp. 146, 149.

[2] "An Inventory of Relics," in Henry Beveridge (ed.), *Tracts and Treatises on the Reformation of the Church* (Edinburgh: Oliver & Boyd, 1958), p. 341. For Calvin it appears the confusion of the event caused the most consternation (he says "So all was mixed up"), underlining Calvin's insistence that

existence of such things testified to the blindness of medieval believers to the message of the gospel.

At the same time Farel took his first pilgrimage, Geiler von Kaysersberg was making very different use of such pious practices, and especially, of the cheap devotional images that were proliferating during this time. As preacher in the Cathedral of Strasbourg he drew crowds who came to admire his piety and his preaching. He was always careful to kneel and recite the Ave Maria before mounting the pulpit to preach. At times he would carry a woodcut with him into the pulpit, explaining to his audience: "If you cannot read, then take a picture of paper where Mary and Elizabeth are depicted as they meet each other, you buy it for a penny. Look at it and think how happy they had been, and of good things . . . Thereafter show yourself to them in an outer reveration [*sic*], kiss the image on the paper, bow in front of the image, kneel before it . . ."[3]

That Geiler should approve of such practices is especially interesting in the light of his role as an early reformer. After coming to Strasbourg as the Cathedral Preacher in 1478, where he stayed until his death in 1510, he was fearless in taking on abuses especially of the monks and priests and the desecration of cathedral services.[4] Geiler, like the major reformers after him, was very concerned with teaching the common people. He assumed they knew little about the Christian faith and so wanted to use any means available to instruct them in the truth.[5] While he was concerned with the abuses of medieval worship practices, he wished them to be reformed rather than abolished. Indeed one might say the use of images he described above was developed in the service of teaching and reform. Although an important figure in late medieval reform, unlike Farel and Calvin, Geiler's

such things were useless for the orderly teaching of what is true. As Calvin (b. 1509) was twenty years younger than Farel so this reminiscence must have been at least a decade after Farel's.

[3] Quoted in Sixten Ringbom, *Icon to Narrative: The Rise of the Dramatic Close-Up in Fifteenth Century Devotional Painting* (Abo, Finland: Abo Academi, 1965), Acta Academiae Aboensis, series A, 31/1, p. 29n40; after O. Clemen, *Die Volksfrömmigkeit des ausgehenden Mittelalters*, Studien zur religiösen volkskunde 3 (Dresden and Leipzig, 1937), p. 14.

[4] Murray and Marian Cowie translate an important letter written by Strasbourg humanist Peter Schott on behalf of Geiler to the papal nuncio Emmerich Kemel, probably around 1483 ("Geiler von Kaisersberg and Abuses in 15th c. Strassburg," *Studies in Philology* 58 (1961), pp. 483–95). The abuses Schott lists include the monks taking more into the monasteries than was allowed, tolls exacted from clergy, disruption of services by bawdy songs (sung from behind statues), and the mayor hearing cases in the Cathedral while services are going on.

[5] E. Jane Douglass notes that it would not be accurate simply to refer to Geiler as a reformer, *tout simple*, though he did play a role in the Reform, especially, through his influence on people like Jacob Sturm. His writings were placed on the Index during the 1490s. See *Justification in Late Medieval Preaching: A Study of John Geiler of Kaisersberg* (Leiden: E. J. Brill, 1966), pp. 13–14 and 205–8; she discusses his concern for teaching the common people on page 32.

idea of reform was one of manner rather than substance; it does not portend the radical imaginative upheaval that the reactions of Farel and Calvin precipitated.

These incidents illustrate two very different reactions to the growth (and, both would agree, the abuses) of popular piety in the later Middle Ages. Their depth of feeling, their setting in their own cultural situation and in the Christian tradition, will all be important for us to reflect upon. The differences of their responses, moreover, reflect tensions that had run through the Christian tradition since the time of the apostles – indeed that in some cases preexisted this tradition, and that would break into the open in the early sixteenth century. It is critical to understand something of these preexisting tensions to properly assess the changes (and continuities) featured in the Reformation. For they reflect not only divergent views of worship practices, but more fundamentally different convictions about the ability of the human mind to experience God and, we will argue, give shape to the world. In this chapter we review some of the precedents for these very different ways of imagining God's relation to the world. We will argue that the understanding of "vision" that comes from Augustine provides both the general framework for understanding God and the devotional practices which developed in the Middle Ages, and an important backdrop for understanding the Reformation. Because of this shared framework we will question two commonly held assumptions about the Reformation: that it represented a shift from a "visual" to an "aural" spirituality; and that it proposed simply an inner appropriation of spiritual reality over against the external piety of the medieval period. Rather we will argue in the conclusion that the particular developments of late medieval devotional practices, and the preaching of the reformers, fundamentally challenged the imaginative world in which believers lived and stimulated some to actively dismantle that world and to reconstruct it with different materials.

THE MEDIEVAL USES OF VISION

The pilgrimages and processions, which the Reformers recall, reflect a long-standing view of the way the sacred comes to expression in the world. Geiler von Kaysersberg, for his part, was reflecting an honored tradition in which images were placed in the service both of teaching and worship. Both the symbolic potential of the physical world, and the role of vision in comprehending these symbols, had been shaped by the thinking of Augustine of Hippo around 400 AD, and by the pastoral practices that grew up under his influence in the succeeding centuries. In his work *On Christian*

Doctrine, Augustine described the relationship between the world and God that would become influential throughout the Middle Ages. He notes that "all doctrine (or teaching) concerns either things or signs, but things are learned by signs." A sign is a thing that causes us to think of something beyond the impression the thing itself makes on the senses. Further, he argued, God has made reality in such a way that things can become signs and these signs can reflect – and even lead us to – the God who is our true home. But to return to our "native country," Augustine notes, we should use this world, in order to "employ it in obtaining that which you love." One does this by seeing the objects of this world as signs: "So that the 'invisible things' of God . . . may be seen, that is, so that by means of corporal and temporal things we may comprehend the eternal and spiritual."[6] Augustine recognized, of course, the danger of idolatry, which is mistaking the sign for that divinity to which it points. "He is a slave to a sign who uses or worships a significant thing without knowing what it signifies. But he who uses or venerates a useful sign divinely instituted whose signifying force he understands does not venerate what he sees and what passes away but rather that to which all such things are to be referred." Such a man, Augustine argues, "is spiritual and free."[7]

In a later work, *De genesi ad litteram* (probably completed after 420), Augustine distinguished the kinds of human vision that are appropriate to this sign-filled view of creation.[8] There are, he argues, three ways in which it can be said humans see: corporal, spiritual and intellectual. The first is the level of sight when things are physically present – this is sight of things themselves "by which we see the letters"; a second level, "through the spirit, by which we think of our neighbor even when he is absent," is the recollection of objects not present at the moment of perception, and which are given a verbal description or are in memory – that is appropriated by signs; the final and highest form is intellectual vision, which is the perception of abstract entities – "through an intuition of the mind, by which we see and understand love itself."[9] Augustine here lays out for medieval thinkers

---

[6] *On Christian Doctrine,* trans. by D. W. Robertson Jr. (New York: Library of Liberal Arts, 1958), bk. 1, ch. ii–iv, pp. 8, 10.

[7] Ibid., bk iii, ch. ix, pp. 86, 87.

[8] Augustine, *The Literal Meaning of Genesis,* trans. by John H. Taylor (New York: Newman Press, 1982), bk. xii, chs. 1–30; see esp. ch. 6:15.

[9] Ibid. 6:15. It is clear that what we call now imagination is dependent on memory to do its work, even in its "creative" capacities. See Gerard O'Daly, *Augustine's Philosophy of Mind* (Berkeley: University of California Press, 1987), pp. 106–13. This hierarchy led Augustine to subordinate physical sight to intellectual comprehension – and, inevitably, image to word. See William J. Diebold, *Word and Image: An Introduction to Early Medieval Art* (Boulder: Westview, 2000), p. 106. Diebold shows that even at this stage the relation between word and image was complex.

the way sight is capable of grasping, at least analogically and symbolically, the divine reality that lies behind the visible world. The latter for its part has been fashioned by God to accommodate itself to the proper use of human vision. Notice in this intellectual and spiritual process sight is given a prominent place. Indeed already in antiquity it was considered the highest of the senses. But the physical sight was valued primarily as a way station *en route* to a higher (spiritual and finally intellectual) vision. As Augustine says concluding this section: "If . . . we think of some corporeal image, it is not love that we behold."

As important as the theological framework are the practices that grew up as this theology encountered the pagan faiths of Europe. Churchmen during the early Middle Ages were regularly confronted with amulets and talismans which pagans believed communicated power and, often, healing. What were Christians, who were taught by Augustine that the world was filled with signs of God's power, to make of these practices? Most missionaries of this era came to see them as an "opportunity to be seized and savored."[10] Even St. Colomba (d. 597) of Iona, known for his encounters with the local magicians, carried with him a "white stone" which had featured in one of his miracles. For him this relic had become a vehicle of God's power. Colomba would probably have called this object a "cretair" which was the Old Irish word for "amulet or talisman," but which, in a fascinating semantic shift, had come to mean "a Christian relic."[11] The pastoral practice this represented was given support in the famous letter of Pope Gregory the Great to the English mission in 601. There he gave careful advice to his missionaries:

The idol temples of that [English] race should by no means be destroyed, but only the idols in them. Take holy water and sprinkle it in these shrines, build altars and place relics in them. For if the shrines are well built, it is essential that they should be changed from the worship of devils to the service of the true God. When this people see that their shrines are not destroyed they will be able to banish error from their hearts and be more ready to come to the places they are familiar with, but now recognizing and worshipping the true God.[12]

Preserving the outward form was important to Gregory. Later in the letter he even encouraged them to form their own equivalent to pagan sacrifices, slaughtering animals to the "praise of God." "Thus while some outward

[10] Richard Fletcher, *The Barbarian Conversion: From Paganism to Christianity* (New York: Henry Holt, 1997), p. 251.
[11] Ibid.
[12] *Bede's Ecclesiastical History*, I, 30, ed. Bertram Colgrave and R. A. B. Mynors (Oxford: Clarendon Press, 1969), p. 107.

rejoicings are preserved, they will be able more easily to share in inward rejoicings."[13]

So the external object became a means of stimulating the inward "vision" of God's presence. This understanding of the relic transformed the pagan use of the amulet. Still a mediation of power, for the Christian believer it became a symbol of a new understanding of spiritual geography. For late Roman people, Peter Brown notes, there was an unbridgeable gulf fixed between this world and the spiritual upper world.[14] The martyr and the saint redrew that map, opening this world to the intervention of God's merciful presence. The relic soon became a detached fragment of this spiritual linkage; people began pilgrimages to martyrs' graves or the site of their relics, where, now, altars had been built. Brown notes that relics did more than the amulets could ever have done to serve the diffusion of the holy.

More than simply allowing these practices, Gregory believed relics and images had positive value in helping people understand the "true God." In another, equally famous letter, Gregory stresses the value of images in teaching. Writing to Bishop Serenus of Marseilles in 600 (who had been inclined to destroy such images), Gregory explained that what Scripture was to those who read, pictures can become to the uneducated who look at them. Clearly the concern for Serenus was idolatry. Gregory, for his part, worried that Serenus' iconoclastic zeal might be counterproductive ("Say, brother, what priest has ever been heard of as doing this?"). Gregory explains: "it is one thing to worship a picture, another to learn from the story depicted what should be worshiped. For what a book (*scriptura*) is to those who read, a picture (*pictura*) presents to the uneducated who observe, since in it the unlearned see what they ought to follow, and in it those who know no letters can read."[15]

Clearly, even at this stage, the use of images represents a concession to those who cannot come to the truth in other ways – for example in reading Scripture for themselves. Though both Augustine and Gregory allowed a role for images, these were a means to a higher intellectual apprehension. This led to a persistent worry over images, especially in the West – as Gregory's exchange with Serenus illustrates. Meanwhile in the seventh-century East the superstitious practices had become so blatant that a council was called in Constantinople in 754. From these proceedings it is clear

---

[13] Ibid., p. 109.
[14] Peter Brown, *The Cult of the Saints: Its Rise and Function in Latin Christianity* (University of Chicago Press, 1981), pp. 2–5; and for what follows, pp. 86–90.
[15] *Nicene and Post-Nicene Fathers*, series 2 (New York: Scribners, 1900), vol. XII, p. 53.

that the worry was these images would detract from the centrality of the Eucharist. So the council decreed:

The only admissible figure of the humanity of Christ . . . is the bread and wine in the holy Supper. This and no other form, this and no other type, has he chosen to represent his incarnation . . . And as the body of Christ is made divine, so also this figure of the body of Christ, the bread, is made divine by the descent of the Holy Spirit.[16]

Around this time a completely different reading of Christ's incarnation was being described by a monk living near Jerusalem, John of Damascus (d. 750), that would mark subsequent developments in the Eastern Church. In his First Apology John wrote that:

I adore three persons: God the Father, God the Son made flesh, and God the Holy Spirit, one God. I do not adore the creation rather than the Creator, but I adore the one who became a creature, who was formed as I was, who clothed Himself in creation without weakening or departing from his divinity.[17]

Since he became flesh to renew our flesh, John says:

When the invisible One becomes visible to flesh, you may then draw His likeness. When He who is bodiless and without form . . . empties Himself and takes the form of a servant in substance and in stature and is found in a body of flesh, then you may draw His image and show it to anyone willing to gaze upon it. (Par. 8, p. 18)

He follows Augustine by noting that as visible things are corporeal models which can be used to understand intangible things, so we "are able to construct understandable analogies . . . by making an image using what is common to nature and so bring within our reach that for which we long but are unable to see" (par. 11, p. 20). Finally, this means that, though we use all our senses to produce worthy images of Him, we especially "sanctify the noblest of the senses, that of sight. For just as words edify the ear, so also the image stimulates the eye . . . it brings us understanding" (par. 17, p. 25).

These theological grounds were to be further elaborated in the Second Council of Nicea in 787, which settled, at least for the Eastern Church, the iconoclastic struggles of the preceding century. There the orthodox view of images triumphed: based on the teachings of the Fathers, icons are to be

[16] Ibid., vol. xiv, p. 544.
[17] St. John of Damascus, "First Apology of St. John of Damascus against Those who attack the Divine Images," in *On the Divine Images: Three Apologies against those who attack Divine Images*, trans. David Anderson (Crestwood, N.Y.: St. Vladimir's Seminary Press, 1980), par. 4, p. 15. Subsequent page numbers in the text are from this work.

made and venerated "for the more continually these are observed by means of such representations, so much more will the beholders be aroused to recollect the originals and to long after them, and to pay to the images the tribute of an embrace and a reverence of honor."[18]

The continuing opposition to images came to expression in the so-called Caroline Books (*Libri Carolini*) written in 790–2, purportedly by Charlemagne, but more likely by skilled theologians of his court. In many ways the *Libri* anticipate the iconoclastic arguments of the Reformation, and perhaps even the development of a uniquely western epistemology.[19] These books are important not only for their role in the earlier iconoclastic controversy, but for their role in Reformation polemics. They were cited as authoritative by Calvin and Elizabethan reformers. Two elements stand out in the argument of these texts. First, for these authors, it is the text which is the source of meaning, and therefore the written statement must always take precedence over the image. Following Augustine, these theologians argued that the very act of understanding proceeds from the soul. So, it follows in the second place, the "interior" person is given precedence over the "exterior." For it is the former which is made in the image of God and renewed in Christ, and which is addressed by the written text. The latter, dealing with physical sight and thus with images, is corrupted after the image of the first Adam. As the *Libri* says: "Thus the exterior is according to the body, that the interior may be resurrection and renovation which will bring about the death of the first life, that is the life of sin, and effect the regeneration of new life."[20] This new life is only to be found in the incorruptible inner world.

What is especially interesting is the Christological grounding both of the rationale of images that triumphed in Nicea and of its opponents. Like the Reformers after them the writers of the *Libri* were more interested in the regenerating work of Christ than in his physical nature. Significant too is the special role that was given to sight in the practice of piety, according to Nicea, as well as the suspicion of "external sight" among its opponents. While the Middle Ages continued to make use of Augustine's definition of

---

[18] Henry Bettenson (ed.), *Documents of the Christian Church,* 2nd edn. (Oxford University Press, 1963), p. 130. The definition of the council goes on to warn that this does not mean we pay the images actual worship.

[19] This is the argument of Anthony Ugolnik in "The Libri Carolini: Antecedents of Reformation Iconoclasms," in Clifford Davidson and Ann Nichols (eds.), *Iconoclasm vs. Art and Drama*, Early Drama, Art and Music Series 11 (Kalamazoo: Western Michigan University Press, 1989), pp. 12–15. This paragraph reflects Ugolnik's argument.

[20] *Libri Carolini*, I, vii, quoted in Ugolnik, "Libri Carolini," p. 15. Ugolnik traces the textual prejudice back to the "tolle lege" Augustine heard during his conversion in the garden in Milan (pp. 24–5).

a sight that is more than physical, the Christological grounding of creation was not given prominence as a rationale for images. Christological reflection came to focus almost entirely on the sacrament and, later, on the passion narrative. As a result most treatments of relics and images reflect the earlier worries of Constantinople that the Eucharist should in no way be compromised. And positively much of the imagery that developed was associated with the Mass, the feast of the Corpus Christi or the image of Veronica, especially as these were interpreted and promoted by the Franciscan and Dominican orders.[21]

A critical point was reached in 1215 at the Fourth Lateran council, called by Pope Innocent III in the interest of reforming and unifying the Church. There the doctrine of transubstantiation – Christ's body and blood are "contained in the sacred species" – and the requirement for yearly confession and communion are promulgated (Canons 1 and 21 respectively). These emphases made certain that the development of religious imagery, and its increasingly penitential emphasis, maintained a close relationship to the Mass and confession. Just as one was to "see" beyond the Eucharist to the Christ present in the bread so one should look at images in order to see the spiritual realities which were enacted in the Mass. The Synod of Paris, already in 1203, had called for the host to be raised and carried in procession; in the century following the Lateran council processions associated with the feast of the Corpus Christi multiplied.[22]

Throughout all the developments of liturgy and devotional practices, vision obviously played a central role. In one sense, by Thomas Aquinas's time, images could be valued more highly than books since vision was more important than hearing – the goal of life being, for Thomas, the vision of God in heaven. Thomas's empiricism contributed to this support for visual mediation. For the only way we reach knowledge is through the senses (*ST*, 1, 1, Ques. 1, Art. 9): "It is befitting Holy Writ to put forward divine and spiritual truths by means of comparison to the likenesses of material things. For God provides for everything according to the capacity of its nature. Now it is natural to man to attain to intellectual

---

[21] On the development of the Feast of the Corpus Christi see Miri Ruben, *Corpus Christi: The Eucharist in Late Medieval Culture* (Cambridge University Press, 1991). Ringbom discusses the way Veronica's devotion to Christ's passion led her to take on, even become, the "true image" of Christ (*Icon to Narrative*, p. 23).

[22] See André Venchez, "The Church and the Laity," in *The New Cambridge Medieval History* (Cambridge University Press, 1999), vol. v, pp. 187–8. He notes this devotion to the Host was intended "to supplant the devotion towards the relics of the saints, which had always been ambitious and inclined to veer towards the superstitious" (p. 187). See also Paul Binski, "Art and Architecture," in the same volume, pp. 90–2.

truths through sensible things, because all our knowledge originates from sense."[23]

Thomas is working here with the three levels of sight that Augustine had outlined. For he goes on to say that God cannot be seen by the sense of sight or "by any other sense." "Hence, He cannot be seen by the sense or the imagination but only by the intellect" (Quest. 12, Art. 3). And for this to happen, "since the natural power of the created intellect does not avail to enable it to see the essence of God . . . it is necessary that the power of the understanding should be increased further by divine grace" (Art. 5). This can only happen, Thomas believed, in the life to come when the intellectual vision of God will be unmediated. Meanwhile this spiritual reality appears to us under the likeness of material things.

The grounds for this continued to be Augustine's view of the world as capable of symbolizing divine reality, though in the Middle Ages this framework was as often mediated by the sixth-century Dionysius (believed in the Middle Ages to be written by the Dionysius Paul encountered on Mars Hill) as well as Augustine. The world, as Dionysius described it, is the image of the spiritual world. For Dionysius, as for Aquinas (who was much influenced by the Areopagite), the process of passage through an image to divine reality, is spiritual and not aesthetic. Moses, Dionysius reminds us, had to undergo purification before he could hear the "many voiced trumpets and see many lights flash forth." Even then he did not see God but the place where God dwells. For "the divinest and highest of the things perceived by the eyes of the body or the mind are but the symbolic language of things subordinate to him who himself transcendeth them all. Through these things his incomprehensible presence is shown walking upon those heights of his holy places which are perceived by the mind."[24]

For the medieval believer all things are potential vehicles to this divine vision. As Emile Mâle puts it, "in the Middle Ages form always clothed a thought. One might say that thought worked within matter and formed it. For it can never be separated from the idea that created it and animated it."[25]

---

[23] *Summa theologicae*, Part I, Question 1, Article 9, trans. Fathers of the English Dominican Province, revised by Daniel J. Sullivan (Chicago: Encyclopedia Britannica, Inc., 1952), vol. I., pp. 8–9. Thomas, interestingly, goes on to quote the pseudonymous sixth-century writer Dionysius' *Celest. Hierarch.* I, rather than Augustine. The following quotes are also from *ST* I, I.

[24] Dionysius the Areopagite, *The Mystical Theology*, trans. C. E. Rolt (New York: SPCK, 1920), pp. 193–4.

[25] *L'Art religieux du XIIIe siècle en France: étude sur l'iconographie du Moyen Age et sur ses sources d'inspiration* (Paris: Librairie Armand Colin, 1925), p. vi; cf. the first chapter "The Mirror of Nature."

Nature and history make up a grand unified vision which the theologians sought to capture in their Summas. Similarly architects and craftsmen sought in building the cathedrals to make these structures a microcosm of this sign-filled world. As Mâle notes, "while the Church Doctors were building the intellectual Cathedral that would shelter all of Christianity, the stone cathedrals were being built as visible images of it . . . in them all Christian doctrine found plastic form."[26]

The medieval believer before 1500 took it for granted that the human relationship to God and the supernatural world was visually reflected and mediated through this visible order of things.[27] Moreover this experience was a holistic one in which moral, metaphysical and spiritual elements all played a role.[28] This is seen best in what is arguably the highest expression of medieval art, the *Divine Comedy* (1314) of Dante Alighieri. In this epic Dante, who read Thomas Aquinas with the Dominicans in Florence, portrays the dramatic ascent of the soul to God in vivid visual and dramatic forms. Dante's world, Erich Auerbach notes, presents a figural view of things. Even in the other world, appearances "fulfill" those on earth. Beatrice's appearance in the other world is a figure of the appearance of beauty on earth, but in such a way that the reality of the one reinforces the other.[29] "A figural schema," says Auerbach, "permits both its poles – the future and its fulfillment – to retain the characteristics of concrete historical reality, in contradistinction to what obtains with symbolic or allegorical personifications, so that figure and fulfillment – although the one 'signifies' the other – have a significance which is not incompatible with their being real." This is particularly true of the human person which directly reflects God. As Beatrice explains to Dante in the Paradiso:

> That Good, which from Itself spurns every trace
> of envy, in Itself sends out such sparks
> as manifest the everlasting grace.
> Whatever is uttered by Its direct expression
> thereafter is eternal; His seal once stamped,
> nothing can ever wipe out the impression.

---

[26] Ibid., p. 25.
[27] Ringbom says, in something of an understatement, "The ideal of imageless devotion proved somewhat impracticable on the medieval scene" (*Icon to Narrative*, p. 19).
[28] Umberto Eco, *Art and Beauty in the Middle Ages*, trans. Hugh Bredin (New Haven: Yale University Press, 1986), p. 5.
[29] Erich Auerbach, *Mimesis: The Representation of Reality in Western Literature* (Princeton University Press, 1968 [1953]), p. 195.

Whatever is poured directly from Its spring
is wholly free; so made, it is not subject to
the power of any secondary thing.
(Paradiso, VII, 64–72)[30]

Note that the figural makes reality into something that may be experienced in a vision. As T. S. Eliot noted, Dante had a visual imagination, he lived in an era when people still saw visions as a mental habit. All his similes serve the purpose of helping us see more definitely the scene he puts before us. "Dante's attempt is to make us see what he saw."[31] But it is a kind of seeing that involves us totally, body and spirit; we are drawn into its "imaginings." We can feel them with our eyes.

This feeling with our eyes will finally issue, in the Paradiso, in Dante's vision of God. But meanwhile this world can become the locus of beauty and love that points beyond itself to God. In the *Comedy* Dante's love for Beatrice serves as an earthly symbol and even a divine pointer toward that vision of God. Toward the end of the Purgatorio, the three theological virtues call on Beatrice to lead Dante to the further, second, beauty:

"Turn, Beatrice, oh turn the eyes of grace,"
was their refrain, "upon the faithful one
who comes so far to look upon your face.

Grant us this favor of your grace: reveal
your mouth to him, and let his eyes behold
the Second Beauty, which your veils conceal."
(Purg., xxxi, 133–8)

HEARING AND SEEING IN MEDIEVAL DEVOTIONAL PRACTICE

At its best, medieval worship reflected this grand vision of a world that was theologically and dramatically ordered. For the medieval worshiper, attendance at the Mass provided a central focus for this world. The allegory of the Mass, from its introit and the gloria through to the dismissal, along with the times celebrated during the year, provided a corporate structure in which the community oriented itself. As Eamon Duffy argues, "the liturgy was in fact the principle reservoir from which the religious paradigms and beliefs

---

[30] *The Divine Comedy*, trans. John Ciardi (New York: Norton, 1961), p. 432. Subsequent citation from the *Comedy* is from this edition p. 283.
[31] T. S. Eliot, *Selected Essays* (London: Faber & Faber, 1932), p. 229.

of the people were drawn." In this liturgy their lives took shape in a "vast and resonant world of symbols which . . . they both understood and controlled."[32] Similarly Pamela Graves argues the "mass acted as the medium by which a whole cosmology was revealed, with the Christian subject, the lay participant, morally implicated in its revelation and relevance."[33] This was a total experience in which vision, hearing, even physical movement (pews having not yet been introduced) played a role.

The view that medieval spirituality was "visual" while Reformation faith became "aural" and verbal, while widely accepted, is clearly a distortion of a complex reality. The holistic experience which Dante recounts underlines the complex interrelationship that existed between the visual and aural in medieval worship. Moreover the relationship between text and image was not unidirectional. Michael Camille has pointed out the importance of hearing and reading (*lectio*) in medieval spirituality. Reading in the Middle Ages was never a silent matter, but was always a mouthing of the words orally. In the eleventh century, he argues, the visual was primarily an expression of the spoken word rather than the visual world. The context in which images were produced and viewed was the practice of *lectio*, the reading, hearing and meditating on Scripture. Meditation was a matter of mouthing each word, which was spoken and performed in the liturgy. The laity, Camille notes, were in a sense reading between the lines when they looked at pictures. He concludes: "Medieval pictures cannot be separated from what is a total experience of communication involving sight, sound, action and physical expression."[34] Margaret Aston similarly has argued that reading, for the literate person in the Middle Ages, was for believers a passage to visual memory – a calling to mind things that were absent, as Augustine had put it. Reading, she noted, was for the sake of imaging.[35]

---

[32] *The Stripping of the Altars: Traditional Religion in England c.1400–1580* (New Haven: Yale University Press: 1992), pp. 2, 591. He writes as one who feels the destruction of this at the Reformation was a tragic loss.

[33] Pamela Graves, "Social Space in the English Medieval Parish Church," *Economy and Society* 18 (1989), p. 309. She sees the breaking up of this fluid space and movement by the proliferation in the fifteenth century of private chapels (enclosures) and the private reading of missals (pp. 317–18).

[34] M. Camille, "Seeing and Reading: Some Visual Implications of Medieval Literacy and Illiteracy," *Art History* 8 (1985), pp. 26–49; quote p. 43. Elsewhere Camille has noted that fear of idolatry was constant during this period, which kept medieval believers from simple embrace of the visual. He says Christians were caught between the denial of the body and its feared materialization in the idol; see *The Gothic Idol: Ideology and Image-Making in Medieval Art* (Cambridge University Press, 1989), cf. pp. 338–40.

[35] Margaret Aston, *Lollards and Reformers: Images and Literacy in Late Medieval Religion* (London: Hambledon, 1984), pp. 116–20. "The reading led to imaging" (p. 120). She refers to Frances Yates

For medieval worshipers the most common experience of this integrated world, visually speaking, was the experience of attendance at the Mass. Not only was the context often the visually elaborate imagery of the church and cathedral, but the liturgy itself was a visual and dramatic experience of a high order – it was the summation of what in the Middle Ages would have passed for what we call today "the media."[36] But in contrast to our media, the experience of medieval worship had the high spiritual function of mediating salvation. As we have noted, the performance of the Mass became the central transaction of the liturgical life of the people. Christ's work was focused, not on the renewing of creation, as in the Damascene, but on his sacrificial death. We noted that transubstantiation was first defined in 1215 at the Lateran Council, but even before the host was being raised so that all could visually participate (since actual participation in communion, before the Lateran Council, was rare).[37] Since actually viewing the host was essential to the experience – and often stood for actual participation – a bell was rung to call distracted (and perhaps sleeping) worshipers to attention. So much so that magical effects were felt to attend one who had witnessed the raised host. When worshipers could not see the host, they pushed and shoved until they could, sometimes calling out to the startled priest: "Lift it higher." This gesture of elevation created what Miri Ruben has called a center of eucharistic action in which all the senses were involved – seeing the host, hearing the bell and perhaps music, clapping the hands and even smelling incense.[38]

In all these developments then the eye was given a privileged though not exclusive role. Visual mediation was felt to be more effective for remembering and recalling things that were absent from the mind, than words alone. In the fifteenth century Reginold Pecock claimed in his answer to the Lollards: "The eyesight showeth and bringeth into the imagination and into the mind within the head of man much matter and long matter sooner, and with much less labor and travail and pain, than the hearing of the ear

---

(*The Art of Memory* [University of Chicago Press, 1966]) to point out that memory at the time was "predicated on a stock of mental pictures or memory places, in which the mind's collection could be housed" (Aston, *Lollards and Reformers*, p. 117).

[36] Emile Mâle has pointed out how the iconography of this period is tied directly to the liturgy and often grows directly out of the liturgical dramas enacted in the church; see *L'Art religieux*, ch. 4, pp. 121–50.

[37] Richard Kieckhefer makes this point in "Major Currents in Late Medieval Devotion," in Jill Raitt (ed.), *Christian Spirituality: High Middle Ages and Reformation* (New York: Crossroads, 1987), p. 97. In the same volume James McCue draws the analogy between seeing the host and the vision of God in heaven (p. 432).

[38] *Corpus Christi*, pp. 54–5. See Graves, "Social Space," pp. 309ff.

doth."[39] A further example of this line of thinking comes from a sermon attributed to St. Bernardino of Siena, an observant Franciscan, preached early in the fifteenth century. In an interesting echo of Augustine's levels of vision, he argues there are four kinds of letters, each better than the other:

The first kind are gross letters for the rude people, such as pictures; the second, for men of the middle sort, are middle letters, and such are written letters; and these are better than the first. The third are vocal letters, found by those who desire actively to busy themselves for charity's sake, pleading and discoursing, in order that they may be learned and may teach others; and these are superior to the first two. Fourthly and lastly come the mental letters ordained by God for those who desire to persevere always in contemplation; and this sort is more perfect than the others and surpasses them all, since they were ordained for this end not the other way around.[40]

Notice once again the interaction of text and image. On the one hand, even with the development of printing, late medieval culture was – even into the reformation period – an oral culture. And it was therefore a religious culture in which preaching was a dominant feature of worship. In the fifteenth and sixteenth centuries, notes Eamon Duffy, "lay people were enthusiastic sermon goers."[41] People flocked to hear famous preachers as cities, as a matter of civic pride, sought to have the best preacher in their cathedral. But, on the other hand, the experience of hearing a preacher was integrated into the drama of the liturgy and was surrounded visually by the everpresent crucifix, the images of the saints and the stories of biblical history. Even the rise of printing did not seem to threaten the centrality of preaching in this culture. Books were simply integrated into the worship practices of the time. Indeed, even those who could not read had access in one way or another to books. There were always occasions for them to be in places – in church, or at home – where books would be read aloud,

---

[39] Reginold Pecock, *Repressor of our Blaming of the Clergy*, vol. 1, pp. 212–13; quoted in Margaret Aston, *England's Iconoclasts* (Oxford: Clarendon Press, 1988), vol. 1, p. 150. Pecock's comments have a peculiarly modern ring in the light of references to our contemporary visual culture. See Mitchell Stephens, who argues: "the future belongs to a single, inclusive medium for which humankind has repeatedly demonstrated a preference: video" (*The Rise of the Image and the Decline of the Word* [Oxford University Press, 1998], p. 170). Interestingly he notes that print looks inward, visual media outward, raising the question that might have been posed to the reformers: why do we assume there is more truth inside than outside (pp. 213–15)?

[40] Quoted in Aston, *Lollards and Reformers*, p. 114. Note again the role of "mental letters" as the highest form of knowing.

[41] *Stripping of the Altars*, p. 57. And see Richard Kieckhefer: "The religious culture of the later Middle Ages was in large measure a preached culture" ("Major Currents in Late Medieval Devotion," p. 77). And see Laniel Lesnick. "Civic Preaching in the Early Renaissance" (in Verdon and Henderson [eds.], *Christianity and the Renaissance*, pp. 208–21), though the Church sought to suppress these popular preachers in the Fifth Lateran Council early in the sixteenth century.

and, often, committed to memory.[42] Similarly the interaction between printed and oral texts was very close. Books of sermons were copied out and circulated so that people could "re-hear" the performance. So the growing appetite for books did nothing, at least initially, to undermine the role that the oral and visual culture played in the religious lives of the people. As Margaret Aston notes, people during this time yearned to hear, as well as see.[43] The Reformation, in this respect at least, did not so much provide a radical break as an intensification of trends that were already evident.

MEDIEVAL REFORM AND THE INNER APPROPRIATION OF IMAGES

However important the visual mediation of piety, there was a persistent worry that images instead of encouraging faith would stand in the way of an inner appropriation of spiritual reality. Already in the twelfth century the movements that sought to reform monastic spirituality, the Cistercians and Carthusians, were suspicious of the growing opulence of many churches and monastery chapels. Their opposition was not to images as such, but to the lavish lifestyles often associated with their display. St. Bernard of Clairvaux (d. 1153) asks his colleagues:

Tell me, poor men, if indeed you are poor men, what is gold doing in the holy place? . . . We who have left behind all that is precious in this world for the sake of Christ, we who regard as dung all things shining in beauty . . . in order that we may win Christ. Whose devotion, I ask, do we strive to excite in all this? What interest do we seek from these things: the astonishment of fools or the offerings of the simple? Or is it that since we have mingled with the gentiles, perhaps we have also adopted their ways and even serve their idols?[44]

In another place Bernard makes it clear that he does not oppose imagery altogether, even giving it a Christological grounding. But notice that Bernard bases his argument, not as John of Damascus had done, on the visual fact of the incarnation, but on the narrative of Christ's life:

The soul at prayer should have before it a sacred image of the God-man, in his birth or infancy or as he was teaching, or dying, or rising, or ascending. Whatever

---

[42] See on this the classic study by Frances Yates, *Art of Memory*. Even Dante, she argues, "could be regarded as a kind of memory system for memorizing" theological reality (p. 95).

[43] "Popular Religious Movements in the Middle Ages," in *Faith and Fire: Popular and Unpopular Religion 1350–1600* (London: Hambledon Press, 1993), p. 23.

[44] *Apologia*, XII.28, trans. Conrad Rudolph, in *"Things of Greater Importance": Bernard of Clairvaux's Apologia and Medieval Attitudes toward Art* (Philadelphia: University of Pennsylvania, 1990), pp. 279, 281. The reference to "poor men" is an allusion to the monks' vow of poverty.

form it takes this image must bind the soul with the love of virtue and expel carnal vices, eliminate temptations and quiet desires. I think this is the principal reason why the invisible God willed to be seen in the flesh . . . He wanted to recapture the affections of carnal men who were unable to love in any other way, by first drawing them to the salutary love of his own humanity, and then gradually to raise them to a spiritual love.[45]

So images can serve the role of "arousing the soul" as the definition of the Second Council of Nicea put it; but they must always be used in the service of this higher end: to bind the soul with love of God.

Henry Suso (d. 1366), who had studied under the Dominican mystic Meister Eckhart, underlined the transitory nature of images. Suso noted that however precious the image of Christ is to us, "we must bid farewell to it in order to partake of the Holy Spirit – just as the disciples had to part from the master."[46] Among those who sought to reform the monastic movement, priority is always given to the inward vision. For example, Guigo I, the fifth Prior of the Carthusian Charterhouse, in a way reminiscent of the *Libri Carolini*, noted in the middle of the twelfth century: "Lack of interior vision, that is of God . . . causes you to go outside your interior . . . and spend your time admiring the exterior forms of bodies or the opinions of men. To gain an interior vision of God and to receive his benefits one must deny the world and himself."[47]

Implicit in these instructions is the awareness of the danger of what the reformers would later call "idolatry," that is dependence on any visible mediation which can distract the heart from its encounter with God. This tradition found perhaps its clearest expression in the so-called Devotio Moderna, associated with the Brethren of the Common Life. The founder Gerard Groote (d. 1384), who became an itinerant preacher and began to translate the bible for the people, approved of public art, but not private images or book illustrations.[48] These smaller images posed the most danger to the personal devotion which was, he felt, to be direct and unmediated.

[45] "On the Song of Songs," Sermon 20. 6, in *The Works of Bernard of Clairvaux*, trans. Kilian Walsh (Spencer, Mass.: Cistercian Publications, 1971), p. 152.

[46] In Ringbom, *Icon to Narrative*, p. 17. Notice that in these mystical traditions the suspicion of the external image is kept alive.

[47] *Meditations of Guigo, Prior of Charterhouse* (Milwaukee, Wisc.: Marquette University Press: 1951), pp. 46–7, 13–14; quoted in Otto Grundler, "Devotio Moderna," in Raitt (ed.), *Christian Spirituality*, p. 180.

[48] See Albert Hyma, *The Christian Renaissance: A History of the "Devotio Moderna,"* 2nd edn. (Hamden, Conn.: Archon Books, 1965). Grundler argues that the Devotio Moderna is more a revival of monastic spirituality than an innovation (*Christian Spirituality*, p. 179; and Ringbom, *Icon to Narrative*, p. 20).

In a way consistent with the mystical traditions of Dionysius, but which also anticipates arguments of the reformers, Groote does not argue that "images" are unnecessary, but that, if they are true and pure, they should ultimately be internal and intellectual. This point is clearly made in the best-known product of this school, Thomas à Kempis's *Of the Imitation of Christ*.[49] At the beginning of Book III Thomas describes how Christ speaks inwardly to a faithful soul.

Blessed is the soul that hears the Lord speaking within her, and receives from His mouth the word of consolation. Blessed the ears that catch the pulses of the divine whisper and take no notice of the whisperings of this world. Blessed, indeed are those ears that do not listen to the voice which sounds without, but attend to Truth itself teaching within. Blessed the eyes that are shut to outward things but intent on inward things.[50]

A large part of the concern over the use of (external) imagery lay in its ability to move the emotions. As one of Aquinas's contemporaries, Bishop Durundus put it:

It is seen that a painting moves the feelings more than what is written. In a painting some action is placed before the eyes; but in literature that action is recalled to the memory as it were by the hearing, which touches the feelings less. And so it is that in church we do not show as much reverence to books as we do to images and pictures.[51]

This fear of the emotional power of images was not a new thing; it dated back to Plato. But it was to become even more important in the development of the devotional image in the fifteenth century, and will attract the special attention (and suspicions) of the reformers. It is precisely this ability of images to move the emotions, in the view of the reformers, that highlights their danger with respect to true worship.

In these mystical circles there were ample cautions directed toward the proliferation of images, especially those for devotional use. Without much change one can readily imagine them affirming elements of Farel and Calvin's response to relics and pilgrimages. Even if Calvin and the other reformers were to draw the boundary around these things more tightly, the impetus toward an inward and spiritual appropriation of God, even

---

[49] There were more than 250 manuscript copies existing when he died in 1471, many of which circulated anonymously. The book was first printed in Venice in 1472. By 1779 there were 1,800 editions and translations. See *Of the Imitation of Christ*, trans. Abbot Justin McCann (New York: Mentor Books, 1957), p. v.

[50] Ibid., bk III, ch. 1, p. 72.   [51] Quoted in Aston, *Lollards and Reformers*, p. 116.

the drawing of internal images of spiritual reality, was clearly present long before the Reformation.[52]

Despite these worries, the dominant view would still have been that images can be useful even to promote the interior piety which was the goal of spirituality. Indeed much of the mendicant revival of piety was associated with the use of religious imagery. Even the growing use of individual prints and prayer books, which we look at presently, could encourage this kind of devotion. Often centering on Mary, these prints encouraged a deeply emotional identification with the person and sometimes led to mystical experiences.[53]

This use of prints and, later, prayer books marks an important shift not only in the use of images, but also in the view of God's activity that is implied. Earlier, for the average worshiper, medieval religion consisted of certain prescribed rituals and practices – attendance at the Mass, saying particular prayers and, for the more devout, making pilgrimages. These engendered, we noted, a certain communal feeling and a commonly shared vision of life and the world. But such rituals may or may not have been accompanied by deep feelings (as is obvious, for example, from Chaucer's account of medieval religious life). The act of going to Mass, or on a pilgrimage, itself expressed what they would have called devotion. But by the time we reach the fifteenth century, under the influence of mystical movements, and the proliferation of prayer books and the religious prints Geiler referred to, it was becoming increasingly common for worship experiences to include deep emotional feelings. One way of describing this is to point out that there is a gradual movement from an objective piety toward a subjective one.[54]

---

[52] Though this does not mean that one can establish any clear link between these movements and the Reformation. Cf. Carlos Eire: "It is difficult to trace a direct line of development from these earlier iconoclastic movements and the Reformation" (*War Against the Idols* [Cambridge University Press, 1986], p. 23).

[53] As a modern artist, Julian Schnabel, put it: "Duccio and Giotto were painting in a society in which there was actually faith in God. People had religious experiences in front of paintings. The painters were connecting people to something bigger than life, something bigger than their individual existences. I think people still have religious experiences in front of paintings. The only difference today is that the religion isn't organized or prescribed – it's consciousness. To get religion now is to become conscious, to feel those human feelings" ("Plate it as it Lies," *Art News*, April 1985, p. 69). Eamon Duffy argues these practices represent a democratization of Brigitine and Carthusian spiritual direction (*Stripping of the Altars*, p. 265). Richard Kieckhefer believes they are a halfway house between bare liturgical practice and contemplation ("Major Currents in Late Medieval Devotion," p. 76).

[54] Simon Tugwell argues that earlier the Dominicans resisted this interiorizing, "stressing that what matters is what one does, not what one feels like while doing it" ("The Spirituality of the Dominicans,"

So Geiler von Kaysersberg could encourage his congregation to use these prints to deepen their faith. His admonition demonstrates a reform-minded medieval piety which could make use of imagery to connect the worshiper in a "deeply emotional experience" with the object portrayed in the image (or with the relic).[55] Images then could be used not simply to teach people who could learn in no other way, they could also be used to deepen the faith even of those who were able to read. In the minds of Geiler and many others, there was no incompatibility between a deepening faith and the careful use of images. Indeed the focus on the affective side of faith was actually enhanced, they believed, by visual imagery.

Though there are surely examples of aniconic mystics – one thinks of Meister Eckhart – who sought a pure (and imageless) experience of God, picturing God and his grace became a dominant means of spiritual ex-pression in the later Middle Ages, even for reformers. By and large the development of this interior piety was accompanied by the use of images, especially those which were used to stimulate an inner vision. It is this tra-dition which Geiler represents in his preaching, and which later will find expression in the spirituality of Ignatius Loyola.[56]

While these developments anticipate some of the devotional emphases that the reformers would later encourage, their use of imagery would be very different. While the reformers would insist that it is the preaching of the word that elicits true faith, they insisted that this should lead to an inner vision of God. But Calvin's stress would be not so much on the imaginative and emotional identification with this inner vision as on the call to live it out in one's life in the world.

in Raitt [ed.], *Christian Spirituality*, p. 29). John Drury has pointed out, by the time we reach the imagery of the Renaissance, "Devout seeing is now a religious subject" (*Painting the Word: Christian Pictures and their Meaning* [New Haven: Yale University Press, 1999], p. 32). But this was already the case by the end of the medieval period, as his own study makes clear. Timothy Verdon and John Henderson even argue that this transition to subjective piety was beginning to take place already in the twelfth century under the influence of the reforming orders (see *Christianity and the Renaissance*, p. 10).

[55] The importance of Sixten Ringbom's work, *Icon to Narrative* (1965), is to trace the development of what he calls the "devotional image" and which he places alongside the didactive image of Gregory and the theological image of John of Damascus (pp. 11–15).

[56] One hears echoes of Geiler's preaching in the Spiritual Exercises of Ignatius on the crucifixion: "The first point is to see the persons in my imagination, contemplating, meditating in detail the circumstances surrounding them, and I will then draw some spiritual profit from this scene" (Ignatius Loyola, *The Spiritual Exercises* [Garden City, N.Y.: Image/Doubleday, 1964], p. 72). David Freedberg goes so far as to question the possibility of an aniconic religious experience. The will to express in figures cannot be suppressed. Indeed, the ability to make mental images is parasitic on physical image making. Loyola's exercises could not have worked except against a background of "stored visual experience" (*The Power of Images*, pp. 55, 179–80).

THE INDIVIDUALIZATION AND EXTERNALIZATION
OF PIETY

Such constructive use of imagery unfortunately does not represent the whole story. Alongside these developments, tensions which had been present all along in the worship life of the people were beginning to break into the open. Although the use (and abuse) of images figures centrally in these developments, there were important theological concerns as well. In this paragraph and the next we briefly trace this part of the story.

It goes without saying that not all images were used in the way that the early reformers approved. With the development of woodcuts images became both portable and more widely available, and began to play an increasingly important role in devotional practices. In a sense they made possible a widely dispersed lay spirituality, that soon exceeded the ability of the Church to exercise control. In this, too, Innocent III had played a critical role, when he offered the first indulgence to any who would pray before the image of Veronica (the "true image" identified in the Middle Ages with the woman who wiped Jesus' face on the way to Calvary).[57] For most the use of images was connected more to traditional votive practices than to the piety we examined above. Prayers were offered, candles were lit, as what Luther would later call a "good work." Nor were aesthetics factors of great importance to most of these worshipers. Aesthetic considerations, when they were present at all, were entirely secondary.[58] While Geiler was probably not offering indulgences to his hearers, he was working at the further end of the developments that Innocent initiated. Clearly people used paintings, and later prints, in ways that were critical to their spiritual lives.

The most common form of this lay devotion was the use of prayer books, or books of hours, that began in the fourteenth century and proliferated in the fifteenth century. All kinds of these primers were produced – though because of their popularity and heavy use most have not survived. The development of printing from about 1460 was a major factor that contributed to the spread of such prayer books. But seventy years before this, woodcuts

[57] Discussed in Ringbom, *Icon to Narrative*, p. 23. Ringbom points out that many of the mystics, for example Teresa and Catherine of Sienna, experienced the formative power of images. The visions of some, such as Julian of Norwich, preceded any exposure to literary models (p. 19). See on this Eco, *Art and Beauty*, pp. 5, 18.
[58] On this whole development see Hans Belting, *Image and Likeness: A History of the Image before the Era of Art*, ed. and trans. Edmund Jophcott (Chicago: University of Chicago Press, 1994). The whole notion of an isolable "aesthetic response" as we understand it would have been foreign to people in the Middle Ages. Arguably this notion was not articulated until Alexander Baumgarten's *Aesthetica*, which appeared in 1750. See Nicholas Cook, *Music, Imagination and Culture* (Oxford University Press, 1990), pp. 4–5. And see Eco, *Art and Beauty*, ch. 6 on "Aesthetic Perception".

had begun to circulate, first used for printing religious pictures on wood-blocks. Many of these contained Scripture and sermons along with images which could aid worshipers in their prayers, either in their homes or at church. Here again, the images and the text, for those who could read, worked together to assist the worshiper to re-hear the words of Scripture or the sermon in light of the image that accompanied it.[59]

This was significant because for the first time people could take the images, previously seen only in the cathedrals, to their homes and contemplate them at leisure. Lucien Febvre and Henri-Jean Martin note the "need for this kind of simple visual resource was felt long before the need for printed literary, theological and scientific texts, interest in which was restricted to a small group of clerics and scholars."[60] One of the most popular of these was called the Biblia Pauperum, which was a small collection of prints of biblical scenes, juxtaposed with contemporary images, as resources for illiterate priests who needed to preach.[61] As soon as books began to be printed they immediately made use of these prints which were easily incorporated into the printing process. But the images continued to circulate separately, as Geiler's reference indicates, and by 1500 broadsheets had become an independent medium. The continuing prominence of this imagery is critical because at most 5 percent of the population could read by 1500.[62]

On the other hand, those who could read soon were able to have their own copy of a "Book of Hours" with its prayers and Scripture portions. Most of these which have survived are those made by artists for wealthy families, but all kinds of such prayer books were written and, later, printed during this century. Margaret Aston calls these books the most common form of lay instruction during the fifteenth century.[63] What is most

---

[59] Aston, *Lollards and Reformers*, pp. 126–33.

[60] Lucien Febvre and Henri-Jean Martin, *The Coming of the Book: The Impact of Printing 1450–1800*, trans. David Gerard (Atlantic Highlands, N.J.: Humanities Press, 1976), p. 46.

[61] Many versions of this circulated, and these prints were later incorporated into printed texts and bibles. By placing biblical images beside contemporary ones and putting Old Testament and New Testament images side by side, the book also served to suggest interpretive schemas that preachers could use in their preaching. The influence of these is mentioned, though not studied in any detail, in James Strachan, *Early Bible Illustrations: A Short Study Based on Some Fifteenth and Early Sixteenth Century Printed Texts* (Cambridge University Press, 1957). And see Febvre and Martin, *Coming of the Book*, p. 49; and David Landau and Peter Parshall, *The Renaissance Print: 1470–1550* (New Haven: Yale University Press. 1994), ch. 1.

[62] See Keith Moxey, *Peasants, Warriors and Wives: Popular Imagery in the Reformation* (University of Chicago Press, 1989), p. 24, though he notes up to a third of the population of cities could read. Ozment puts the figure in Germany at 3–4 percent at 1500 (*The Age of Reform 1250–1550* [New Haven: Yale University Press, 1980], p. 201).

[63] *Lollards and Reformers*, p. 122. See on this development Roger S. Wieck, *Painted Prayers: The Book of Hours in Medieval and Renaisssance Art* (New York: George Braziller and the Pierpoint Morgan

interesting for our purposes was the growing practice in which worshipers took these books with them to church. This practice, which may have had something to do with the increasing use of pews (so that the worshiper could sit and read her/his prayer book), allowed the believer to "read along" with the performance of the Mass. But it also encouraged the solitary believer to increasingly focus on her own thoughts and reactions to what was going on. This growing independence over time made it possible for believers to develop their own ideas about what they were hearing – and not incidentally to begin to question what their priest was saying. As Aston comments on these developments: "For lay people to prove themselves capable of theology, direct auditors of God, was to change the world."[64] Little by little the use of images by individual worshipers either in prayer books or circulating independently, rather than connecting one with others around them in a unified worship experience, was encouraging an individual devotional experience. Engrossed in the image, and the book, the worshiper could be cut off, even from the neighboring worshiper.

A further evidence of the individual experience supplanting the communal is to be found in the changing shape of the worship space itself. Pamela Graves, in a study of religious space in medieval England, points out that original structures were designed to promote a fluidity of space in which the Mass and the Liturgy could create a "unity of allegory" that was reiterated in the space and structure of the building. The changing religious practices we have surveyed served to articulate this space in ways that distracted worshipers from the unity of the experience of worship – their practice of private reading of primers, and of sitting in pews, changed not only the worship experience but also the experience of space. Graves notes that these practices "dislodged allegory from the spatial associations the action of the priest in the mass proposed."[65] At this time, because of the increasing wealth of parishioners, donors began to endow private chapels in churches (often with their own elaborate altarpieces). According to Graves, this further divided the space into separate places where individuals and families could gather in their worship. Graves concludes that these contributed to breaking apart the cohesive elements of worship. Use of space itself, she concludes, and its influence on the imaginative construal of

---

Library, 1997). They note "more Books of Hours were produced, both by hand and by press, than any other type of book, even than the Bible" (p. 9).

[64] *Lollards and Reformers*, p. 132.

[65] Graves, "Social Space," p. 318. She notes of the primers that they enabled the worshiper to "muster their own thoughts, rather than construct a communal memory of the passion through the memory of the mass."

reality contributes to the transformation of worship, and, often uncon-sciously, to historical change.[66]

The growing practice of endowing chapels and sculptured images had its counterpart in more popular forms of devotion. As the wealthy built their own chapels, or commissioned their own sculptures for their domestic worship spaces, the poor found more and more opportunities for proces-sion and pilgrimage. Pilgrimages had previously been available only to the wealthy, who could travel to Rome, Compostela or Jerusalem, but as local towns gained prominence, people were increasingly able to go to the next town, or a nearby mountain, as Geiler's family was able to do, and visit a relic. And cities and Church vied with each other in offering indulgences for such practices. The feast of the Corpus Christi grew in importance, fasts became obligatory, bleeding hosts appeared and miracles at the site of relics were reported from city to city.[67]

But the very multiplication of these images and processions tended to devalue their religious value. As the spaces of the parish church were filling with altars and images donated by wealthy parishioners, the crowds at the pilgrimage sites were growing worse. Economic activity and travel increased, and made more visible, the growing gap between the rich and the poor. As the year 1500 approached there was, for many, a sense of apocalyptic ending.

Johan Huizinga, in his classic study *The Waning of the Middle Ages*, suggested almost a hundred years ago that this period represents a wearing out of forms and a lassitude in devotion.[68] This study of what Huizinga called "the forms of life, thought and art" was a pioneering and influential attempt to develop a cultural history of this period. Especially interesting for our purposes is his argument that the art of the period, especially in its highest forms, in for example the Flemish painters, the brothers van Eyck (Hubert, d. 1426? and Jan, d. 1441), reflected, not the apogee, but the waning of medieval culture. He sees the quattrocento representing the culmination of the medieval tendency to "accentuat[e] every detail, of developing every thought and every image to the end of giving concrete form to every concept of the mind."[69] For the devout, as we have noted,

---

[66] Ibid., pp. 318–22. Though one should perhaps not generalize Graves's findings. There is evidence that elsewhere, in Italy for example, such private practices served to actually open up spaces that had previously been closed (Ena Heller, in private correspondence, November 11, 2003).

[67] Duffy, *Stripping of the Altars*, pp. 40–3; Eire, *War Against the Idols*, pp. 13–25.

[68] *The Waning of the Middle Ages: A Study of the Forms of Life, Thought and Art in France and the Netherlands in the Fourteenth and Fifteenth Centuries* (London: Edward Arnold, 1927). The original Dutch title, published in 1924, meant literally the "Autumn" of the Middle Ages.

[69] Ibid., p. 255–6.

Figure 1　Jan van Eyck, *The Virgin of Chancellor Rolin*. Oil on wood, 66 × 62 cm. Louvre
(Museum), Paris, France, 1435.

beauty was a reflection of the splendor and perfection of God, enlivened by
brightness and movement. But, says Huizinga, the almost perfect expression
of the miniatures of Jan van Eyck represented, not a coming triumph of
realism, but an expiring mode of thought. "Are not unity and harmony lost
in this aggregation of details?"[70]

Consider one of Jan van Eyck's most famous pieces, the exquisite *The
Virgin of Chancellor Rolin* (painted about 1435, now in the Louvre) (Figure 1).
Its size (about 66 cm square) and the presence of the donor kneeling before

---

[70] Ibid., p. 256 and see pp. 243–4.

Mary indicate its use as a privately commissioned piece.[71] This piece lends support to Pamela Graves's thesis that the growing private patronage was impacting the use of images in worship and even the nature of the worship itself. Here the worshiper, without sponsorship of one of the saints as would have been common previously, has intruded on – broken up – the sacred space which previously belonged to the Holy Family.

Of particular interest is the fact that Chancellor Rolin was a powerful and unscrupulous member of the court of Philip the Good. Yet here he has been allowed to enter the throne room as it were, decorated in sumptuous décor (with its Romanesque architecture, which Panofsky believes is symbolic of the heavenly Jerusalem). Outside a beautiful garden is visible, reminding one of the Garden of Paradise, and beyond that the sparkling Meuse river, recalling the river of water "clear as crystal" running through the New Jerusalem. That this painting is meant to be an act of penance is clear from the fact that originally there was a large purse hanging from the side of Rolin which was painted over. In the garden are peacocks, symbolic of worldly pride, and the buildings which the two figures look out on may well be some of the many from which the Chancellor collected his immense rents.[72] Van Eyck then manages to capture something of the ambiguity that this event suggests. Medieval worship is being transformed before our eyes. Here the donor performs his penance, but, as one art historian proposes, it is "an incomplete penance."[73] The splendor of the setting is undermined by the symbolic ambiguity the artist pointedly includes.

Something similar happened, according to Thomas Crow, in the exquisitely carved limewood sculptures made in Germany later in the century by, among others, Tilman Riemenschneider.[74] Consider this *Altarpiece of the Holy Blood* from St. Jakobskirche in Rothenburg (Figure 2). Most of these were made not for the corporate worship of the Church but for wealthy individuals or the newly powerful fraternities. All such commissions, Crow writes, illustrate "the same fragmentation of social sense engendered in the economic boom with all of its attendant dislocation of settled statuses and habits."[75] Crow argues that both the capitalist forces and the pious anxieties

[71] See Erwin Panofsky, *Early Netherlandish Art* (New York: Harper & Row, 1971), vol. I, p. 139. Though he notes that eventually it was donated to Autun Cathedral.
[72] Craig Harbison, *Jan van Eyck: The Play of Realism* (London: Reaktion, 1991), pp. 109, 111.
[73] Ibid., pp. 115, 116.
[74] See Michael Baxandall, *The Limewood Sculptors of Renaissance Germany* (New Haven: Yale University Press, 1980); and Thomas Crow, *The Intelligence of Art* (Chapel Hill: University of North Carolina Press, 1999).
[75] Ibid., p. 64; in the first part of the sentence he is quoting Baxandall, *Limewood Sculptors*, p. 62.

Figure 2   Tilman Riemenschneider, *The Altarpiece of the Holy Blood: Last Supper* (center),
Christ Entering Jerusalem (left), *Christ in the Garden of Olives* (right). Limewood, 9 m high.
St Jacob's Church, Rothenburg ob der Tauber, Germany 1500–1504.

of the time (which were themselves not unrelated) conspired to push these sculptures further in the direction of delicate beauty of form and "florid" elaboration that soon called down the wrath of the reformers – and indeed the larger population. These elaborate sculptures "rendered all too visibly the compromises of pre-Reformation piety and thus lost all persuasion for a large part of the population suddenly vigilant against visible luxury." Michael Baxandall shows how these altarpieces became an "instrument for self-registration by the patron, and open to criticism as a disagreeable expression of pride." One might even say, Baxandall notes, the florid beauty itself was brought into existence by the very forces that would eventually destroy it. Sculptures such as these would become, in less than a generation, the object of the iconoclasts' wrath.[76]

Other examples could surely be given, but these show that the highest expressions of late medieval art were often formed out of tensions that threatened the very existence of that tradition, quite apart from anything the reformers would later do. In Zurich, for example, the commissioning of ecclesiastical art increased one hundredfold between 1500 and 1518,[77] only a few years before Zwingli began his work of "purifying" the worship of that city. All of this lends support for Carlos Eire's assertion that this period represented the "externalization of piety."[78] Or to Eaman Duffy's conclusion that late medieval worship was a "religion in which there was little evidence of . . . deep religious introspection and interiority . . . concentrating rather on the objective things of religion; the observance of feast and fast, the changing patterns of annual liturgy."[79]

Consider the van Eyck painting to which we referred above. Outside the interior space into which the donor has inserted himself, lies the enclosed

---

[76] Baxandall, *Limewood Sculptors*, pp. 66 and 83. One can begin to see how iconoclasm may be viewed, among other things, as a rational response to the excess and arrogance of the wealthy donors and not just as a philistine movement. Baxandall argues that while iconoclasm does not result from these excesses, they do "backlight" this response (p. 69). See also the emphasis that Lee Wandel gives to the motive of social justice that appeared in the iconoclastic movement – this extravagance should have been used for the poor (see *Voracious Idols and Violent Hands*, p. 95).

[77] Eire, *War Against the Idols*, p. 13.   [78] Ibid., p. 16.

[79] *Stripping of the Altars*, p. 75. Ironically his conclusion, to his mind, supports the fact that the old religion showed a remarkable ability to adapt to changing circumstances, and was not in need of the major (and devastating) transformation that followed (see pp. 87, 256, 337). Similarly Margaret Aston has taken issue with Huizinga's characterization of late medieval piety. In a reflection on the influence of Huizinga's book after fifty years, she argues all this complexity suggests an exuberant growth to religious experience and devotion at the end of the Middle Ages. While expressing gratitude for the sensitivity to the forms that Huizinga introduced, she takes issue with the fundamental premise. Is not the chief characteristic of this period one of vitality rather than decay, of moral fervor rather than lassitude, she asks? Beyond this, was this not a period of unstructured personal experience *par excellence*? ("Huizinga's Harvest: England and *The Waning of the Middle Ages*," in *Faith and Fire*) pp. 146–52. But whether this can be taken as a sign of religious depth and promise is debatable.

garden which stands between this sacred space and the world beyond. Within the sacred space inside, the donor kneels with the prayerbook open before him, attention focused on the virgin and her child, while angels hover overhead with a crown which is about to be placed on her head. Outside figures look out on a teeming world. But what, in the symbols which the picture contains, connects these worlds? How does one bridge the gap between the secular and sacred worlds? Is that sacred space one in which we too are invited? Van Eyck is ambivalent. The integration is made in typical late medieval fashion, by symbolically absorbing this world into the heavenly Jerusalem, whose imagery controls this picture. It is this move which, in some way, the Reformation will reverse. For Calvin at least this world itself is meant to display the glory of God.

While not everyone could afford the penance suggested by Chancellor Rolin or the display of the Limewood Sculptures, comparable efforts were being made on every hand. Devotional practices multiplied of those seeking assurance of salvation in the midst of the turmoil of late medieval society. While various movements of reform continued, the medieval system of worship was being strained. The crowds visiting the relic of the sacred cross near Tallard did not worry about the levels of seeing which Augustine defined, nor about the fine points of adoration. They had more deep-seated anxieties – about their family, health, especially about their own soul's salvation, and for them this was somehow connected with the relic they went to see as if they were seeing God himself. Margaret Aston admits, whatever the authorities taught, "for the unsophisticated believer who knelt before a statue there existed a practical identity between the image and the saint."[80] Such devotional outlets continued to multiply. By this time there was little the ecclesiastical authorities could do to control it, even when on rare occasions they would try. Indeed, in their rush to offer indulgences, the orders, the Pope, even the towns, sought to outdo each other, inadvertently contributing to the confusion and growing anxieties.

THE CRISIS OF FAITH: WHERE WAS GOD TO BE FOUND?

It is commonly assumed that the Reformation represents a radical break from a unified world of medieval piety. Historian John Bossy, for example, believes the reformers' focus on the word represents a "devaluation of the collective existence represented by sacraments, saints, and the 'unwritten' tradition of the Church, in favor of a naked confrontation with

[80] "Popular Religious Movements," *Faith and Fire*, p. 13.

Scriptures."[81] While it is not hard to find evidence for this in the Middle Ages, we have seen that this characterization is an oversimplification. For one thing we have observed currents at work which anticipated the inward faith that the reformers would later celebrate. For another, in many respects the unified medieval world had already been breaking up long before the reformers appeared on the scene. The hundred years leading up to the Reformation witnessed some of the most important social changes of all the Middle Ages.[82] On the economic and political front it was an age of major upheavals. Population growth began to recover some of the losses from fourteenth-century famines and recurring outbreaks of the plague. By 1500 the population of Europe reached 60 million (growing to 95 million by 1600). And while only a small percentage of these lived in the urban areas, because of growing trade, these centers played an increasingly important role, and became the centers for social and (eventually) religious change. Meanwhile the monarchies were able to consolidate their national territories at the expense of the Pope and the Bishops. All of this meant that traditional religious authority was being undermined and a new, unprecedented, openness to new practices and even beliefs became possible.

The role of towns will become so important in the Reformation that it calls for some comment. With traditional sources of religious authority being challenged, the cities began to take on a new role, not only in the economic and social lives of the people, but even in the moral supervision of their communities. The magistrates and city councils began to take "direct responsibility for education, welfare and morals."[83] They restricted the right of criminal asylum in the churches and monasteries. The practice grew of lay people endowing a preacher in the local cathedral, who would be employed by the city to preach a specified number of times a year.[84] Cities and cathedrals vied with each other to have the best preacher, and the people crowded in to hear their sermons. All of this reflects a growing dissatisfaction with the medieval Church and especially with the orders, who vigorously opposed these "secular" preachers – that is those who preached outside the monasteries in parishes. While lay donors were satisfied that such endowments were counted as a good work which might secure divine

---

[81] *Christianity in the West*, p. 97. Eamon Duffy similarly argued the Reformation represents more a 'violent disruption' than a fulfillment of medieval piety (*Stripping of the Altars*, p. 4).

[82] On this period see Ozment, *The Age of Reform*, and *The Reformation in the Cities* (New Haven: Yale University Press, 1975); Burke, *Popular Culture in Early Modern Europe*; and Euan Cameron (ed.), *Early Modern Europe: An Oxford History* (Oxford University Press, 1999).

[83] Ozment, *Age of Reform*, p. 205; and see *Reformation in the Cities*, pp. 34–5. The population estimates are Ozment's.

[84] *Reformation in the Cities*, pp. 37–42. Usually they would have to preach about a hundred sermons.

favor, the ecclesiastical authorities were increasingly losing touch with the longings of the common people.[85]

Steven Ozment argues the social upheaval, the economic growth and mobility, and the educational reforms all provide the means, even the opportunity, for the Reformation that was coming, but they did not provide its impetus. Even the moral failings of the clergy, or their tepid attempts to reform, was not the spark. That lay deeper. Ozment concludes: "The failure of the late medieval church to provide a theology and spirituality that could satisfy and discipline religious hearts and minds was the most important religious precondition of the Reformation."[86] In the final analysis the impetus came from the widespread hunger that the people felt for connection with the spiritual world, a world which, despite proliferating pilgrimages and devotional opportunities, seemed to be receding before their very eyes.

The deep dissatisfaction with aspects of the medieval Church and the widespread longings must be borne in mind when facing the question of how those who eagerly visited these pilgrimage sites could, only a few year later, join the crowds destroying these very images. How could those who stood quietly listening to Geiler von Kaysersberg one day, come to have such bitterness toward the very images he had so often used? Or similarly, what made a William Farel, raised by pious parents who took it upon themselves to visit a shrine and ensure their young son went along, come to have such horror toward practices of this kind? What made those who worshiped the images as a child turn on the image in iconoclastic rage as an adult?

The issue goes to the heart of people's search for salvation, and the elements they believed mediated this search. The issue for them, which the reformers would address, was the following: where is God to be found? Is God truly accessible through these medieval practices? Uncertainty about these questions would strike terror in the heart of those who were finding no satisfaction in their common rituals. Something of the depth of feelings these things aroused is shown in a play written by the Swiss Protestant Nicholas Manuel, *Die Totenfresser* (in 1523). In one scene the characters reflect on the indulgence market, one recalling that Christ chased the money

---

[85] Ibid., pp. 40–1; and Ozment, *Age of Reform*, p. 205; cf. Baxandall: "The altar pieces endowed by a parish had much in common with the town preachers endowed by the citizens to preach on the level they wanted, a gesture of independence and diminishing confidence in the clergy" (*Limewood Scultures*, p. 88).

[86] *Age of Reform*, p. 208. His analysis of the order of events in the Reformation is as follows: (1) the reformers' preaching provided the spark; (2) the popular response made it necessary; and (3) the grudging support and sanction of the government consolidated it (see *Reformation in the Cities*, pp. 124–5).

changers out of the temple, another claiming he never had believed in them anyway. One must have spoken for many when he recounted his experience of being placed under a ban for insulting the Pope. In mortal fear he and his wife took their precious egg money and rushed to Bern to buy an indulgence. When they returned home exhausted and hungry they fell on their knees and worshiped the indulgence. "I believed I had seen the very God himself," he confessed. But later after he understood that this was worthless, and realized the depths of his deception, he became enraged and took the letter of indulgence and "wiped my ass" with it. "I am still sick to my stomach about it," he confided to his friends.[87] He had been taught that God came to him in this way, but, when he thought more and looked harder, God was absent.

Deep-seated feelings were being aroused by the devotional practices, but an even deeper sense of anger, bitterness and betrayal resulted when these were questioned. Of course this relates to the fear of death and damnation which led to the profound melancholy that, Huizinga points out, was the constant companion of late medieval life. But I would argue that it also relates to the feelings aroused when one imaginative construal of the world, one way of understanding God's relationship to his creation, is shaken. In one sense the unified picture of the world which had been defined by Augustine was still reigning. But the practices that were supposed to navigate that world seemed not to be working. This was because the social, economic and religious changes taking place were conspiring to make this imaginative structure increasingly improbable. For it is precisely this picture of the world which facilitated or obstructed the way to salvation. This picture moreover came to expression most clearly in the forms by which medieval believers chose to express their devotion. For in these visible forms and practices, the complex of hope and vision, the tension between idolatry and worship was felt the strongest. Here images played a pivotal role. For, as David Freedberg points out, the impulse to image the divine is perennial and cannot ever be completely eradicated. Indeed the persistent attempts at suppression are themselves testimony to the inevitable urge to picture.[88]

But the break which occurred was not simply a matter of abandoning an older form of imagining the world in favor of a new one. The old world did not have to be merely left behind, it had to be destroyed. The motives and dynamics of iconoclasm are complex. But one thing seems

[87] Recounted in Ozment, *Reformation in the Cities*, p. 45. He notes, "the violent anticlericalism of the early period of the Reformation may be the response of those who were convinced that they had been religiously burdened in vain. Iconoclasts care."
[88] *The Power of Images*, pp. 54–65.

clear: when the crowds entered the churches to take down the images, they were ordinarily not entering the worship space of another, they were going into what was once their own space. They were desecrating spaces where they themselves had worshiped. Even if they would not have put it in these terms, for many this deconstruction was an act of corporate and visible repentance for the mistaken ways they had sought to understand God's presence. This deconstruction, or repentance, had to precede the turning to the world with a new vision and a new imagination. This explains why Farel and Calvin should feel the way they did about the ritual practices they knew when they were young, and why the crowds could gather at the cathedrals to take down images. Since the relic, and the image, are not media of spiritual power (Farel goes on at great length in his description of this event to show the folly of the supposed miracles at this site), they must be rooted out before a better way to come to God could be put forward.

But all of this still does not explain why Calvin or Farel could not see in Geiler's use of imagery a possible means of instruction, even of nurture. Why could they not believe this was something which the Holy Spirit could use, even as he used the verbal preaching of the word? For the image Geiler holds up recalls the encounter of Mary and Elizabeth which is part of a larger story which itself carries the spiritual meaning. Perhaps the image could encourage reflection on that larger story. But if others could find help in this way, Calvin and Farel could not. They were intent on – indeed obsessed with – the abuse, and so there could be no compromise. So, later, when they gave themselves to redrawing the spiritual map, for better or worse, there would be no place on that map for the woodcuts, images and pilgrimages.

CHAPTER 3

John Calvin: seeing God in the preached word

As Calvin recalls it at the end of his life, when he arrived in Geneva in August 1536, he did not have much to work with: "When I first arrived in this church there was almost nothing. They were preaching and that's all. They were good at seeking out idols and burning them, but there was no Reformation. Everything was in turmoil." From one point of view this was certainly true. Only the previous May 25 had the people accepted the reform, agreeing at a citizens' assembly on that day to "live according to the law of the Gospel and the word of God and to abolish all Papal abuses."[1] Indeed up until 1532, when William Farel arrived to preach for the first time, the challenge Geneva faced had been almost exclusively a political struggle for independence from the Prince Bishop of the House of Savoy and neighboring Bern. The first Reformed service was not held until Good Friday in 1533.

Before Calvin's arrival, Farel and his protégé Pierre Viret, when the authorities tolerated their presence in Geneva, were trying their best to hold things together, preaching and teaching in the churches. When Calvin made a detour through Geneva in the summer of 1536 on his way to a quiet scholarly life in Strasbourg, Farel immediately recognized the promise of this young scholar and, in a famous encounter, prevailed on him to throw in his lot with the reformers in Geneva.

The destruction of idols, to which Calvin referred, consisted of two episodes of iconoclasm in 1534 and 1535, which the timid magistrates condemned.[2] Contrasting the destruction of idols with genuine reformation

---

[1] Calvin's reminiscences are from the account of the last visit of the Company of Pastors to Calvin in April, 1564, composed by Pastor Jean Pinault, in Monter, *Calvin's Geneva* (New York : John Wiley & Sons, 1967), p. 95. Reference to the citizens' assembly is on p. 56. On Geneva during this period, in addition to Monter, see Ozment, *Age of Reform*; John McNeill, *The History and Character of Calvinism* (Oxford University Press, 1967); and Henri Naef, *Les Origines de la réforme à Genève*, 2 vols. (Geneva: Librairie Droz, 1936).
[2] Monter, *Calvin's Geneva*, pp. 50–4.

should not be taken to imply Calvin believed the removal of images was a matter of indifference. As we will see images were regularly and unconditionally condemned in his writings. Indeed, while he did not advocate iconoclasm as a Christian duty (thinking it was the magistrates' work to remove images from churches), we will argue that Calvin's project was at heart iconoclastic in the broader sense. That is he proposed removing not just the images but the whole medieval system of worship, root and branch. This removal, however, was not an end in itself, but was part of a larger project: reconstructing the Church and society after a new blueprint provided by Scripture. Thinking of his calling in terms of this reconstruction led Calvin to use "architecture" (cf. the use of "plan" and related terms in the *Institutes*), as a kind of master trope by which he imagined God's redemptive work.[3]

The fact that Calvin should insist there was no "reformation" is an important indication of his view of real reform. For, while there was much to be done, from one point of view, the reform of worship had already taken place. The magistrates had approved of abolishing the Mass and requested a vote by the people to live by the Gospel, and most of the images had already been removed from the churches.[4] Of equal importance is the fact that Calvin belongs to the second generation of reformers. Those who sought to purify the church and its worship from the accumulation of practices and devotions that we reviewed in the last chapter had already accomplished a great deal. Luther's writings had been widely distributed – indeed Calvin himself had certainly read many of these while still a Catholic in Paris.[5] Moreover Zwingli had already brought about the reform of the Church in Zurich during the 1520s and, when Calvin arrived in Geneva, that reformer had already been dead for five years. It is important then for us to review briefly the struggles that these reformers had over the question

---

[3] See *Institutes*, ii, xi, 1 and ii, xxiv, 16 *et al.*, trans. Ford Battles, ed. John McNeill (Philadelphia: Westminster Press, 1960). And "all things will tend to this end, that God, the Artificer of the universe, is made manifest to us in Scripture" (i, vi, 1). Cf. Catherine Randall, *Building Codes: The Aesthetics of Calvinism in Early Modern Europe* (Philadelphia: University of Pennsylvania Press, 1999), p. 27.

[4] A good discussion of these events is in Eire, *War Against the Idols*, pp. 135–40. Eire points out that these activities reflected the growing strength of the Reformation supporters. In all this, François Wendel notes, "one should be careful not to underestimate the work that Farel had already done. In most of the directions which were to claim Calvin's activity, Farel appears as the precursor" (*Calvin: The Origins and Development of his Religious Thought*, trans. Philip Mairet [London: Collins, 1963 (1950)], p. 49).

[5] *Calvin: Origins and Development*, p. 20. Wendel goes on to point out that Calvin had no real relation to the reform until 1533, which was the probable time of his conversion to the Evangelical cause – a mere three years before his arrival in Geneva (pp. 37–9).

of images and the visual mediation of faith, as a precedent for the work of Calvin.

THE PRECEDENTS OF LUTHER AND ZWINGLI

Martin Luther's position on images and, indeed, on the role of creation, in religion, grew out of his own struggles as an Augustinian monk to find a righteous and merciful God.[6] The luxuriant growth of medieval practices had been all too familiar to Luther and, as a monk, he had tried unsuccessfully to find satisfaction through many of these practices. As a professor at the University of Wittenberg between 1513 and 1516 he began a series of biblical lectures, first on the Psalms and then on Paul's letter to the Romans, that was to radically change his perspective on these things. In the Psalms Luther first glimpsed the powerful righteousness of God which the Psalmist compares to the "mighty mountains" (Ps. 36:6). In his lectures on the letter to the Romans he came to his central theological insight that the just have access to this righteousness by their faith (Rom. 1:17). Human teaching, he notes, can only help one become righteous before others. "But only the gospel reveals the righteousness of God (i.e. who is righteous and how a man can be and become righteous before God) by that faith alone by which one believes the word of God."[7] The whole of Luther's theology, and his view on any visual mediation, grew from this foundational preoccupation with the righteousness of God and justification by faith. Since God's righteousness can only be made available to the believer by faith, any external mediation is wrong, not because it is physical, but because it constitutes a kind of works righteousness that violates justification by faith. Indeed Luther here makes a fundamental break with the medieval dualism between the spiritual and material, insisting – in a way that even Calvin will not – that the fundamental dichotomy is not between matter and spirit but between faith and works.[8] Thus in his commentary Luther

---

[6] On Luther's theological development see Roland Bainton, *Here I Stand: A Life of Martin Luther* (New York: Abingdon-Cokesbury, 1957); Philip Watson, *Let God be God: An Interpretation of the Theology of Martin Luther* (Philadelphia: Fortress, 1947); G. Ebeling, *Luther: An Introduction to his Thought*, trans. R. A. Wilson (Philadelphia: Fortress Press, 1970 [1964]). On his theology of images see Carl C. Christensen, *Art and the Reformation in Germany* (Athens, Ohio: Ohio and Wayne State University Presses, 1979); and John Dillenberger, *Images and Relics: Theological Perceptions and Visual Images in Sixteenth Century Europe* (Oxford University Press, 1999), ch. 4.

[7] Luther, *Lectures on Romans*, ed. and trans. by Wilhelm Pauck (Philadelphia: Westminster Press, 1961), pp. 17, 18.

[8] In contrast with Calvin, Wendel notes: Lutheran theology "had never admitted the strict dualism that Western theology had affirmed ever since St. Augustine" (*Calvin: Origins and Development*, p. 347). Carlos Eire points out that since Luther changed the spirit–matter dualism to one of faith–works, he always considered iconoclasm a form of works righteousness (*War against the Idols*, pp. 68–9).

goes on to describe the way sinful people exchanged the glory of God for the worship of creatures:

Their error was that in their worship they did not take the God-head for what it is in itself, but changed it by fitting it to their own needs and desires. Everyone wanted the Godhead to be in him whom he happened to like, and thus they turned the truth of God into a lie.[9]

The error is a lack of faith in the living God. Even the Old Testament worshipers of Baal erred by an idolatry of the heart: "Thus they worship this idol of the heart as if it represented God himself and as if it were the very truth and righteousness."[10]

Two theological warrants, which Luther was to develop later in support of this view of idolatry and images, call for special comment. The first is Luther's view that all created things are really masks of God (*larvae Dei*). This means on the one hand that they are not anything in themselves, but are only "veils" or media in which the creator is concealed, and in and through which this creator can speak to us. But this means, on the other hand, that these masks, which include all the "stations" in life (magistrate, schoolmaster, parent, etc.) as well as all created objects, can be honored as those through whom God may be reverenced and honored.[11] This has obvious and critical importance, secondly, for Luther's view of Christ's continuing presence in the world (and especially in the sacrament). The God who as creator is "unrestingly active in all his creatures" is also the God who is revealed in Jesus Christ. This led Luther to assert the "ubiquity" of Christ's presence in the world even as he is at the right hand of God.[12] While all of creation can speak of God's love in a general way, it is only in the historical intervention of God in Christ that we glimpse God as he is in himself. So in the word and sacraments we can see and hear the glory, not of the invisible God, but of the God incarnate in Jesus Christ. Of this Philip Watson concludes: "That is why Luther insists the true and complete body of Christ is present in the Eucharist."[13]

---

[9] *Lectures on Romans*, pp. 23–4.

[10] Ibid., p. 307. The resulting openness on questions of decorations and images also appears in this early work. As he says of the "new law": "Nor does it belong to the new law to build such and such churches and to adorn them thus and so and to sing in them in one way or another. Nor are organs, altar decorations, chalices, or pictures required" (p. 381).

[11] See *Luther's Works*, ed. J. Pelikan (St. Louis: Concordia, 1963), vol. XXVI. In his lectures on Galatians Luther says: "Now the whole creation is a face or mask of God . . . there must be masks or social positions, for God has given them and they are his creatures," p. 95 (on Gal. 2:6). See the discussion in G. Ebeling, *Luther: An Introduction to his Thought*, trans. R. A. Wilson (Philadelphia: Fortress Press, 1970), p. 198, and in Philip Watson, *Let God be God: An Interpretation of the Theology of Martin Luther* (Philadelphia: Fortress, 1947), p. 76.

[12] See Watson, *Let God be God*, pp. 162–3.   [13] Ibid., p. 163.

This view of Christ's bodily presence has clear implications for Luther's developing openness to the use of images and pictures in worship. For his view of creation as a "veil" of God allows him the freedom to see elements of creation as "mental signs" which can potentially witness to God's loving presence.[14] At the same time his fear of "works" made him wary of any use of images that would imply they have any spiritual effect, or provide any means of gaining God's favor. The tension between these two themes produced a recurring pattern in the thought of Luther. The insistence that everything must grow out of his fundamental conviction about justification, while it allowed him to be open to the issue of images, at the same time kept him from developing a consistent doctrine either of creation or of images.[15]

In his famous Ninety-Five Theses of 1517, for example, Luther addresses the issue, not of images, but of indulgences, noting – in a common theme in the Protestant polemic about images – that this money would be better used to care for the poor than to build elaborate churches. Later, when more radical elements led to outbreaks of iconoclasm, Luther was forced to pay more attention to the question of images. His maturing views on images were articulated in a series of sermons preached upon his return from a year away from Wittenberg, where he had been under the protective custody of Frederick the Wise at Warburg Castle. During his absence Andreas Karlstadt, in defiance of Frederick's policy of moderation, incited people to attack images. Karlstadt argued, for example, that a crucifix reminds one only of Christ's physical sufferings, not of the more important spiritual struggle – it is therefore an actual barrier to right understanding.[16]

In a famous series of eight sermons preached the week of March 9, 1522, upon his return from Warburg Castle, Luther seeks to sketch in his major views of worship and the liturgy as a means of taking control of a volatile situation. He makes two major points relating to images. First he argues that it is the preaching of the word, grasped by faith, that changes lives and even shakes the authority of princes. Since the word as it is preached has real spiritual power, the response of faith to this word must be without compulsion – therefore all violent means of removing obstacles to faith

---

[14] Watson insists that ubiquity is really a testimony to the conviction that where God is at work, he is at work in love (*Let God be God*, p. 163).

[15] See Sergiusz Michalski, *The Reformation and the Visual Arts: The Protestant Image Question in Western and Eastern Europe* (New York/London: Routledge, 1993). "It is hard to overemphasize the influence of the doctrine of justification on Luther's attitude towards art" (p. 9). He also notes that Luther did not develop a consistent theology that related to images (p. 37).

[16] See Bainton, *Here I Stand*, pp. 158–62. Notice how Karlstadt reinforces the older dualism that Luther has discarded.

(as in iconoclasm) are misguided. He notes then in the second sermon: "I opposed indulgences and all the papists, but never with force. I simply taught, preached, and wrote God's Word; otherwise I did nothing."[17] Thus he can say that images in themselves are not a problem for the believer, for having understood by faith God's goodness, nothing can be seen to compete with the power that is resident in God's word of grace. In the third sermon he addresses images specifically: "We are free to have them or not, although it would be much better if we did not have them at all. I am not partial to them." All the struggles over this question, he goes on to say, amount to making a "must" over what is free. The first commandment, he points out, can be construed either to condemn all images, or simply the worship of images. In the face of such uncertainty "who should be so bold as to destroy images?" Paul certainly was not emphatic on the issue; in fact he seemed to tolerate them because "he wanted to show that outward things could do no harm to faith, if only the heart does not cleave to them or put its trust in them."[18]

Clearly they can do no harm, but are they of no positive use? Luther came gradually to believe they did have some positive role to play, so long as one did not trust in them – indeed Luther was realistic enough to know that when we think about biblical stories we inevitably form pictures in our minds. His German Bible (1534) was filled with many woodcuts of the biblical stories. Of these he says:

Pictures contained in these books we would paint on walls for the sake of remembrance and better understanding, since they do no more harm on walls than in books. It is to be sure better to paint pictures on walls of how God created the world, how Noah built the ark, and whatever other good stories there may be, than to paint shameless worldly things. Yes, would to God that I could persuade the rich and mighty that they would permit the whole Bible to be painted on houses, on the inside and outside, so that all can see it.[19]

As we will note below, such images did in fact multiply in Luther's Germany, numerous woodcuts adorned the German Bible, Luther's catechisms, and a variety of Reformation tracts.[20] Inexpensive broadsheets which circulated widely provided a visual analogue to the reformers' preaching and constructed a kind of visual universe that reflected the

---

[17] *Luther's Works*, ed. John Doberstein (Philadelphia: Muhlenberg Press, 1959), vol. LI, p. 77.
[18] Ibid., pp. 81–3.
[19] Ibid., vol. XL, p. 99 quoted in John Dillenberger, *Images and Relics* (Oxford University Press, 1999), pp. 91–2. The passage goes on to say, "Images are preaching for the eyes."
[20] Christensen notes that Luther's first complete German Bible contained 117 different woodcuts (*Art and the Reformation in Germany* [Athens, Ohio: Ohio University Press, 1979], p. 170).

struggle of the reformers' scriptural preaching with the lies of the Pope and his minions.[21] Something similar could be said of the altarpieces that were commissioned for the new Lutheran churches.[22] The congregation at Wittenberg commissioned Luther's friend Lucas Cranach to paint an altarpiece, which was installed in 1547, the year after Luther's death (Figure 3).

This is a graphic display of the art that followed from Luther's theology. It is in fact a visual image of the church as the place where the word is rightly preached and sacraments administered according to the Scriptures. Luther felt that altarpieces should be about the sacraments; paintings of God and Christ can be shown elsewhere.[23]

On the right side of the predella Luther points to the cross which stands between the preacher and the congregation (which includes the Cranachs and Luther's wife and children). Above are three panels which portray the three sacraments which Luther had accepted: Baptism, Lord's Supper, and absolution (or penitence). In the larger central panel Christ sits with John on his chest; across the table from him a servant has just given Luther the communion cup. On the left panel Melancthon baptizes an infant by sprinkling water over it and on the right Bugenhagen, pastor of the Wittenberg city church, stands holding keys, while a penitent kneels before him. Note how scriptural events are made contemporary, Luther receives the cup at the supper, Melancthon rather than John the Baptist administers that sacrament, and their colleague Bugenhagen, rather than Peter, holds the keys to the kingdom.[24] For these it is the preaching of the word and right administration of the sacrament that controls the use of this imagery. One sees a Protestant translation of imagery of medieval altarpieces, which serves to reinforce the preaching and activity of the church in which it is placed.

[21] See Robert W. Scribner, *For the Sake of the Simple Folk: Popular Propaganda for the German Reformation* (Cambridge University Press, 1981). Scribner points out that this medium was clearly an extension of the reformers' preaching ministry, indeed it was from the beginning a hybridized medium of print and imagery (pp. 2–6).

[22] Significant altarpieces were painted for Protestant churches in Schneeberg, Wiemar, Dessau and Wittenberg (see Dillenberger, *Images and Relics*, pp. 96–107). Though Christensen discusses these as well, he refers to others not as well known (*Art and the Reformation*, p. 135).

[23] Dillenberger, *Images and Relics*, p. 93.

[24] Christensen, *Art and the Reformation*, pp. 139–40. The Apology on the Augsburg Confession, Article xiii, on the number and use of the sacraments, says: "The sacraments, therefore, are Baptism, Lord's Supper, and Absolution (which is the sacrament of penitence), for these rites have the commandment of God, and the promise of grace, which is the heart of the New Testament" (*The Book of Concord: The Confessions of the Evangelical Lutheran Church*, ed. and trans. by Theodore G. Tappert [Philadelphia: Fortress, 1959], p. 211). In the previous section absolution is specifically connected with the power of the keys.

Figure 3   Lucas Cranach, the Elder, *Wittenberg Altarpiece: The Last Supper and Scenes from the Life of Martin Luther*. Marienkirche, Wittenberg, Germany, 1547.

This altarpiece demonstrates the way a Protestant iconography is being formed. A prominent emphasis of the Reformers was a focus on the incorporation of children into the believing community – the major reformers often issued catechisms in the earliest stages of their ministry. Pictures of Christ receiving the children, or the baptism of children, themes relatively rare in the medieval period, thus became important subjects of Protestant paintings and woodcuts. The Last Supper, often with the chalice prominently placed, also becomes a prominent theme in areas influenced by Luther. This probably was to emphasize the contrast between the Lutheran communion of both kinds with the previous practice of distributing only the wafer.[25]

But if these images do suggest a new iconography, they do not present a new symbolic image of the world, apart from what can be found in medieval altarpieces. The material they present is preaching under another form. As Neil MacGregor notes in his discussion of Cranach, "This is art as argument. And the clue to this pictorial puzzle lies in the proper understanding of Scripture."[26] Indeed while under Luther's influence certain Christian practices – preaching, catechizing, and support of Christian marriage, and Christian views of work – are developing new (and eventually revolutionary) shapes, the reformer insists that other cultural practices, such as the production of images and pictures, are of minor importance – they belong to the freedom of the Christian. But are they a matter of indifference? If idolatry is not simply a matter of misplaced worship but also a confluence of cultural and religious values concentrated in symbolic images, might not fresh images also potentially portray the power of a new worldview? While he is speaking of the popular imagery of the German Reformation, one can apply Robert Scribner's conclusion more generally to this stage of the Protestant revolt: "It did not produce the powerful new symbols of allegiance which might have created a new 'symbolic universe' distinctly different from that of the old faith."[27]

A very different, more radical, view of the use of imagery is to be found in Ulrich Zwingli's teaching in Zurich during the 1520s. Zwingli (1484–1531) was trained as a humanist in Vienna and Basle before coming to Zurich in 1518, after ten years as a parish priest in Glarus and three years at the pilgrimage center of Einsiedeln. A poet and musician, Zwingli had studied and reflected deeply on questions of church music, but his careful study of Scripture had led him to the view that music, along with any other form that served to distract from the simple preaching of the word, should

---

[25] See Christensen, *Art and the Reformation*, pp. 147–54. He points out that of 441 pre-Reformation pictures analyzed only 4 were found to portray the Last Supper (p. 149).

[26] MacGregor with Langmuir, *Seeing Salvation*, p. 202.

[27] *For the Sake of the Simple Folk*, p. 248. It could be argued that Luther did in fact inaugurate a new tradition in music in his role of organizing choirs and introducing hymns and congregational singing, but this did not happen in the visual arts (see Michalski, *The Reformation and the Visual Arts*, p. 40). The only exception to this is the work of Albrecht Dürer, though his superb work did not contribute to developing a tradition of Protestant art. In fact Erwin Panofsky notes a decline in North German art in the late 1600s and through the 1700s ("Comments on Art and Reformation," in Craig Harbison [ed.], *Symbols in Transformation: Iconographic Themes at the Time of the Reformation, An Exhibition in Memory of Erwin Panofsky* [The Art Museum, Princeton University, March 15 – April 13, 1969], p. 12). See Christensen, *Art and the Reformation*, pp. 177 and 181ff.

not be allowed in worship.[28] During his time at Einsiedeln he had been appalled at the devotional abuses and had come to believe that the common people were too often distracted by many things that had nothing to do with true worship or the salvation of their souls. In his *Account of the Faith* which he prepared at the request of the Emperor for the Diet of Augsburg, Zwingli describes his view of God's power in a way that anticipates Calvin: "I know and believe that this most excellent majesty, which is my God, freely determines all things, so that his counsel and determination hangeth on no cause or occasion of any creature."[29] When the time came, this God "sent his son to take on him our nature on every part, except that is disposed and ready to sin . . . [so that he might] be a mediator, which for us, by offering his innocent body unto death, might satisfy God's most upright justice."[30] This sovereignty and unique mediation led Zwingli to believe that the preached word of this gospel must be central to worship, while a sacrament could be nothing other than "an initiatory ceremony or a pledging . . . A sacrament therefore, since it cannot be anything more than an initiation or public inauguration, cannot have any power to free the conscience. That can be freed by God alone."[31] The worship experience then should focus the heart and mind on the mediating presence of Christ who is experienced through faith in the preached word. The theology that grounded Zwingli's view of images therefore rests on the two sides of a single assertion: Only God as he uniquely offers himself in Jesus Christ can properly be the object of trust; only a whole-hearted and unconditional response on the part of the believer can properly appropriate this offer of grace.

For Zwingli it was in worship above all that this true faith is nurtured and expressed. In 1523 the question of images led to a disputation. Here Zwingli professed himself willing to delay abolishing images until the preaching had won over the hearts of the people: "Let us labor to restore to their creator hearts that are given over to this world." For Zwingli seeking forgiveness by any other means than through the death of Christ is of a piece

---

[28] Charles Garside, *Zwingli and the Arts* (New Haven: Yale University Press, 1966), pp. 21, 22, 54. Walter Köhler, an earlier biographer, notes: "Of the three great reformers, he was musically the most gifted; technical knowledge and power brought to fruition his native ability, and he played the lute with especial fluency" (quoted in Garside, *Zwingli and the Arts*, p. 22n61).

[29] *An Account of the Faith*, trans. Thomas Cotsford (Geneva: n.p., 1555), Second Article, p. 8. It is clear that Zwingli here depends more on the medieval tradition of Duns Scotus, where the regularity of the world rests uniquely on God's will, rather than his reason as in Thomas Aquinas.

[30] Ibid., p. 10.

[31] *Commentary on True and False Religion*, ed. Samuel M. Jackson and Clarence N. Heller (Durham: Labyrinth Press, 1981), p. 181.

with idolatry, whether this involve a trust in images, the Pope, or even oneself.[32]

While this led Zwingli to exclude any traditional role for images, it did not keep worship in Zurich from taking on a particular visual and dramatic character. Lee Palmer Wandel has argued that this theology resulted in an experience in which this grace was intended to be made visible in the clearest possible way, but only as each element served the word that is heard. In the Zurich Munster which was Zwingli's parish church, the people gathered in the nave of the church, men to the right, women to the left. After the sermon there was a short prayer, and the reading of the communion narrative in I Corinthians 11:20–29. Then thanksgiving was made by the congregation, the men and women alternating. The minister then read John 6:47–63 and the people recited the Apostles' Creed. After another prayer the elements were distributed.

On some of Zwingli's written works simple woodcuts underline in a straightforward manner the truth that Zwingli wanted to guide evangelical worship. In his vernacular work on the Lord's Supper, which would have been read in many homes, the title page is adorned with simple images that illustrate the Christian Lord's Supper (Figure 4). At the top is a Jewish passover supper, on each side the collecting of the manna over against the feeding of the five thousand (as the illustrations of this supper in the Old and New Testaments) and then, below, the last supper of Christ with his disciples. These images portray and elaborate this special meal in a clear and simple way, making visible that central tenet of the Christian faith in a way that would have been accessible to all who participated in the worship experience. It was teaching by pictures the narrative connections between these miracles and the communion meal. Protestant religious culture in Zurich, Wandel concludes, "was visual but not in the place we have traditionally looked."[33] Clearly the images here play the role of helping people envision the theological meaning proclaimed in the preached word and in the sacrament.

But for Zwingli the symbolic connection between God and the world has been broken; only Christ appropriated by faith makes that connection for us. And he comes to us in the preached word. Unlike Luther the critical dichotomy is not between faith and works, but between the invisible and

---

[32] W. P. Stephens, *The Theology of Huldrych Zwingli* (Oxford: Clarendon Press, 1986), pp. 67, 155; Zwingli quote p. 37.

[33] Lee Palmer Wandel, "Envisioning God: Image and Liturgy in Reformation Zurich," *Sixteenth Century Journal* 24/1 (1993), pp. 21–40; quote p. 40. She notes the stark contrast between this and elaborate settings for the Eucharist in the late Middle Ages.

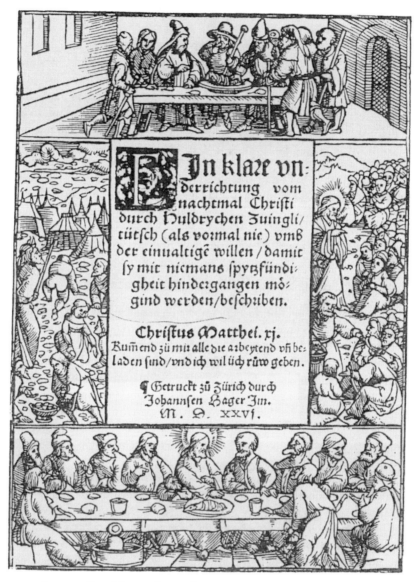

Figure 4   Hans Hager, title page from Zwingli's book *On the Lord's Supper.*
Zentralbibliothek, Zurich, Switzerland, 1526.

visible, the one belonging to the realm of faith, the other to that of unbelief. If the visual element is present, as Wandel argues, it is clearly subordinated to the word, invisible and heard. In his famous response to Valentin Compar, 1525, Zwingli argues that the true believer is one who trusts in God alone. Anything that one places between oneself and God immediately takes on the character of a substitute. By this time Zwingli had come to realize that such substitutes could include either inward mental idols, or external forms. Images in the Church are clearly forbidden because, in that setting, they will always be subject to religious interpretation. Whether or not these things are actually worshiped, Zwingli notes, when fear grips their hearts, the people go to them for help, betraying where their trust truly lies.[34]

The argument that Zwingli develops appears to operate on two levels. On a fundamental level he attacks the rampant superstition that characterized the Church at the end of the Middle Ages. Faith in God, he believed, had been seriously compromised by the devotion paid to the saints and by the elaborate system of penance. This was inappropriate because only God was worthy of a person's trust, and this trust must be unconditional and unmediated. But this implies a second level of argument. Zwingli's preference for the mystical and nominalist aspects of the medieval tradition stimulated him to take his desire to reform worship a step further. Not only are images a distraction, or (potentially) idolatrous,[35] they are actually incapable of conveying the truth that God's word contains. Images simply cannot play any religious role; their role is merely illustrative or possibly educational. The arts of the eye cannot express the holy because, Zwingli insists, they are bound to time, which is an aspect of this world, a material thing. Whereas the believer is bound to God by faith in a relationship that transcends time. So nothing we learn from the senses has power to bring us to Christ. Even if we had an image of Christ, Zwingli argued, we would

---

[34] It appears that these things are forbidden largely on the grounds that they have been made objects of worship. Persons and stories may be displayed outside the church provided that they do not give rise to any act of reverence. Garside notes that "the artist's activity is to be limited henceforth to the representation of historic events" (*Zwingli and the Arts*, p. 150). This emphasis Calvin will develop further with important implications. As with Calvin, all ecclesiastical art is forbidden. Zwingli, with all his reforming zeal, appeared to have a keen sense of meeting people where they were. He wanted as little ceremony as possible, but allowed that one should "use some, so that we don't keep the act from being completely dull." He consistently made allowances for what he regarded as human weakness. See the discussion in P. Auksi, "Simplicity and Silence," *Journal of Religious History* 10 (1978), p. 344.

[35] Zwingli assigned the word "strange god," *Abgott* (rather than *Götze*), to anything which, as an external or material phenomenon, turns one's mind away from true belief (Garside, *Zwingli and the Arts*, p. 164).

only learn from it that he was handsome, not that he was our Lord and God.[36]

The two kinds of belief stand in absolute contrast to one another: "Right, true, brave, and steadfast reverence for God is when a man carries his God with him in his heart." The false believer is one who by "looking at images or idols induces devotion for no longer than one sees them and mumbles a meaningless word." Thus, Charles Garside concludes, for Zwingli: "the prime symbol of true belief is the word, invisible and heard; the prime symbol of false belief is the image, visible and seen."[37]

CALVIN'S PROGRAM OF RECONSTRUCTION

All of these struggles and debates were in the past when Calvin arrived in Geneva in 1536. What exactly their influence was on him is hard to establish, though he must have been aware, at least, of much of what was written by these reformers.[38] As we have noted, Geneva had gone through its own anguish and come out openly with the reform. Indeed the city had taken a number of steps that would provide the basis for Calvin's work. We noted in the last chapter that cities at the end of the Middle Ages had come to play a growing role in the economic, social and even moral life of their citizens. Geneva was no exception, and indeed may have excelled over other cities in this respect. Henri Naef shows that from the beginning of the sixteenth century the magistrates of Geneva were often men of deep faith who were concerned for the welfare of the citizenry. They sought out preachers who would edify the people; they fought heresy.[39] And in the end, as we have seen, after some vacillation, they supported the people's decision to side with the Reformation. In many respects then the entire apparatus of medieval devotion had already been dismantled – the monasteries had been closed, the images were gone, the Mass had been abolished. In a single generation, the world of the medieval Church in which most of the citizens

---

[36] Stephens, *Theology of Huldrych Zwingli*, p. 174.

[37] *Zwingli and the Arts*, pp. 147 and 175. This latter distinction recalls the *Libri Carolini*.

[38] Michalski argues that Karlstadt and Zwingli did not influence Calvin as much as we might think: "They arrived at similar positions by very different paths" (*The Reformation and the Visual Arts*, p. 43). We do know, however, that Calvin read much that Luther wrote, and he must have been aware of the debates over images; it is also well known that he was not impressed with Zwingli's theology – which implies at least a familiarity with it (see Wendel, *Calvin: Origins and Development*, p. 135–7), though Carlos Eire argues that via Farel, Calvin was surely influenced by Zwingli on the question of true worship (*War Against the Idols*, p. 123 and 218n102).

[39] Naef, *Les Origines de la réforme à Genève*, vol. I, pp. 135–218. Though he notes that heresy "n'est jamais affaire de doctrine, mais de fait. C'est l'éternel pacte avec le diable, la participation au sabbat les crimes commandés par Satan" (p. 216).

of Geneva had been raised had disappeared. The question was not simply what kind of preaching would replace that of the monks, but what kind of world would the people live in? And more importantly, since the older images were being destroyed, what kind of images would shape their world?

So Calvin came to Geneva at a propitious time in its history. And he came at an opportune time in his own development as a young theologian and reformer. Amazingly the first edition of his *Institutes* had already appeared – in March 1536, five months before his arrival in Geneva, and only two or three years after his conversion. There he had already laid down the fundamental lines of his thinking. The second edition that appeared in 1539, however, was three times longer, and included the critical opening chapters on the knowledge of God and the knowledge of Self.[40] This growing work was to provide the structure not only for Calvin's thought and practice, but for generations of Reformed Christians after him.

a. Theological grounds

Calvin's views on the visual and images throughout his life were based consistently on his theological vision. While briefly described in the 1536 edition, the 1539 edition lays out the definitive structure of Calvin's theology around two poles: the knowledge of God and the knowledge of ourselves. An early commentator Caspar Olevianus described this in an introduction to the 1585 edition (which became the standard seventeenth-century edition) as follows:

The central intention [scopus] of this Christian Institutes is twofold: First, that knowledge of God which leads to blessed immortality; and, second, in connection with this [the knowledge of] ourselves. In order that we might understand this [scopus], [Calvin] simply sets before us the arrangement [methodus] of the Apostles' Creed as something familiar to all Christians.[41]

---

[40] These were, of course, in Latin; a French edition appeared in 1541, a further Latin edition in 1550 (translated in 1551) and a final edition in 1559 (translated in 1560). See Wendel, *Calvin: Origins and Development*, pp. 112–18. Interestingly for our purposes, much of the most substantial discussion of images does not appear until the 1550 and 1559 editions. Clearly he considered that other issues were more immediate and pressing.

[41] Quoted in Richard Muller, "In the Light of Orthodoxy: The 'Method and Disposition' of Calvin's *Institutio* from the Perspective of Calvin's Late Sixteenth Century Editors," *Sixteenth Century Journal* 28/4 (1997), p. 1217. Modern interpreters have picked up on both elements as critical to Calvin's intentions. In his classic work, Edward A. Dowey argued that the twofold knowledge of God and self structures the work (see *The Knowledge of God in Calvin's Theology* [New York: Columbia University Press, 1952], pp. 41–2); T. H. L. Parker argued that it was the Apostles' Creed that gave Calvin his structure (*The Doctrine of the Knowledge of God: A Study in Calvin's Theology* [Grand Rapids, Mich.: Eerdmans, 1959 (1952)], pp. 119–21). As is clear from Olevianus' summary,

In another sense one might argue that all of Calvin's thought is related in one way or another to the active direction and transcendence of God. Consistent with the reformers generally Calvin begins with the insistence on the "otherness" of God and opposes any thought of mixing God with anything created – an impulse that, in part, responds to all the spiritual practices that had grown up in the Middle Ages.[42] Of necessity then Calvin begins his theological reflection with the knowledge of God: "It is certain that man never achieves a clear knowledge of himself unless he has first looked upon God's face and then descends from contemplating him to scrutinize himself" (I, i, 2). As John McNeill notes, the knowledge of ourselves, to which Calvin refers, may be taken to include all mankind and indeed all of creation, since Calvin argues elsewhere the person is a microcosm of creation.[43] So all knowledge of oneself, and consequently all right knowledge of creation, must ultimately come from God. But this does not mean that such knowledge is directly revealed by God, for Calvin goes on to argue that it is, first, naturally implanted in the person's mind (I, iii), and, secondly, it shines forth from creation for all to see (I, v). The problem then is not that the knowledge of God is unavailable, but the human mind is so blinded by ignorance and malice that it fails to grasp it. Human minds, Calvin argues, "neglect sound investigation": "Out of curiosity they fly off into empty speculations. They do not therefore apprehend God as he offers himself, but imagine him as they have fashioned him in their own presumption" (I, iv, 1).

Here at the beginning Calvin lays out both the essential structure of our knowledge of God and the world, and the severe limitation of the human mind in comprehending either. On the one hand God has graciously granted an awareness of himself in the human heart and his glory shines through every aspect of creation (a fact we focus on in some detail below). But, on the other hand, apart from God's intervention, human eyes are blind to this splendor. So the problem of knowledge does not lie in creation, but in the human heart. Left to its devices it will "imagine" what only can reflect the human arrogance and pride that is a result of its fallen condition – which he goes on to describe in the sections which follow in great detail,

---

sixteenth-century interpreters accepted both views. See Muller, "In the Light of Orthodoxy," p. 1222. I am dependent on Muller for much of the discussion of the structure. See also Richard Muller, *The Unaccommodated Calvin: Studies in the Foundation of a Theological Tradition* (New York: Oxford University Press, 2000); and Wendel, *Calvin: Origins and Development*, part two: "The Theological Doctrine."

[42] It also reflects certain medieval philosophical traditions such as those associated with the name of Duns Scotus, though the influence of this has been disputed. See the discussion in Wendel, *Calvin: Origins and Development*, pp. 127–9.

[43] *Institutes*, I, i, 2., note 5. On the person as microcosm see I, v, 3.

including extended references to images and idolatry. Calvin never makes any positive reference to what we would call the work of "imagination." The nearest equivalent is "fantasy" (fantasia) which he attacks as a lesser faculty. "Since he only is true God, it follows that the inventions of men are utterly insane and therefore deceptions and mockings of the devil to deceive mankind."[44]

Over against this pursuit of human illusion and superstition, there is "sound investigation," which alone can lead to a true knowledge of God and his creation. Calvin generally assumed that the human mind, when its moral capacity had been repaired, was capable of grasping the world as it actually is.[45] This sound method was dependent on a particular view of the centrality of the understanding over against the will: "The understanding is, as it were, the leader and governor of the soul; and . . . the will is always mindful of the bidding of the understanding, and its own desires awaits the judgment of the understanding" (I, xv, 7). This sound method of applying the understanding to grasp the ordered world Calvin will illustrate both in the substance and method of his own work.

In substance sound method is laid out in the ordering of the chapters and books which follow. In Chapter 6 of Book One, Scripture is described as the only means by which one can come to right knowledge of God. This knowledge is further conveyed to us in Scripture by the ministry of the Holy Spirit who is uniquely present in the reading and preaching of Scripture (Chapter 7 and following). Then in Book Two Calvin elaborates the knowledge of God as redeemer which is given to us in the law and then the Gospel. In the latter Christ is sent to uniquely bridge the (moral) gulf between God and ourselves. Book Three then goes on to describe the merits that come to us as we receive the grace offered to us in Jesus Christ, the mediator. Here Calvin discusses the nature of regeneration and the Christian life. But since people cannot be grafted into Christ by the Holy Spirit without the use of "means," Calvin concludes in Book Four with a discussion of the means by which the redemption of Christ is applied to the human heart, i.e. by the Church and the sacraments. Under the guidance of Scripture, these external means become the proper way in which believers come to know God and live out the grace of God which is offered to all in Christ. This theological structure constitutes the "sound investigation" which alone leads to true knowledge.

---

[44] Commentary on Jer. 51:19. On "Fantasia" as the lowest of the human faculties see *Institutes*, I, xv, 6–7. See the discussion in William J. Bousma, *Calvin: A Sixteenth Century Portrait* (Oxford University Press, 1988), p. 80. Bousma notes that Calvin omits any positive treatment of imagination and creativity, attacking them under the label of fantasy.

[45] Bousma points out that this was generally assumed throughout the Middle Ages. *Calvin*, p. 98.

But Calvin also seeks to show this "sound investigation" in the structure itself of the *Institutes*. From his training as a humanist and a lawyer in Paris, Calvin was consistently interested in proper order and method. He intended the *Institutes* as "disputationes dogmaticae," that is a continuation of the medieval method of the statement of the doctrine, then an objection, and finally a reply to the objection. But he also wanted it to be a "loci communes," that is a book of "commonplaces," a standard ordering of doctrines as they are properly related to one another.[46] In the progressively elaborated ordering of the *Institutes* Calvin is developing an order and structure, an architectural plan, which he believes captures and illustrates the essential truth of Scripture. And this was an order that he believed was replicable within the worship experience of the congregation and, beyond that, to life in the world that God made. As the congregation regularly recited the Apostles' Creed, they were to remember this narrative ordering of their lives; as this story was disseminated through the catechism, which the children of Geneva studied every Sunday, its structure was meant to embody the ordering principles of life for the believer.[47] This is true not only for what is usually called the "religious" part of one's life, but it is meant to shape all of life. The implications of this for the developing imaginative construction of the world will be large.

This method animates the development of the *Institutes* as Calvin worked it out. The *Institutes* was to embody both in its content and its structure this "sound way" of knowing God and the world. Thus in a sense the text itself is taking on some of the iconic functions that were previously carried by the ceremonies, images and even the drama of worship. We have observed the way that textual aids to devotion began to develop well before the Reformation, and even before the development of printing. But the growing centrality of such texts in the lives of believers has now reached a new stage. The text of the *Institutes*, which Calvin believed faithfully reflected the ordered truth of Scripture, as complemented by and reflected in the preaching of that Scripture, is now meant to play a shaping role in the thinking of God's people. In giving centrality to this ordered presentation

[46] See Muller, "In the Light of Orthodoxy," 1997, pp. 1215–18. He notes that the modern tendency to insert paragraph headings gives the work a more discursive form than Calvin may have intended. This twofold question and answer method has led some commentators to see a tendency to bifurcation which anticipates Peter Ramus, whom we discuss below. But Muller believes this is rather a continuation of the place logic of the late Middle Ages, influenced by Agricola (see *Unaccommodated Calvin*, pp. 110–11).

[47] Wendel points out that Calvin expended his "best energies" on the doctrine that he believed animated the Church as on the training up of that Church. "His doctrinal work, as he has expressed it in the different editions of the *Institutes* and in his Biblical commentaries, thus went hand in hand with his properly ecclesiastical work" (*Calvin: Origins and Development*, p. 70).

of God's truth, Calvin wanted to give the world a particular mental shape. This shape was embodied in the architectural "plan" by which Calvin ordered the *Institutes*. Despite Calvin's disparagement of "invention," this text and the visual and oral performances of the sermons based thereon had their own constructive and even aesthetic role to play in the lives of believers.[48] From his humanist background, of course, Calvin inherited a variety of rhetorical strategies by which to move his hearers. But beyond this the structuring both of the *Institutes* and subsequently of the worship experience, as these reach out to embrace the larger world, may be said to encourage a new aesthetic sensibility. The role of images alongside texts, the place of the visual in worship (and indeed in the Christian life as a whole) and the way the imagination is encouraged to comprehend God and the world will all be transformed in the process.

b. Calvin's views of worship

Calvin certainly cannot be accused of not reflecting deeply on the meaning and shape of worship. The consistent theological vision and the ordering structure it represents lead Calvin to clear views of worship that will have implications (not always consistently developed) for the role of images and especially of beauty. In his Catechism he distinguishes four parts to true worship.[49] First worship consists of putting our whole faith and trust in God; this is represented by the congregation's reciting the Apostles' Creed. Second we are called to serve and obey him with the whole of our lives; this is symbolized by the instructions contained in the law as elaborated in the preaching of the word. Third we are to invoke God's name and take refuge in him at all times; this is recalled by reciting the Lord's Prayer. Finally we are united by faith to Christ in accordance with the promise that is preached; this is "imaged" and sealed to us in the sacraments. Although the focus of true worship lies in the activities of the gathered community, its reference is extended to the whole of the believers' lives.

    In the three places where Calvin discusses the nature of true worship in the *Institutes* (I, xii, I; II, viii, 17–18; IV, x, 7–29) he develops the implications of his view of God's complete holiness and transcendence, and elaborates

---

[48] John Bossy claims that John Calvin did more than anyone to explore the use of printed word as "art": "[He] wrote more eloquently than was decent for a theologian." So Luther's audible word gave way to visible, portable, quotable text (*Christianity in the West*, p. 102). But we argue that this use of text as art appears in the context of: (1) the experience of hearing and seeing the preached (i.e. performed) word; and (2) the newly invigorated sense of the importance of everyday life.

[49] See the "Geneva Catechism" in *Theological Treatises*, ed. and trans. by J. K. S. Reid (Philadelphia: Westminster Press, 1954), pp. 91–139.

this view of worship. This God demands that we not only reflect on him, but also honor him in ways appropriate to his transcendence. In worship it is critical then that nothing belonging to God's glory be usurped by any earthly object or ceremony. He reiterates this point frequently:

As often as Scripture asserts that there is one God, it is not contending over the bare name, but also prescribing that nothing belonging to his divinity is to be transferred to another. (i, xii, i)

In his discussion of the first commandment he says:

[This] restrains our license from daring to subject God, who is incomprehensible, to our sense perceptions, or to represent him by any form. (ii, viii, 17)[50]

And in Book Four on the nature of the Church he insists:

If we duly weigh this, that it is unlawful to transfer to man what God reserves for himself, we shall understand that the whole power of those who wish to advance themselves to command anything in the church apart from God's Word is cut off. (iv, x, 7)

As this implies Calvin believed that in worship, as in all other parts of the Christian's life, Scripture must be our guide. But more than this Scripture is to be "set forth" in the preaching that will become for Calvin the focus of worship and that now supplants previous visual mediation:

In the preaching of his Word and sacred mysteries [God] has bidden that a common doctrine be there set forth for all. But those whose eyes rove about in contemplating idols betray that their minds are not diligently intent upon this doctrine. (i, xi, 7)

What is this "doctrine" that Calvin intends to be put in the place of all the various "images" of the medieval Church? It is the true preaching of the Word of God that is faithful to Scriptural teaching. Calvin says pointedly, in such preaching "Christ is depicted before our eyes as crucified . . . From this one fact they could have learned more than from a thousand crosses of wood and stone" (i, xi, 7). In an important sense, when Christ is rightly preached, we "see" the truth in a way that is not possible by simply looking at images. Only now the work of "seeing" is done in our minds – it is a mental work, in response to what is heard.

Calvin is not saying simply that certain images (those of Scripture) ought to replace others (those shaped by human hands), he is saying something

---

[50] As David Steinmetz comments on Calvin's exposition of this commandment, "The weight of Calvin's exposition falls on the prohibition of sensible images of God" (*Calvin in Context* [Oxford University Press, 1995], p. 60).

more far-reaching that recalls Zwingli's argument. There is a higher way of comprehending than that provided by the sense of sight, and that is a grasping of the preached word by faith in one's heart. Barbara Pitkin has pointed out that for Calvin faith was a special kind of perception for which he often resorted to metaphors of sight. Calvin invites his readers, once the Spirit has opened their eyes, to "see" themselves and the world through the eyes of faith.[51] This faith Calvin defines as "a firm and certain knowledge of God's benevolence toward us, founded upon the truth of the freely given promise in Christ, both revealed to our minds and sealed upon our hearts through the Holy Spirit" (III, ii, 7). Working in and through the preaching of Scripture, and as imaged in the sacraments, it is the Holy Spirit that reveals the reality of Christ to the mind.[52] This revelation is restricted uniquely to Scripture as illumined by the Spirit; no other mediation or even metaphoric elaboration is necessary. For only here can God's true majesty be grasped by a faculty which is far above mere visual perceiving. Calvin explains this in more detail in his instructions on preaching in the Catechism (1541):

In the preaching of the word, the external minister holds forth the vocal word and it is received by the ears. The internal minister the Holy Spirit truly communicates the thing proclaimed through the word that is Christ to the souls of all who will, so that *it is not necessary that Christ or for that matter his word be received through the organs of the body*, but the Holy Spirit effects this union by his secret virtue, by creating faith in us by which he makes us living members of Christ.[53]

No bodily organ is necessary, Calvin wants to claim, but of course some organ must be used. For apart from actual hearing (in the actual perfor-mance of worship), one could never receive the truth of the preached word, with or without a believing heart. So in fact the ear *is* privileged over the eye (the function of which has been reduced to a cipher for comprehension). And it is the word that becomes especially joined to the work of the Holy Spirit. But one wonders: why should the ear be any less capable of mis-hearing or falling for obstinate superstition than the eye? Or contrariwise, if faith involves a special kind of perception, why must the Holy Spirit be joined only to the aural word of preaching and not to some parallel word

---

[51] Barbara Pitkin, *What Pure Eyes Could See: Calvin's Doctrine of Faith in its Exegetical Context* (Oxford University Press, 1999), pp. 128–30. Calvin viewed faith as a special kind of perception that involved new ways of understanding even seeing (p. 3).

[52] H. Jackson Forstman argues that the conviction of the divinity of Scripture and its witness to Christ comes by the secret witness of the Holy Spirit, and this fact saves Calvin from any literalism in respect to Scripture (*Word and Spirit: Calvin's Doctrine of Biblical Authority* [Palo Alto: Stanford University Press, 1962], pp. 71–4).

[53] *Theological Treatises*, p. 173; emphasis added.

made flesh (visible)? After all in the earlier history of the Church such a relationship found ample support in the biblical doctrines of creation and incarnation. One could argue of course that Calvin, along with the other reformers, is recovering an emphasis that is biblical and which results from his own careful rereading of the texts. But clearly his own reactions to medieval practices, which we have reviewed, provided an important component of the context in which he did his exegesis.

Calvin comes closest to giving space for an "image" in worship in the sacraments. They are given to "show forth" Christ who is joined to the believer by the Holy Spirit. In fact Calvin uses the language of touch and sight frequently with respect to the sacraments. The purpose of these signs is "to direct and almost lead men by the hand to Christ, or rather, as images, represent him and show him forth to be known" (IV, xiv, 20).[54] But here again these senses become metaphors for the inward appropriation of Christ by faith. In this way alone, Calvin insists, the believer is joined to Christ.

His conviction about the exaltation and return of Christ led Calvin to deny that there was any sense in which Christ was bodily present in the elements. Here Calvin emphasized the importance of the ascension, insisting that "the body of Christ from the time of his resurrection was finite, and is contained in heaven even to the Last Day" (IV, xvii, 26). And "when he is borne high into the air, and by the cloud beneath him, [Acts 1:9] teaches us that he is no longer to be sought on earth, we safely infer that his abode is now in heaven" (IV, xvii, 27). In Calvin's view as the believer faithfully partakes of the elements she or he is lifted up by the Spirit to share communion with Christ in the heavenlies.[55] This spiritual understanding of our present experience of the incarnation sets Calvin apart from the Eastern tradition, and even from Luther – and it makes any actually "imaging" of Christ in this period of history unthinkable. The Eastern tradition believes that the icon painter makes the holy figures present in drawing an icon; the medieval tradition believed Christ was set

---

[54] In this, Calvin goes on to say, they are like the Tabernacle, except the latter referred to what was to come, while these signs refer to what has already come. In his French writings he even described the sacraments as a "peinture" (painting) of the gift of Christ (*Three French Treatises*, cited in Aston, *England's Iconoclasts*, vol. I, p. 7). The sacrament as "image" was a common patristic description, but Stephen Gero believes Calvin came to it independently ("Byzantine Iconoclasm and the Failure of a Medieval Reformation," in Joseph Gutmann [ed.], *The Image and the Word: Confrontations in Judaism, Christianity and Islam* [Missoula, Mont.: Scholars Press, 1977], p. 54).

[55] See Douglas Farrow, "Between the Rock and a Hard Place: In Support of (Something Like) a Reformed View of the Eucharist," *International Journal of Systematic Theology* 3/2 (2001), pp. 169–71. This article surveys much of the current literature on the Eucharist during the Reformation and concludes the strength of Calvin's emphasis on the absence of Christ lies in invoking the Church's cry of "Maranatha," even if the emphasis is more often spatial than temporal (p. 178).

forth as the bread became the body of Christ. For Calvin only the true preaching of the word makes Christ spiritually present.[56]

The centrality of the preached word, received by faith in the power of the Holy Spirit, determines for Calvin not only the way grace can be "signified" in the sacrament, but also specifies the way any image can signify spiritual truth. For Calvin the sacrament of the Lord's Supper had first to be stripped of all medieval associations with sacrifice, and reinserted into his rereading of the biblical narrative. In this narrative it becomes a sign of the grace offered to the believer through the death and resurrection of Christ. B. A. Gerrish has argued that Calvin's reinterpretation of the sacraments as a Eucharistic feast, in which the believer partakes of the life-giving flesh of Christ, lies at the center of Calvin's theology.[57] Calvin does not deny efficacy to the sacraments, but this efficacy is dependent, argues Gerrish, on "the sacramental word." Its sign function is subordinated to the promise which is offered in the preaching of the word. Gerrish goes on to say:

The indispensable component in a sacramental action is not the sign but the word, which the sign confirms and seals; and we are not to imagine that the sacrament adds to the word an efficacy of a totally different order. The sacraments are efficacious precisely as a form, though not the only form, of the word.[58]

So the image cannot signify on its own, it must be joined, as Calvin says, to the word.

Here Calvin is consistent with his basic theological orientation. His emphasis on Christ's bodily "absence" resonates with his iconoclastic resistance to any physical mediation of grace. The way that Christ images God is not in his being as the Godman, but in what he does for the believer – as the reformers frequently put it, to know Christ is to know his benefits. Christ has to be God to accomplish the work of redemption, but this work is not, as in the Eastern tradition, connected with God's incarnation in human flesh. So Calvin claims in his commentary on the First chapter of Colossians that "Christ is the image of God because he makes God in a manner visible to us." But it is in his role as savior, not as the human image

---

[56] P. Auksi notes, "ultimately Calvinistic worship drives toward a religion where the flawed sense of corrupt man can neither apprehend nor cultivate the supersensible glory of God" ("Simplicity and Silence," p. 353). Since the Holy Spirit can use the preached word, as we noted, this is not completely true. Cf. Michalski, *The Reformation and the Visual Arts*, pp. 171–9. David J. C. Cooper goes so far as to suggest: "The sermon echoes the verbal logos as the icon reflects the visual icon" ("The Theology of Image in Eastern Orthodoxy and John Calvin," *Scottish Journal of Theology* 35 [1982], p. 234).
[57] *Grace and Gratitude: The Eucharistic Theology of John Calvin* (Minneapolis: Augsburg/Fortress, 1993), pp. 1–5.
[58] Ibid., p. 162.

of God, that this visibility consists. Calvin can even claim that "Paul is not concerned here with those things which by communication belong also to the creatures, but with the perfect wisdom, goodness, righteousness and power of God for the representing of which no creature would suffice." With Christ we glimpse God as in a mirror; to seek the divine anywhere else is idolatrous.[59]

So Calvin's restrictions on the Eucharistic imaging of God are consistent with his view of God's aseity and his instrumentalist view of the incarnation. In comprehending God's mercy and grace in the elements, Calvin insists, the believer "sees" the splendor of God. But this can only happen when the false associations of the elements – as sacrifice, as real presence – have been pared away. Elsewhere Calvin has a great deal to say about God's generous communication of the divine beauty throughout the whole of creation. But here it is Christ's role as redeemer, not mediator of creation, that comes to expression and becomes visible. One wonders: does Christ's limited "mirroring" of God fit with what Calvin says elsewhere about the broader communication of God's beauty?

c. Beauty in Calvin

Calvin does not limit his discussion of beauty to the experience of the worshiping congregation – though it is not absent from that event. In fact the theme of beauty and the splendor of creation play a major role in his theology as a whole. In his discussion of creation he is careful to insist that the glory of God shines through all that he has made. Even in the ordered way that he creates over a deliberated period, God intends to "fix our attention." God distributes the work over six days "that our mind might the more easily be retained in the meditation of God's works."[60] The glory of creation, Calvin says in a formulation that is clearly central to his aesthetic theology, is a "mirror in which we can contemplate God, who is otherwise invisible" (1, v, 1). Everywhere we look, there are signs of his glory. Even in the arts and sciences we see evidence of his wisdom (1, v, 2); "For there are as many miracles of divine power, as many tokens of goodness, and as many proofs of wisdom as there are kinds of things in

[59] Calvin, *Epistle of Paul the Apostle to the Galatians, Ephesians, and Colossians: Calvin's New Testament Commentaries*, trans. T. H. L. Parker (Grand Rapids, Mich.: Eerdmans, 1965), p. 308.
[60] Calvin, *Commentaries on the First Book of Moses called Genesis*, trans. John King (Edinburgh: Calvin Translation Society, 1847), p. 92, On Gen. 1:26 see Susan Schreiner, *The Theatre of His Glory: Nature and the Natural Order in the Thought of John Calvin* (Grand Rapids, Mich.: Baker, 1991), pp. 15–16.

the universe"(I, xiv, 21); food and clothes are not simply for necessity but for "delight and good cheer/comeliness and decency"(III, x, 2). And all of this is meant, not simply to point to God, but to be enjoyed:

Has the Lord clothed the flowers with great beauty that greets our eyes, the sweetness of smell that is wafted upon our nostrils, and yet will it be unlawful for our eyes to be affected by that beauty, or our sense of smell by the sweetness of that odor? What? Did he not so distinguish colors, as, to make some more lovely than others. (III, x, 2)[61]

While sin and pride have deformed these things, they are not incapable of showing, in spite of this, the beauty of God himself. So it is natural that the highest expression of God's splendor should appear in his intervention in Christ for the salvation of the world. But this glory resides, we have seen, in what Christ does, not in what he is – Calvin does not see him partake of the splendors of creation. Indeed Calvin believes that in the story of salvation God is painting an intricate and beautiful "narrative scene." In his classic elaboration of Calvin's aesthetics, Léon Wencelius describes the way God intends to work out in creation the harmony that exists in the trinity, creating an "immense fresco which unfolds itself across all of time."[62] Calvin himself refers to the world as a theatre where God's glory can be seen. So it is fitting, he says, to turn one's "eyes to contemplate God's works, since he has been placed in this most glorious theater to be a spectator of them" (I, vi, 2). "Let us not be ashamed to take pious delight in the works of God open and manifest in this most beautiful theater" (I, xiv, 20). The contexts of these citations stress the superior value that attends the one who "pricks up his ears to the Word" of Scripture. For, as Barbara Pitkin reminds us, "the word as the ultimate object of the providential faith is God's Logos ordering creation and history, revealed especially in Scripture, but also, for redeemed eyes, in God's works in nature and history."[63] Scripture is the remedy that "not only makes those things plain which would otherwise escape our notice, but almost compels us to behold them; as if he had assisted our dull sight with spectacles."[64]

---

[61] In the next section he goes on to attack any extreme asceticism: away with all those who would not allow lawful use of these gifts which "robs a man of all his senses and degrades him to a block."

[62] *L'Esthétique de Calvin* (Paris: Société d'Edition "Les Belles Lettres", n.d. [1937]), p. 94. Wencelius is writing to counteract the common view of his time that Calvin was insensitive to the arts and beauty. He notes that only Emile Doumergue and Abraham Kuyper had sought to defend Calvin in this regard.

[63] *What Pure Eyes Could See*, p. 130. Calvin's reference to "pricked ears" is in I, vi, 2.

[64] Calvin, in the "Argument" to his *Commentaries on the First Book of Moses Called Genesis*, trans. John King (Edinburgh: Calvin Translation Society, 1847), p. 62.

Wencelius goes on to make two points about Calvin's developing aesthetic that are critical to our argument. First Calvin's strong doctrine of creation encouraged him to subordinate artistic activity to the order of creation. He always encouraged his reader to "listen to creation" and thus felt the best art would "follow nature." This would encourage an attitude on the part of the artist of humility and moderation that best suited the human situation before God.[65] Calvin stipulated that "only those things are to be sculptured or painted which the eyes are capable of seeing: let not God's majesty, which is far above the perception of the eyes, be debased through unseemly representations"(I, xi, 12). This is consistent with Calvin's conviction that the human mind is capable of grasping the world as it is, which we noted above. But Calvin also reflects here the newer thinking of the Renaissance that reason can discern the way the world works.[66] This ordered splendor reflects the glory of God, but it does so as it exhibits the order that God built into it; it does not do so as God is attached to special places or objects, as the medieval believers thought. As Susan Schreiner points out, Calvin basically believed that "a reliable God controlled a rational universe."[67] Of course God could still intervene, though Calvin believed the special gift of miracles had ceased with the apostles.[68]

Léon Wencelius then goes on to draw out the implications of this splendor of creation. Since creation shines with God's glory, if the artist carefully followed the order that God had instituted there, she or he would discover the essentially "spiritual" character of art. If one follows the traces of divinity that God has put in creation, Wencelius insists, "it is unthinkable that art not be rich in spiritual possibilities."[69] Of course these possibilities have been distorted by the medieval developments of art, especially that which had been allowed into the Church. A clean break must be made from all of this. But there are aesthetic values which reflect God's character, which not only animated Calvin's written description of the truth of Scripture and the austere order of worship, but which, he believed, could be discerned (and followed) in the created order. These involved, Wencelius argues, certain fundamental characteristics: clarity, harmony, purity and transcendence.[70]

---

[65] *L'Esthétique de Calvin*, pp. 103–11.

[66] In his references to superstition, Calvin constantly contrasts "right reason" with such meanderings, a view, Eire notes, that reflects the humanist tradition (cf. *War against the Idols*, p. 231).

[67] *Theatre of His Glory*, p. 33. As a result, she notes, Calvin was ambivalent about the role of secondary causes (p. 30).

[68] So Calvin and the other reformers abandoned the use of chrism as a means in praying for healing, fearful that it be seen as a talisman. See Eire, *War against the Idols*, p. 223n130.

[69] *L'Esthétique de Calvin*, p. 106.

[70] Ibid., p. 89. Umberto Eco argues by comparison that the medieval triad that, coming from the *Book of Wisdom*, forms the basis for understanding beauty: Number, Weight and Measure. For the

Creation is a "mirror" and a "theatre" for God's glory. But is this glory visible to all or only to those with eyes enabled by redemption to see it? This question is important, and will appear again in the theology of Edwards. The answer to it determines ultimately the significance that art and cultural production more generally plays in the overall program of God. On the one hand Calvin says that the brightness of God's presence in the mirror of creation is visible to everyone – it is "borne in upon the eyes of all" (I, vi, I). On the other hand, God saw that another "better help" was needed to direct people into the very presence of God, which is the Scriptures. Here Calvin employs the metaphor of spectacles, as we have seen. In the classic passage he notes:

Just as old or bleary-eyed men and those with weak vision, if you thrust before them a most beautiful volume, even if they recognize it to be some sort of writing, yet can scarcely construe two words, but with the aid of spectacles will begin to read distinctly; so Scripture, gathering up the otherwise confused knowledge of God in our minds, having dispersed our dullness, clearly shows us the true God. (I, vi, I)

But do these spectacles allow us to see, say in science or beauty, qualities that cannot be seen by unbelieving eyes? Susan Schreiner argues the spectacles do not function "to make nature more knowable in a scientific way." Calvin largely accepted and appreciated the science of his day.[71] Similarly his comments on beauty indicate that this too is visible to believers and unbelievers alike. What is not visible to the untutored eye is the narrative by which God wants people to find mercy and forgiveness. Insight into this "painting" of God surely sharpens what is seen in creation, but it does not make visible something that was previously invisible.

It has been argued that Calvin, even if he can allow a role for visual art in recording the beauty of creation, is really making impossible any visual art that could be called religious.[72] For the split between the world of God and this world is so great and the worry over idolatry so profound that no image or architectural space can refer, even symbolically, to God. In one sense this is so; the world cannot "hold" God, and therefore no image can be transparent to the Divine, as icons are for the Orthodox. But in another

---

medieval person, then, all creation can reflect God insofar as it participates in God's being which is, ultimately, one, true and good (*Art and Beauty*, pp. 20–1).

[71] *Theatre of His Glory*, p. 106. Edward Dowey argues that, with Scripture as guide, "we actually see God at work in creation." But he goes on to say, with respect to general revelation, it is a means God uses to reach man, it is not yet a new source of knowledge about God (*Knowledge of God in Calvin*, pp. 144–5).

[72] Cooper, "Theology of Image," pp. 219–41.

sense Calvin wants to redefine what is religious. It is true God's presence has been removed from particular images and practices. But a better way of putting this is to say God's presence has been displaced so that it can be glimpsed in a larger sphere of activity. This displacement will have a great significance for how reformed believers will understand themselves in relation to God's presence. It issued, for example, in the visual and dramatic components to both worship and life that are consistent in the vision of Calvin – even if in Calvin's mind these had nothing to do with what we call art or aesthetics. Previously believers sought out special times and places where God's power, and even salvation, were to be found. Now believers are not directed to particular images or places, but having their eyes opened by faith they are directed to see the world and their lives as potential material for God's saving activity. Erwin Panofsky makes the illuminating distinction between Ignatian "ecstasy" and protestant "absorption."[73] That is, Ignatian spirituality directs believers' meditation on the events of the life of Christ to identify themselves, ecstatically, with these events – as though they were there. Protestants who follow Calvin, by contrast, will imagine themselves as players in the theater of creation, to see themselves, in other words, as being "absorbed" by and into the redemptive story that God is directing.

d. The role of images

On the basis of these convictions, Calvin developed his views on the role of images. The controlling conviction is the belief that God has given us the true image of the divine, insofar as we can apprehend this, in creation and in our neighbor. Any other attempt to "picture" God or his truth is not only unnecessary but positively harmful – a view that is progressively emphasized as he produced further editions of the *Institutes*. His review of Scriptural teaching, which is elaborated in the 1550 edition of the *Institutes*, leads him to conclude: "Man's mind full, as it is of pride and boldness, dares to imagine a god according to its own capacity" (I, xi, 8). And, he adds in 1559: "We see how openly God speaks against all images, that we may know that all who seek visible forms of God depart from him" (I, xi, 2).

In his development of the *Institutes* Calvin had to confront the fact that Scripture itself is filled with images that God revealed to symbolize his presence and power. What, for example, is the meaning of the Cherubim placed over the altar in the Temple? Calvin seems to become impatient in

---

[73] "Comments on Art and Reformation," in Harbison (ed.), *Symbols in Transformation*: p. 14.

his answer. Using these "paltry" examples, he insists, one becomes a "raving madman." These show only "that images are not suited to represent God's mysteries. For they had been formed to this end, that veiling the mercy seat with their wings they might bar not only human eyes but all the senses from beholding God, and thus correct men's rashness" (I, xi, 3). Besides, Calvin goes on, these signs belong to "the antiquated tutelage of the law." Later Calvin explains the signs (and parables) of the prophets – the figurative expression of physical things – especially those which describe the destiny of those who reject God. These are to "confound all our senses with dread" (III, xxv, 12); they enable us to "conceive" (that is to grasp mentally) in physical metaphors what we might not otherwise understand – apparently here the fact they belong to the Old Testament does not count against them. In still another place Calvin deals with signs which God uses in Scripture to reveal elements of his truth, such as the rainbow or the tree of life. Interestingly he deals with these as "sacraments in the wider sense." They render us "more certain and confident of the truth of his promises" (IV, xiv, 18). But even these are marked by the Word of God as sacraments: "Cannot God mark with his Word the things he has created, that what were previously bare elements may become sacraments?" Though God can do this, clearly we cannot. Their character as signs is dependent on God's decision, not on any quality inherent in the object.

But why are practices which were so important, even central to Scripture, forbidden to us?[74] Here it is clear that, in addition to his theological convictions that we reviewed, the setting in which Calvin worked – which we described in the last chapter – was influencing his reading of Scripture. The knowledge of God, Calvin believed, was mostly missing from the worship experience of most people. What was called implicit faith Calvin attacked as another name for ignorance. He frequently refers to the corruption that had been introduced in the medieval period. He believed that during the first five centuries church walls were empty of images, as its ministers faithfully held to Scripture (I, xi, 13).[75] So that the instructions of

---

[74] John of Damascus is one who would see them as essential to the way Scripture communicates. See his discussion of the cherubim in the context of a reference to the second commandment: "[God] allows the image of cherubim who are circumscribed, to be made and shown as prostrate in adoration before the divine throne, overshadowing the mercy-seat, for it was fitting that the image of the heavenly servants should overshadow the image of the divine mysteries" ("First Apology," p. 15). In his brief discussion of the Second Nicene Council, Calvin makes only the briefest mention of John's argument for images based on the incarnation, but does not interact with it in any way. Indeed, because of his unique view of the ascension, which we noted, the incarnation does not serve any positive theological role for Calvin with respect to images (see I, xi, 14).

[75] Though Calvin, at this point, was clearly mistaken. The situation is best surveyed in Thomas Matthews, *The Clash of Gods: A Reinterpretation of Early Christian Art* (Princeton University Press,

Pope Gregory, which we surveyed earlier, correspond in Calvin's eyes to the beginning of the degeneration of ministry. For "whatever men learn of God from images is futile, indeed false" (1, xi, 5 added in 1550). He scoffs at the "madness" evident in the instructions of Nicea II – which he believed to be effectively refuted by the *Libri Carolini* (1, xi, 14). Beginning at the time of Gregory, Calvin believed, ministers in the Church turned over to idols the teaching office because they themselves had become mute! "Not content with spiritual understanding, they thought that through the images a surer and closer understanding would be impressed upon them" (1, xi, 9). This section ends with a reiteration of the central theme of this discussion: that God's glory cannot be divided and shared with any object. "What God rigorously reserves for himself alone, we distribute among a great throng" (1, xii, 3).[76]

We have noted above that Calvin is always careful to point out, in a move that Puritans after him would employ, that painting, sculpture, even what we would call fashion design, are "gifts of God" (1, xi, 12). These can be used and enjoyed: they have a legitimate use. Painting should portray what can be seen (not things which one cannot see, such as God's majesty). Within the class of visible things are histories and events, and images or forms of bodies not depicting past events. The former may have some use for admonition and teaching. But it is the second category which has most commonly appeared in churches, and which have not been used out of "judgment and selection" but out of "foolish and thoughtless craving." Quite apart from the misuse that has been made of these, they have a further weakness: "I don't see what they can afford other than pleasure" (1, xi, 12). So Calvin concludes of images that do not portray events or history: "if the use of images contained nothing evil it still has no value for teaching." Likewise in his discussion of instrumental music, he concludes it is too much like an unknown tongue which distracts from true worship and thus is not to be allowed. "It may minister to our pleasure, rather than our necessity."[77] These – images, accompanied by music evoking as they do

---

1993). Stephen Gero argued a generation ago that "No theological consensus evolved for, or against, image-worship, during the patristic period" ("Byzantine Iconoclasm," p. 51).

[76] This is elaborated in Calvin's treatise "An Admonition Showing the Advantages which Christendom might derive from An Inventory of Relics," in *Tracts Relating to the Reformation*, ed. Henry Beveridge (Edinburgh: Calvin Translation Society, 1844), vol. 1, pp. 289–341. This is a tirade against these superstitions, whose possible advantage of increasing piety is vastly outweighed by the dangers they entail. Here he is careful to distinguish those images made by artists and those supposedly possessing spiritual power – attacking only the latter (p. 314).

[77] In *Commentaries on the First Book of Moses, On Genesis 4:20*, p. 218. The view that art served pleasure was, from one point of view, an innovation – it anticipates some of the discussion on the arts and aesthetics that will take place in the eighteenth century.

our pleasure – must then be excluded from the worshiping congregation. For Calvin the line is clearly drawn, not only between visual imagery, but also between pleasure and worship.

But the line is pointedly not drawn between pleasure and life. Here there appears a profound ambivalence in Calvin's thought. His suspicions about pleasure lead him to exclude particular things from worship which, with the right use, he can praise in life. The gifts of God, it appears, like the goods of creation, have been scattered about where they can be seen and enjoyed. But the ancient connection between these gifts and the worshiping community has been severed. Whatever Calvin's good wishes might have been for those gifted in these arts, Calvin gives them no positive encouragement or guidance. As a result, artists and sculptors were mostly out of work in the Geneva of Calvin's time.[78]

Whatever his personal views on art, beauty and images, Calvin's time in Geneva, at least initially, was spent building a new worship life that would replace medieval practices. In this setting more constructive work on the arts was simply not possible, or at least did not fall within the priorities that pressed upon him. As we noted Calvin considered that the work of truly reforming the Church had barely begun when he arrived in Geneva. The first work he took on was the organization of the churches according to the theological principles he was developing in the *Institutes*.[79] Though his ideals soon foundered on the reality of a recalcitrant population, they are nevertheless important to note. He first wanted to increase the frequency of the celebration of the Lord's Supper. He proposed weekly celebration, but agreed on a monthly schedule "so as not to bring contempt" (in the event it was celebrated quarterly). All pilgrimages were forbidden, all paternosters, keeping of feasts, even treating one another to drinks in the tavern. Anyone caught in possession of an idol was to be brought before the consistory. He proposed further to do away with Christmas, New Year, Annunciation and Ascension.[80]

Calvin was appalled at the state of prayer in the Church: "Certainly as things are, the prayers of the faithful are so cold that we ought to be

---

[78] Michalski, *The Reformation and the Visual Arts*, p. 72. This was true even in areas influenced by Luther. Christensen points out that in some areas artists were even persecuted. The sculptor Riemenschneider we discussed in the last chapter had his arms and hands broken (*Art and the Reformation*, pp. 177–8).

[79] The Articles for organizing the Church were submitted to the Magistrates in January of 1537; reprinted as "Articles concerning the Organization of the Church and of Worship at Geneva," in *Theological Treatises*, pp. 48–55.

[80] "Articles," in *Theological Treatises*, pp. 80–1. It is little wonder the magistrates felt he had overstepped his authority, and in April 1538 expelled him from Geneva. He was recalled in September 1541. See Ozment, *Age of Reform*, pp. 362–6.

ashamed and dismayed." As an antidote he proposed that the congregation sing Psalms. "The Psalms can incite us to lift up our hearts to God and move us to an ardour in invoking and exalting with praises the glory of his name."[81] Though Luther had initiated congregational singing before him, Calvin's innovation of the singing of Psalms, as we will see, was to have a great impact on the developing worship life of Reformed congregations, and indeed a larger cultural impact. Note that the singing which Calvin allowed was in fact sung prayer in unison. This innovation – that prayers could not only be spoken but "joined to music" – was so striking that it needed justification. In his instructions that were to be used in the English Congregation at Geneva, Calvin, writing in 1556, felt it necessary, after giving proper scriptural documentation, to explain this form of prayer:

As if the Holy Ghoste wolde saye that the songe did inflame the heart to call upon God, and praise him with a more fervent lyvely zeale and as musike and singing is naturall unto us, and therefor every man deliteth therein: So our merciful God setteth before our eyes, how we may rejoyce and singe to the glorie of his name, recreation of our spirites, and profit of ourselves.[82]

Though this would touch the emotions, Calvin allowed it because with music added, such prayer served to turn worshipers' hearts wholly to God.

Sunday services in Geneva were to begin with sermons "at break of day" at St. Peter's (Calvin's parish church) and St. Gervais, then again at the usual hour at all three churches. At noon the catechism was to be taught to children at all three churches. At three o'clock there would be a third sermon at St. Peter's and St. Gervais. Additionally at St. Peter's, services were to be held three times a week, on Monday, Tuesday and Friday. For these services ministers were appointed – this schedule needed, at the beginning, five ministers and five coadjutor ministers. Additionally elders were appointed to provide oversight, and deacons who were to care for the growing number of poor in Geneva.[83]

---

[81] "Articles," in *Theological Treatises*, p. 53.
[82] *The Form of Prayers and Ministrations of the Sacraments, used in the English Congregation at Geneva: And approved by the famous and godly learned man John Calvin* (Geneva: John Crespin, 1556), pp. 17–18. Though he quickly goes on to note how the Papists have corrupted this gift with their strange music.
[83] *Theological Treatises*, pp. 62–6. Throughout, the phrase "good order" appears frequently; while ample provision was made for the poor, begging was totally prohibited.

e. Calvin's aesthetic reconstruction

These reforms made possible a new way of experiencing both worship and the broader world. In the first place worship now was oriented around the performance of the preached word. In Calvin's Geneva the instruction in the catechism, the prayers even the singing, all were a dramatic elaboration of the preached word (which itself rested on the structure outlined in the *Institutes*). Victor Turner has argued that every society has a primary aesthetic-dramatic "mirror" by which it understands (and judges) itself. Every community has a particular movement through time, he notes, which is obviously "dramatic."[84] In the case of Calvin's community this was constituted by the performances surrounding the preaching of the word – in singing, reading Scripture, praying and reciting the creed.

The whole population was enjoined to come to the services provided, even the servants; children were to be taught the catechism each Sunday (which was finally published in 1542 after Calvin returned from Strasbourg); parents were to lead families in regular prayers; and new ministers were instructed in theology and the bible (initially by Calvin alone but eventually, in 1559 when the Academy was formally founded, by a team of distinguished ministers). All this was to complement the regular preaching of the Scripture which was the focus of the services. This was supported by the celebration of the sacrament as a "sign and seal" of faith in Christ, and in the exercise of discipline, both in excommunication (which instilled greater fear in people of the sixteenth century than a modern person can imagine) and moral oversight.

The services were probably not the dull and dreary thing they are often made out to be; indeed, from what we can tell, the singing of the congregation made a deep impression on all who visited. But its beauty was an austere one – clarity, harmony and transcendence were its characteristic marks. This was because this worship "performance," while central to the believers' week, was directed toward shaping worshipers' lives throughout the week. Calvin emphatically insisted that the splendor of the Church is not meant to be shut up there, but it should spill out into the world. People were encouraged to take their gifts and graces with them out into the world, even as they carried their Christ in their hearts; but they were

---

[84] V. Turner, "Are there Universals of Performance in Myth, Ritual and Drama?" in Richard Schechner and Willa Appel (eds.), *By Means of Performance: Intercultural Studies of Theatre and Ritual* (Cambridge University Press, 1990), p. 8.

nowhere invited to bring these same gifts into the sanctuary and exercise them there.

While there is great beauty in St. Peter's church, which is visible to this day, the space and environment of worship did not play a major role in the thinking of Calvin. It was to the ear, and the mental construction this stimulated, that worship was meant to appeal. In what amounts to a metaphor of his view of worship space, he insisted that, outside of regular worship hours, the church buildings should be locked. This was to be done so that "no one outside the hours may enter for superstitious reasons. If anyone be found making any particular devotion inside or nearby, he is to be admonished; if it appears to be a superstition which he will not amend, he is to be chastised."[85] But what if one wanted to go in to the church to pray? But that is precisely Calvin's point: one does not need a special space in which to pray. All of life has become an arena of faith and spirituality. No particular space is sacred; but all spaces are potentially sacred.

This suggests the second aspect of Calvin's reconstruction: the shape of his theology was meant to find its primary embodiment, not in the experience of worship alone, but in people's life in the world. Clearly a major contribution of Calvin's reconstruction was to affirm the value of everyday life. In the breadth of ordinances of worship and instruction, Calvin sought to make Geneva, in all of its life, "a Saintly City." In any discussion of the visual imagery and aesthetics, one must not lose sight of the fact that Calvin believed God's glory should be manifest in the whole of life. The ordered structure which was so important to his understanding of truth and which shaped his *Institutes* was to be carried out consistently in the worshiping life of the people. But beyond that it was to be lived out in the homes and workplaces of Geneva. And, little by little, Calvin did succeed in giving a unique moral and spiritual tone to Geneva. This vision of society included equal justice before the law, especially for the weak; and special provisions for the sick and poor, who, Calvin believed, were God's "receveurs."[86] As the modern economic and political structures were

---

[85] *Theological Treatises*, p. 79.

[86] Many people believe Calvin succeeded in his attempts at social control to a fault. But Monter points out that it was only after Calvin's death that the moral and religious legislation for which Geneva became famous (or notorious depending on one's perspective) was codified into law. Even then its stringency was matched by legislation elsewhere in Europe, even in Italy (*Calvin's Geneva*, p. 216). See the discussion of the social dimension of Calvin's work in Fred Graham, *Constructive Revolutionary: John Calvin and his Socio-economic Impact* (Richmond, Va.: John Knox Press, 1971), pp. 62–6. "It was, for Calvin, the treatment of the weak in society that really determined the value of a political regime" (p. 62).

struggling with older patterns of life and thought, Calvin's greatest contribution may be in giving a new way of understanding everyday life under the watchful eyes of God. William Monter believes Calvin's "basic achievement . . . was to instill Christian discipline upon a refractory and even revolutionary population that had just uprooted her traditional spiritual leader."[87]

But this calling itself was not unrelated to the role of images and imagination. External images and ceremonies were not valued precisely because the believers' human life in the world was itself to "image" the reality and glory of God's work in Christ. Calvin's treatment of the cross provides an important insight into this dynamic. In the *Institutes* his treatment of the cross as an historical event is limited to little over a single page (II, xvi, 6). But later Calvin proceeds in a long ten-page section to describe how our lives should take on the character of the cross (III, viii, 1–11). Each must bear his own cross; it teaches us patience and obedience; it chastises us; it teaches us to rest on God alone. And so on. Here then is one critical component of a protestant imagination. For followers of Calvin it is not in the contemplation of an image, nor in an Ignatian meditation on the events of Christ's life, that spiritual nurture and godliness are to be found. These spiritual benefits are sought as believers live out – reenact – this life-giving cross in their everyday life.

These innovations in worship and in the perspective on everyday life, in Calvin's mind, rested on solid theological grounds. The basic conviction was that God is immeasurable and cannot be contained or controlled by any human service, whatever the motive. Only in the lively preaching of the word, in singing, in the visible sacraments and in a godly life can this immeasurable God be "glimpsed." But the bodily essence of Christ, as the physical cross, has no implication for aesthetics. Rather it is the benefits of these things wrought in the heart of the believer by the Holy Spirit that would, little by little, shape a new aesthetic.

Sergiusz Michalski has argued that this central contention and its tension with traditional Catholic (or even Orthodox) views, is really about the post-resurrection presence of God, and therefore with the way the Holy Spirit

---

[87] *Calvin's Geneva*, p. 235. Many have pointed out the significance of the Reformation for giving value to everyday life. Among the most articulate has been Charles Taylor in *Sources of the Self: The Making of the Modern Identity* (Cambridge Mass.: Harvard University Press, 1989). He points out that, in contrast to the medieval view that some forms of life were higher than others, the Reformation emphasized that "the fulness of Christian existence was to be found within the activities of this life, in one's calling and in marriage and the family." And "the hallowing of life was not seen as something which takes place only at the limits, as it were, but as a change which can penetrate the full extent of mundane life" (pp. 218 and 221).

is allowed to work. He argues: "The basic difference between the Lutheran and the Calvinist understanding of the Eucharist on the semiotic plane consists primarily in a synecdochic understanding of the sacrament by [Luther] and the metaphorical-allegorical conception of [Calvin]."[88] The Orthodox argued that the icon painter, through prayer and proper preparation, can "write" an image of Christ that communicates the presence of God; the Catholics believed that the priest does this by consecrating the bread and wine. But for Calvin, Christ has taken his humanity with him to heaven, and the Spirit now works, primarily, through the preached word – which is the reformed theological equivalent to the icon or the raising of the host. In the sacrament the promise of the preached word is added to the outward sign by the Holy Spirit who joins the believer to Christ in the heavenlies. The objects of the sacraments have no intrinsic importance, either aesthetically or theologically – these aspects have been stripped away. Rather the performance of the preached word enacted in the sacraments becomes a unique mediation of grace, and it is the theological center of Calvin's cultural-aesthetic identity.

But at the same time the experience of worship is not the complete reference of that identity. For that, one has to look to the world and one's life in the world. This insistence is consistent with Calvin's conviction that we are not to create images of God's splendor, because God has already done this in our neighbor. In serving our neighbor, wife, child, friend, we are serving God and creating a world – making images – which in some way can reflect the splendor that belongs to God. The world then is given a new, and radically different importance. Our work can point to God; but it is not enchanted with God's presence.[89]

CALVIN AND THE WIDER WORLD

As a symptom of this changing emphasis, the gulf between the reformers' view of worship and images and that of the Catholic Church was only to grow wider toward the end of the century. Two events might be said to mark this divergence. First between 1545 and 1563 Pope Paul III convened an Ecumenical Council in Trent to draw up their response to the growing Protestant movements. In one of its last sessions it took up the

---

[88] *The Reformation and the Visual Arts*, pp. 176 and 177; quote p. 177.
[89] See Andrew Greeley: "God is sufficiently like creation that creation not only tells something about God, but, by doing so, also makes God present amongst us" (*The Catholic Imagination*, p. 6). Calvin would have said: God is sufficiently unlike creation that, outside of the holy life of God's people, it can only dimly reflect that presence as in a mirror.

issue of images, giving a much more positive face to the 'factory of idols' which Calvin deplored:

Since the nature of man is such that he cannot without external means be raised easily to meditation on divine things, holy mother Church has instituted certain rites . . . [and] made use of certain ceremonies . . . whereby both the majesty of so great a sacrifice might be emphasized and the minds of the faithful excited by those visible signs of religion and piety.

The council then decreed that:

The images of Christ, of the Virgin Mother of God, and of other Saints, are to be had and retained, particularly in the churches, and that due honor and veneration are to be given them . . . That by means of the stories of the mysteries of our Redemption, portrayed by paintings or other representations, the people are instructed and confirmed in the habit of remembering, and continually revolving in mind the articles of faith.[90]

But these instructions are given with the awareness that reform was necessary. So the council went on to carefully outline what was to be avoided, addressing much of what had concerned the Protestant reformers. First no false doctrine was to be taught or inferred from the image. People were to be carefully taught that God cannot be seen "with bodily eyes." All superstition, or any quest for monetary gain is to be avoided. Images are to be decent, suitable for veneration (though they are not to be worshiped – *veneratio* only is allowed, not *adoratio*).[91] Clearly there was a sincere recognition of the dangers of imagery and of the need for reform. Johannus Molanus, the most influential commentator on the Tridentine Decrees, writing in 1570, noted that indecent images are a complete distortion of the original purpose of images which was to "excite devotion" (St Thomas).[92] Indeed one must be stricter with painting than with books because of the greater impact of images. Molanus concludes by quoting Canon 100 of the council: "For the sensuality of the body easily spreads to the soul. We therefore forbid hereafter making in any way pictures which offend the eyes, corrupt the mind and kindle base pleasures."[93] Others interpreting

[90] *Canons and Decrees of the Council of Trent*, ed. H. J. Schroeder (St Louis: Herder, 1941), quoted and discussed in Aston, *England's Iconoclasts*, vol. 1, pp. 44–5.
[91] In Aston, *England's Iconoclasts*, pp. 44–5. See also Anthony Blunt, *Artistic Theory in Italy* (Oxford University Press, 1962), pp. 107–10. Blunt points out that the Church had been relatively lax about these things in the Middle Ages, and only with Trent became concerned about orthodoxy in its imagery.
[92] David Freedberg, "Johannus Molanus on Provocative Paintings," *Journal of the Warburg and Courtauld Institutes* 34 (1971), pp. 229–45.
[93] Ibid., p. 243. Ironically Molanus frequently quotes Erasmus with approval, even though that scholar had been placed on the index promulgated by Trent.

the Canons for the Church went on to insist that artists needed to hold strictly to Scripture in what they portrayed. Raffaello Borghini, for example, insisted in 1584 that artists should "paint subjects derived from Holy Scripture simply and purely."[94]

Notice that for Catholics the stipulations laid down for images were directed toward the disciplining of the unruly imagination – which they too worried over – and its tendency to shape illicit images. For the Reformed Party such discipline of image-making involved its elimination. But meanwhile they would come to privilege inward images, which were to be shaped by God's Word and Spirit. But why are these inner visions any more to be trusted than those made of visible materials?

Calvin was not impressed with the results of Trent – in many ways it was too late for these reforms to make a difference. In his lengthy response he argues that Trent did not represent the best thinkers of the Church. The Pope and his minions controlled the process from the start.[95] He acknowledges that Nicea and Trent both sought to ground images in Scripture, using – inappropriately in Calvin's eyes – verses like Genesis 1:26: "Let us make humankind in our image." Calvin will have none of it. His intolerance of any external ceremony is expressed in his tract "On Shunning the unlawful rites of the ungodly." There he refers to Isaiah 45:23, where God says: "To me every knee shall bow, every tongue shall swear." This means "an image receives worship due to God when reverence for it is expressed by any bodily gesture." No, we must keep every part of our body "untainted by any sacrilegious rite,"[96] for one simply cannot do these things in appropriate ways, without dividing the honor that is due God alone.

But there was another straw in the wind at this time, which highlighted the growing distance between Protestants and Catholics over the issue of images. In an attempt to mediate the growing divisions in France, in September of 1561 Catherine de Medici, widow of one king, Henry II, and mother of another, the reigning King Charles IX (then aged eleven), called a Colloquy at Poissy between Catholic and Reformed leaders, which met again in St. Germain-en-Laye in January of 1562. In September Theodore Beza, who would become Calvin's successor, was called upon to present the Reformed side. He began by laying out points where there was fundamental agreement between the two sides – with respect to the Trinity and the Chalcedonian unity of the divine and human

---

[94] Quoted in Blunt, *Artistic Theory*, p. 111.   [95] *Tracts* (1851), ed. Beveridge, vol. III, pp. 30–188.
[96] Ibid., pp. 369 and 377.

nature, even the perpetual virginity of Mary! Then he moved on to describe the sacraments noting that they are signs that Christ is truly offered to us. Nor do the Reformed deny Christ's real presence there. But, he went on:

If we regard the distance of things (as we must when there is a question of his bodily presence and of his humanity considered separately), we say that his body is as far removed from the bread and wine as is heaven and earth.[97]

At this point the meeting almost broke up. One of the cardinals in attendance shouted: "Blasphemy!" Beza, who seemed not to realize his mistake, was only repeating Calvin's view of the ascension and bodily presence of Christ. But was it consistent with the Chalcedonian formula to which Beza had just subscribed?[98]

In the January meeting they discussed images in particular, which the irenic Catholic Claude d'Espence considered one of the "principal points which separate us."[99] Catherine dearly wanted to avoid any further conflict between these parties in France and called on the Colloquy to reach some kind of agreement. On February 11, the Reformed side issued a statement that summarized their position. It began:

Since the explicit Word of God completely condemns all use of images, when it comes to serving them inwardly or outwardly, we cannot in good conscience depart from such an explicit commandment of God and approve what is explicitly prohibited.[100]

They proceeded to propose that all images therefore be abolished from the churches. But, in a conciliatory gesture, they allowed that if the king wished to tolerate images, they would propose a series of safeguards – that interestingly parallel those which were to be included in Trent within a year of this Colloquy: illicit images are to be removed; people are to be warned not to make offering to such images; that images be removed from places where abuses are clear; etc. Then they concluded, strangely, by requiring all crosses be removed: "Considering the worst superstition is committed at the place of the cross, we cannot tolerate the cross any more than we can other representations and images, and we are content to gaze upon Christ

[97] Quoted in David Willis-Watkins, *The Second Commandment and Church Reform: The Colloquy of St. Germaine-en-Laye of 1562*, Studies in Reformed Theology and History, no. 2 (Princeton: Princeton Theological Seminary: 1994), p. 9.

[98] Willis-Watkins notes that Beza seemed not to be even aware of this possible inconsistency (*The Second Commandment*, p. 9).

[99] Ibid., p. 17.   [100] Quoted in ibid., p. 21.

and his passion depicted in a living way in his Holy Word [dépeinte au vif en sa sainte parole]."[101]

This judgment may be taken as symptomatic of developing Reformed attitudes toward images and ceremonies. To Beza, and Calvin before him, the image of the cross would have been a matter of relative indifference. Indeed Beza in his response goes so far as to allow that images might be retained for a time. But it was the superstitious use to which these objects were put that was intolerable to these reformers. This intolerance led them to disallow all forms not specifically endorsed by Scripture. But in this reaction to artificial ceremonies they were not only denying that God's presence could be mediated by an external image or practice, but they were implying further that these could not even play any teaching or symbolic role.

The Catholic response was in the form of a majority report and a minority report, the latter written primarily by Claude d'Espence. In this d'Espence concluded that since adoration of images and burning of incense

constitute one part of the adoration which is made out of respect for religion, we wish that all images, except the simple cross, would be removed from the altars and put in such places in the parishes where one can no longer adore them. Kiss them, clothe them . . . or carry them about on shoulders.[102]

"Except for the simple cross" covers the main differences that existed between this party and the Reformed. For this moderate Catholic party, which was rapidly to lose favor in France, reform was as urgent as it was necessary, but this would not deny a role to images in places where they could not be adored. But for the reformers, reform of the abuse of images was not really possible. For these "reform in connection with images was their elimination."[103] This opportunity to consider their differences was to be the last the situation in France would provide. The gulf between their worlds had grown too wide. Indeed the ways in which they imagined the world to work had become incompatible. The one, while holding to what was good in the tradition, sought through various means to reach an understanding whereby bloodshed would be avoided; the other felt no peace would really be lasting until the king promoted the true worship of God, which allowed no compromise on the question of images.

---

[101] Ibid., p. 22. Willis-Watkins notes this was formulated in what the Protestants hoped would become a royal decree, especially since it matched some of what the moderate Catholic party of D'Espence wanted.
[102] Ibid., p. 30.   [103] Ibid., p. 33.

In 1564, when Calvin was dying, he called in the company of pastors for a last visit. He warned them in biblical terms: "I have been in the midst of battle, and you will experience ones not less but greater. For you are in a perverse and unhappy nation . . . You will have your hands full after God has taken me away."[104] Perhaps he sensed that some of the godliness had already begun to wear off. A second generation of pastors was in place, with Beza in the position of leadership. The Academy was running, but, with Calvin gone, it would soon begin to weaken. By the 1580s the pastors began to experience what Gillian Lewis has called a failure of morale. By 1600 the Academy was closed, and "Geneva was . . . swept into irrelevance by the force of international politics and war."[105] But the reconstruction had been accomplished and the resultant mental picture of God's presence in the world had already begun its work, and this was, by 1600, anything but irrelevant. What exactly these ideas did and what kind of world they began to shape is the subject of the next chapter.

---

[104] In Monter, *Calvin's Geneva*, p. 96. Later Calvin pleads with them to "change nothing, to make no innovations, for novelty is often requested . . . but all changes are dangerous" (p. 97).

[105] Gillian Lewis, "Calvinism and Geneva: 1541–1608, in the Time of Calvin and of Beza," in Menna Prestwich (ed.), *International Calvinism: 1541–1715* (Oxford: Clarendon, 1985), pp. 52–60; quote p. 60.

CHAPTER 4

England and the visual culture of the Reformation

To work our way back into the world picture of people raised in Calvin's Geneva we might look at the questions he prepared for the children. As the most important means of teaching Calvin's ideas was certainly his Catechism,[1] we might begin with this question from his 1542 Catechism on the Second Commandment:

Does this prohibit us from painting anything or sculpting any likeness?

No, but it does forbid these two things: that we make images either for representing God, or for worshiping him.

Why?

Because there is no resemblance between him who is spirit eternal and incomprehensible, and corporeal, corruptible and dead figures.[2]

In the English version of Leo Jud's 1541 short catechism, the explanation is more emphatic. "Why does God forbid this?" the teacher asks:[3]

CHILD: Because that he being an everlasting good that cannot be seen, will not be figured and drawn out in any bodily thing. He forbiddeth it under great punishment through the mouth of all the prophets. He that draweth the image of God in a creature despiseth God, and falleth into blindness of mind and horrible vice, as Paul sayeth to the Romans.

---

[1] Among the first things Calvin did in Geneva, alongside his *Articles of the Church*, was to produce a catechism for teaching children. The first version appeared in 1537, the second more definitive edition (which was considerably influenced by that of Martin Bucer) was published in 1542. Calvin took the substance of the catechism from his *Institutes* (see Wendel, *Calvin: Origins and Development*, pp. 52, 80).

[2] Calvin, *Theological Treatises*, p. 109.

[3] In Aston, *England's Iconoclasts*, vol. 1, p. 447. The English version of Jud's catechism was published (in Zurich) in 1550. Calvin's catechism was not translated into English until 1556 (printed by Crespin in Geneva), but as a minister in Zurich, Jud was clearly influenced by Zwingli and, almost certainly, by Calvin.

But, the teacher asks, "may we not bring the children and unlearned to God through images?"

CHILD: In no wise. For images draw men from God and cause them to forget him.

Sunday by Sunday, as these questions were reiterated, attitudes toward the visual mediation of truth were formed, a process that might be called a pedagogy of iconoclasm. It is difficult for a modern person to understand the impact of such teaching. As Margaret Aston notes, "the very persons who had once been expected to learn through imagery were now expressly taught to reject as spurious the very idea that pictures can teach."[4] Memories of childhood encounters with images, and their supposed power were still fresh in the minds of the reformers. Indeed, as we have seen, those most vehement on the removal of images often had the most involvement with them previously. Andreas Karlstadt, for example, recalls in his tract on images (1522): "My heart since childhood has been brought up in the veneration of images, and a harmful fear has entered me which I gladly would rid myself of, and cannot."[5] If he had not heard the voice of God, he explains, and experienced the liberation of the Spirit he would not have realized how deeply images were rooted in his heart. So this teaching grew out of deeply held anxieties and was formed out of a profound sense of liberation. The theological warrant for this, according to Calvin, was the transcendence of God over his creation which cannot be bridged by any image the creature may form. But while religious images were not allowed, this did not remove all value, even all religious value, from the created order. Indeed Calvin had insisted that creation could be a mirror of his glory. If certain kinds of images were forbidden, others were allowed, even encouraged.

Our argument then is that the Reformation teaching and practice constituted a – sometimes systematic, sometimes impulsive – dismantling of an old way of thinking about God's presence in the world, and an equally intentional construction of a new way of imagining God and the world. As Peter Matheson has argued, "the iconoclasm of the Reformation was not just a concern to remove superfluity and 'stubble', but was complemented if not overshadowed by its iconopoesis, its vision of a human world which

---

[4] *England's Iconoclasts,* p. 447.
[5] Quoted in Carl Christensen, *Art and the Reformation,* p. 25. Segiusz Michalski argues that iconoclasm "was in the most general sense a form of struggle in effigy with the entire system of the old faith" (*The Reformation and the Visual Arts,* p. 90).

mirrored the divine in its banal, day to day reality."[6] This dismantling and remaking moreover was based on theological convictions about God's transcendence and the inward and personal appropriation of that God through preaching and reflection on Scripture. It was as though the very elimination of the sacramental presence of God from the world kindled a call to remake the world in its edenic purity; and the external removal of divine images stretched an internal canvas on which God's presence could be painted.

An important early expression of these values, and one that was to have important influence on England, was Martin Bucer's *Treatise on Images*, which appeared in an English translation in 1535.[7] Bucer, writing in defense of the removal of images in Strasbourg, echoes many of the themes we found in Calvin. He appeals to Scripture, especially the second commandment, and to the impiety caused by these images. They do nothing, Bucer argues, to promote the praise of God; they do not stir up our minds either "of the workes or of the benefits of God." And they are the main cause of our negligence of true worship.

The power of images, in Bucer's mind, rests on their ability to distract the believer's attention from works that are truly acceptable to God: genuine praise of God and works of charity. "The goodness of God," Bucer says, "shineth in all his creatures." The true image of God is to be found in our neighbor. All the goodness we see around urges us to "be to others as God is to us." Images necessarily impede this work. "For suche expenses which ought to have been made upo [*sic*] poore nedy folke (whom as beynge the very lyve image of God it was convenyent to have socoured and made our frendes with our lyberalyte) we have wastefully bestowed upon styckes and stones."

As for the use of images in teaching, like Calvin, Bucer sees no need. For we have the whole frame of the world as "a monument and token to put us in remembrance of God." Nor does the fact Christ took on bodily form justify images, for "his bodily presence was nothing profytable." For it is the Spirit that quickens, which is why Christ ascended to God. "It is stark madnesse to desire to be put in remembrance of the benefits of Christ by images." For it is in our own following of Christ that the true image is to be

---

[6] *The Imaginative World*, pp. 74–5.

[7] Martin Bucer, *A Treatise Declaring and Showing . . . that Pictures and other Images are not to be Suffered in the Temples and Churches of Christian Men* (London: W. Marshall, 1535), STC 24238. W. Marshall translated J. Bedrohte's Latin translation of Bucer's German original, *Das einigerlei Bild* (1530); quotes in the text are from the English edition, which is not paginated. Eamon Duffy describes the commotion this work caused, leading the Lord Chancellor to complain to Thomas Cromwell about the book. But it was immediately popular and went into a second printing the following year (*Stripping of the Altars*, p. 386).

formed. As often as God tries us and lays his cross upon us, Bucer stresses, in a theme that will be picked up by William Perkins, we have "this Jesus nayled faste upon the crosse set before the eyes of our mynde."

In this chapter we focus on the cultural practices that developed from this theological and imaginative transformation in England. We focus on England as the scene where Calvin's influence took its most distinctive shape, especially as this was to influence puritan America.[8] As the people formed by this worship and this catechesis began to shape their culture, what was the result? What kind of visual culture was constructed? Here we look primarily at the places most influenced by Calvin's worldview, especially at England and France up to 1580.[9] We want to ask not only what cultural practices resulted, but what "images" were to replace the visual media that were so central to medieval life, and how these began to reshape people's lives.

CHEAP PRINTS AND WOODCUTS

For most believers the most obvious effect of the Reformation was the disappearance of images from their own churches and the new worship patterns that were introduced.[10] Outside of church, cultural practices changed more gradually. And, while they played a different role than they had done previously, images by no means disappeared from people's everyday lives. There is a growing amount of evidence for the continuing role that images – and other art forms – played in the culture, even among those closest to the Reformation.[11]

---

[8] We recognize other influences were at play in England during this time, but the influence of Calvin was surely important to the cultural developments we sketch. Bucer was a close colleague of Calvin and was influential especially on the latter's view of the sacraments. Though Calvin does not quote Bucer's work on images, it is clear their views were similar.

[9] Though reference will be made to later practices, we will note that, by 1580, fundamental changes in cultural practices were underway that were central to what would later be called Puritanism.

[10] "The Reformation for most believers meant the reformation of their parish church" (Aston, *England's Iconoclasts*, p. 16).

[11] The more traditional view is expressed by John Bossy: the Reformation was a "devaluation of the collective existence represented by sacraments, saints and the 'unwritten' tradition of the Church in favor of a naked confrontation with Scripture" (*Christianity in the West,* p. 97). The continuing role of the visual among common people has been described in a pioneering work by Scribner, *For the Sake of the Simple Folk,* and was developed in greater detail for England in Tessa Watt, *Cheap Print and Popular Piety: 1550–1640* (Cambridge University Press, 1991). See also Anthony Wells-Cole, *Art and Decoration in Elizabethan and Jacobean England: The Influence of Continental Prints, 1558–1625* (New Haven: Yale University Press, 1997). These have shown the importance of a more inclusive approach that describes the way popular culture has both responded to and altered the teaching of the reformers.

The Protestant art of this period has not fared well at the hands of students of art history. Roy Strong can claim of England that "few periods have been more inimical to the visual arts than the middle years of the sixteenth century."[12] But scholars who have paid more attention to the reception of the Reformation by the people have corrected this simplified picture. Robert Scribner and Tessa Watt among others have demonstrated how the practices of the people responded to or adapted the teachings of the reformers. For the people, it could not have been a question of simply allowing or promoting art that was good and rejecting the rest. They saw clearly that finely wrought images had been taken captive by the developing economic elite and their attempts to assure their own salvation. In people's eyes, therefore, the production of these images had appropriated resources which would have been better used in caring for the growing number of poor, and in any case served interests that did not match their own.[13] As a result they frequently responded by invading their churches and dismantling the images and altars, but they also began to shape a visual culture that more closely matched their own developing faith.

The issue then is not a complete rejection of the visual, so much as the new theological orientation and the corresponding change that resulted in the way culture was formed. The visual element, as cultural practices generally, may appear in places one does not expect to find it, or in forms that have less prestige – at least from our modern perspective. Printing, for example, made possible the production of inexpensive prints which, often, were put with a text and distributed in broadsheets. From evidence that has survived, such prints were cheap enough so that even the poorest could buy them to decorate their homes. Robert Scribner has argued that, in Germany, these popular images were used as propaganda to promote the Reformation cause.[14] Their imagery created, he argues, a kind of symbolic universe in

---

[12] *The English Icon: Elizabethan and Jacobean Portraiture* (New York: Pantheon, 1969), p. 1. Strong notes that the English court did little in the way of patronage after Henry VIII, due to the collapse of the crown finances. But he goes on to note that standards foreign to that century ought not to be applied, for there were aesthetic developments in England even in the visual arts that proved to be significant. There developed, Strong argues, an "isolated, strange, exotic and anti-naturalistic style which is more akin to the aesthetics of Byzantine art" (p. 3). Erwin Panofsky echoes this caution by pointing out that representational arts had been in decline in England from the beginning of the fifteenth century ("Comments on Art and Reformation," p. 10; see also the comments of John Dillenberger, *Images and Relics*, p. 190).

[13] Cf. Peter Matheson, "The removal of images was part of [a] leveling campaign, because they were seen as the legitimation of privilege and hierarchy" (*The Imaginative World*, p. 74).

[14] Scribner sees these as allied and subordinate to the preaching mission of the Reformation (*For the Sake of the Simple Folk*, p. 249). Emile Doumergue describes similar prints that appeared in Calvinist areas (*Iconographie calvinienne* [Lausanne: Georges Bridal, 1909], part III).

which the truth of the Reformers' preaching was often contrasted with the lies (and immorality) of the monks and priests.[15]

Something similar appeared in the ballads and broadsides distributed in England by traveling minstrels – called then vagrants – at fairs, alehouses and town squares. This phenomenon underlines the interconnection of print and image and the close connection between oral and print culture. Often the broadseller would use his vocal performance of the ballad to sell the printed text of his song, which may or may not have been decorated with images.[16] Alehouses and private homes would certainly have been decorated with these and the painted cloths that were popular in England, reinforcing in imagery the beliefs and ideas of the developing Reformation. Because of their popularity and the composition of the materials, very few of the popular prints survive.[17] A large percentage of these ballads, up into the 1570s at least, conveyed a moral, or religious lesson. All of this spoke of the widespread impact of Reformation ideas,[18] as well as the continuing tolerance for visual imagery.

A more significant example of the role of visual imagery was the use of woodcuts and, later, etchings in printed books. This was common both on the continent and in England. In some cases prints of very high calibre appeared in works of Protestant scholars and publishers. Luther's catechism appeared adorned with prints illustrating many of the commandments and doctrines – even with images of God and the trinity.

Even Calvin's works frequently had images on the title page. Typical is the title page of the 1553 edition of the *Institutes*, which appears more than once, of an axe at the base of a tree, with the Latin inscription around it: "Now the axe is laid at the root of the tree, every tree that does not bear good fruit, is cut down and thrown into the fire" (Matt. 3:10). Another on the Commentary on the Gospels (1561) pictures an angel (with a scythe, representing the final judgment) pulling someone from a cave. Around this is written in French, "From deep places and full of obscurity, God in time extracts truth." Or the image on both the English translation of

---

[15] *For the Sake of the Simple Folk*, pp. 8–10. Craig Harbison quotes an Italian in Padua who commented that Lutherans there refused to look at any image "except those printed on paper" ("Introduction" to *Symbols in Transformation*, p. 15).

[16] See Watt, *Cheap Print*, pp. 11–14, 23.

[17] Wells-Cole, *Art and Decoration*, p. 5. He notes that it was from this medium, especially in Germany and the Netherlands, that the fine print developed, which, because of its quality and ownership, has survived in greater number. Watt notes that, in England, as the century wore on, the calibre and class of the writers declined: "Writing of godly ballads was on the wane by the middle of Elizabeth's reign" (*Cheap Print*, p. 41).

[18] Though these ideas were often modified, Tessa Watt notes, "by the more conservative outlook of the larger public" (*Cheap Print*, p. 4).

the *Form of Prayers* (1556) and the *Catechism* (1556), of a man pointing
his walking stick, with a banner over him saying (in Latin), "Enter by the
difficult way" and around him (in English), "the way to life is straight, and
few finde it" (Matt. 7:14). The close connection of text (usually of Scripture)
and image underlines the fact that the image served to support the verbal
message.[19]

In England Thomas Cranmer's *Catechism* had prints, several of which
were by Hans Holbein. Printed in London in 1548 during the reign of
Edward VI and the growing Protestant influence, his work had a large
following.[20] But the *Catechism* illustrates some of the multiple influences
at play in the English Church and the confusions which resulted. The
Catechism is really a translation of a German devotional book by Andreas
Osiander published in Nuremberg in 1533.[21] Cranmer's only original contribution is a long chapter addressing images, which did not really cohere with
the Lutheran eucharistic theology propounded elsewhere in the document.
But the *Catechism* is notable for its inclusion of fine prints. For example, in
Figure 5 note the simple print illustrating the first sermon which pictures
a Pharisee (shaven with a tonsure) praying at the altar, while an unshaven
lay publican stands alongside with his head down. In another illustrating
the Seventh petition of the Lord's Prayer – "Deliver us from Evil" – Jesus
delivers a demoniac of a spirit which is pictured emerging from the mouth
of the man, as amazed and skeptical leaders look on.

In the "sermon" Cranmer added on the second commandment, in good
Calvinist fashion, he cautions against bowing down to any creature. "For
what can be more contrarie to the dignitie of man, than he, whom God
hath made Lorde over all creatures to kneel or do reverence to the image
of a creature."[22] For we are made to stand and look up to God not to
kneel before a creature. As to images of Christ and the saints, he admits
their bodily nature and allows images of them, "I will not utterly deny
but they may be had. Still for charity sakes they should be kept out of the

---

[19] John King refers to these as a handmaid of biblical understanding (*English Reformation Literature:
The Tudor Origins of the Protestant Tradition* [Princeton University Press, 1982], p. 147). In general,
more images appear in the vernacular texts than those in Latin, and the numbers in general decline
until images in books are outlawed in 1580. See Collinson, *Birthpangs of Protestant England,* p. 117.

[20] See Diarmaid MacCulloch, *Thomas Cranmer: A Life* (New Haven: Yale University Press, 1996).

[21] MacCulloch says this was "the only purely Lutheran devotional work to take any official place in
the English Reformation" (ibid., p. 387). The catechism was, MacCulloch believes, a "fiasco."

[22] *Catechismus: That is to say a short Introduction into Christian Religion* (London: W. Lynne, 1548);
pagination is inconsistent and, in this section, missing. Unlike Calvin's (and Bucer's) catechism, he
does not adopt the dialogue method, but includes lengthy sermons on the areas covered. Though
designed for "children," the level of difficulty indicates they were probably read to rather than by
children.

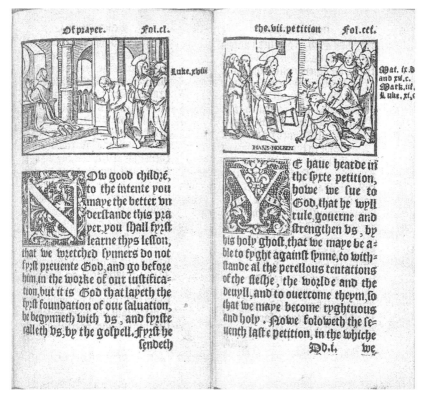

Figure 5   Hans Holbein, the Younger, *An Instruction of Prayer, The First Sermon, Plate XVIII* and *An Instruction of Prayer, The Seventh Petition, Plate XXV*. Huntington Library Museum, San Marino, Calif., 1548.

church. For the goodness that may come from them is not comparable to the evil of idolatry. Why not lift your eyes and your hands to heaven where God is?"

Of more significance was the fact that the two most influential books of the English Reformation – the bible and John Foxe's *Acts and Monuments* – were illustrated with a large number of prints, some of which were of a high quality.[23] In an important sense these books came to stand in place of the teeming medieval imagery that filled the imaginative world of the medieval believer. By mid-century in England most images and crucifixes

---

[23] See Strachan, *Early Bible Illustrations*. He notes that before the Reformation most bibles printed in Europe contained illustrations: "Of the seventeen German bibles before Luther fifteen were illustrated" (p. 9).

had been removed from the churches. "Their place in the Church," writes Ernest Gilman, "would now be filled by scriptural verses painted on the walls and altar cloths, and by the literary monuments of the Reformation, the English Bible and Foxe's Book of Martyrs."[24] Most famous of these prints was the title page of the Coverdale Bible, printed in 1535 (probably in Cologne), and attributed to Hans Holbein (Figure 6).

Dominating the images at the top, where in medieval iconography God would preside, stands the Hebrew word for God: Jahweh – who could not be "pictured." On one side Adam and Eve, on the right a victorious risen Christ – banners read: "In what day so ever thou eatest thereof thou shalt die," and "This is my deare sonne in whom I delight, heare him." Down the left side Moses appears receiving and Ezra (?) reading the law, on the other side Christ sends out the disciples to "preach the Gospel" and an image of Acts 2 shows the disciples receiving the Holy Spirit. Below clerics receive the scriptures from the king. Banners there reiterate: "O how swete are thy words unto my throte, yeh more than hony" (Ps. 119:103) and "I am not ashamed of the Gospell of Christ, for it is the power of God" (Rom. 1:16). Additionally in this 1535 bible there are prints of God creating Eve out of Adam's side (with God actually pictured as an old man); Cain killing Abel; even Bathsheba at her bath!

In the Great Bible of 1541 the frontispiece reverses the Coverdale image and features the king receiving the bible from the translator, along with lively images of Pharaoh's dream, the burning bush (in which other events from the life of Moses are also portrayed), and David slaying Goliath. The famous Geneva Bible, so-called for its having been printed in Geneva (by Rowland Hall, in 1560), is less lavishly illustrated though there are images of Israel following the cloud through the Red Sea as the frontispiece, under which is written, "The Lord will fight for you, therefore holde you your peace" (Ex. 14:14). Among other images are the Ark during the flood, and the encampment of Israel with the tabernacle. Images in this bible are particularly significant as this became the most widely read bible up to (and even for a while after) the famous King James version in 1611.[25]

---

[24] Ernest B. Gilman, *Iconoclasm and Poetry in the English Reformation* (University of Chicago, 1986), p. 7.

[25] Wells-Cole contends the 1560 edition is the bible "people would have read at home and it remained so until well after the publication in 1611 of the Authorized Version" (*Art and Decoration*, p. xii). James Strachan notes, however, that the woodcuts dropped out of later editions of the Geneva Bible. "In later editions the maps remained while the woodcuts tended to disappear." Indeed by the time the AV appeared, "the fashion for small woodcut illustrations had died out" (*Early Bible Illustrations*, p. 86).

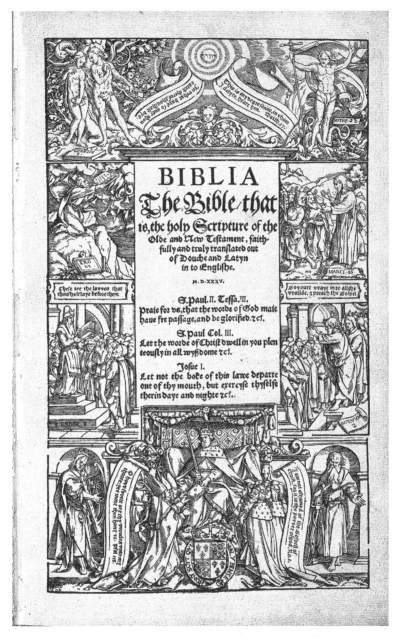

Figure 6   Attributed to Hans Holbein, title page of Coverdale Bible. Huntington Library Museum, San Marino, Calif., 1535.

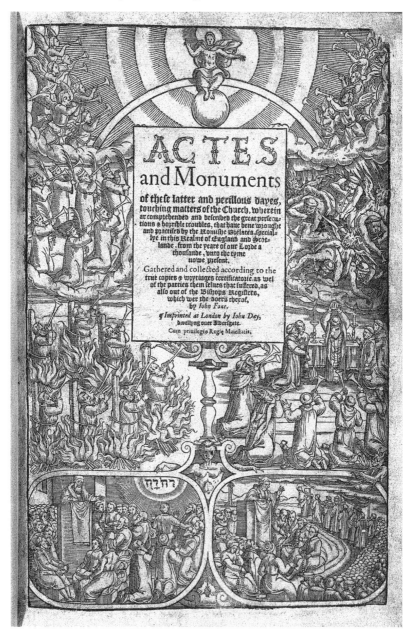

Figure 7 Anonymous, title page, in John Foxe, *Actes and Monuments of Matters most Memorable*, 1583 edn. Huntington Library Museum, San Marino, Calif., 1583.

Equally prominent in the shaping of Protestant thinking was the enormous *Actes and Monuments of Matters most Memorable*, by John Foxe (1516–87), which first appeared in 1563 in a single folio volume.[26] Here the history of the Church is interpreted in terms of the persecutions visited upon the true followers of Christ. Foxe's purpose was to extol the martyrs of the reign of Queen Mary, but he put this in the context of a history of the Church in which Satan has regularly attacked God's servants. The book opens with a calendar of martyrs' anniversaries in what is clearly intended to provide an alternative list of Protestant saints. The images on the title page (Figure 7) clearly delineate the true from the false church. On the left-hand side martyred souls wave palm branches and blow trumpets as they praise God. Below martyrs are burned at the stake and a preacher preaches the pure word of God – the Hebrew letters for God the only "image" to be seen. Meanwhile on the right side demons descend toward a priest celebrating the Mass. Below pilgrims follow their endless pilgrimages while people fingering rosaries listen to false preachers.

The graphic and detailed descriptions of the martyrs' deaths were accompanied by the equally graphic prints, as in this print of the burning of Wyclif's bones (Figure 8), images and words reinforcing one another. The teaching purpose of the prints is underlined by the fact that critical persons and places are labeled in the picture, including especially the primary villains of the drama. The great influence of Foxe's work was enhanced by its being approved and recognized by the Bishops of the Church of England, who in 1571 placed chained copies in every church. It probably did more than any other book to develop the notion of England and its people as having been especially chosen by God.[27]

Protestants then during the first generation of the Reformation would have been confronted with graphic images of the stories they heard read in church and of the testimonies of those who suffered during the reign of Mary.[28] In the images in catechisms, the bible and Foxe's "Book of Martyrs" one might describe the beginning of a Protestant iconography.[29] On the

---

[26] Printed in London by John Day; an expanded (and larger) version appeared in two large volumes in 1583, which was later updated and reprinted into the seventeenth century.

[27] William Haller, *The Elect Nation: The Meaning and Relevance of Foxe's Book of Martyrs* (New York: Harper & Row, 1963); and see King, *English Reformation Literature,* p. 428.

[28] During this period (1553–8) the influence of Calvin was reinforced as many leaders spent their time in Geneva in Exile. But Dan Danner argues in his study of this period that English Reformed thinking, while influenced by Bucer and Calvin, sprang from indigenous roots, and was not strictly Calvinist (*Pilgrimage to Puritanism: History and Theology of the Marian Exiles at Geneva: 1555–1560* [New York: Peter Lang, 1999], pp. 141–3).

[29] The themes of such an iconography were suggested by Craig Harbison in the exhibit he curated in 1969 at Princeton University. This exhibit was arranged under the following themes: "Spirit and

Figure 8   Anonymous, *The Burning of Wyclif's Bones*, in John Foxe, *Actes and Monuments*, 1583 edn, p. 105. Huntington Library Museum, San Marino, Calif., 1583.

one hand these images primarily reinforce the centrality of Scriptural texts and events. These events, or their contemporary equivalents, are clearly and simply pictured, in ways that would be accessible to anyone, often with accompanying words. On the other hand, in Foxe's *Acts and Monuments*, the so-called "Book of Martyrs," the saints of the church featured in medieval iconography are replaced by martyrs and "heroes of the faith" who suffered for their faith. In many ways Foxe develops a Protestant hagiography. Pictures often appear with accompanying legends to underline the significance of the person, and to emphasize that the human figure is now the proper "image" of God.

    In all instances, the images were not meant to stand alone as "works of art" – even if some would qualify as fine prints. For they were not made to call attention to themselves. Here words and images reinforce each other, to

Flesh," "Man [*sic*] and Idol," "Grace and Fate," "Suffering and Revelation," and "the Human Image" (see *Symbols in Transformation*).

make the impact of the event clear – especially for children and lay readers.[30] The images function something like Anthony Gilby's famous annotations on the side of the Geneva Bible, to underline the newly appropriated meaning of these texts. As John King puts it, the "illustrations serve to break down whatever barrier may exist between reader and text."[31] Lying behind this of course are the theological convictions that the transcendent God is mediated only by a faithful (and internal) appropriation of Scripture. It is through the word, read, preached and heard that the saving truth of God's love is brought home to the hearts of the hearer by the ministry of the Holy Spirit. Images, when they are allowed, are subordinated to this much more important work. Reformation art, like medieval philosophy, functions *ancilla domini* – a means to a higher end.

The art historians are right in one sense: no particular artistic tradition is begun by the use of images we have described. Reformed Holland in the seventeenth century is arguably an exception to this, but even there the ambiguity persists, as we will see in the next chapter. Nor does the use of imagery flower as the sixteenth century goes on; quite the opposite. In 1580 all biblical images were banned in Geneva, even in printed books; in England a clear reaction to imagery takes hold after that date.[32]

HANS HOLBEIN, NICHOLAS HILLIARD AND THE HUMAN IMAGE OF GOD

Part of the ambivalence art historians have toward this period, we have argued, lies in the fact that the visual does not appear in ways that correspond to modern aesthetic hierarchies. So the art of the period, especially in England, is dismissed as expendable and utilitarian, as one historian put it: part wall furniture, part social and political record.[33] Such judgments would have been puzzling to sixteenth-century persons for at least two reasons. First, such practical standards would have been the only ones available to them. Renaissance notions of painting as high art only entered England

---

[30] Gilman believes that the biblical frontispiece functions as a kind of emblem. He points out that in the Renaissance emblems do not simply illustrate the text; word and text interrelate in a synaesthetic way (*Iconoclasm and Poetry*, p. 16).

[31] *English Reformation Literature*, p. 129; cf. "Protestant images represent the word visibly" (p. 152).

[32] Michalski, *The Reformation and the Visual Arts*, p. 72. On the situation in England, see Collinson, *Birthpangs of Protestant England*, pp. 99ff; though also see the qualifications suggested in Watt, *Cheap Print*, p. 135.

[33] This is the argument of Lacey Baldwin Smith, " 'Christ What a Fright!': The Tudor Portrait as Icon," *Journal of Interdisciplinary Studies* 4/1 (Summer 1973), p. 119; she is reviewing the work of Roy Strong.

late in the reign of Elizabeth, most notably in the writings of Philip Sidney
in the 1590s. But more importantly, in the developing Protestant view, it
was precisely painting's utility that gave it value. It was widely assumed, and
not just by Protestants, that works of art had value because of their utility.
Earlier images had religious value, but when this was given up other uses
needed to be found. In the work of Hans Holbein and Nicholas Hilliard
these other uses, based on Reformation values, came to expression.

Though a native of Basle, from 1532 until his death in 1543 Hans Holbein
lived and worked in England and exercised an enormous influence on
the development of English art during his century. Holbein's developing
interest in the reform was influenced both by his home in the center for
dissemination of Luther's ideas in Switzerland and southern Germany, and
by his close friendship with Erasmus.[34] Little is known about the details
of his faith, but he declared publicly for the reform in June of 1529, while
still in Basel, and clearly chose to move to (and remain in) England to
work for the reforms he saw in progress.[35] Already in 1526 he had given up
specifically religious subjects and turned almost exclusively to portraits.

Why did Holbein turn to portraits? Of course the immediate answer
is that this is what his patrons wanted, but why were they now seeking
this visual record? In the larger culture the rising humanism and the newly
wealthy families placed a new emphasis on the achievement of individuals
and families, and portraits were a reasonable way to record this. Such
careful recording of important people was of course not a new thing; as
in other areas of Renaissance culture, the reemerging of portraits marked
a recovery of ancient models, especially the portrait medal. Meanwhile the
impetus to record nature in a careful and precise manner, deriving from
the illuminated manuscript, led to a growing desire to depict people as
they were at a particular moment in time. But this also built on medieval
traditions which included symbols of the transience of life. A portrait then
could both celebrate earthly life and lament its brevity.[36]

All of this would have had religious overtones, but there are even more
important reasons to link this developing interest specifically with the Reformation ideas that we have been tracing. Derek Wilson, in describing
the attacks on images that were taking place in Holbein's native Basel,

---

[34] Derek Wilson, *Hans Holbein: Portrait of an Unknown Man* (London: Weidenfeld & Nicolson, 1996).
    Wilson argues Holbein certainly shared the utilitarian attitudes of art then common (cf. p. 113).
[35] Ibid., pp. 167–8 and 274–5. Wilson argues, against those who believe Holbein left Basel because
    reforms had become overly restrictive, that he went to England specifically because he was drawn to
    the reforms in progress there and his contacts there offered greater opportunities for work.
[36] See the discussion of Renaissance portraiture in Oskar Bätschmann and Pascal Grienen, *Hans Holbein*
    (London: Reaktion Books, 1997), p. 153.

argues that the artists themselves (Holbein included) certainly came to support the removal of images. It was a recurring theme of Reformation (and related humanist) polemics that more care should be given to God's human image than those made with human hands. Erasmus himself, while he was repulsed by the extreme forms of iconoclasm, could say in terms that anticipate Bucer: "I wonder what possible excuse there could be for those who spend so much money on building, decorating and enriching churches . . . when meanwhile our brothers and sisters, Christ's living temples, waste away from hunger and thirst."[37] It would have been natural, then, when other religious subjects were forbidden, for artists to record human subjects. We have seen both in Calvin's writings and in Bucer's attack on images that this focus on the neighbor as the true image of God was a central factor in developing attitudes toward morality and culture. Indeed it is significant that the two elements that characterize British art up to the present, portraits and landscape, are precisely those elements that were celebrated by Calvin as the site of God's splendor.[38] In contrast to the more colorful style of his earlier paintings, Holbein's portraits are well known for their graceful and restrained focus on the person, as in this portrait of a merchant from 1538 (Figure 9).

The sitter, no doubt a prominent figure in London, is shown half length with his pensive eyes averted, dressed in plain costume and hat. The stark simplicity of the figure is emphasized by the plain dark green background, which seems to push the figure toward the viewer. The portrait during this period, Roy Strong argues, is both symbol and allegory. It records the sitter's position in society, but it also recorded the inexorable process of aging – even as photos do today. Moreover, it was meant to spur the viewer to greater virtue. As Strong says: "Lessons of virtue and of vice were to be read from the countenance of the great."[39] Although elements of these conventions were inherited from previous traditions of portraiture, there is a new impulse at work in Holbein's later portraits. What is celebrated is the dignity and reserve of the sitter, his or her humanity rather than their status. Under the religious influences we have traced, emerging portrait

---

[37] Quoted in Wilson, *Hans Holbein,* p. 110. Erasmus wrote this in 1526.

[38] So one should not be too quick to see these elements as "secular," as in this description of British painting: "Since the sixteenth century when the Protestant Reformation in Britain swept away the religious images that were the mainstay of art in the Middle Ages, British art has been dominated by the secular genres of portraiture and landscape" (Malcolm Warner, "Anglophilia into Art," in Malcolm Warner and Robyn Aselson [eds.], *Great British Paintings from American Collections: Holbein to Hockney,* Catalogue of the Exhibit at the Yale Center of British Art and the Huntington Library [New Haven: Yale University Press, 2001], p. 2).

[39] *The English Icon,* pp. 29, 38–9; quote p. 46.

Figure 9   Hans Holbein, the Younger, *A Hanseatic Merchant.* Oil on oak panel, 49.6 ×
39 cm. Yale University Art Gallery, New Haven, Conn., 1538.

conventions began to suggest that great lessons may be learned from the
countenances of those who would not qualify as great in the world's eyes.

While Holbein may be the most influential of these new portrait painters,
his follower Nicholas Hilliard (1547–1619) also provides an important example. After twenty-five years of confusion in English art following the
death of Holbein, it is generally felt that Hilliard brought a fresh impetus
to visual art, though he followed the manner of Holbein.[40] Hilliard's connection to the reform was even closer than that of Holbein. He was born to

[40] Graham Reynolds, *British Portrait Miniatures* (Cambridge University Press, 1988), pp. 8–10; and see
Erna Auerbach, *Nicholas Hilliard* (London: Routledge, Kegan, Paul, 1961).

Richard Hilliard who was a zealous supporter of the reformed religion. He even lived for a time with Thomas Bodley in Geneva during the Marian exile, and presumably shared in the humanistic and theological education given to Bodley.[41] He returned to England in 1559 and was apprenticed to Robert Brandon, a goldsmith. The best of his mature works date from the 1570s when he enjoyed the – sometimes fickle – patronage of Queen Elizabeth I.

Hilliard is best known as a miniaturist, and this medium shows his florid neomedievalism in its best light. Miniatures attracted the attention of patrons as a way of memorializing loved ones in a form that could be worn as jewelry. But Hilliard also excelled in book illustrations and full-sized panel paintings. Throughout, his greatest strength and the basis of his originality is in his glowing, almost calligraphic drawing. Cut off from Italian influence, Hilliard's lineage is more properly placed in the medieval books of hours.[42]

As can be seen in this portrait of a young man (Figure 10), Hilliard is unmatched in the careful recording of detail, lively color and design, and the developing fashions in clothing and jewelry. But the central focus of his work is always the person, who appears in this portrait with a calm dignity. Though Hilliard is famous for his portraits of Queen Elizabeth, he paints here an unnamed man against a plain background. The motivation for his work as a portraitist can be seen in Hilliard's treatise on the "Art of Limning" which, though written around 1600, was left unpublished at his death.[43] Here Hilliard argues strongly for a more exalted position for the artist. He should be a "gentleman" for art is a special gift of God, "the author of wisdo[m and] . . . all good gifts and goodness" (p. 16). As God gave the Spirit to Oholiab and Baselel in Exodus 31, so he gifts artists today. "Here is a kind of true gentility when God calleth" (p. 17). In good reformed fashion he goes on to celebrate the calling of God in all these issues, even those who gave up painting for the "liberty of the Gospel" and became ministers (p. 18).

He proceeds to give more practical advice for those called to become painters (who are superior he argues to carvers!), which includes their own comportment and the layout of their workspace. Then he turns to the subject of painting. "Now knowe that all Painting imitateth nature or the life in everything, it resembleth so fare forth as the Painters memory or

---

[41] Reynolds, *British Portrait Miniatures,* p. 10.   [42] Ibid., p. 20. See Strong, *The English Icon*, p. 14.
[43] N. Hilliard's *The Art of Limning: A New Edition of a Treatise concerning the Art of Limning,* transcription by Arthur F. Kinney, commentary by Linda Bradley Salamon (Boston, Mass.: Northeastern University Press, 1983). Subsequent references to this work are given as pages in the text.

Figure 10   Nicholas Hilliard, *A Man Aged 24*. Victoria and Albert Museum, London,
England. Photo: Art Resource, New York.

skill can serve him to express" (p. 22). But above all the painter must favor
our divine part, which is the human face. "Of all things the perfection is
to imitate the face of mankind, or the hardest part of it, and which carieth
most prayess and comendation" (p. 22). This is, he says, the highest work,
and one should not undertake it until he or she has had much experience
in "story work." For with persons it is not the events but the "graces and
countenance" that matters. This is expressed, Hilliard goes on to explain, in
three ways: in "fair and beautiful couler or complection"; good proportion
which he calls "favor"; and grace in countenance by which "afections apeare"
like a strike of lightning (p. 23). Interestingly it is the eyes that are the life of
the picture, and sad countenance is not to be recorded: it is a sign of some

evil (p. 24). He goes on to develop his theory of the primacy of the flowing line as the principal part of drawing after life, as that which best captures the life that is the truth the painter seeks, and the importance of light as the counterpart of good favor. Shadows, like a sad countenance, are a sign of a bad cause, like Judas meeting Christ at night (pp. 28–9).

Clearly for Hilliard the beauty of line and color was by no means inconsistent with his faith, indeed it belonged to the many gifts given by God. And the calling of the artist, to his mind, was equal to that of any other vocation. Even the style of painting, based as it is in Calvinist fashion on drawing after life, embodies principles that grow from his understanding of God as the source of goodness and light. But notice that it is in the human countenance that this light is especially to be seen. This, Hilliard believed, is our "divine part" – that place where the image directing us to God is most clearly to be seen.

PROTESTANT ARCHITECTURE AND GARDENS

The influence of Reformed thinking on the imagery of the seventeenth century clearly is greater than is ordinarily thought. But one must look beyond the explicit imagery to see the theological influence of Reformed ideas on the developing culture. For Calvin, the impact of the performance of worship and of Christian discipleship was to extend to the reforming of the structures of everyday life. The theological plan of the *Institutes* was to be reflected in the structures that became visible in the communities and cultures that lived by this plan. As a result the visual culture that we need to examine appears not only in the specific images that might be placed in books or hung on walls of house or church, but, above all, in the structuring of the spaces in which believers were to live.

It has been known for some time that some of the most important architects in seventeenth-century France were French Calvinists, or Huguenots, but the religious aspect of their work has been almost entirely ignored. In fact when the Calvinist Bernard Palissy's works were edited and published in 1888 the editors expressed their amusement at his attempts to mix his Protestantism with "ancient truth." His placing of biblical passages on the four fountains of the garden, they note, may come from his piety, but it is also odd ("de bizarrerie").[44] But recently Catherine Randall has argued that Palissy and others worked out of a specifically Calvinist conception both of

---

[44] Bernard Palissy, *Les Oeuvres de Maistre Bernard Palissy*, ed. P. Fillon (Niort: Clouzot Librairie, 1888), vol. 1, p. li. "C'est peut-être de la piété, mais c'est aussi de la bizarrerie."

space and the natural world. For them Calvin's *Institutes* provided a kind of blueprint that served as a (usually hidden) agenda for their work for the Catholic Court of France. Randall notes of Palissy: "Scripturally modeled structures and spaces provide the theatre for the enactment of salvation in the text of this Calvinist architect."[45]

The most famous of the Huguenot architects was Bernard Palissy (1510–1590). He was born in Saint-Pons in the south of France, where he became a part of the newly formed Reformed congregation, though he spent much of his life working for the French Court in Paris. Perhaps his most famous work was in planning the Tuileries palaces and Gardens for Catherine de Medici. In *La Recept veritable* published in 1563 he lays out his views (what he calls his philosophy) of architecture and agriculture.[46] In this work he expresses what must be called modern ideas of working with nature, and respecting the dignity of creation – he has harsh words for those ignorant people who destroy the forests and by this their own future (pp. 101–3). But the central notion of the work is the elaborate plan for his "delectable garden." In a description that recalls Augustine's conversion experience, he remembers hearing Psalm 104 beautifully sung. He begins to contemplate the sense of this Psalm ("[J]'entray en contemplation sur le sens dudit Pseaume"). In what must be an early use of "imagination" in the modern sense, on the basis of this Psalm, he "pictures" to himself a garden where exiles from persecution can come and find rest. Interestingly he says that he contemplated drawing ("figurer") the landscapes of the Psalm in some pictures. But seeing that paintings do not last long, he decided to find a convenient place to construct a garden, which matched the design and beauty of the Psalm. Having already drawn this garden in my mind ("ayant desjà figuré en mon esprit ledit jardin"), he says, I considered how I might be able to erect such a palace or amphitheatre (p. 24). Interestingly he imagines this beautiful place serving as a refuge for Reformed exiles in France during times of persecution.

His plans are based on the fact that God has made the earth to replenish itself, an activity that goes on all the time (p. 46). His garden is built as a square with arboreal arches at each side, intersected with pathways that meet at a pyramid in the center (pp. 71–95). There are four fountains inscribed with biblical phrases such as "the fountain of wisdom is the word of the Lord" and "the fear of the Lord is the beginning of wisdom" (pp. 85, 86).

[45] Catherine Randall (Coats), "Structuring Protestant Scriptural Space in Sixteenth Century Catholic France," *Sixteenth Century Journal* 25/2 (1994), pp. 341–53; quote p. 349; and *Building Codes.*
[46] Palissy, *Oeuvres*, vol. 1, pp. lix, lx. *La Recept veritable* is found in vol. 1, pp. 1–129. Page numbers in the text are to this work. Translations are mine.

Though never explicitly stated, it is clear that the garden for Palissy is an image of salvation. For he notes it is a "refuge" (p. 24) from those who would destroy him, and a retreat from these "perilous and evil times" (p. 95). Sometimes when I'm asleep, he says, I seem to be already in my garden enjoying its fruit. So much so that when he "comes to consider the marvelous actions that the Lord has asked his creation to perform . . . I am completely amazed by the providence of God" (pp. 97, 98). Even when he leaves the garden he is able to see wisdom everywhere: all is clothed with wisdom (p. 99). After lamenting those ignorant and foolish people who despise those who work with their hands and spend their time seeking benefices to purchase, he concludes there will always be those who persecute the righteous. "Take your refuge then in your chief, protector and captain, our Lord Jesus Christ, who, in his time and place, will know how to avenge the wrongs done to him, and to us" (p. 114).

The object then of his work in planning, planting and building, is to make his work an image of his "delectable garden," that is an image of redemption. For when one has found his or her refuge one can see the world in terms of the wisdom that God has placed in it. But this vista can be missed! One can only "see" this natural symbolism if one's eyes are purified, that is if one sees through the eyes of faith. As if to give flesh and blood to his "image of salvation," at the end of his work he tells the story of his own Reformed Church at Saint-Pons beginning in 1546. Little by little it prospered and became widely admired in spite of suffering and much persecution, like Daniel in the Lion's Den, he notes (p. 118). But on Sunday these folk, "take walks in the meadow, woods, or some other pleasant place, and in such places they love to sing all kinds of holy songs" (p. 125). For, despite their enemies, having found their peace in Christ, they are able to go out and enjoy that peace in the world – to see it as a theatre for God's glory.

Catherine Randall points out how closely Palissy follows the structure implied in Calvin's *Institutes*. Indeed his imaginary garden, Randall argues, is an "entexted structure" that reflects the transformation that Christ has made possible. Though fallen, through artifice the world can be restructured, in the same way that the invisible church for Calvin may be superimposed on the visible. "Palissy's garden render[s] literal Calvin's conception of believers as a new 'garden of Eden'."[47]

A further example is the French architect Salomon de Caus, a French Hugeunot who came to England in 1611 to redesign the gardens of

[47] *Building Codes*, pp. 45–55; quote p. 55.

Richmond Palace in the "new manner." De Caus's views on his work are laid out in his work on perspective published in London in 1612.[48] Interestingly, like Palissy, de Caus makes no explicit reference to Calvin, but, also like that architect, he seems at times to be repeating sections of the *Institutes*. All that is built should be, de Caus asserts in his notice to the reader, for utility and pleasure. This is true for all the work of architects, engineers and painters. Especially the latter, he says. "The art of painting consists in representing a natural thing and making it appear natural when it is seen. This cannot be well done without using appropriate reasons which are unique to this science and which serve to put all lines and traces in their place." Nothing gives pleasure when it is seen like perspective, he notes, both in writing and drawing. But it is not easy to sense by writing alone when dealing with natural objects, these must be "pictured" and built. In his only reference to God he says simply at the close of the introduction: "May God guard you." Then follows a discourse, amply illustrated with drawings, on properly drawing and building in perspective and in the proper relation to light and shadow. All centers on the eye, lines represent the surface of the earth or right angles to that surface, light and shade come from the rays of the sun or fire. Palissy interestingly had similarly noted that all structure in architecture comes from the tree and the human body.

Much of this of course is not original and could have been said by anyone trained in the classic sources rediscovered in the Renaissance, especially, in this case, Vitruvius. But that is just the point. This is not an art that intends to call attention to itself. Catherine Randall notes that these architects coded a hidden agenda in their work, which was intended to leave no trace. They mean their efforts to be not so much a finished product as the "paradigm of a process which will enact the reformation of the created order (and will then be no longer necessary)."[49] Art here serves religion, but not at all in the medieval sense. It now serves what is to these architects the higher calling of religion, that program of making right a distorted created order. Walking in a "delectable garden," strolling in a well-ordered space, one does not necessarily think of God. But these are spaces that can, to these builders, "picture" God nevertheless.

Notice further the role of the creative capabilities of the mind in this emerging view. The human imagination, or the picturing function of the

[48] Salomon de Caus, *La Perspective avec La Raison des ombres et miroirs* (London: Norbon, 1612), the book is not paginated. See the discussion of his work in England in Strong, *The English Icon*, p. 56.

[49] "Structuring Protestant Scriptural Space," p. 346. In the introduction to *Building Codes*, Randall argues that this indirection has largely to do with these architects' minority (and persecuted) status, which certainly must have been critical. But it also positively reflected the natural way Christians were now to understand and remake the world. We discuss this further in Chapter Seven.

mind, is challenged to play, if anything, a greater role in making and building than it did in making devotional images. In the medieval period, for
example, the image of the labyrinth served as a microcosm of the soul's
journey toward God. Indeed the labyrinth placed in the floor of cathedrals
served as an external means of encouraging systematic prayer. With Calvin
(and Milton among others) this image became a symbol of human lostness
apart from the guidance of the word of God. Huston Diehl in his discussion
of this transformation concludes: "In its rejection of external aids, Protestantism alters man's relation to the objective, visible world, encouraging
believers to look inward."[50] This is true as far as it goes, but there is more
to be said. Though they rejected such external aids, Reformed theologians'
understanding of faith provided inner leverage for a new way of comprehending the world and thus a greater scope for the work of imagination.
Believers were not limited to traditional imagery, they could seek to find
and construct images of God's grace and of salvation in all aspects of life.

Nor was this work of "imagining" something optional or unimportant.
Recall that it was only after Palissy had pictured this garden in his mind,
on the basis of the "sense" of Scripture, that he was able to begin the actual
design of projects. The irony of the Protestant imagination may be said to
lie precisely here: while denying the right to picture anything that might
be mistaken for God, and by forcing faith inward, into the deepest recesses
of the human spirit, religion was creating a space for the mind to operate –
to picture a new world. Rather than allowing the imagination to picture
what was absent, in an important respect this imagination is encouraged to
picture what never existed. And in many respects this space, this new world,
is precisely what the subsequent generations of Reformed Protestants set
about to construct.

A NEW (PROTESTANT) CULTURE

Modern students who associate art with museums and galleries may be
forgiven for not finding much of interest in those places influenced by
sixteenth-century reformed Christianity. For the reformers of this period,
and the artists they influenced, had a larger project in mind: the structuring
of a new order of society that better reflected their (newly appropriated)
understanding of Scripture. To their minds, of course, the art which survived from the Middle Ages not only did little to promote this project, it

---

[50] Huston Diehl, "Into the Maze of Self: The Protestant Transformation of the Image of the Labyrinth,"
    Journal of Medieval and Renaissance Studies 16/2 (1986), pp. 281–301; quote pp. 297–8. Calvin uses
    the image frequently, the labyrinth first appears in *Institutes*, I, vi, 3.

actually stood in the way. Though for a while they tolerated a great deal of imagery – as long as it was purged of older associations – they were working on a larger canvas.

The influence of the Reformation in England, which we consider now, was carried by those most influenced by Calvin, who later became known as Puritans.[51] These shared with Protestants generally in England an antipathy to the Pope and the sense that England was a chosen nation. But they wanted to take the reformation further and deeper. They shared Calvin's sense of the corruption of human nature and the need for a radical conversion and a continuing dependence of God's grace. They worshiped in plainly decorated churches and looked to the bible as their primary authority, spending much of their time reading and memorizing it.[52] What kind of impact did these believers have on the development of English culture?

Thomas Cranmer made clear in the beginning of his 1548 catechism the larger purposes he had for the teaching of children. Despite the heavy going of the "sermons" of this catechism and the confusion of its sources, it was not written for priests, but for the young child who in wise and measured words might have "the beginning of Christian religion and doctrine and learne as well howe they should live, as also what they shoulde believe."[53] Thus the teaching was meant to reorient their lives in accordance with the teaching of Scripture. This reorientation involved a new appreciation for children and family life, as the catechisms themselves demonstrate, and a life ordered by Scripture. In general this introduction of discipline and order into communal life was to have an immense impact on the development of western cultural generally, and capitalism in particular.[54] Patrick Collinson has called attention to the way that the misrule and violence that characterized pre-Reformation society – and that accompanied the many practices of popular culture – was replaced by the reformers with a busy workweek, followed by a rigorously controlled Sabbath. The latter for

[51] Those who initially were called "radical" Protestants later came to be called "Puritans," which was initially a term of reproach. On the development and use of this term see Hill, *Society and Puritanism*. He notes it was first used of those who sought to reform the Church by separating from the Church of England but later of those who sought reform from within the Church. "For contemporaries the word had no narrowly religious connotation" (p. 24). See also Christopher Durston and Jacqueline Eales (eds.), *The Culture of English Puritanism, 1560–1700* (New York: St. Martin's, 1996), intro., pp. 1–31.

[52] These characteristics constitute, Durston and Eales argue, a "distinctive cast of mind," a kind of *mentalité* (*Culture of English Puritanism,* p. 9).

[53] *Catechismus,* from the preface.

[54] This of course has been argued most famously by Max Weber in *The Protestant Ethic and the Spirit of Capitalism* (1905 and many subsequent editions) and R. H. Tawney in *Religion and the Rise of Capitalism* (1957). These writers have found more favor with social scientists than economists, though their thesis continues to be influential.

many writers constituted the central element in their cultural program, for it underlined the new order of discipline and worship. Collinson concludes: "Calendarwise the Reformation amounted to the intrusion of the working season into the months traditionally associated with a kind of holy play."[55] In some senses this involved a secularization of life, but as we have argued with respect to Calvin's aesthetic, it also involved a new spiritual understanding of that larger world. Collinson again noted: "it paradoxically involved the sacralization of the town, which now became self-consciously a godly commonwealth, its symbolic and mimetic order replaced by a literally articulated, didactic religious discipline." Assuming that this was the social project to which Puritan leaders would commit themselves, what was the implication of this for cultural production more narrowly conceived, and, in particular, what shape did it give to the developing Protestant imagination?

In the same year that Cranmer's Catechism was published, an important book appeared by John Bale, *The Image of Bothe Churches*.[56] Bale composes a meticulous commentary of John's revelation on Patmos, which is set against the background of the struggle of Bale's time between the "Church washed without spot" and the "Proud Church of the Hypocrites," that is between the Protestants and the Catholics. All belief, he asserts, is summed up in this book (i.e. The Revelation of John), in the light of the current "treacherous times" in which the "wrath of God shall be declared." Bale develops the "images" first of all of the true and false church: "For the one is mayntayned by the onlye preacynge of Gods pure word, the other by all kyndes of Jewyshe ceremonyes and heytenishe supersticyons." But the book also "images" many of the figures of John's vision. Most interesting is Bale's description of the risen Christ as John portrays him in the Revelation, chapter 1 (Figure 11). The head of Christ is his marvelous godhead; the eyes his godly wisdom and knowledge; the feet his human "affeccions"; his voice is the Gospel; right hand his power and so on.

As it is the "image" of these churches Bale underlines, so it is the figurative character of Revelation that he emphasizes. John King argues that Bale here seeks to reveal what is hidden to the reprobate, and is dependent

[55] *Birthpangs of Protestant England,* p. 54. The following quote from p. 55. Cf. R. H. Tawney, who characterizes their goal as: "the attempt to crystallize a moral ideal in the daily life of a visible society, which [could] be at once a church and a state. Having overthrown monasticism, its aim was to turn the secular world into a giant monastery" (*Religion and the Rise of Capitalism* [New York: Mentor, 1959], p. 101; quoted in Monter, *Calvin's Geneva,* p. 235).

[56] Published in London in 1548 by Richard Fugge, no pagination, though it is divided into chapters that correspond to the chapters of Revelation. The book is small format (4″ × 6″) and the pictures are small (1 1/2″ × 2″).

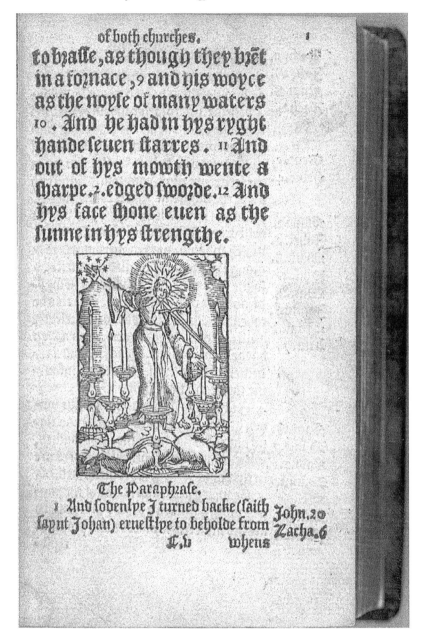

Figure 11   John Bale, *Image of Bothe Churches*. Huntington Library Museum, San Marino, Calif., *c.* 1548.

on the Joachimist argument of the seven ages of the Church, that is the story of the Church in the last days.[57] The book is illustrated with a dozen prints, some of them reproduced at several points in the book. The image of Christ in the first chapter is illustrated with this small print of Christ standing in the midst of the seven lampstands, with a sword coming out of his mouth; chapter 21 verse 2 is illustrated with the print of John being shown the city coming down from heaven and from God. Interesting as these prints are, these "images" are not those that Bale refers to in the title. These merely are included to underline visually the images which are carefully described in the text. "Image" here takes on a particular meaning that grows out of the developing theological convictions, that of a clear and graphic description of truth, which is meant to serve a religious end. Moreover these images were to be internally grounded, in order to provide motivation for a proper external ordering of life.[58] John N. King describes this shift in mimetic theory in this way: "In opposition to the artistic externalization of religious feelings, Protestant subjectivity demands inner faith predicated upon spiritual understanding." As Bale notes in the conclusion, these images are to provide the soul's consolation from the Eternal Trinity in picturing the universal estate of the Church from Christ's ascension to the end of the world.

John Bale is a critical force, according to John King, in developing "a distinctively Protestant literary tradition [which] took root in England under Edward VI."[59] But to Bale the larger concern was not with literature, to which he probably did not consider he was contributing much, but to the Church and beyond that to society. Again it is critical that we understand the social context which faced the reformers in England. Even leaving out of account the royal vacillation with respect to the reform, English society in the first half of the century faced enormous problems. Margaret Aston, in her important study on the Lollards and early reformers, notes that at the time of Wyclif the reformers were not primarily worried about heresy, but about the whole of society.[60] This is true of sixteenth-century reformers as well. And it is true of them in two senses. First, in contrast to the medieval superstitions, they believed they had discovered theological grounding for a new and positive evaluation of everyday life, for the family and community.

---

[57] *English Reformation Literature*, pp. 61–2.   [58] Ibid., p. 16.

[59] Ibid., p. 407. King notes that Bale's influence was particularly strong on John Foxe, especially in his sense of the "two churches," and eventually even on Spenser and Milton. "Mid century reformers embraced poetry as a powerful vehicle that combines aesthetic pleasure with didactive instruction" (p. 210).

[60] *Lollards and Reformers*, p. 2.

But secondly this means that when they looked at the larger society they did not find much to encourage them. Christopher Hill has described the character of social and economic life during the first part of the century as a backward economy with a voluntarily underemployed workforce. The common attitude was that one needed to work only until one had enough to eat and drink. Drunkenness was a constant problem, and a large number of idlers spent their time (and money) on amusements offered by games and the frequent (and bawdy) civic celebrations.[61] In addition, as we noted in the first chapter, the development of trade and rise of the cities led to the impoverishment of peasants beginning in 1450. This situation grew worse during the course of the sixteenth century. By late in that century each city had an increasingly large number of poor, in some cases reaching as high as 50 percent of the population.[62]

Clearly the challenges facing the culture were enormous – in this Catholics and Protestants agreed, and it is in this context that the Puritan efforts at reform must be understood. As with visual imagery, most of the celebrations and games were intricately connected with the religious calendar and were even sponsored by the Church. At the beginning of the century the Church sponsored many festivals, plays and what were called "church ales." These events, or better what had become of them, were considered by Puritans not only dangerous to individual piety, but more importantly a threat to the family and community.[63]

The fate of drama during the century may be taken as representative of Puritan attitudes toward popular culture. As with images, there seems to have been a tolerance for religious drama up through the middle of the century. In fact plays based on Scripture were written and performed, which, John King argues, "developed organically from the medieval

[61] *Society and Puritanism,* pp. 124–6. The most notorious of these perhaps was the maypole celebration.
[62] See Alison Rowlands, "The Conditions of the Life for the Masses," in Cameron (ed.), *Early Modern Europe,* pp. 55–9. She notes that the resultant rise in mortality rates and increasing mobility made care for the poor a major urban issue after mid-century.
[63] Jeremy Goring notes that Catholics often joined Protestants in opposing the depths to which the frequent celebrations had reached (see *Godly Exercises or the Devil's Dance? Puritanism and Popular Culture in Pre-Civil War England,* Friends of Dr. Williams Lecture, 37 (1983), London: Dr. Williams Trust, pp. 14–17, 19). But see P. Burke; he notes that where Catholics modified a practice, the Protestants often abolished it (*Popular Culture in Early Modern Europe,* p. 213). As Tessa Watt explains: "Protestant reformers directed their energies within a closed godly culture centered on the church and private household, rather than more public and 'popular' forms of recreation" (*Cheap Print,* p. 70). Though John King argues: "The general impulse of the sixteenth century was toward the public reformation of the Church and State rather than private sanctification" (*English Reformation Literature,* p. 7). We have argued that the impulse from Calvin was on the inward transformation having a visible and reforming impact on the public world.

religious stage." Clergymen were, he argues, the driving force behind this drama, which was to have some influence on the later developments of theater. But this openness did not last long. By 1560 this kind of religious drama had all but died out in Puritan-influenced areas.[64] What accounts for the growing suspicion toward the theater? Clearly there were important theological reasons, which we will describe below. But there were other factors as well. Jeremy Goring argues that there were probably a variety of reasons behind the decline of religious theater.[65] Prominent among them may have been economic factors. Apparently these performances and the accompanying celebrations had become increasingly expensive, until other priorities (such as the growing charitable programs for the poor) made them appear impractical. There were also social factors at play that reflect the responsibility that communities (and not simply churches) were taking for the life of their citizenry. Beyond the moral problems associated with many plays and the accompanying festivities (which apparently were considerable), these events often caused civic unrest that the authorities were anxious to control. As in the case of Geneva, religious factors were not working in isolation.

It is true, however, that later in the sixteenth century Elizabethan Divines began to apply a stricter interpretation of the Sabbath and widened the interpretation of the seventh commandment. So that anything that encouraged libidinous feelings or even kept one from church was likely to be forbidden.[66] But plays may have come under closer scrutiny than other cultural forms, precisely because they appealed so unashamedly to the eye. Watching drama one may be moved more deeply than the reformers of that day wanted to allow. As Shakespeare knew, the play is the thing to catch

[64] *English Reformation Literature*, pp. 272, 275; quote p. 273. These were in turn adapted to the Elizabethan stage. Even a certain sexual frankness was allowed by these early divines (p. 281). Collinson describes their decline in *Birthpangs of Protestant England*, p. 54.

[65] *Godly Exercises*, pp. 7–8. Peter Burke suggests, by this time, the role of religious drama was declining, and rising literacy also may have made it less important. The history of the religious image, he notes, "followed similar lines" (*Popular Culture in Early Modern Europe*, p. 228). The growing consensus is that the Protestant reformers could not have had the impact they did if they were not promoting values that were widely shared in their communities. They were not simply exercising a form of social control. The famous church courts that were established to raise morals in the community, Martin Ingram has concluded, enforced values which were "broadly consensual" and in line with the wide spectrum of unspectacular orthodoxy that was widely shared (*Church Courts, Sex and Marriage in England, 1570–1640* [Cambridge University Press, 1987], pp. 94, 124; discussed in Watt, *Cheap Print*, p. 325).

[66] Goring, *Godly Exercises*, pp. 10, 13. He notes that there was not a unanimity in this regard. Some ministers, as time went on, supported games at "seemly times" to support good fellowship (pp. 15, 16).

the conscience not only of the king but all who watch. We have seen how suspicious of the "eye" the major reformers were, and therefore plays were more easily captured by idolatrous functions – and this may have to do with the religious roots of the drama. As Michael O'Connell notes: "Theatre is not worship, but as a cultural institution, its roots lay deep in the centuries in which it performed a religious function."[67] As in other areas of culture then, the reformers were not satisfied until this ancient connection between drama and religion was completely severed.

Brian Crockett even suggests that the suppression of religious drama may have had something to do with the flowering of secular theater in Elizabethan England. When Protestant ministers forbade all religious or sacred drama, playwrights were pushed to secularize their writing, even if they did not leave their religious convictions behind altogether. In the development of the forms of drama during this time, Crockett believes, many were applying to secular themes some of the "root paradigms" that they had learned in their catechism instruction. The exploitation of paradox, of incarnation, of sin and grace, Crockett suggests, all might have been behind many of the dramatic techniques that powered this golden age of theater.[68] The subjects had to be secular of course, to avoid any charge of blasphemy. But this may have forced playwrights – most of them surely believers themselves – to shape their work into a kind of secular liturgy. G. K. Hunter has described the theological elements that are "hidden" in Shakespeare's plays – grace, repentance, mercy, forgiveness, all elements which require a theological gloss. He concludes his study noting that "the government's requirement that the writer avoid doctrinal matters (in a vocabulary still loaded with doctrinal echoes) looks like an extraordinary boon, and may be one part of the means by which Shakespeare was able to move into the 'modern' world of psychological creativity."[69] Circumstances may have forced Elizabethan playwrights, like the Huguenot architects, to become masters of indirect communication.

[67] "The Idolatrous Eye," *English Literary History* 52 (1985), p. 307. His conclusion could equally apply to the developing visual culture: "Its . . . status was ambiguous . . . not religious in the same sense it had been, and yet . . . not secular either" (p. 307).
[68] " 'Holy Cozenage' and the Renaissance Cult of the Ear," *Sixteenth Century Journal* 24/1 (1993), pp. 47–65, especially pp. 61–3. See Collinson: "Unwittingly, the about face in Protestant cultural attitudes emancipated the English theater by completing its secularization" (*Birthpangs of Protestant England*, p. 114).
[69] G. K. Hunter, "Shakespeare and the Church," in John M. Mucciolo (ed.), *Shakespeare's Universe: Renaissance Ideas and Conventions: Essays in Honor of W. R. Elton* (Aldershot, England: Scolar Press, 1996), p. 27.

A SCRIPTURE CULTURE

But all of this speaks largely to the negative (or indirect) influence of Reformers in England. What can be said of the positive cultural influences
of their theological convictions? In light of the concern of the reformers
with the larger issues of society, it is clear that they based their evaluations
and their strategies squarely on the teachings of the bible. In fact one can
characterize their culture, as it would form itself, as through and through a
Scripture culture. But it is important that the constructive impact of Scripture, and not only its restrictions, be borne in mind. As Patrick Collinson
remarks, the bible was for the Puritans not a straitjacket, but a "rich and
infinitely varied source of imagination and formal inspiration."[70] We have
seen already that it stimulated the imagery that was allowed, and it may
have been a stimulus for architectural design, even drama. But the source
of this influence was not, in the first instance, the application of biblical
truth to cultural practices, but the reading, hearing, singing, even memorizing of Scripture, all of which formed the center and focus of Protestant
worship life. This focus, as it worked its way into people's consciousness,
soon developed its own set of cultural practices.

The most public (and dramatic) contact with Scripture for most people
would have been the regular preaching of the word in worship. Peter Burke
notes that "Protestant culture was a sermon culture. Sermons might last
for hours and they might be a great emotional experience involving audience participation, with members of the congregation exclaiming, sighing
or weeping."[71] As the century wore on, the performance of the sermon
took on more and more importance until it became for many people their
primary cultural experience. Since the ear was more to be trusted than
the eye, late sixteenth-century preachers could pull out all the stops and
use any dramatic technique available to catch the attention of the congregation. Brian Crockett argues that, despite frequent complaints against
plays and showy sermonizing, the sermon became an important dramatic
event for most worshipers. "It is clear that the rhetorical ties between the
performative modes of the sermon and the stage play are strong."[72] The
modern attention given to the Elizabethan theater may serve to obscure

---

[70] *Birthpangs of Protestant England,* p. 95.
[71] *Popular Culture in Early Modern Europe,* p. 226. Christopher Hill says: "In the absence of other media
of communication, sermons were for the majority of Englishmen their main source of political
information and political ideas" (*Society and Puritanism,* p. 32).
[72] Crockett, "Holy Cozenage," p. 64.

the contemporary significance of preaching as a cultural event. Paul Seaver points out that "even in sophisticated London the popular preachers attracted larger audiences week after week than Shakespeare or Jonson did in their prime."[73]

Scripture reading, preaching and memorization not only occupied the Sabbath times of believers' lives but created a unique form of popular culture.[74] This culture centered of course on the preaching of Scriptural sermons, which in many ways became dramatic performances. So important was this that people would travel long distances in the company of "friends in the Lord" to hear an unusually good preacher. On the way they would share and receive hospitality. And along the way they would sing the Psalms, which they had grown to love at the services. As the dignified and majestic singing of Psalms became their hallmark, Calvinists were often called "Psalm singers." They sang everywhere, at home, at work, in prison, even on the way to their death. Even their enemies called their haunting tunes melodious and delectable, and many were attracted to their services because of it.[75]

In many ways the center of this popular culture was to be found in the special fasts which the Puritans held. These were not the regular fasts of the Church calendar (nor were they sanctioned by the Bishop) but specially organized fasts for some particular purpose. They often amounted to a kind of religious rally, where special preachers would be invited and offerings received for special causes, leading to a general time of religious awakening – sometimes including ecstatic experiences and exorcisms. Often people would travel great distances to these fasts, in a kind of Protestant version of the pilgrimage. Indeed Patrick Collinson points out that in many respects these were a kind of Protestant version of the old, now forbidden, festival days.[76]

---

[73] Paul Seaver, *The Puritan Lectureship: The Politics of Religious Dissent* (Palo Alto, Calif.: Stanford University Press, 1970), p. 5.

[74] See the description in Patrick Collinson, "Elizabethan and Jacobean Puritanism as Forms of Popular Culture," in Durston and Eales (eds.), *Culture of English Puritanism,* pp. 32–46.

[75] W. Stanford Reid. "The Battle Hymns of the Lord: Calvinist Psalmody of the Sixteenth Century," in *Sixteenth Century Essays and Studies* 2 (1971), pp. 44, 53. The first Reformed Psalter was published in 1539, but the complete Psalms were published in 1562 in French – also in an English translation in the same year (pp. 38–41). Though others were not so kind, the ecclesiastical authorities in Paris said such singing was "to the great scandal of the Christian religion" (p. 45). Even Queen Elizabeth scoffed at them as "Genevan jigs" (p. 52).

[76] "Elizabethan and Jacobean Puritanism," pp. 50–56. Leigh Schmidt traces the rise of such Holy Fairs in Scotland and the changed form they took in their transfer to America, even the role they played in the eventual rise of the revivals. See *Holy Fairs: Scottish Communions and American Revivals in the Early Modern Period* (Princeton University Press, 1989).

A NEW IMAGINATIVE STRUCTURE

In terms of cultural production Protestants did not so much deny culture, as is sometimes argued, as transfer their cultural energies into new forms. Traditional recreations were out, though there remained a residue of these – they did allow horse-racing, foot races, bonfires, gala dinners and, above all, sermons. Traditional forms of graphic art and painting, by late century, were not encouraged, but in general, as Tessa Watt shows, they "transferred their efforts to other forms of print, to be used in very different contexts."[77] Prayer books, psalters, books of sermons, handbooks of devotion, religious treatises of various kinds proliferated. These are not without their own literary value, nor without influence on the development of literature, as we have hinted. But clearly the growth of these forms accompanied a decline of more traditional media. By this time all religious drama was banished. Already in the 1560s all pictures were being eliminated in "almanacs" published in Geneva and Lyon, and by 1580 all images were banned from books published in Geneva. After this time, in areas influenced by Calvinism, bibles and other books were no longer illustrated (and those that were continued to use prints previously produced). What was happening around 1580 to cause this retreat from traditional imagery?

Patrick Collinson has argued that this date marks the beginning of a period that he calls, after Karl-Josef Höltigen, iconophobic. This momentous change he describes as a change from the visual to "the invisible, abstract and didactic word." He accounts for this by noting: "We are making a journey from a culture of orality and image to one of print culture: from one mental and imaginative set to another."[78] Tessa Watt, while acknowledging that a tightening takes place in mid-Elizabethan Protestant culture, thinks the thesis of Collinson (and Ong) is misleading. She argues that "Collinson has exaggerated the 'visual anorexia' of English culture in this period, and overstated the extent to which people were cut off from traditional Christian imagery."[79] For one thing Collinson and Ong also overlook the way that the visual and the oral are interrelated in culture. We have argued that while reformers tried cutting the ancient link between worship and the visual (and even the dramatic), this did not keep the people from responding

---

[77] *Cheap Print,* p. 69. Cf. Collinson, "Elizabethan and Jacobean Puritanism," p. 44.

[78] *Birthpangs of Protestant England,* p. 99. Collinson's thesis is similar to that of Walter Ong; see *Orality and Literacy,* esp. ch. 4, where Ong argues that writing and printing restructures and interiorizes consciousness.

[79] *Cheap Print,* p. 136. Her argument is that visual communication continued to play a role in mainstream Protestant culture, even if the forms and meanings were different.

to visual and dramatic elements in the worship. Moreover, in the prints, wall hangings, even in the published books a – sometimes rich – visual culture survived amidst the strictures of the reformers' teaching.

Nevertheless visual media in general seemed to be declining as the century came to an end. What lies behind the changes that occurred toward the end of the century? Perhaps, up to this point, the question that the reformers had faced from the beginning had not been finally answered: After giving up the complex iconography of the Middle Ages, how is one to embody and communicate the truth to the faithful? How is one to think about or picture the world? Preaching the Word was central of course, but what visible shape will this take? Calvin provided an important part of the answer to that in proposing the shape of the creed, as embodied in the *Institutes*, as a kind of "icon" by which the truth of God and the world may be accessed. We have suggested that certain architects and dramatists may have, perhaps unconsciously, developed the implications of this new understanding of God's "invisible" presence in creation and human affairs. But beyond these isolated (and unsystematic) instances, all attempts at using imagery, drama, even cultural festivities, in the service of the communication of Christian truth appeared to be given up by around 1580.

We might think of the change in terms of two influences that came together during this time: the cumulative impact of the iconoclastic polemics and the initiation of a new way of ordering and thinking about the world. On the one hand the continuing polemic against what the reformers saw as decadent forms of popular culture finally bore fruit in closing down any possible creativity in these areas. Only the purely Christian subcultural practices that we have described were now to be encouraged. On the other hand a new way of "imagining" the world was emerging that would take the place of previous ways of thinking about truth and, eventually, about culture. The reformation of cultural practices felt to be harmful was leaving a cultural void that needed to be filled, and new ways of thinking were shaping new cultural practices that became available to fill this void. These developments would gradually begin to influence the larger culture in respect to the visible shape that Christian truth should now take. Let us see what evidence there might be for this hypothesis.

First it is clear that polemics against a decadent culture were not new: they appear in Calvin, and, in England, in William Tyndale, among others.[80] But around 1580 such attacks seemed to proliferate. In 1581, for example,

---

[80] See Tyndale's famous exchange with Sir Thomas More: *The Dialogue concerning Tyndale*, facsimile from the collected edition of *Thomas More's English Works* (1557), ed. W. E. Campbell (London: Eyre & Spottiswoode, 1927).

Thomas Lovell published *A Dialogue Between Custom and Veritie concerning the use and abuse of Dauncing and Minstrelry*.[81] In the Epistle to the Reader, Lovell notes that the benefits which God bestowed upon us are so great that our weak wits are not able to comprehend them. For this reason our best and wisest course is to follow the law (in Scripture) which is given to us "pure and whole" and not at any time seek to "please ourselves." He goes on to elaborate this point: pleasing ourselves means to speak our own words and go after our own imagination, and seek our own will. This "going our own way," focusing especially on "imagination" used in an entirely negative sense, which might be said to accompany a certain kind of cultural production, is contrasted simply with the encouragement that we "do good." He concludes: "For when we do more practice our vain pleasures, then do we more after our own wicked imagination." He focuses in particular on the Sabbath, he notes, because it is a "figure" of our endless life with God which he grants us in his mercy. By contrast to common practices of popular culture, the Sabbath is decidedly not consecrated to the abominable idol of fleshly pleasure.

In the following dialogue between "custom" and "veritie," Lovell proceeds (in rhymed verse!) to describe the contrast between these two approaches to culture. Dancing comes in for particular attack. David danced before the Lord, but, alas, "in these days in this dance few delight." Dancing should be avoided because it arouses passion, and, besides, there are better ways of finding a wife. Even if the rare person can partake of such activities safely, many others would fall. He concludes: not against right use, but the abuse

> Of things has been my fight.
> God grant his spirit may quicken us
> Good fruit our trees may bring.
> We may not fall in firey lake
> Where doth no mercy spring.

As is typical of Puritan polemics, Lovell insists the activity itself is not wrong. But no guidance or encouragement is made as to what shape such "right use" might take. Indeed any mental activity which might be used to think about this in a wholesome way is forbidden as vain imagination. Whatever young readers might have thought about such a treatise (the "poetic" form Lovell uses surely is meant to attract wide attention to what

---

[81] London: John Allde, 1581, not paginated. In this and the following reference I have modernized the English.

he has to say), they would find there no help in "transforming" such cultural practices.[82]

Two years later Phillip Stubbes published his work: *The Anatomie of Abuses, a briefe summarie of notable vices and Imperfections, as now raigne in many Christian Countries of the World.*[83] Stubbes in the address to the reader considers plays, dancing, gaming and "such like." Not as though he is opposed to "any kind of exercise in general," he pleads, "but only their abuses." When these are cut away, Stubbes argues, these practices are "not only of great ancestries, but also very honest and commendable exercises" (pp. 1, 2). A dialogue follows between Spudeus and Philoponus. The latter has just returned from a long journey abroad to an imaginary land, which is clearly meant to describe the "wordly" life of many of his contemporaries, and which he proceeds to describe: it is a blessed land, with a wicked people. But why can't we just let them be, Spudeus asks? We cannot, Philoponus responds, for their sufferings are our sufferings, and we are called to weep with those who weep. Of the abuses that are listed, pride heads the list, as the beginning of all evil of heart, mouth and apparel (p. 10). The latter, he argues, offends God worse than other things. Going even beyond Calvin he argues that decency is enough in respect to our dress, we must reject "novell inventions and new fangled fasions" (p. 14). He goes on for pages about make-up, ruffles, shoes, socks, earrings, coats, even perfume. Anything which serves to paint our living sepulchre is clearly meant to "delight the eyes of unchaste beholders whereby God is dishonored" (p. 24). All inventors of such things are clearly guilty of the evil which follows (p. 83) – an indictment that surely must have discouraged any creativity among tailors and jewelers!

All forms of sexual impurity and gluttony are attacked. As to the latter food is given to sustain us. We are "not to delight and wallow therein continually" (p. 113). As in Lovell, this way of life should be replaced by one in which we do good to our neighbor. In contrast to practices that appeal to our lust and vanity, he argues forcefully, we should give liberally to the poor (p. 115). Then he proceeds to attack especially those things which increase the burden of the poor: drunkenness, enclosure of the commons, usury (which he likens to murder) and the abuse of the Sabbath.

Turning to stage plays he has particularly strong words for the divines who had (previously) written what he calls sacriligious plays. Profane plays

---

[82] Though it may not have been Lovell's intent, soon after his attack even godly popular songs dropped out of fashion (Collinson, *Birthpangs of Protestant England,* p. 110).

[83] London: Richard Jones, 1583; pagination added in the copy in the Huntington Library, which is noted in the text.

only nourish vice and feature mostly vagrants and beggars. Of maypole activities he claims, on good authority he says, that of a hundred women who go, only a third return undefiled. Though there could be a dancing for joy before the Lord (p. 189), dancing, in general, is an introduction to whoredom (p. 196). Even music which is a good gift of God has been abused by minstrelry. Bearbaiting is forbidden as the abuse of one of God's creatures, as are cockfighting and hunting (p. 210). God is abused when these creatures are! All of this suggests, Stubbes concludes in a typically millennial vein, that the latter days of which Scripture speak are at hand.

What is striking to the modern reader is the mixture of relatively radical social views, concerning care for the poor (and the social and economic adjustments that are needed) and the treatment of animals, along with what appears to be a reactionary refusal to allow any rethinking or reworking of the contemporary popular culture. The worry is clearly not about the absence of creativity in the cultural sphere! It is a more deep-seated anxiety about society itself. Cultural energies were being refocused toward these more pressing needs, and any art that might survive would of necessity be subordinated to this larger social and cultural project.

But paralleling, and in many ways shaping, this cultural critique is the de-velopment of what is nothing less than an alternative religious imagination that would have repercussions on every area of culture. This is the project of giving the world a new mental shape, after the "icon" of the *Institutes*. This fresh way of "imaging" truth, we argue, diminished the prospects in some cultural areas, but may have enhanced them in others.[84] We noted earlier that it was around 1580 that the structuring of the *Institutes* took its final shape, always accompanied by "epitomes" which "summed up" the argument of the work. The 1585 edition includes a long complex structure of the argument in the preface of the work, that was to become definitive into the seventeenth century. At about this same time other epitomes of Calvin's works began to appear, some with elaborate charts. All of this was clearly the result of the influence of the "logic" introduced by Peter Ramus, a French Huguenot who died in the St. Bartholomew's massacre in 1572.[85]

---

[84] Watt points out that the "religious reaction against certain aspects of 'pop culture' coincided with a changing 'renaissance' aesthetic, and the two movements were inextricably intertwined" (*Cheap Print*, p. 54).

[85] See Muller, "In the Light of Orthodoxy," p. 1204. He calls the 1585 edition and its structuring the "culmination of the sixteenth century process of creating an apparatus." He describes other epitomes and their charts on p. 1219, and see p. 1221. On Ramus's life and work, see Walter J. Ong, *Peter Ramus, Method, and the Decay of Dialogue: From the Art of Discourse to the Art of Reason* (Cambridge, Mass.: Harvard University Press, 1958); R. Hooykaas, *Humanisme, science et réforme: Pierre de la*

Ramus was an extremely popular and influential professor of rhetoric and logic in Paris. His first published works in 1543 attacked Aristotle's logic and the whole university curriculum as confused and disorganized. As might be expected the university authorities were not pleased and he was forbidden from teaching publicly. In 1545 he quietly began teaching in the Collège de Presles where he sought to develop a more effective method of teaching. Eventually Ramus gained the favor of King Henry II who lifted the ban against him (in 1547) and appointed him Professor of Eloquence (in 1551) to the college that was to become the Collège de France. He converted formally to Protestantism in 1562.

Always the educational reformer, Ramus believed the logic that he developed was the key to all right knowledge and that it was the natural extension of Calvin's understanding of the world as ordered by God. There were 1100 separate printings of ramist works between 1550 and 1650; his *Dialectic* (1555) alone went through more than 100 editions during that period.[86]

Like the major reformers before him Ramus was deeply concerned to discover a way of escaping the scholastic subtleties and teaching the truth clearly, especially to young people. Always lecturing to large classes, he sought to make his teaching immediately practical and to be as closely related as possible to the natural sense of things. In many respects his most important work was as an educational reformer, especially in his influence on Jacob Sturm and Philip Melancthon. Education, he believed, should henceforth be freed from the need to learn a list of abstract concepts by heart. The goal of teaching must be changed to include the practical application of things. "The practical," he would say, "is both the source and the end."[87] He insisted that following this "natural method" was what makes great artists and architects. They become masters, not by learning the rules, but by following usage, and making masterpieces.[88]

Ramus's thinking was heavily influenced by an earlier humanist, Rudolph Agricola (b. 1544). Agricola's first teacher may have been Thomas à Kempis, and he was strongly committed to educational practice of these Brothers of the Common Life. Nourished by the new "typographical culture," Agricola sought to accommodate teaching to real life. He felt reality could best be

Ramée, 1515–1572 (Leyden: E. J. Brill, 1958). For the general background of Renaissance logic, see Neal W. Gilbert, *Renaissance Concepts of Method* (New York: Columbia University Press, 1960).

[86] Hooykaas believes it was one of the three or four most influential works in the sixteenth century (*Humanisme, science et réforme: Pierre de la Ramée* [Leyden: E. J. Brill 1958], p. 3.; and Ong, *Ramus, Method and the Decay of Dialogue*, p. 5).

[87] Quoted in Hooykaas, *Humanisme*, p. 30.   [88] Ibid., p. 31.

explained by analogy to "mechanical constructs" for which he developed the notion of "topics" (topoi or loci) which would replace medieval categories as the means for organizing human knowledge. From Agricola, Ramus derived the goal of dialectic, which he separated from rhetoric, as teaching pure and simple. And like Agricola he sought to replace older "categories" which he considered abstract, with more concrete "places." Places ("topoi") are those key notions or headings to which one looks to find out what is available in one's store of knowledge.[89] What are called "loci communis," as we noted in connection with Calvin's *Institutes*, are the "common places" according to which one can organize one's knowledge in an orderly way. The fact they are called "places" is significant – the visual element is quite intentional. Placing things in their proper order in relation to one another was felt to make knowledge more stable, and more easily grasped and remembered. This was because in Ramus's mind the places into which things were being placed were more "natural." His central idea, according to Hooykaas, resonates with Calvin's teaching: "The truth reveals itself in 'natural reasoning' in the human intelligence, and, at the same time, in the natural order of things in the universe."[90] But this will only happen as the method is used in one's actual living. For logic is to truth, as art is to life. As Ramus says in his *Dialectic*: "It is the business of 'use' to draw out into a 'work' these 'precepts' in a way which will 'shape and express' in examples the force contained within the precepts."[91]

His logic is, following Agricola, a discrimination by dichotomies (Figure 12). The basic parts are first "invention" that is a discovery of the questions, arguments and places into which reality is ordered; and second "judgment" which is "the doctrine of collocating (or assembling) what invention has found, and of judging by this collocation concerning the matter under consideration."[92] Exactly what this process consists in was never made clear to his contemporaries, and has remained unclear. But what is clear is Ramus's attempt to revise the way the mind grasps and orders the world. As Ong notes, the power of adaptation of Ramus's work shows that it is best described as a "state of mind arising within a complex of established intellectual and cultural traditions and exhibiting them in new aspects."[93]

[89] Ong, *Ramus, Method and the Decay of Dialogue,* pp. 103–9. Ong's discussion of Agricola is on pp. 96–104. Agricola's *Dialectical Invention* (1479) became especially influential in Paris after 1535.
[90] *Humanisme,* p. 51. If one follows one's nature, Ramus is implying, there will be a precise correspondence between our conceptions of things and the things themselves (p. 58).
[91] Ong, *Ramus, Method and the Decay of Dialogue,* p. 190; quoting *Dialectic* (1542 edn), fol. 53.
[92] In Ong, ibid., p. 184; quoting *Dialectic*, fols. 19–20.
[93] *Ramus, Method and the Decay of Dialogue,* p. 7.

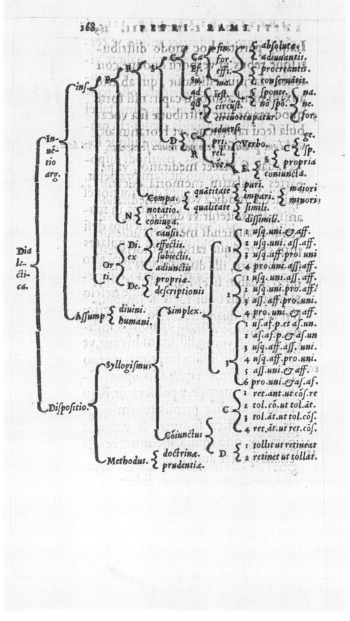

Figure 12   Peter Ramus, *The First Ramus Dichotomies*. Harvard University Houghton
Library, Cambridge, Mass., 1543.

Ramus's logic of organizing by dichotomies has not fared well at the hands of logicians and philosophers. Ong notes that while his *Dialectic* was the most influential element, it is hard to specify what this actually is, though it is not anything that a competent logician would take seriously. His best sense is that Ramus:

represented a drive toward thinking not only of the universe but of thought itself in terms of spatial models apprehended by sight. Dialogue itself will drop more than ever out of dialectic. Persons . . . will be eclipsed insofar as the world is thought of as an assemblage of the sort of things which vision apprehends – objects or surfaces.[94]

While Ramus's work has an appearance of appeal to the natural order, Ong says, it is not really suggesting the experimental method which Francis Bacon was to introduce a generation later. R. Hooykaas, on the other hand, has a decidedly more positive take on Ramus's work. While admitting that his science was still bookish, Hooykaas believes Ramus's work was an important step in the direction of the inductive method. He points out that medieval science had totally lost touch with the natural reality. And while he did not see the full implications of what he was doing, Ramus did move the understanding of logic toward an openness to the real world. Hooykaas sees Ramus as a transitional figure from a "literary empiricism" to the truly "empirical science" of modern times.[95]

But to judge his importance strictly as a logician is to miss the point of his influence. Even to challenge his originality is beside the point. For in a sense he was codifying a growing openness to the natural world and, more importantly, suggesting a mental structure that, to his mind, corresponded to that natural order. The nature of his influence is well illustrated in a little vignette that Ong recounts in his book. As a young man, Richard Mather, who would rise to prominence later in New England, for a few months read Ramus with great relish while he was at Brasenose College, Oxford. He found the experience so significant that he promptly left the university for good to pursue his ministry first in England and eventually America.[96] The incident captures nicely the practical turn of Ramus's thought, and also the immediate usefulness to which students believed it could be put.

---

[94] Ibid., p. 9. Neal Gilbert says of Ong's logic: "Originality was not one of its chief merits" (*Renaissance Concepts of Method* [New York: Columbia University Press, 1960], p. 221).

[95] *Humanisme*, pp. 58, 122–3. Hooykaas notes that Bacon was surely exposed to ramist battles at Cambridge, so would have read Ramus, though he should not be considered a Ramist (pp. 116–17).

[96] *Ramus, Method and the Decay of Dialogue*, p. 303.

Two elements of Ramus's work call for special attention, both having to do with the implications for the developing mental habits of Protestants. The first is the emphasis on following the natural order of things as a way of reaching their true essence. Those who studied and followed Ramus had a sense of being liberated from the accretions of medieval logic and pedagogy. While traditional scholars read and reread texts in order to write their commentaries, Ramus said that one must learn what is actually practical. In light of the definitions, partitions, digressions and axioms by which medieval reasoning proceeded, it is not hard to imagine that Ramus's ordered structure seemed to be a breath of fresh air. Like the spiritual liberation Reformation believers experienced from the confusing mediations of medieval saints, their teachers must have felt a similar intellectual release by following Ramus's model of approaching material directly and ordering it clearly.

A particular aesthetic style of course followed necessarily from this direct method. Ramus, writing in 1569, had this to say about the work of poets:

This is what the poet does as a major part of his tactics, when he sets out to sway the people, the many-headed monster. He deceives in all sorts of ways. He starts at the middle, often proceeding thence to the beginning, and getting on to the end by some equivocal and unexpected dodge.[97]

As a result those poets who would "delight and move" will not, except indirectly, be able to teach. And clear teaching of course is a driving motive of Ramus's (and other reformers') thinking. Such thinking did not discourage poetry altogether, but it surely discouraged a certain kind of poetry. Indeed subsequent Protestant poets would boast of their liberation from elaborate metaphoric strictures. See for example the following poem of George Herbert (1593–1633), Jordan I:

> Who says that fictions onely and false hair
> Become a verse? Is there in truth no beautie?
> Is all good structure in a winding stair?
> May no lines pass, except they do their dutie
>   Not to a true, but painted chair?
>
> Is it no verse, except enchanted groves
> And sudden arbours shadow coarse-spunne lines?
> Must purling streams refresh a lover's loves?
> Must all be vail'd, while he that reades, divines,
>   Catching the sense at two removes?

---

[97] Quoted in ibid., p. 253.

> Shepherds are honest people; let them sing;
> Riddle who list, for me, and pull for Prime:
> I enjoy no man's nightingale or spring;
> Nor let them punish with losse of rime,
>   Who plainly say, "*My God, my King.*"[98]

Is there in truth no beauty? This could be a summary of the developing Puritan aesthetic. There is beauty, the Puritan who read Calvin and now Ramus would say, only in truth. Because this best suits the order of things which God has made.

But the second element which derives from Ramus is equally important. There is not only a practical and natural directness to Ramus's *Dialectic*, but also a handy way that this can be put down in a visual form. The truth can be readily "outlined" – to give it its modern term – so that one can tell at a glance the structure of the material under consideration.[99] While this may seem strange to us living on the near side of the scientific revolution, Ramus and those who followed him, when they put objects or concepts down in this clear and ordered way, felt that they were getting closer to the things as they actually are.

Ramus himself uses a metaphor that helps us understand something of the euphoria he felt over this new approach to truth and reality. All the rules and principles are there, we can learn them but they may still do us no good. Imagine then that you put all of them on small slips of paper and placed these in a giant urn and mix them thoroughly. Now what dialectic can help one order these all properly? The method is simple. Place them all around and discover the universal and general first, then the secondary and special afterward. So pick from the urn what is most general of all, then that which is a part (or parts) of that, and so on until all has been laid out.[100]

Ramus's influence in England was large, especially among the Puritans. Partly this is due to the way his practical orientation connected with ideas that preexisted him there.[101] But as his works became more widely known it is possible to note specific ways his thinking made its impact. Professors at Cambridge were already reading him during the 1560s,

---

[98] *The Works of George Herbert,* ed. F. E. Hutchinson (Oxford: Clarendon Press, 1941), pp. 56–7.

[99] Ong's attributing this to the change in technology, specifically the printing press, is at best partially true. If anything, this would apply more accurately to Agricola, who developed the original idea of ordering through dichotomies just as the printing press was coming into use (see *Orality and Literacy*).

[100] In Ong, *Ramus, Method and the Decay of Dialogue,* pp. 245–6.

[101] See Hooykaas, *Humanisme,* p. 115.

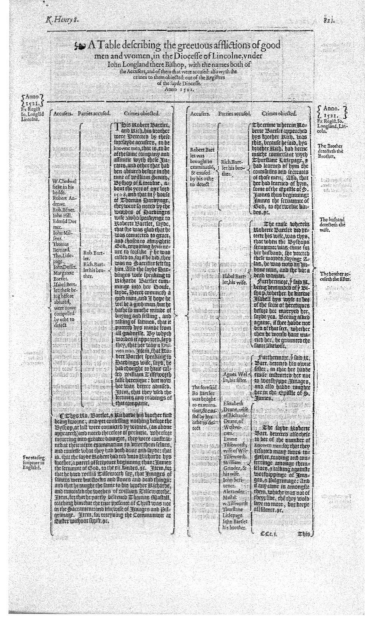

Figure 13   Anonymous, diagram, in John Foxe, *Actes and Monuments*, 1583 edn. p. 821.
Huntington Library Museum, San Marino, Calif., 1583.

but the first English translation appeared in 1581 as *The Logik of the Most Excellent Philosopher P. Ramus Martyr.*[102] Here Ramus's work is condensed into one hundred pages, for a generation of eager readers. Something of the sense of entering a new world is captured in the address to the reader. There the various aspects of Ramus's work are correlated with justice (leaving aside rhetoric including only what is unique to logic), verity (use only the rules and precepts which are necessarily true), and wisdom (treat general matters generally and particulars particularly without mixture).[103] Then follows book one, "invention" – or settling the argument, and book two, "judgment" – arguments so ordered that we can judge rightly.

And last he shall knit and join together with apt transitions the end of every declaration with the beginning of the next. And so having defined, divided, and knit together the parts of the etymology, he shall make everything more manifest and plain, with most fit and special examples. All poets, orators, and historiographers follow such good order so that things be plainly set forth.

Any violation of this through insertion of digressions and irrelevancies "is preposterous and out of all good fashion and order."[104]

The influence of ramist thinking was soon visible in the lay out of published works in England. The 1983 edition of Foxe's *Book of Martyrs*, now expanded to two large volumes, while continuing to reprint the images from the earlier work, now has a number of ramist diagrams added at significant points to "sum up" the argument (Figure 13).[105]

As early as 1586, in bibles printed in England, ramist diagrams begin to replace pictures. The diagram in Figure 14, which faces the first chapter of Genesis of a bible printed in 1583, lays out the structure of Scripture – the running commentaries of Gilby now have been reduced to this 'epitome' of the teaching of Scripture. This same diagram appears in the 1603 edition of the popular Geneva Bible which was commonly used even after the introduction of the King James Version a few years later. Tessa Watt comments of this period: "All of the author's or publisher's visual creativity has gone into arranging the brackets and exploiting the possibilities of . . . different fonts, which organization is somehow meant to render Scriptural precepts more accessible."[106]

---

[102] Translated by M. Roll and M. Hamlini (London: Thomas Vantrolier, 1581).
[103] *The Logik of the Most Excellent Philosopher,* pp. 7–12.   [104] Ibid., pp. 96, 101.
[105] The original 1563 edition had a single chart describing the nature of the sacrament, on p. 994.
[106] *Cheap Print,* p. 242. "The English were known for being particularly unsophisticated in their use of Ramism, already a rather unsophisticated method in itself."

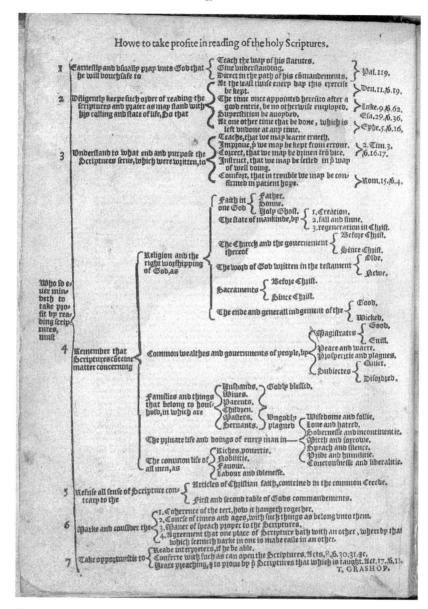

Figure 14   Anonymous, chart facing Genesis 1:1, in bible, O.T. Psalmes. Enlish, Sternhold & Hopkins. Huntington Library Museum, San Marino, Calif., 1583.

Broadsides which combined this new "visual order" with the teaching of Scripture became common. An early example is "the gloves" which are to be used to teach the young (Figure 15). Each finger, as it is ticked off, recalls one of the ten commandments. To this image is added a godly poem by William Powell (d. 1567):

> Who loveth and wolde vertues increase
> And vices seke to over throwe
> Loe heare be gloves that wyl thee teache
> All evyl in tyme to laye full lowe.

This new appropriation of reality, Frances Yates has argued, is really an appropriation of the ancient art of memory.[107] Every subject is now to be laid out and arranged in a dialectical order and then memorized in this order. It has become an epitome. But, she notes, the older idea of putting actual images in the places to be memorized has gone. In its place are divided and composed items in their order. Ironically, she notes the actual images in their medieval presentation had been employed to convey moral and religious truth. But they are banished, she claims, by an internal "iconoclasm," corresponding to, and following from the outer one.

Notice that it is no longer theological categories that shape the order of things, as in Calvin's *Institutes*, but the arbitrary dichotomies of ramist logic. Though there is perhaps a kind of openness to the natural world and to God's work there, this Presence does not – as in Calvin – shape the way we think about things. Worse, as we will see, the order risks becoming an end in itself rather than a means to other more substantial ends.

Something is clearly lost, and we are right to point it out. But at the same time is there not something that is encouraged? William Perkins writing near the end of the century suggests what this might be. In his famous work, *A Reformed Catholike: Or, a Declaration shewing how neere we may come to the present church of Rome in sundrie points of religion and wherein we must forever depart from them*,[108] Perkins writes what would have passed for ecumenical discussion in the late sixteenth century. Responding to the suggestion of some that the Protestant and Catholic churches may be reunited he suggests points in which there is agreement and others where there is none – where the difference is as between light and darkness. As one of the points in which they differ, he proceeds, in the ninth part, to address images in particular. He acknowledges the civil use (in buildings and on coins) and even the private use to which images may rightly be

---

[107] Which she argues has a long tradition behind it going back to Cicero; see *Art of Memory*, pp. 232–5.
[108] John Legat, Printer to the University of Cambridge, 1598. Page numbers in text are to this work.

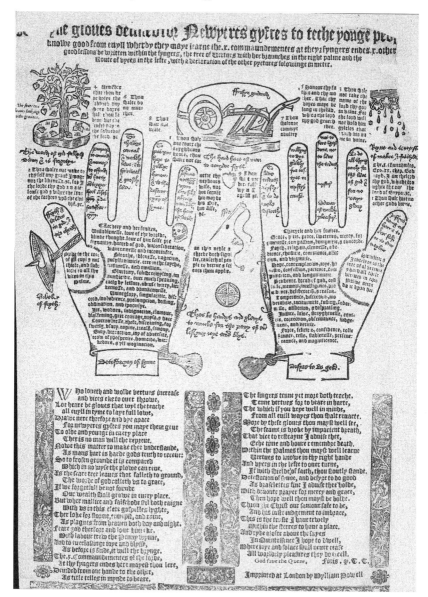

Figure 15   William Powell, *Some Gloves*. Broadside, Huntington Library Museum, San Marino, Calif., 1500s.

put. He reiterates Calvin's point: "We hold the historical use of images to be good and lawful that is, to represent to the eye the actes of histories, whether they be humane or divine: and thus we thinke the histories of the Bible may be painted in private places" (p. 172). These pictures however are mere illustrations. The true pattern of virtue, he insists, comes not by an artist but by the word of God. Here Perkins seems to go beyond Calvin. For this pattern, Perkins claims, is what provides us by a kind of mental transubstantiation with a "true and reall presence of Christ": when the word is uttered "the sound comes to the eare; and at the same instance the thing signified comes to the mind; and thus by relation the word and the thing spoken of, are both present together."[109] This is no "iconoclasm of the mind." To the contrary, the mind is actually allowed, and now absent the surrounding visual cues, given space and opportunity, to "picture" what is being said.

An important instance of this inner picturing is found in the writing of Richard Bernard, a radical though nonseparating minister at Nottinghamshire, in 1610. His devotional work is pointedly entitled: *Contemplative Pictures with wholesome Precepts*.[110] Following Ramus he contrasts "disputation" with the kind of practical religion that follows from an inward grasp of God's truth. "By troublesome disputations men get knowledge to approve the good, but by quiet meditations men grow to more conscience [*sic*] in their ways, and do increase in grace" (Epistle Dedicatory). What now will be the focus of this meditation? One is to meditate on the "pictures" that Bernard proceeds to draw (the book has no images). These inward "images" are contrasted with the external ones which the Catholic Church approves. As he describes his purpose in the preface:

Here . . . of all these are certain pictures, not popish and sensible for superstition, but mental for divine contemplation; Whereto are added wholesome precepts for direction after godly meditation, God's picture, to behold him, that is good; to admire his excellency, to fear his majesty, to praise his bounty.

The first chapter is "the Picture of God." This includes a graphic description of God based on biblical language: "His face is a flame of fire, his voice thunder, his wrath, dread and terrible horror" (p. 5). Then he describes how creation also speaks of this God, concluding: "Fear this God, believe him to be, know him rightly, behold him invisibly, conceive him without

---

[109] *Reformed Catholike*, p. 185. Perkins goes on to say that when we take it the body and blood of Christ are both present "to our mind" (p. 186).

[110] London: William Hall for William Welbie, 1610, first part. Pages in the text; Epistle Dedicatory is nonpaginated.

idolatry" (p. 12). Then there is the "Picture of the Father": "Did ever a loving father put his darling to death, to prevent from his enemy the force of his wrath? We see it not, stories record it not, nature suffers it not. Yet this father killeth his best son, to kiss his worst creature; forsaketh the Gracious, for a time, to receive the Graceless to mercy for ever" (pp. 24, 25). There follow "pictures" of the Devil, and evil ("the creature's deformity"). To the latter is appended the precept: "Love not (reader) the works of darkness, lest thy eyes cannot behold the light" (p. 84). Upon reflecting on heaven the reader is admonished: "O mortal man, do thou often meditate of [*sic*] this happiness. Let it eat up thy heart with desire to enjoy it...neglect not this felicity, the things heere are transitory vanitie" (p. 103). Finally he paints the picture of hell as darkness, or a lake burning in a hollow cave striking "terrour with lamentation" (p. 108).

One can imagine an early seventeenth-century family reading this around the dinner table. Or a believer, carrying the small book with them on a journey. This is the contemporary prayer book. Visible imagery is missing, identified as it is with superstition. But the visual dimension of faith is nevertheless present. For the inward appropriation of truth, by faith, does nothing to discourage and everything to encourage the imaging of this truth. And the figures encouraged are to be drawn in the most graphic and emotional terms possible. After forming an image of heaven one is to "let it eat up thy heart." But for these readers it is not only God's truth, but God himself which is apprehended this way. When the peasant fled home with his indulgence, he bowed down before it as before the very God. But for these Protestants there was no sense that visible images could cultivate a proper awareness of God, as Geiler had taught. Nor is there any inquiry as to why internal images are more to be trusted than external ones. Rather each believer, at the hearing of the truth and by the prompting of the Holy Spirit, is encouraged to draw the image for herself, within. And, somehow, on this assessment, God is there to be drawn and found.

David Freedberg has argued that the will to image the world figuratively cannot be suppressed – the very notion of aniconism is, he says, a myth.[111] The development of reformed influences gives ample evidence for Freedberg's thesis. While external visual mediation of spiritual reality was forbidden, indeed often physically removed, the inward imaging of God was not only acknowledged but encouraged – and that on the highest authority of God's word itself. In this sense iconoclasm and inward imaging,

[111] *The Power of Images*, p. 55. The persistent fact of suppression itself, from the time of Plato, testifies to this inevitable urge to picture.

if Freedberg is right, are two sides of the same reality. For some this inward ordering received its impulse from Calvin's *Institutes*, for others from the dichotomous structure of Ramus. We have noted some of the ways that these influences were in tension with one another, and we will see that this tension will mark the subsequent development of reformed thinking on these things. In the seventeenth century, moreover, this tension is well represented by the contrasting influences of William Ames and John Cotton, to whose work we turn in the next chapter.

At the same time we have seen that this imagining of God and his Word was in the service of a larger cultural project. This calling involved a re-ordering of life according to God's Word. According to Ignatian spirituality believers are to place themselves into the biblical story. Reformed believers face a different challenge: they seek to remake the world after the biblical patterns, to read their story as an extension of biblical narratives. This becomes clear especially in the seventeenth-century Puritans we examine next.

CHAPTER 5

William Ames, John Cotton and seventeenth-century puritanism

Lady Margaret Hoby's diary provides one of the best available depictions of Puritan women of landowning families in England at the turn of the seventeenth century. Her day was laid out in a pattern that encompassed both ordinary and devotional activities. The following excerpt, written around 1600, gives a sense of the flow of her day:

Alter private praier I read of the bible and wrought tell dinner time, before which I praied: and, after dinner, I continued my ordinarie course of working, reading, and disposing of business in the house, tell after 5: at which time I praied, read a sermon, and examened myself.

Or consider this entry from sometime in 1601:

After private praier I was busie about the house, and dressed my servants foot and another poore mans hands, and talked with others that came to aske my counsill: after, I went into the garden, and gave some hearbes unto a good wiffe of Erley for his garden: after, I came to diner, praied, and went to diner: after, I talked a while with Mr. Rhodes and his brother, and, after that, went to worke, and heard Mr. Rhodes read of Mr Perkins new book: and, after, went to walke, and about the house, and then went into my clositt, and then examened myselfe and praied.[1]

Life was a serious proposition during this time – it was a period of economic depression in England. Externally Lady Margaret carefully planned her life to balance time for devotions with oversight of the house and gardens and care for those in need. Recreations were few, apart from bowling, boating and playing the alpharion; much of the day was spent in useful occupations – especially in serious reading. Internally life was articulated by devotional times, prayer and "self-examination."[2] But these spheres were

---

[1] *Diary of Lady Margaret Hoby: 1599–1605,* ed. Dorothy M. Meads (London: George Routledge & Sons, 1930), p. 67, section from 1601, pp. 169–70. Mr. Rhodes served as a live-in chaplain to the family. Some spelling modernized.

[2] Speaking from her modern point of view, Dorothy Meads notes that, though there was introspection, there was little real self-knowledge (*Dairy of Lady Margaret Hoby,* p. 47).

held together by a widely shared understanding of the way God's word structured both one's outer and inner life. This was all nurtured by the reading Lady Margaret did, both in Scripture and theology.

Two elements of Lady Margaret's life are typical of the emerging Puritan ethos. First the fact that her "worship" now was centered in the domestic life of the house was of great importance. From the time of Calvin the family played an increasingly important role as a center of religious devotion. While worship did occur in regular services, its performance was extended to the home and family. Moreover this performance structured the domestic sphere – its practice punctuated the day and, these believers would argue, shed light on the activities of the household. Second, notice that this devotion featured prominently the practice of reading, or hearing texts read by others. In Lady Margaret's day reading – especially of Scripture but also sermons – had become not only a central devotional practice, but a kind of metaphor for the whole of life. Though, according to Calvin, God had inscribed the divine nature on creation in a clear language, since human eyes are blurred by sin, one cannot read this off unassisted. The solution of course was to understand creation in terms of Scripture, which is, in Calvin's words, like a pair of eyeglasses (*Institutes*, I, vi, I). With these glasses the believer can read the signs of God's presence which are scattered throughout creation. This means, as Thomas Luxon points out, "looking at *things* is presented under the metaphor of reading and interpreting *words*."[3] Reading these living words stands in contrast to previous practices of seeing things as images of religious meaning. The one sheds meaning, the other, these Puritans believed, obstructs it. Nor does the trope of reading diminish the emotional impact of what is read and understood. If anything this impact is increased. "Words, we see, are to be preferred to images," Luxon argues, "but faith in the word plants a new image on the heart, a lively image that speaks far more clearly than mere words, notionally understood."

The book which Lady Margaret heard read was surely William Perkins's *A Warning against the Idolatrie of the Last Times: And an instruction touching Religion and Divine Worship*,[4] which was published that year. There the famous teacher and preacher in Cambridge continued his efforts to "stirr up loathing against Popish religion," and inform the ignorant of the nature of true worship. This instruction focused much of its attention on the role of images – which are equated with "idols"(p. 2). But in this work Perkins

---

[3] Thomas H. Luxon, "Calvin and Bunyan on Word and Image: Is there a Text in Interpreter's House?" *English Literary Renaissance* 18 (1988), p. 441; his emphasis. Subsequent quote from p. 451.

[4] Cambridge: John Legatt, at the University of Cambridge, 1601. Page numbers in the text are to this work.

expands the danger of such images to the inner world. If one is encouraged to shape inward images, one must recognize the possibility of misusing this faculty. An idol, Perkins argues, is properly "any such image as is erected to represent either [a] false or true God" (p. 2). These may appear in any of three forms. First, Perkins says, to conceive of God in any way other than he has revealed himself to us – such as making him all mercy and no justice – is to erect an idol in our heart, or as he puts it, an "idol of the braine" (p. 4). Thus any intellectual misconception of God or Christ is a form of idolatry. Secondly, idolatry involves any attempt to worship God by other means than those which he has revealed to us in Scripture (p. 11). In what would become a common stricture, he notes that one could in fact make a visible image of Christ, since he was after all a real man. But this image necessarily is only of his manhood – his divinity could not be captured in this way – and would have no use in religion (p. 15). But thirdly idolatry exists when anything which is God's property is given to another – such as bowing before the sacrament, making vows or burning incense to the saints and so on (pp. 31, 45, 51). And of course, Perkins concludes, the "masse is an abridgement and compendium of all superstition and idolatrie" (p. 79).

Then Perkins turns to a description of the true worship that is to replace this popish confusion of imagery. This is laid out in Scripture's pattern of virtue and the resulting frame that is to shape the Christian life. Following Calvin, he argues this is founded on the knowledge of God and of ourselves (p. 106). This proper service of God for Perkins characteristically returns the emphasis of human reflection on life – "imagining" – to life in the world. For this knowledge of God and ourselves, Perkins insists, is known "experimentally": for the faith and confidence in Christ "are but fictions of the braine, so long as they are severed from amendment of heart and life" (p. 115).

Here Perkins displays a fundamental struggle that will both trouble and stimulate the Puritan imagination. We observed in the last chapter that in the *Reformed Catholike* (1598) Perkins actually directed the mind to "picture" what the word says. For when the word comes to the ear "the thing signified comes to the mind; and thus by relation the word and the thing spoken of, are both present together." When we take the body and blood of Christ both are present "to our mind."[5] For as he said in that earlier work, "it is not meet that a Christian should be occupied by the eyes, but the meditation of the mind."[6] As Bryan Spinks points out, for Perkins there is both an external and internal working out of God's purposes. The signs of the sacraments, for example, affect the senses both externally and internally. For these signs reflect the visible outworking of the will of God expressed in election and point to the believer's sanctification.[7]

But here in this later work Perkins goes on to define the nature of this meditative work. One might properly wonder: if these internal "images" or descriptions of God are allowed, cannot external images accurately simulate these? By no means, Perkins exclaims, for to allow this would be to misconceive the nature of these inner images. For the "right way to conceive God, is not to conceive any form: but to conceive in mind his properties and proper effects."[8] What is "conceived" then is the truth in the form of proper teaching about God, not any external, or visible, aspect of God, nor even any inner imagined form. Of course, the bible itself uses images of God and his affects – Perkins like Calvin before him had to deal with this troublesome fact. But, unlike Calvin, Perkins seems not to believe that creation itself, even if authorized by biblical use, can be an adequate theater for God's glory. The signs of Scripture, Perkins argues were really only signs or indications of God's presence: "The forms in which the Sonne and Holy Ghost have appeared were not their images, but only sensible signes and pledges of their presence: and signes not forever, but only for this present time, when they appeared."[9] Their outward "symbols" then are only a kind of pledge of the inner sphere where the definitive revelation of God takes place. Perkins can be defended against the apparent docetic implications of this statement, since he refers to the types and symbols of Christ and the Holy Spirit not the actual incarnation or the Pentecost. Still it is the words and concepts of Scripture that "signify" God's presence. God can speak in creation, but only as this is put into appropriate verbal and conceptual forms – there is no nonverbal imagining of God beyond this. Christ's continuing mediation and the working of the Holy Spirit in creation both seem to be limited to working through proper intellectual formulations.

---

[7] Bryan D. Spinks, *Two Faces of Elizabethan Anglican Theology: Sacraments and Salvation in the Thought of William Perkins and Richard Hooker* (Lanham, Md. and London: Scarecrow Press, 1999), pp. 67, 72–3. He quotes from *Reformed Catholike*, in *Workes* (Cambridge: Legatt, 1912), vol. 1, p. 610: "The signes and visible elements affect the senses outward and inward: the minde directed by the Holy Ghost reasoneth on this manner, out of the promise annexed to the sacrament" (p. 72). Spinks also reproduces some of Perkins's ramist charts on baptism and salvation, which illustrate how internal baptism corresponds to the external one, and which are further broken down, "ramified," in these parallel spheres (p. 74). On the impact of ramist logic on Perkins, see Donald K. McKim, *Ramism in William Perkins' Theology* (New York: Peter Lang, 1987).

[8] *A Warning against the Idolatrie,* pp. 107–8.

[9] Ibid., p. 15. Besides, Perkins goes on to say, although God can always make such images this does not mean we can (p. 16).

Perkins goes on to detail this proper use of the imagination in sermons which were published after his death in *A Treatise of Man's Imagination.*[10] Imagination is defined as "that which is devised and plotted in the thoughts of man's hearts" (p. 20). Taking his starting point from Genesis 8:21 which says that "man's imagination is only evil continually," Perkins notes that human imagination, "the frame of man's heart by nature," is naturally wicked and against the law of God (p. 21). Such framing assumes there is no God or naturally turns the true God into an idol (p. 35), which is to say it denies in practice the reality of God (p. 41). To such imagination the word of God is foolishness. "By this wicked imagination we may see how hard a thing it is truly and soundly to convert a sinner unto God" (pp. 78–9). But even if the imagination is so corrupted that it can be of no positive use, it seems that it can play a kind of negative role. The use of imagination has been much abused by papistry, of course, leading to a salvation by works. But it appears the remedy also must start with imagination: We must "first seek to rectify the imagination by bringing the minde to a right conceit of [its] affliction" (p. 145). For by considering one's final state and God's mercy one might be moved to consider God. For if the "judgment be well informed . . . then the cure is halfe wrought and the crosse half removed" (p. 146). Of course this movement of the mind must be a response to God's internal work as, according to Perkins and Calvin before him, there is no free will to do good within the person (pp. 159, 162). It must moreover serve the larger purpose of developing proper notions of God's presence and grace.

This inward reflection is central to Puritan devotional practices and is key to understanding the developing cultural life of Puritan America. Just as there is a proper role that the mind can play in the process of salvation, so there is something parents and teachers can do to appropriately stir up the mind. Perkins goes on to develop this process at some length. An examination of his exhortation to self-examination does much to illumine the subsequent development of the Puritan imagination, especially in those influenced by William Ames. Perkins insists that the minds of the young can be encouraged to examine their hearts with respect to God's mercy and their own evil imagination. The means for this of course are the faithful preaching of God's word and prayer for pardon, as part of a larger program to reform the imagination and life (pp. 174–7). He writes: "We must heare Gods word preached attentively, and apply not only our outward senses, but our minds also thereto, that so it may enter our hearts"(p. 175). This

---

[10] *A Treatise of Man's Imagination: Shewing his natural evill thoughts; his want of good thoughts; the way to reform them* (Cambridge: John Legat, 1607). Pages in the text are to this work.

program consists in the systematic reformation of thinking by bringing all thoughts captive to the obedience of Christ (II Cor. 10:5; Phil. 4:8); it includes a careful guarding of one's heart; and, finally, since the believer's conversation is in heaven, it culminates in the lifting up of the heart to God (pp. 181, 186). While this is encouraged by external means – hearing God's word, the participation in the sacraments and continual prayer – these means have their internal counterpart, as they stimulate us to focus on God's love and on reconciliation with our neighbor. The external means are instrumental to the inner work. Perkins is emphatic that meditation is central to this process, as we seriously think over those things which relate to our salvation: on God's works, his ways and his word. In all this "we must give ourselves to spirituall consideration or meditation" (p. 191). As Lady Margaret's diary frequently attests, this includes praying, reading and hearing sermons, and above all examining oneself. This implies, Perkins explains, on the one hand, making oneself aware of God's presence, of his judgments, his great works (pp. 194–201). But it also involves, on the other hand, reflecting on one's sin: the misery this brings, one's temptations and final end, when we will give our account before God (pp. 211, 214, 223). One reflects then in increasing intensity, and gratitude, on our knowledge of God and ourselves.

But the tension remains that will be worked out in the subsequent development of Puritan thinking. Perkins in one sense does as much as anyone of his generation to encourage an internal reflection on the reality of God; indeed his writings often contain striking images. In one sense this opened the way for the creative use of the imagination that was demonstrated, for example, in Richard Bernard, and that would come to have such influence on the literature, even the visual culture of the seventeenth century. Yet Perkins insists on contrasting this meditation with "being occupied with the eye": "It is not meete that a Christian should be occupied by the eyes but by the meditation of the minde." For such practices he cannot help associating with the popish traditions against which the Puritans had long fought. Visible images, he says, kindle corrupt affections, and thus by dulling wit and memory, actually impede the proper development of the spiritual imagination. This latter imagination is to be occupied not with stories and pictures, but with the "truths" of God's word, which are to be put to the good use of one's own spiritual examination.[11]

---

[11] *Reformed Catholike,* p. 177; quote pp. 171–2.

Brian Spinks argues that Perkins's tension reflects a tradition that is indebted more to Thomas Aquinas than to Augustine. Perkins, in beginning with the three persons of the Trinity, argued that God's will was not ruled by justice or love, or indeed by anything outside itself,

but itselfe is an absolute rule both of justice and reason . . . [therefore] affections of the creature are not properly incident unto God, because they make many changes, and God is without change. And therefore all affections and the love that is in man and beast is ascribed to God by figure.[12]

Perkins then rejects the view of God as infinite love that Richard Sibbes will hold, and that goes back to Augustine – indeed he argues that God's nature is free of all passions. Similarly for Perkins grace, as with Aquinas, is "commodity like" leading to a tendency to establish "one's righteousness through righteous actions, based on grace."[13] While most subsequent Puritan theologians are indebted in some way to Perkins as to Calvin, there will be an important difference in what some theologians will find in this tradition – with critical significance for the understanding and role of the imagination. Some will focus on the experimental character of his faith and the signs this gives of election; others will develop the inner focus of life in the Spirit and the nature of God as grace and love.

Since Calvin there had been an implicit tension between the strong emphasis on external order and structure, and the inward focus on life in the Spirit and with Christ. Both sides of the tension were fed not only by what they saw as biblical teaching and the theological convictions that grew out of this, but also by the reformers' rejection of the medieval mediation of spiritual reality, represented by the cult of images and the Mass. The latter needed to be entirely eliminated and replaced by a reordering of life by the Word of God. But this reordering would be variously interpreted. On the one hand, Perkins and Ames would focus on the experimental life ordered by God's word; on the other Richard Sibbes and John Cotton will stress the affective life with Christ. For both groups any external mediation of spiritual truth was excluded, but for Sibbes and his followers this did not necessarily exclude a visualization of God's presence within the boundaries of symbols provided by Scripture. The practices that resulted, especially of worship and meditation, carried their own theological meaning that shaped

[12] Spinks, *Two Faces of Elizabethan Anglican Theology*, p. 55, 59, he quotes from Perkins's *Workes*, vol. 1, p. 278 and p. 742.
[13] *Two Faces of Elizabethan Anglican Theology*, p. 66. Spinks quotes from R. N. Frost's dissertation, "Richard Sibbes' Theology of Grace and the Division of English Reformed Theology," London University (1996), pp. 94–5. This line of argument, and the division Frost traces, becomes the central issue in subsequent Puritan debates, coming to special focus during the antinomian controversy.

not only Puritan minds and hearts, but impacted the culture that would be planted in the New World. In this chapter we examine the theological shape these tendencies took in the seventeenth century; in the next the cultural shape this took.

We will examine first William Ames, who despite the fact he ministered in Holland and died there in 1633, was to become the most influential theologian among the first-generation clergy in New England. As a student not only of Perkins, but also of the Cambridge Ramists, he would articulate the side of the tradition that sought good order and the careful structuring of life, both individually and communally. John Cotton, on the other hand, we take to represent the side of the tradition that developed the implications of the inner life, and its affective potential. There is much that these parties shared, of course: the central emphases of Calvin on God's sovereignty and the incapacity of the creature to adequately reflect God. But their different styles and sensitivies would lead to differing aesthetics. As Janice Knight describes this difference: one side channeled God's sovereignty into rational structures, while the other modified this into affective modes.[14]

The irony we will trace is that though Puritan theology in America has been interpreted largely in terms of Ames's influence, in many respects this side of the tradition proved culturally constricting. Meanwhile the sensitivities of John Cotton, and Richard Sibbes before him, while apparently eclipsed in the later seventeenth century, became central in the thought of Jonathan Edwards and in the First Great Awakening more generally. And it would be these influences that would eventually have a much larger, and more important, impact on the development of American culture, even after they are cut loose from their theological framework.

WILLIAM AMES AND THE MARROW OF THEOLOGY

If Calvin had sought to give the world a mental shape, it would be William Perkins and, especially, William Ames (1576–1633) who would draw the map of this new world. Ames belonged to the second generation of Puritans who came of age during the period of growing repression against

[14] Janice Knight, *Orthodoxies in Massachusetts: Rereading American Puritanism* (Cambridge, Mass.: Harvard University Press, 1994), p. 32. My argument has been influenced considerably by this important book, though I would insist the tension goes back further than she suggests, not only to Perkins, but implicitly to Calvin himself. Her argument is inevitably subject to some oversimplification, as she would admit, such as the simple designation of Ames's tradition as rationalist. See the more nuanced view in Norman S. Fiering, "Will and Intellect in the New England Mind," *William and Mary Quarterly* 29 (1972), pp. 515–58.

the program of purifying the Church: what Keith Sprunger calls Puri-tanism's "slough of despondency."[15] Indeed this repression, and the dis-couragement it produced, did much to influence the character, perhaps even the thought, of William Ames.[16] Born in 1576 in Puritan-dominated Ipswich, he knew the Winthrop family while growing up. In 1593 he en-tered Christ's College, Cambridge, where he received his BA in 1597/8 and became a fellow in 1601. During the early 1590s he experienced the light-ning and thunder of Perkins's preaching and was dramatically converted. Perkins, who became his tutor and good friend, and Peter Ramus whom he never met, had probably the greatest influence on his thinking, though he was exposed to a wide variety of Puritan thinking while at Cambridge. Ames's more distant heroes were Augustine and Calvin, though it was a Calvin mediated by Perkins and one that found expression in the Synod of Dort, where Ames was a theological consultant.[17]

Beginning in 1604, James I and Archbishop Bancroft insisted on strict conformity to the Anglican Church and began to track down Puritans whose dissent was too outspoken. Ames was already a marked man for hav-ing translated into Latin William Bradshaw's *English Puritanism*, adding a supporting introduction of his own. In 1609 he was considered for the mastership of Christ's College but the appointment of someone who had so visibly refused to wear the surplice proved impossible. At about the same time the Bishop of London blocked an attractive call that came to Ames from the Church at Colchester. It soon became clear that Ames's prospects in England were anything but promising, and, in 1610, pursued by some who "would have willingly shortened their journey," Ames was escorted by friends to Gravesend and across the North Sea to Holland.[18]

In Holland he supported himself by ministering to congregations of ex-iled Englishman. In 1611 he married the daughter of John Burgess, whom he had succeeded as chaplain to the British community in The Hague, but she soon died leaving him childless. The long arm of the British authorities pursued him even in Holland, blocking an appointment at the University of Leyden, which had been making serious overtures to Ames, and even suc-ceeding in 1618 in having him dismissed from his chaplaincy. Fortunately,

---

[15] Keith L. Sprunger, *The Learned Doctor William Ames: Dutch Backgrounds of English and American Puritanism* (Urbana: University of Illinois, 1972), p. 4. For the details of his early career I am dependent on Sprunger's first chapter. But see also John D. Eusden's introduction to *The Marrow of Theology* (Boston, Mass.: Pilgrim Press, 1968), pp. 1–66. On Ames's Calvinism see Sprunger, *Learned Doctor*, pp. 8, 12, 60–4.

[16] This is argued well by Knight, *Orthodoxies in Massachusetts*, p. 62.

[17] Eusden, introduction to *Marrow of Theology*, pp. 6–8.   [18] Ibid., p. 4.

because of the sponsorship of Dutch Prince Moritz, a recommendation of the Synod of South Holland that he be appointed Professor at the newly formed University of Franeker succeeded and in 1622 he gave his inaugural address on the deeper meaning of the high priest's attire in Exodus 28. The ten years remaining to him became the most fruitful of his life. During this period he wrote his most important theological treatises, and, upon his appointment as rector in 1626, sought to bring order and morality to the school. In 1633 he wavered between travel to New England, at the encouragement of his old friend John Winthrop, and removal to Rotterdam where another friend, Hugh Peter, was beginning a theological academy. The shorter trip proved the most dangerous and while settling in with his family at Rotterdam in October 1633, his home was flooded, and the cold water and air gave him a fever from which he did not recover. In 1637 his second wife and their three children finally made the trip to New England without their husband and father.

Amidst an array of personal and professional tragedies Ames was remarkably productive, though he never got over the bitterness associated with the arbitrary exercise of power by Church authorities. While he became one of the dominant theological voices in New England, his influence on the Dutch Church was limited.[19] While at Franeker he attracted a wide following among students from outside of Holland, and his influence can be seen, for example, in Johannes Cocceius, known as the father of federal theology, who studied with him. René Descartes was also a student at Franeker during Ames's time, and, while he was clearly not influenced by the orthodoxy of the university, its methods may have had some influence on the system he was already developing there.[20] Clearly Ames reflects the major theological emphases of his generation of Puritans, especially Perkins's concern for "experimental" Christianity and the need to reform the Church.

THE SHAPE OF THEOLOGY: A MAP OF DIVINE TRUTHS

The core idea in Ames's theology is the practice of living to God. Theology is to be both experimental and practical. He defines this in the *Marrow of Theology* as people living in accord "with the will of God, to the glory

---

[19] Sprunger, *Learned Doctor,* p. 26. Though Sprunger argues that Ames's insistence on practical theology "worked its way into the life of the Dutch Church at different levels, especially in the pietistic movement" (p. 94), his memory has all but disappeared in Holland today.

[20] Sprunger notes he enrolled in April 1629 and began work on his *Discourse on Method* in Franeker and worked on *Meditations* somewhat later in Friesland (*Learned Doctor,* p. 80).

of God, and with God working in them."[21] But his theology is intended to be "practical" in quite another sense: it is ordered in such a way that it is clear and unambiguous – it consists in an order that is easily "seen" and grasped in the charts and outlines that structure his work. We examine these two senses of the practical in reverse order, looking first at the practical structure, then at the practice of living to God.

Ames's most important work in developing his method, *The Technometry*, though probably first written while he was a student at Cambridge, was not published until after his death.[22] In this treatise of theological methodology Ames applies literally Peter Ramus's system of arranging the content of the arts curriculum (which would have included the sum total of human knowledge as it was then understood) into a "technometria" or ordered dichotomous structure. This aspired to provide a complete "map" of knowledge of living to God and the ways in which this knowledge – indeed all knowledge – could be accessed.

In the outline of the work (Figure 16), all knowledge is divided into its nature and its use, each subsequently subdivided into the more and less general. A taste of this may be gained by examining his description of the notion of "eupraxis." "Good action," Ames says at the beginning of the *Technometry*, is fundamental to all art[23] and is methodically delineated by universal rules (*T.* 1). This "idea" of good action existing in God is not so much a Platonic form as a model or exemplar. It is: "The form of a model formed in the mind of an artificer before action and for the sake of action" (*T.* 3). This model of course exists uniquely in the mind of God and secondarily in humans as "a refraction of rays" (*T.* 15). All art then is grounded archetypically in the mind of God, and exists "ectypically" in humans, and "entypically" in things. Interestingly, in the *Marrow*, he likens this process of good action specifically to the work of an artist: "In every artist, or anyone who expresses himself after taking counsel, there exists beforehand an idea which he keeps in mind as he is about to work so that he may fit his work to it" (*M.* 1, vii, 13). This "idea" is brought to action in the creation of things and exists in them as "opus" (work done). These objects contain their "types," "in which all art shines and from which its

---

[21] *The Marrow of Theology* [definitive Latin edn, 1627, first English edn 1643], translated from the Latin by John Eusden (Boston, Mass.: Pilgrim Press, 1968), 1, i, 6. Subsequent references will be indicated by *M.* followed by the book, chapter and section.

[22] See Ames, *Technometry,* trans. and intro. by Lee W. Gibbs (Philadelphia: University of Pennsylvania, 1979), composition and sources discussed pp. 14 and 18–30. Hereafter cited as *T.* followed by the paragraph number given by Ames.

[23] Ames uses art in its more traditional sense of any ordered human practice, though the idea of artist as "artificer" in a special sense had already come into use in the Renaissance.

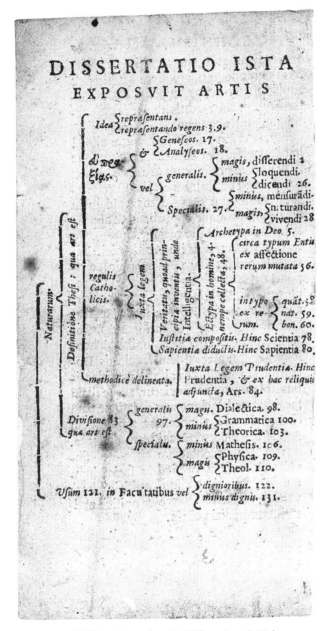

Figure 16   William Ames, chart in William Ames's *Technometry*.
British Library, London, England, 1633.

principles, which produce human understanding, are gathered by man" (*T.* 48). Ames in more than one place defines the six practices which make up this "gathering" in a variation of the classical liberal arts (*T.* 117): "These six arts perfect the whole man: logic directing his intellect; theology his will; and the remaining arts – grammar, rhetoric, math, and physics – his locomotion according to rule in their eupraxae" (see also *T.* 30). The end of all things, that toward which they look, Ames says, is the universal goodness and glory of God (*T.* 60). While people are able in principle to gather this knowledge and arrange it properly, in practice they cannot do so because of sin. Since the race is fallen the "types" shining in objects are inadequate, they have become illegible. So God has substituted Scripture "for the type deficient in that part of things" (*T.* 62). Even though "analysis" by logic is useful, no one can *inwardly* perceive these things apart from the ministry of the Holy Spirit working through and with the truth of Scripture (*T.* 65).

Ames takes note of the inductive method of Francis Bacon (*T.* 70) and believes that the analysis that he proposes is an equivalent procedure. A person proceeds from sense experience, through induction (i.e. Ames's analysis) to experience. Here he rejects Aristotle's distinction between the theoretical and practical. For, he says, in terms that sound strikingly modern, "there is no contemplation that should not be practice and have its own work; nor is there any action in general such as to exclude all contemplation" (*T.* 89). But having argued for a practice-based integration he goes on to subvert this insight by saying that the preferred distinction is between the general and the special, reflected in the six good practices noted above and also in the all-inclusive map of their application. Everything Ames believes can in principle be located according to its location within this dichotomist system. So Ames rejects the distinction between theory and practice, ironically, by making everything theoretical – making its real meaning dependent on its location in this vast map of reality. As Lee Gibbs points out, Ames's notion of integration is not an organic unity, but a search for the best distribution of parts in their proper dichotomous relationship.[24]

The structure that resulted from this impulse to map can be seen in much of Ames's work, and it came to have enormous influence on the development of New England theology. As with ramism generally, it was accompanied by the sense of breaking through to a new and fresh conception of the nature of things. As Perry Miller notes, the New England Puritans believed they were not merely thinking about things, they were

---

[24] Introduction to *Technometry,* p. 33. Ames's procedure is clearly not the scientific method that Bacon was developing, though it can be argued, as in the case of Ramus, that he is moving in that direction.

achieving access to things as they objectively were. They were persuaded that "the laws of God found in the Bible were hypothesized by the logic of Ramus into never failing realities, as endurable as facts, and from that assurance Puritanism got its strength and its confidence."[25] But whatever their sense of things, we must be clear as to what is happening: the conception of the thing has taken the place of the thing itself. Basil Wiley's characterization of this process in the seventeenth century may not be exaggerated: "We must expect to find the rationalizers largely concerned with putting an *idea*, and *abstraction*, where formerly there had been a *picture*. For only the abstract, only what could be conceptually stated could claim to be *real*: all else was shadow, image or at least 'type' or 'symbol'."[26]

This order can be discerned, for example, in *The Marrow of Theology*, especially when its contents are laid out in the form of a chart (Figure 17). Interestingly this chart only appeared in the 1642 edition, and was not used in this form during Ames's lifetime.[27] But it clearly lays out the structure that Ames intended – all theology is divided into faith and observance, which are described in books one and two, and so on throughout the work. Ames may have specifically avoided using such a chart, because, as with the gardens of Palissy, he may have intended the structure to be hidden, given only to those whose eyes have been opened to see it. This may also account for the fact that Ames did not seek to publish *The Technometry* during his lifetime, though its structure clearly informs his work. But significantly, as becomes clear in the *Marrow*, the ordering principles are structural rather than theological, abstract rather than concrete. Faith/observance are further defined in terms of sufficiency/efficiency and virtue/good works respectively, that is in terms of the general and the special; unlike Calvin's *Institutes* in which the order follows generally from that of the Apostles' Creed – an order that is theologically (and one could argue biblically) defined. For Ames, there is no sense in which, say, God's glory or Christ's incarnation are given any structural significance – these notions find their place in this great map of general and special knowledge.

Consider for example Ames's treatment of creation and the incarnation, theological themes obviously central to the human cultural project. Since in the schema creation falls under efficiency or working power of God, creation can only be understood as an expression of efficiency or God's power. He explains this as follows: "The proper order for conceiving these things is,

[25] *The New England Mind: The Seventeenth Century* (Boston, Mass.: Beacon, 1961 [1939]), p. 148.
[26] *The Seventeenth Century Background: Studies in the Thought of the Age in Relation to Poetry and Religion* (London: Chatto & Windus, 1949), p. 133, emphasis his.
[27] See Eusden, introduction to *Marrow of Theology*, pp. 71–3.

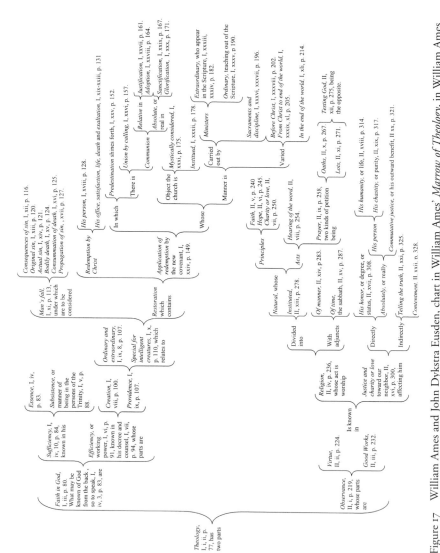

Figure 17   William Ames and John Dykstra Eusden, chart in William Ames' *Marrow of Theology*, in William Ames and John Dykstra Eusden, *The Marrow of Theology*. Boston: Pilgrim Press, 1968, pp. 72–3.

first, to think of God's *posse*, his power; second, his *scira*, knowledge; third, his *velle*, will; and lastly his *efficere potenter*, efficient power" (*M.* I, vi, 8). So all is construed in terms of God's omnipotence and his action, and, in the following chapter, his freedom. Creation then can only be understood in terms of "kinds" of efficiencies: dichotomized as direct creation and providence. All the actions of God toward creation are expressions of power, all action is transitive. But what of creation as an expression of God's love or his wisdom? Or creation, as Calvin saw it, as the theater of God's glory? In fairness, Ames briefly alludes to such themes later by saying: "Now natural things tend towards God, first, in that they declare God's glory . . . and give occasion for us both to know and seek God" (*M.* I, viii, 22), but this cannot be elaborated, or made into a central theme as they will in Edwards, because the structure that has been imposed does not allow it.

Similarly for the Incarnation, consistent with the instrumentalist view of Calvin, Christ is the extension of the restoration side of the fall/restoration dichotomy. But other than a brief assertion that in creation the Trinity acts together (*M.* I, v, 21–4),[28] Christ's role is limited to obtaining salvation for humanity by his death "establishing man in freedom from the bondage of sin and the devil by payment of a just price" (*M.* I, xviii, 6), just as the Holy Spirit is said to work the application of this atonement in the believer (*M.* I, xxiv, 2). Their structural relationships do not allow them any continuing role in politics or culture. Ames pointedly closes the chapter on the kingship of Christ: "The kings of the nations are not properly subordinated to Christ in their authority, but rather to God" (*M.* I, xix, 31).

But, while we may not agree with the imaginative shape that Ames and his followers sought to give the world, we must pay respect to the importance of their quest. As Robert Blair St. George has pointed out, the seventeenth century was going to witness a great "metaphor transition." Their inherited metaphor was fundamentally hierarchical, stretching from God and heaven, down through the king and feudal lords to the common people.[29] Ames and his contemporaries were reaching toward a new conception of things that would break down this fixed order, and replace it with one they believed was more reflective of God's word. Ames's charts represent what in the

---

[28] Note that this discussion is, according to the structure imposed, under the chapter of the "Subsistence of God" which has been paired with God's "Essence" (*M.* I, iv and v). This arrangement surely owes more of a debt to medieval metaphysics than to biblical exegesis.

[29] Robert Blair St. George, " 'Set Thine House in Order': The Domestication of the Yeomanry in Seventeenth Century New England," in Jonathan L. Fairbanks and Robert F. Trent (eds.), *New England Begins: The Seventeenth Century* (Boston, Mass.: Museum of Fine Arts, 1982), vol. II, pp. 159–60. See also Arthur Lovejoy's classic expression of this hierarchy in *The Great Chain of Being* (Cambridge, Mass.: Harvard University Press, 1936).

seventeenth century would pass for a metadiscipline, making a complex world clear and, more importantly, accessible to anyone who looks upon it – with structuring principles that are graphically visual.[30] This new order was expressed through the catechism instruction the children learned, through the sermons they heard and the devotional books they read, even in the primers by which they learned to read. And this developing order was to have a major impact not only on their devotional life but on the way they shaped their world. Not many New Englanders left us their diaries, they were people of few words. But they did leave us the patterned structures of their lives – their farmsteads, their towns, their personal sense of dress and time, that would, eventually, break up and replace the old world and its hierarchies.

THE PRACTICE OF THEOLOGY: LIVING TO GOD

Critical to the developing vision of human life in the world is Ames's understanding of the "typological" or linear interpretation of Scripture and the role that external forms play in this. This understanding represented the second sense in which Ames's theology is practical: the understanding that human life fits into a larger historical program that God was developing from creation through the end of history. Given the centrality the bible played in the imagination of Puritans, it is not surprising that the hermeneutical understanding called typology played such an important role in their thinking, and, more particularly, their imagination.[31]

A great deal of Ames's writing is occupied with the battle over ceremonies and images that had caused him to leave England.[32] While he was not radical in his ecclesiology, holding to a nonseparating congregationalism, in matters of worship he insisted that only those elements specifically required in Scripture should be allowed. "No instituted worship is lawful

---

[30] Ames's method, and his "technometry" in particular, clearly influenced the development of the notion of the theological encyclopedia, which in its secularized eighteenth-century form developed into the modern idea of the encyclopedia as a compendium of knowledge. See Gibbs, Introduction to the *Technometry*, pp. 45–7.

[31] The importance of this for the literature and culture of the Puritans has been described in two recent studies: see Mason I. Lowance, *The Language of Canaan: Metaphor and Symbol in New England from the Puritans to Transcendentalists* (Cambridge, Mass.: Harvard University Press, 1980); and Theodore Dwight Bozeman, *To Live Ancient Lives: The Primitivist Dimension in Puritanism* (Chapel Hill: University of North Carolina Press, 1988).

[32] One of his first published writings was his long *Reply to Dr. Mortons Defence of three nocent Ceremonies, viz. The Surplice, Crosse in Baptisme and Kneeling at the receiving of the sacramental elements of bread and wine* (Amsterdam: n. p., 1622). At his death he was working on the even longer work: *A Fresh Suit Against Human Ceremonies in God's Worship* ([Amsterdam]: 1633), which reached almost 700 pages!

unless God is its author and ordainer" (*M.* II, xiii, 10). In his *Reply to Dr. Morton* he insists: "There is no necessitie that in any nation the churches should have any religious ceremonies of spiritual signification, beside those which Christ hath appointed to all."[33] The worship of God's people of course looked different in the Old Testament. Ames notes that "although the free, saving covenant of God has been one and the same from the beginning, the manner of the application of Christ, or the administration of the new covenant has not always been so" (*M.* I, xxxviii, 1). The signs or ceremonies given by God in the Old Testament time were in general external aids, a kind of "hornebook" or "prymer." As he says elsewhere, they provided temporary guidance "for the church to be schooled by when it was in its infancy . . . called elements of this world . . . because these were only supplemental to those spiritual ordinances which are called moral and substantial."[34] Here Ames gives voice to his understanding of worship as fundamentally that which is described in the First Commandment: loving and serving God with one's whole heart. This which he calls "natural worship" (*M.* II, v, 7) is contrasted with instituted worship given by God to increase this more fundamental or "natural" worship (*M.* II, xiii, 1).

In general then the ceremonies and signs given in the Old Testament are pointers to the coming of Christ and therefore are no longer necessary after Christ's coming. In a characterization central to the Puritan mind, Ames says, "while Christ was still to appear, all things were more outward and carnal, afterwards more inward and spiritual" (*M.* I, xxxviii, 6). But obviously much of the imagery of the Old Testament is of continuing value in that it can be used to portray our life with Christ. For example, Ames notes all the ways that the Old Testament prefigures the justification, sanctification and glorification that has come to light in the New Covenant. This New Covenant has instituted an order which Ames calls "inward and spiritual," not bound by time, nor constituted by external symbols which are now no longer necessary (see *M.* I, xxxix).[35] But we can still read the Old Testament as picturing our life with Christ under several forms – Abraham is a type of faith, Exodus symbolizes our redemption,

---

[33] *Reply to Dr. Mortons Defence*, p. 3. Moreover, he goes on to say, "not to command in things that pertaine to worship is all one with forbidding" (p. 6). Dr. Morton had appealed to Calvin for support of his more lenient position. Calvin had argued (*Institutes*, IV, x, 30) that after applying those practices that Scripture approves, God leaves the details of ceremonies to the Church, concluding: "If we let love be our guide we will be safe." Ames has to insist that Calvin only refers to minor areas, not "significant circumstance."

[34] Ames, *A Fresh Suit Against Human Ceremonies*, p. 35.

[35] The ceremonies that are temporary he calls ordinary, those with enduring value he calls extraordinary; see *Marrow of Theology*, I, xxxviii and Lowance, *Language of Canaan*, p. 37.

Canaan speaks of promised glorification, and so on (*M.* I, xxxviii, 24–30). The Puritan then can "imagine" herself in terms of these Old Testament stories which throughout her life were preached, retold and endlessly discussed.

But while growing out of an inner and spiritual witness, this living to God was not, for all that, invisible. This covenant life is "diffused throughout the whole world" (*M.* I, xxxix, 13). These congregations are not constituted by visible symbols as they were during the Old Testament period, but they are not without visible signs. At various key points Ames returns to this theme of the "experimental" character of living to God. In fact in the *Marrow* this section on extraordinary types lies at the end of the section of faith, which is concluded by a short chapter on Baptism and the Lord's Supper and on the End of the World. In the discussion of the Lord's Supper Ames reminds the reader that it is not necessary that Christ be corporeally present with us for our "spiritual nourishment" appropriate to this time in history. "It required only that Christ be spiritually present with those who receive them in faith" (*M.* I, xl, 23). Only God can accomplish this work of grace through the sign he has initiated and which he uses to "stir up spiritual grace in us" (*M.* I, xxxvi, 20). But consistent with Ames's "experimental" focus, the sign finally takes its meaning in its use: "illustrated in the distributing, receiving, eating and drinking"(*M.* I, xxxvi, 21). So the sacrament has no value in itself – it does not reflect any intrinsic value in creation as mediated by Christ, indeed, "sacraments do not properly exist apart from their being used, i.e., they are not revered sacraments either before or after their use" (*M.* I, xxxvi, 22). That is, the sacraments' visibility has to do with making visual the communion we have with God and with others who also partake (*M.* I, xxxvi, 34). This embodiment, as symbolized in the sacrament, will be seen more clearly at the end of history, when the image of God will be perfected in all the sanctified and the "glory and blessedness hoped for will shine forth in all fullness, not only in the soul, but in the whole body" (*M.* I, xli, 5, 6).

Book II follows and describes the observance of theology which Ames defines as "submissive performance of the will of God" (*M.* II, i, 1). In this section and in the monumental *Conscience with power and cases thereof*,[36] Ames applies in detail his conception of living well, or living to God, to the major ethical issues faced in the seventeenth century. By a sanctifying grace the believer's will is moved toward the habit of loving the good and hating

---

[36] *De conscientia et eius jure vel casibus: libri quinque* (Amsterdam, 1630); English translation, *Conscience with power and cases thereof, Five Books* (London: 1639). Hereafter, references indicated in the text by *C.*, followed by book and page.

evil, which is not the cause of eternal life "but the ministering, helping or furthering cause of possessing this life . . . the way by which we walk to heaven" (*M.* II, i, 30). In *Cases of Conscience*, which Ames regarded as an essential elaboration of the description of living to God that informs the *Marrow*, he applies all the elements of his theological system in terms of this practical judgment applied to what is good (*C.* I, p. 2). Reflecting in particular on the Dutch Church, he notes a "famine of godliness" exists in many places so that he sets forth a program that includes "these instructions touching the power of conscience" (*C.* To the Reader).

After dealing with general issues of conversion and human duty in general, Ames turns to human duties to God and one's neighbor (*C.* Bks. IV and V). In the former he emphasizes that hearing the word and fearing God must issue in external profession, for, Ames insists, God can see the internal act but internal profession is not enough. In discussing prayer, he notes that sometimes internal prayer is insufficient: "Because God is to be glorified and to be religiously worshipped by us not only by our soules, but also with our bodies and so with our voice" (*C.* IV, p. 39). Most gestures of course are to be avoided in public – they may distract or be an occasion for stumbling. But in private prayer they can be profitable, indeed lifting up one's hands and eyes "is decent in every solemn prayer" (*C.* IV, p. 43). For "by the gesture and habit of the body, affections are excited, supported and continued" (*C.* IV, p. 42). This leads naturally to a discussion of singing of Psalms which, Ames believed, brings a sweet delight to godly minds and leads to mutual edification. Ames is emphatic here that we can put ourselves into these Psalms as though they were spoken to us. "We ought in our thoughts to put on, as it were, the person . . . that what ever is spoken there, we may, in some sort, take it as spoken to ourselves" (*C.* IV, p. 44). As Theodore Bozeman notes, the Puritans were insistent on destroying the accretion of imagery that had accumulated in worship precisely to allow Christians to "return more completely to the intense, richly imagined world of the biblical primordium."[37] Worship centered on a plain reading and description of Scripture, because it was meant to encourage Christians to enter into the scriptural narrative, as though it were telling their own story.

But there was something more that underlined the practical and even the visual dimension of living to God. We have seen that external forms of worship could not be given much importance because they were merely instrumental. They were to lead to a life of visible godliness: instituted

---

[37] *To Live Ancient Lives,* p. 33. "Scripture," he notes, "presented a dramatic panorama which moved from Creation to Redemption to Resurrection and Last things, a panorama that sprang into present life in preaching, biblical study and meditation" (p. 33).

worship was to support natural worship. The Sabbath, for example, one of the central institutions in Puritan life, forbids those things which "hinder a man from attending upon God and his worship" (*C.* iv, p. 98). But the goal is to be manifest throughout the week: "We are to be so employed in those exercises that we may get spiritual refreshment thereby, by virtue of which we may passe the rest of the week holily" (*C.* iv, p. 98). As if to underline this experimental end of worship, Ames notes that our devotion to God takes precedence over our duty to our neighbor (*M.* ii, iv, 10–14). And if justice and piety conflict, the "duties of piety are to be preferred" (*M.* ii, iv, 15). But Ames goes on immediately to qualify this: "God is better worshipped with inward affection than outward deed. But men need the outward deed more. An outward work of religion may, therefore, sometimes be omitted in order that a necessary work of justice and mercy may be done" (*M.* ii, iv, 17). So if an external work of religion conflicts with a work of justice, it is the latter that takes precedence. Religion is not violated in this way, Ames explains, because it insists that external "rite" be omitted in order that something more necessary may be done.

Ames gives expression here to the priority of the inner purpose of worship, of natural worship over instituted worship. Since it is the human creature that is the image of God, care for our neighbor, indeed for all creation, "implies a respect for the image of him found in other living creatures" (*M.* ii, xviii, 4). In performing justice therefore for our neighbor we are said to "love God in men and men in God" (*M.* ii, xvi, 8). This reiterates a theme we have noticed since the discussion of iconoclasm: worship is meant to serve actual godliness, and when it does not do so, no matter how splendid or revered the form it may take, it must give way. Externally wrought images are destroyed so that the true image might be visible. The image of God is best honored in care for the human person, and, by extension, the created order that God has made.

Godliness then is not only the goal of life, but the purpose of the institutions God has ordained for worship. But like the God of the Old Testament, this construal of godliness makes comprehensive claims. It absorbs all of one's attention and becomes, at least for Ames, the focus of immense speculative energy. Long sections specify the circumstances that make good works "good," for "all the circumstances must be good to make the shape or mode [of an act] good" (*M.* ii, iii, 9). Nor can one simply let love rule in all things. For in natural worship faith comes first, hope follows and charity is last: "Charity or love follows faith and hope in natural order as effect follows cause" (*M.* ii, vii, 2). Unlike John Cotton, Ames insists it is faith that is the foundation of our natural worship not love. For it is faith that "sustains and holds together all the parts of the building" (*M.* ii, vii, 3).

In his *Fresh Suit against Human Ceremonies*, which Ames was working on when he died, he returns to this theme. In instituted worship images and ceremonies are not to be appealed to for help – neither cross nor surplice finds support in Scripture. It is true that Beza allowed pictures in his bible, Ames admits, but these are not religious ceremonies. Quoting Alexander of Hales, he says, "these signifie holy things not as they are holy but as they are things."[38] These are not to be used in worship in any way, for if we allow them, how can we condemn those who worship them (p. 291)? In a familiar proviso, Ames assures the reader that God does not require us to give up human significant (or civil) ceremonies, only the use of images and ceremonies in the Church. But why cannot such images be profitable in worship, to call to mind scriptural events and people, one might wonder? Simply because God has not allowed it. "Nothing is profitable in religion," Ames responds, "but that which is instituted by God" (p. 213). Otherwise, he says, we might justify bringing gallows into the Church to remind us of God's justice!

In *Cases of Conscience* duties toward one's neighbor are spelled out in tedious detail in Book v, which follows in a general sense the order of the ten commandments. But the longest section is that on the Seventh Commandment, which is entitled "Luxury" (*C.* v, pp. 211–19). This is violated by an excess of things used to deck the body, which leads one to uncleanness, and which inclines a person to "melt in luxury" (*C.* v, p. 211). These sins are serious Ames believes, and are elaborated at great length, because they lead to many other faults. Even when an immodest act is "represented onely by the imagination and thought" with no intention to perform it, it is "wantonness" (*C.* v, p. 212). Dancing and common revelry which inflame the mind to lust are altogether to be condemned (*C.* v, p. 214). Stage plays mostly show wickedness, poeticizing and internalizing it, and they are utterly to be condemned (*C.* v, p. 216). For, Ames warns in terms modern critics of popular culture would endorse, "vices creep in more easily by pleasure" (*C.* v, p. 217). Not only do these plays consist in things forbidden, which find no support in Scripture, but Ames notes, replaying a typical Reformation complaint against such excess, for the cost of a play "many poore may bee sustained for some months." What about plays of biblical subjects? These too are forbidden, for such solemn themes fit poorly with the lightness

---

[38] *A Fresh Suit Against Human Ceremonies,* p. 287; see also p. 212. Subsequent pages in the text are to this work.

and scurrility of plays, and are spoiled with such use. "If choice of the two were to bee granted," says Ames echoing the feelings of many Elizabethan divines, "it seemeth more sufferable that prophane rather than sacred stories should be acted by players. For the majesty of the Word of God, which ought to be heard, and thought on with feare and trembling, is debated [*sic*], spoiled, and abused in an unworthy manner, if it bee turned into a matter of sport" (*C.* v, p. 219). For all these things may threaten that pearl of great price, with which Ames ends his work: contentment. "Bee not to carefull of those things which belong to the present life," Ames pleads (*C.* v, pp. 292, 293), use them as though you had them not. In this way life can be lived to the good of our neighbor and glory of God, and enjoyed with a peaceful conscience.

William Ames wanted to emphasize the practice of theology over speculation, piety over controversy and the simple explaining of Scripture over philosophy. But ironically he did as much as any seventeenth-century thinker to further a speculative and polemic approach to theology. Perhaps a combination of his temperamental response to his difficult circumstances, together with a constricted theological vision, inclined him in this uncompromising direction.[39] In any case Ames did not exercise a creative influence on the tradition of Calvin; he felt the need of drawing the boundaries and setting the stakes even more firmly than Calvin.[40] But, seen from the perspective of a seventeenth-century person, it was precisely Ames's system and the clarity it seemed to introduce to thought that proved most influential. The thrust of Ames's theology caught the imagination of the Puritans: all truth emanates from God and can be understood in a vast scheme that is reflected both in the world God has made and (potentially at least) in the world that humans reorder by their artifice. This meant that all the projects, the "arts," that people undertook in the new world took on this character of a simple application of God's word.

But this plain order that Puritans followed in home, church and community should not be confused with a lack of what we would call imagination. For as Theodore Bozeman notes: "Movement toward the simpler was, not a careless relaxation, but an act of organized discipline and self-denial."[41] In an important sense it was also an act of imaginative construction of life and the world. And Ames believed this constructed order was theologically grounded. It was precisely their faith in a God who ruled creation and

---

[39] This is an argument that Janice Knight makes in *Orthodoxies in Massachusetts,* pp. 60–1.
[40] Sprunger notes this is true of most theologians of that century, who were "competent systematizers, but not creators of a new theology" (*Learned Doctor,* p. 259).
[41] *To Live Ancient Lives,* p. 44.

history with a strong and loving hand that led these theologians to search for order. As Perry Miller put this, these Puritans were "cosmic optimists" and this optimism led them to look for, and sometimes impose, an order on things.[42]

The centrality of Scripture, both in public and private lives, was critical for Ames and Puritan theology generally. But in the case of Ames, and even more for Cotton whom we review next, Scripture was not so much an answer book for the problems of life, as a rich imaginative source for the living of their lives. Perry Miller, in his pioneering description of Puritan thought, argued that Puritan thought wrestled with two incompatible notions: their intoxication with an absolute and sovereign God and their need to rationalize and explain the world.[43] Recent scholars have shown that this tension was overstated and that Puritans were able to hold both these ideas together quite happily.[44] The reason for this is that the biblical God had laid out the order in the scriptural story that could provide a script for lives well lived.[45] Meditation on this story provided an imagination that was often richly allegorical and figurative.

But Ames's contribution to the development of this imaginative world was limited by his focus on the will and the moral life. Here he reflects a somewhat different tension within the Puritan mind, that between the external focus on order and inner elaboration of images and feelings. Not that Ames did not speak of joy or the pleasure of life lived in the presence of God, but for him the focus came to rest more on the cultivation of the will, which, Ames argued, is the center of theology.[46] Nor did Ames overlook the central importance of the life of prayer for the Christian, but this too is primarily a matter of presenting our will to God (*M.* ii, ix, 1). This focus grew naturally out of Ames's intense desire to see religion practiced, especially in view of a Dutch Church he saw lacking such godliness. It led to what he regarded as his most important work, the *Cases of Conscience*. Conscience he described as a contemplative judgment, belonging to the

---

[42] Perry Miller, *The New England Mind: The Seventeenth Century, and Orthodoxy in Massachusetts, 1630–1650* (1933; reprt. Gloucester, Mass.: Peter Smith, 1965) p. 148; though Knight argues that it was Cotton and his party who are the true cosmic optimists, rather than the more pessimistic Ames (*Orthodoxies in Massachusetts,* p. 159).

[43] See Miller, *The New England Mind.* These two modes of knowing, Miller believed, led to two aesthetics.

[44] See the review in David D. Hall, "A Reader's Guide to the New England Mind and the Seventeenth Century," *American Quarterly* 34/1 (1982), pp. 31–6.

[45] See on this George Marsden, "Perry Miller's Rehabilitation of the Puritans: A Critique." *Church History* 39 (1970), pp. 91–105.

[46] See *Technometria,* par. 117, *Marrow of Theology,* i, i, 9 and also *Conscience with power and cases,* i, p. 3.

understanding and not the will, which works "to the end that it may be a rule within him to direct his will."[47] This leads him to an important sense of religion as leading to the practice of God's will laid out in Scripture, and to a focus on the moral life as the place where God is imaged and seen. As he says in the *Marrow*: "The love toward God contained in religion of its own nature produces love toward men, for they are in some sort partakers in the image of God, therefore we are said to love God in men and men in God" (*M.* 1, xvi, 8). But this focus also carried the danger that the external practice can dominate the life of faith to such an extent that an inward openness to any direct experience with God, any stirring of the emotions, is suspect. Practice becomes the primary sign of godliness. And this tendency did more than anything to create the tension with which Ames's followers would wrestle in New England.

JOHN COTTON: DRINKING FROM THE FOUNTAIN

John Cotton (1584–1652) would pay homage to William Ames throughout his life, but his own theology clearly sprang from different sources. He enrolled in Trinity College, Cambridge in 1597, and so was a slightly younger contemporary of Ames. Perkins was not the means of his conversion, as he had been for Ames, but he was a troubling presence for Cotton. As his grandson Cotton Mather would put it, hearing Perkins preach, John Cotton was deeply troubled by the exclusive claim God seemed to lay on one's life. Cotton worried that "if he became a *godly* man, 'twould spoil him for being a *learned* one."[48] By this time the young Cotton had earned quite a reputation for himself as a preacher. A funeral oration he gave in 1609 was widely considered brilliant and he was called a new Xenophon throughout the university. He admits to breathing a sigh of relief when he heard the bells tolling for the funeral of Perkins.[49]

But another preacher of the time proved even more difficult for Cotton to ignore. In 1609 Richard Sibbes was made college preacher. His preaching was far less popular even than Cotton's but, in Cotton's case, it proved more effective. After considerable exposure to Sibbes's

---

[47] *Conscience with power and cases,* ch. 1, p. 2. Cf. Sprunger, *Learned Doctor,* pp. 169–70, who argues that Ames follows here the medieval tradition in which conscience is an act of practical judgment.
[48] *Magnalia Christi Americana: The Ecclesiastical History of New England* (Hartford: Silas Andrus & Son 1855 [1702]), vol. 1, p. 255; his emphasis.
[49] Larzer Ziff, *The Career of John Cotton: Puritanism and the American Experience* (Princeton University Press, 1962), pp. 18–19 and 28–9. I am dependent on Ziff for the account of Cotton's conversion. The three subsequent page references in the text are from Ziff. Also important is Cotton Mather, *Magnalia,* vol. 1, pp. 252–75. See also Everett H. Emerson, *John Cotton* (New York: Twayne Publishing, 1965).

preaching, Cotton became so troubled he even despaired of his salvation. For Sibbes preached in the plain style against negative righteousness, arguing that one could give all the outward signs of faith and not have that inward application of Christ's work (p. 30). After two years of uncertainty Cotton finally felt the quickening work of the Holy Spirit. The message of Sibbes that finally touched Cotton's heart was one Sibbes repeated frequently: "It is a sin for a child of God to be too much discouraged and cast down in affections." For grief and sorrow are meant to lead us to Christ (p. 31).

This word of Sibbes would become a touchstone of Cotton's own preaching. Sibbes was not the theologian that Perkins was; indeed he called himself a spiritual counselor and a physician of the soul. Similarly Cotton was more a pastoral theologian than Ames was. The relationship between Cotton and Sibbes would continue to be influential throughout their lives, as they worked together in England to bring about not simply reform but an inner renewal to the Anglican Church. Cotton especially was drawn by Sibbes's inclination to preach what Perkins apparently denied: a universal calling from a great and loving God (p. 32).

Not long after his conversion it became Cotton's turn to preach at St. Marie's and he suffered deep anguish. Should he follow the plainness of Sibbes and thus, he felt, confirm the prejudice that conversion stifled the creativity of the intellect? What of the reputation that he had earned for himself? After a long struggle he decided he had to preach the simple truth as he had come to believe it. As Cotton Mather put it: "He considered it was his duty to preach with such plainness, as became the oracles of God, which are intended for the conduct of men in the paths of life, and not for theatrical ostentations and entertainments, and the Lord needed not any *sin* of ours to maintain his own glory."[50] The results were not unexpected. The crowd who came to hear Cotton's eloquence pulled their caps down around their ears and when the preacher had finished his simple proclamation of repentance there was an ominous silence instead of the usual hum of approval. Nevertheless a clear confirmation of God's approval appeared later that day while Cotton sat in his room. One of the wittiest and most eloquent fellows of the university, John Preston, knocked on his door and confessed that God had so touched his heart that morning that he had seen for the first time the uncertainty of his own salvation. He asked Cotton for prayer.[51]

---

[50] *Magnalia*, vol. I., p. 256; his emphasis. Cf. Ziff: Cotton was "convinced that the plain style was the saving style and he realized that he must abandon his elegant oratory" (*Career of John Cotton*, p. 32).

[51] Ziff, *Career of John Cotton*, pp. 32–3. He comments that after Sibbes had brought about Cotton's conversion "it was in this tradition rather than in that of William Perkins that he taught" (p. 41).

John Preston too would work closely with Cotton, Sibbes and later John Davenport, becoming in effect the tactician of the closely knit Sibbesians, as they came to be known. Like Ames these were nonseparating Puritans, but, unlike Ames, they were willing to compromise and make strategic retreats to maintain their positions in the Church.[52] In 1612 Cotton left his fellowship at Cambridge to minister to the largest parish church in England, St. Botolph's in Boston, Lincolnshire, with 1500 communicants. And while he gradually grew in his noncomformist convictions, by subtle indirection, he was able to stay in this strategic position until he left for New England in 1633. Often when challenged on his views he professed himself to be unsure of what Christians should do and willing to listen and learn. During a disturbance at St. Botolph's in April 1621 windows, ornaments and statues were destroyed. When Cotton was called to account, he commented "they might as well refuse the king's coyne because crosses were on it, as forbidd the crosses [in church]." At another point he noted that his congregation was really so large that there was hardly room for them to stand let alone kneel! When further examined by the Bishop Monteigne he was offered restoration if he agreed to kneel just once at taking Eucharist, or "show good reason why he would not." Cotton chose the latter and sent along this simple verse:

> Cultus non institutus, non est acceptus:
> Genuflexio en perceptione Eucharistiae est cultus non institutus;
> Ergo, non est acceptus.[53]

He was promptly restored to his parish.

THE INFLUENCE OF RICHARD SIBBES

Richard Sibbes was clearly the spiritual father of this circle and, because he too kept many of his views on Church order secret, he went on to have a distinguished career at Cambridge, as a lecturer at Trinity then Grey's Inn and eventually as Master of St. Catherine's College.[54] He died unmarried in 1635. His collected works run to seven volumes and are filled with spiritual counsel and admonitions to seek God's mercy. One of the most interesting and positive descriptions of the godly use of the imagination is to be found in a small work of his entitled "The Soul's Conflict with Itself,"

---

[52] Knight, *Orthodoxies in Massachusetts*, pp. 40–2, 65.
[53] Ziff, *Career of John Cotton*, p. 53. A cult that is not instituted is not accepted/Kneeling before the Eucharist is not instituted/therefore it is not accepted.
[54] Knight, *Orthodoxies in Massachusetts*, pp. 41–2.

and written probably in the 1620s.[55] Sibbes acknowledges that the soul is often troubled, searching for the "beauty" of a well-ordered soul, often feeling the lack of spiritual means. He goes on to describe how one can know of victory without yielding to pride, or persevere in testing without despairing. Chapter Thirteen is entitled: "Of Imagination, sin of it, and remedies for it." The imagination he admits is the source of much disquiet in our souls. That is because the imagination is simply "a shallow apprehension of good or evil taken from the senses" (p. 178). It sets too great a store on "sensibly good things." The problem of course is that since the fall, our judgment in these matters is overturned. So what is sensibly good is often evil, and vice versa (p. 179). As a result much of our lives is given over to vanity, what he calls "fancy," that is the search to please or be great "sensibly."

Imagination, however, though it is a "windy thing," does have real effects. It stirs up affections, which move spirits and humours and thus the whole person (p. 180). The remedy is to bring these risings of our souls under the obedience of God's truth and spirit, rather than being led by appearances. These are after all but shadows of the true realities which religion affords.[56] The only way to counter the "sickness of fancy" that lies in all of us is to propose "true objects": the greatness of God, joys of heaven and so on (p. 181). New England poet Ann Bradstreet could have had these words of Sibbes in mind when she wrote this for her children in the 1650s: "The reason why Christians are so loath to exchange this world for a better is they have more sense than faith: they see what they enjoy; they do but hope for that which is to come."[57]

But significantly Sibbes goes on to propose a positive use of the imagination. Though its focus is on what is outwardly pleasant, not what is moral or immoral, we must "make our fancy serviceable to us in spiritual things" (p. 185). For "putting of lively colours upon common truths hath oft a strong working both upon the fancy and our will and affections" (p. 184). God himself presents heavenly things in earthly terms – portraying the Christian life as a great banquet, or a marriage. In a way that recalls Calvin, and even

---

[55] *The Complete Works of Richard Sibbes,* ed. Alexander B. Grosart (Edinburgh: James Nichol, 1862), vol. 1, pp. 130–294. Subsequent pages references in the text are to this work. On the influence of Sibbes generally as well as on Cotton, see Mark E. Dever, *Richard Sibbes: Puritanism and Calvinism in Late Elizabethan and Early Stuart England* (Macon, Ga.: Mercer University Press, 2000). He notes that the "Soul's Conflict with Itself" has been called the first Puritan work on the imagination in the seventeenth century (p. 140n20).

[56] The Platonic influence on this picture is apparent, especially when below he argues that imagination must be "bridled with reason" (p. 183).

[57] *Meditations Divine and Moral,* XIII, in *The Works of Anne Bradstreet,* ed. Jeannine Hensley (Cambridge, Mass.: Harvard University Press, 1967), p. 274

surpassing him, Sibbes is able then to propose a positive and creative role for this faculty. "Whilst the soul is joined with the body, it hath not only a necessary but a holy use of imagination and of sensible things whereupon imagination worketh." But how is this grounded? In our customary use of the sacraments, Sibbes argues, and the theology that undergirds that. For, he goes on to say: "What is the use of the sacraments but to help our souls by our sense and our faith by imagination?" (p. 185). Of course imagination doesn't invent truths, but it is useful in proposing or showing examples that we or others may follow. Indeed we should every morning "strengthen and perfume our spirits with some generous meditations" (p. 186).

Contrary to the argument of Peter Ramus, Sibbes assumes images can embody truth and make it winsome. Sibbes here virtually paraphrases Philip Sidney's defense of poetry published a generation earlier (in 1595). Sydney's work was a direct response to the attack on imagery in people like Philip Stubbs that we reviewed in the last chapter. The philosopher and the historian can only use precept and example, Sidney had pointed out, but the poet "giveth a perfect picture of it in someone by whom he presupposeth it was done."[58] The philosopher (or we might add the theologian) only describes verbally what is to be done or what is true, while poetry yieldeth an image to the mind. "Poetry ever sets virtue so out in her best colors . . . that one must needs be enamoured of her" (p. 90). And since moving is higher than teaching ("For who will be taught if he be not moved with desire to be taught?"), poetry is higher in not only showing the way, but enticing "any man to enter into it" (p. 92). In lines composed in the same years Sibbes was preaching his sermon, George Herbert would write in "The Church-Porch":

> Hearken to a verser, who may chance
> Ryme thee to good, and make a bait of pleasure.
> A verse may finde him, who a sermon flies,
> And turn delight into a sacrifice.[59]

Sibbes's own preaching and teaching could develop striking imagery. For example he speaks on one occasion of seeking God.[60] God comes to us "out

---

[58] *A Defence of Poetry, Miscellaneous Prose of Sir Philip Sidney,* ed. Katherine Duncan-Jones and Jan van Dorsten (Oxford: Clarendon Press, 1973), p. 85. Subsequent pages in text are to this work. For the iconophobic context of Sidney's work, see Collinson, *Birthpangs of Protestant England,* pp. 112–13.

[59] *Works of George Herbert,* p. 6. Janice Knight underlines the strong affinities of Herbert's poetry with the Sibbesians (see *Orthodoxies in Massachusetts,* pp. 72, 114, 148).

[60] "The Successful Seeker," in *Works,* vol. VI. Though published posthumously (1639), this was no doubt from a manuscript of a sermon he had preached (pp. 111–32). Subsequent pages in the text. Mark Dever notes that this gave Sibbes a very different take on the Covenant theology he had

of that hidden light that he dwells in" (p. 111). Sibbes notes that God is not content to come alone to us; everything he has made speaks of his light, so if we are in any dark condition the fault does not lie in God (p. 112). God is willing, indeed anxious to be known; his goodness is communicative, it is spreading. "God useth his creatures . . . for the spreading of his goodness" (p. 113). We too can borrow this goodness and we are most like God when we too communicate this goodness to others (p. 114). This naturally calls to mind the incarnation, and indeed Sibbes goes on to give this a Christological focus. This divine communication is best seen in our savior Christ: "You see what world a were [*sic*] beholding to him; heaven and earth were beholding to him" (p. 114). So the nearer we are to Christ the more self-denial to do good to others will be evident. For "a public mind is God's mind." As so often in Sibbes and Cotton, one can hear rhythms that will be taken up by Jonathan Edwards a century later.

John Cotton was close to many who sailed with John Winthrop for New England in 1630 on the ship *Arbella* and in fact he was asked to preach the farewell sermon on board before it sailed.[61] Pressure on the Puritans had been growing as anti-Calvinist sentiments increased, and Cotton began to wonder how long he could hold out. In 1631 after a long bout of sickness, he lost his wife Elizabeth and was left a widower and childless. In 1632, after remarrying a widow Sarah Hawkridge, word came that he was being summoned before the high court to answer before William Laud – who was about to be made Archbishop. So, as many before him, he disappeared into the Puritan underground. After thinking to go to Holland, in June of 1633 he finally set sail for New England, at 48 years of age beginning a new life barely five months before the revered Ames would die of fever in Rotterdam.[62]

In his sermon to those on board the *Arbella* in 1629 he had urged them not to be "unmindful of the Jerusalem at home," and in his new home he heeded his own advice. While others sought his services he accepted a call from the church in new Boston, where the greater part of immigrants from his home in Lincolnshire had settled. He announced that the faithful

---

inherited. "In Sibbes' sermons God's testaments were testimonies of his love, and the conditions of the covenant were the Savior's wooing of the beloved" (*Richard Sibbes*, p. 115).

[61] Later published as *God's Promise to his Plantation* (London: William Jones, 1630). This sermon ends interestingly with an appeal for concern for the native inhabitants. "As you reape their temporalls, so feede them with your spirituals . . . who knoweth whether God have [*sic*] reared this whole plantation for such an end" (pp. 19–20).

[62] Ziff, *Career of John Cotton*, p. 70. For the general background with respect to cultural developments, see Collinson, *Birthpangs of Protestant England*, pp. 118–20. Collinson notes that after a time when Puritanism seemed growing in strength, Laud introduced a strong anti-Calvinist reaction that was accompanied by major liturgical enrichment and the return of imagery.

at St. Botolph's wanted him to "minister in this country to such of their town as they had sent before hither, and such others as were willing to go along with me or to follow after me."[63] So he was appointed teacher to the church, whose minister was John Wilson. No sooner had he arrived than the seeds were sown for a controversy that would shortly reveal the differences between the followers of Ames and those of Richard Sibbes.

Cotton's ministry immediately met with unusual success, as John Winthrop reports in his journal:

It pleased the Lord to give special testimony of his presence in the Church of Boston, after Mr. Cotton was called to office there. More were converted and added to that church, than to all the other churches in the bay . . . Divers profane and notorious evil persons came and confessed their sins . . . Yea the Lord gave witness to the exercise of prophecy.[64]

Thus began something of an awakening among the churches that Jonathan Edwards would recall one hundred years later.[65] Much to the delight of the population, weekday preaching was instituted not only in Boston but in churches throughout the area. People flocked to hear the sermons, took notes and discussed the fine points of theology in their homes. So popular did the lectures prove to be for colonists eager for entertainment, that they neglected their work and the ministers had to agree to reduce the sermons to two days a week on a kind of rotating schedule.[66]

William and Anne Hutchinson, who had been devoted members of Cotton's congregation in old Boston, followed Cotton to New England in 1634, and immediately joined his church. Soon Anne became known as an effective midwife and spiritual counselor to the women of Boston.[67] At some point she began to hold discussions in her home to discuss the previous week's sermons. These proved so popular that she had to organize a separate series for men (p. 5). She immediately noticed and pointed out a difference between the preaching of her beloved Cotton and the others: one side she called the "legalists" who saw some necessary connection between a person's "works" and redemption; the other side saw grace as immediate

[63] John Cotton, "Reasons for his Removal to New England," in Young's *Chronicles of Massachusetts*, p. 440, quoted in Ziff, *Career of John Cotton*, pp. 81–2.
[64] Winthrop, *Journal*, I, 116; quoted in Ziff, *Career of John Cotton*, p. 106.
[65] Edwards notes of this revival that by a counterfeit of true religion Satan prevailed "to quench the love and spoil the joy of her espousals about a hundred years ago" (see *Religious Affections*, p. 87).
[66] Ziff, *Career of John Cotton*, pp. 106–7. Ziff notes: "For such colonists, sermons were the great episodes in lives of material privations and recreational restrictions" (p. 106).
[67] For what follows see David D. Hall (ed.), *The Antinomian Controversy, 1636–1638: A Documentary History*, 2nd edn (Chapel Hill: Duke University Press, 1990), for the historical background see the Introduction, pp. 3–23. Pages in the text are from this work.

and supernatural preceding any work on the part of the person. It did not take people long to wonder whether Cotton was not behind Hutchinson's accusations (p. 6). And initially Cotton did defend Hutchinson, insisting that God did not demand that one prepare oneself to receive grace. Faith was an effect not a condition of God's grace (p. 19). The Orthodox followers of Ames, represented primarily by Thomas Hooker, Peter Bulkeley and Cotton's own colleague John Wilson, meanwhile insisted that some outward behavior could, indeed must, be taken as a sign that justification has truly taken place (p. 13). The dispute split the New England clergy and led in 1636 to open charges and finally in 1637 to a synod, where a compromise was reached in which Cotton conceded the validity of the major charges of the "orthodox." Still, Hall says, "though his opponents may have agreed to tolerate Cotton's theology, it was their own synthesis of moralism, activism and voluntarism that came to prevail in New England" (p. 20).

Anne Hutchinson was accused of dividing the ministers between those who taught a covenant of works and Cotton who spoke of a covenant of grace – although Cotton himself regretted she had introduced the division in that way. Her trial over this issue dragged on inconclusively for several days. But the issue over which she was finally condemned and banished from the colony was her claim to have received a word from God. She recounted her experience of sorting out the false from the true testifying: "I bless the Lord, he hath let me see which was the clear ministry and which the wrong."[68] Subsequently she asked rhetorically: how could she be condemned for "speaking what in my conscience I know to be truth" (p. 337). But, they wondered, how did she know this to be the Spirit speaking to her? Just as Abraham knew that God asked him to offer his son, she responded. "By an immediate voice?" they asked. "So to me by an immediate revelation," she replied (p. 337). One can almost hear the collective gasp in the transcripts. This admission eventually became the decisive charge in the trial – to allow special revelation was to undermine the order of the whole community. While Cotton would later claim not to support all that Hutchinson taught, the issue on trial was centrally related to his own emphasis on God's immediate work, over against the outward evidence of morality. When asked during the trial if he believed her revelations to be true, Cotton could only reply: "That she may have some special providence of God to help her is a thing that I cannot bear witness against" (p. 341). In an important sense the antinomian controversy was about the ways that

---

[68] "Examination of Mrs. Anne Hutchinson," in Hall (ed.), *Antinomian Controversy*, p. 336. Subsequent page references given in the text.

God's presence can be seen in the world. Hutchinson preferred not to tie God strictly to prescribed forms, a practice she associated with legalism; the orthodox insisted that God's work must be tied to established means: the word of Scripture read and heard and an appropriate ordering of one's life. Hutchinson wanted to preserve the freedom of the Spirit; they were concerned about the order of the community.

Anne Hutchinson, whatever her excesses, had picked up the major thrust of Cotton's (and Sibbes's) theology: the immediate and personal reception of grace in the human heart. The major emphasis of Cotton throughout his writings was on the overwhelming priority and miraculous character of God's work of grace in the believer. In *Gospel Conversion* (1646) he asks rhetorically: how can we bring forth good fruit until we have a good tree? "To works of creation there needeth no preparation; the almighty power of God calleth them to be his people . . . and by calling them to bee so, he maketh them to bee so."[69] The point is that God's grace is so powerful and indispensable that it overpowers believers and makes them new creatures. How then can sanctification be a cause or ground of our justification? This is "to build upon a false and sandy foundation," he says (p. 7). No, God must make us righteous by a "free promise of grace" (p. 9). Nothing, not even a renewed sense of conscience, is possible apart from the witness of the Spirit (pp. 17–18). For we do not even have eyes to see our gifts and duties, apart from this quickening. "No man can see his gifts and duties of sanctification in himself, but hee must first have seen Christ by faith, the Spirit of Christ enlightening his understanding in the knowledge of him" (p. 25). This then begets conditions in which our work becomes possible; the good fruit by which a good tree becomes known is a sign for others not ourselves (p. 29). Besides, the believer who has been made alive by the Spirit does not need this kind of external evidence. For "if John [in *I John*] could give sanctification for an evidence of adoption to such as knew their good estate before by the witness of the Spirit: This were but to light a candle unto the sun" (pp. 20, 21). In one sense this is reiteration of the great Reformation theme of justification by faith alone, but it is put into the context of Calvin's stress on human inability to do anything in respect to our salvation and the necessity of a quickening work of the Holy Spirit.

But a further element that contrasts markedly with Ames is Cotton's understanding of grace as personal. Cotton's grace is centered and

---

[69] John Cotton, *Gospel Conversion: Discovering whether any gracious condition or qualification are wrought in the soule before faith in Christ; How the assurance of a man's salvation is to be evidenced. The Manner of the Soul's Closing with Christ* (London: J. Dawson, 1646), p. 5. Subsequent page references given in the text.

personalized in the believer's relationship with Christ. In 1651 a series of sermons preached in old Boston between 1612 and 1632 was published under
the title *Christ the Fountaine of Life*.[70] Worship, properly speaking, Cotton
says, consists in esteeming Christ highly while we are humbled. But "we
may be sure we could never have thus prized him, but he first prized us"
(p. 8). Significantly the "true worship of Christ," he says, is worked out *in
our minds* in two ways. First we become inquisitive to know all the virtues
that are to be found in Christ. Secondly we come to have a deep affection
of our hearts in Christ as our chiefest good (p. 9). Thus worship consists in
these two elements: the judgment (will) and the affections. The book then
goes on to describe these virtues and this affection.

Being made partakers of the covenant which God has made we are able,
Cotton says, to see his promises in all the blessings of this life, in his supply
of whatever is needful (p. 33). "This do we desire of God when we desire
him to be our God, God is an heape and fountaine of goodness, and he
undertakes so to be to us"(p. 33). This we can come to know and see in our
experience with God. But beyond this, Cotton implies that it is primarily
in our mind, or better our imagination in the sense of our mental shaping
of our world, that we see this rule of Christ realized. To be ruled by Christ
in all things, Cotton says, is to let him be our prince. And this rule is
fundamentally a matter of the way we think about things. Without Christ,
Cotton notes, one does not have good thoughts in one's mind, or if one by
chance comes across something good, it is not given lodging – for "every
imagination of his heart is evil." But by contrast for a godly man "if a good
motion come into him, it is most welcome to his soule and he entertains
it with the gladness of his spirit" (p. 83). And this is a good practice, for,
echoing Sibbes, Cotton notes that "good thoughts are of everlasting use,
and of everlasting durance, and they will continue to everlasting life" (p. 85).
What is true of thoughts by extension is also true of our words and actions.
Such practices center on a continuing meditation on Christ. Cotton goes
on to describe the meditative habit of mind that reinforces this rule of
Christ in our hearts. This is based of course on the word of God which
is preached and heard and which possesses mighty power (p. 199). But
beyond the word preached there is a similar power in meditating on it day
and night. "You should finde a mighty power in it to fructifie, as if you
are planted by the rivers of waters, for the Spirit of God breathing in the
word, and your hearts sucking it up and by meditating upon it, you grow

---

[70] *Christ the Fountaine of Life; Sundry choyce Sermons . . . of First John* (London: Robert Ibbitson, 1651).
Future references will be given as page numbers in the text.

in more knowledge in the object of your faith" (p. 206). By this meditating one may grow in knowledge and in the object of faith and especially in the actions which are the fruit of one's faith.

Cotton, like Perkins, here directs reflection on Christ's rule inward, to the reflections and meditations of the heart. But unlike Perkins it is imagery – hospitality, fountains and rivers of waters – that forms the warp and woof of this process, not as in Perkins the rational reflection on correct doctrine. Indeed, as we have seen, Cotton was remarkably tolerant of those whose views and experiences were unusual – we should not be any quicker to give up on these, he insisted, than Christ is on us! Perhaps this was because of Cotton's stress on grace as a personal welcome, rather than a commodity.

Finally, in Cotton's view this grace as miraculous intervention and as personal presence is meant to become for the believer a lived narrative. In continuity with all the major reformers Cotton believed that Christians were now living in the new order that Christ brought about by his life and death, which was at the same time the "last days" before his return. Cotton also shared with most of his contemporaries the eschatological understanding of the events of the settling of New England. God had directed them to establish in New England a pure church that would realize the Holy Commonwealth. This is seen, for example, in Cotton's treatment of Revelation and of the Song of Songs.[71] The believer is invited to share in these providential events. The theme of living in the light that Christ has brought about runs throughout Cotton's preaching and writing, but is perhaps seen most clearly in *The Way of Life* (1641).[72] In this work he begins by laying out the familiar contrast between the darkness and bitterness in which we naturally lived and the light and life that comes when God opens our eyes. Our darkness can be turned to good account if it forces us to cast ourselves upon God's mercy. Previously (during Old Testament times) one walked in "shadows and vailes," now "the Lord dispenseth a plentifull measure of grace, not only upon ministers, but upon all sorts of Christians" (p. 96). By his Spirit Christ dispenseth more of himself so that the least confessors of Christ "saw more of Christ, then [*sic*] any while he lived on earth" (p. 99). How can we not relish this glory! This involves the Christian then in living a whole new life, which Cotton describes as

---

[71] Mason Lowance says that "John Cotton was clearly the avenue through which . . . the figural reading of Revelation . . . would enter the theological world of New England Puritanism" (*Language of Canaan*, p. 41).

[72] *The Way of Life or God's way and course, in bringing the soule into keeping in and carrying it on the ways of peace and life* (London: By M. F. for L. Fawne and S. Gellibrand, 1641). Subsequent page references given in the text.

"keeping one's heart" (p. 203) in which we resort to God, call on his name and hear his word. This life which is lived in Christ changes everything. So that "whatever proceed from us, whether it be thoughts of the minde or affections of the heart, or words of our lips, or wayes of our whole man, they are lively and spirituall" (p. 213).[73]

Christians then are called to live in the light of Christ's life and death but not simply as events in the past but as that which gives meaning to the present. Images of a daily battle or a journey are common in Cotton's writings. He begins his famous exposition of Revelation sixteen with the following admonition: as you go about settling this new world "take the Lord Jesus Christ along with you, and take rivers and fountaines of waters, that as you look for rivers and fountaines for the refreshment of your cattle, and servants and children, you may finde a living fountaine of the blood of Christ."[74] Note that this use of scriptural imagery was subordinated to the larger purpose of Cotton's sermons, which was to prick the conscience and bring hearts under the obedience of Christ. As Larzer Ziff points out, for Cotton the sermon was more of an act than a product, "having a future in its human consequences rather than in its form."[75] So images were not important in themselves but in what they brought about; they were both the picture and the medium of the history that God was enacting in New England. Christians were not only meant to listen to this history but in a very real sense to participate in it. This led Cotton to introduce during his early years in New England the practice of adding to the usual requirements for Church membership the narrative of conversion.[76] This confession was to narrate the course of the "grace of God to his soule." As Cotton described this narrative: "In the profession of his faith, he declareth not onely his good knowledge of the principles of religion, but also his professed subjection to the Gospel of Christ, with his desire of walking therein, with the fellowship of that church."[77]

---

[73] Notable is the lengthy section in this work in which Cotton deals with the implications and applications of this life of faith to a "warrantable" calling and the public good (for which God gifts one and to which he leads one), pp. 245, 439–40.

[74] *The Pouring out of the Seven Vials or an Exposition of Chapter sixteen of Revelation with an application of it to our time* (London: for R. S., 1642), Third Vial, p. 24.

[75] *Career of John Cotton,* p. 159. He notes the consistency of this with Puritan eschatology, but it also resonates with the desire to "conceal art" within the higher purposes of ministry, which we examine in the next chapter.

[76] See Patricia Caldwell, *The Puritan Conversion Narrative: The Beginnings of American Expression* (Cambridge University Press, 1983), esp. pp. 64–6. She argues that this narrative voice is the beginning of the distinctive American voice in literature.

[77] John Cotton, *The Way of the Churches of Christ in New England* (London: By Matthew Simmons, 1645), p. 55.

The miracle of grace is personalized in Christ and takes shape in the narrative of a person's life. Both of these elements are critical for the way in which Cotton believed we lay hold on God and the world. For Cotton the call to live out the life of Christ is intrinsically figural. But the images we employ must be rigorously disciplined by the narrative in which Christians are to understand their lives, especially as this is grounded in Scripture. In a posthumously published piece, in common with all his contemporaries, he speaks critically of images, which are introduced by human design. There he defines an image as a figure "having relation to the examplar, or certaine pictures with relation of representation."[78] For this purpose only two ceremonies are stipulated, Baptism and Lord's Supper, which stimulate faith. "All signs of men's devising cannot teach or stir up true devotion, but delude and nourish superstition" (p. 9). Nor can anything be needed in the way of ceremony to "perfect" our worship; such additions are always injurious. Whether these images are physical or in the mind, if they are devised by "man" for religious use they are forbidden (p. 23). But, by contrast he asserts, biblical images are means to our spiritual health. So he says, echoing Calvin: "Christ crucified set before our eyes in the word and sacraments, is life and salvation" (p. 23).

This unique use of imagery marks a special contribution of Cotton to the development of the Protestant imagination, and to American art and literature more generally. On the one hand Cotton would have agreed with Perkins that we are to seek the single and literal meaning of Scripture. We have seen that he also endorsed the Puritan goal of the plain style, that is the iconoclastic scraping off the accretions of symbol or imagery that, over time, had come to obscure the simple truth of Scripture. But Cotton took a slightly different approach to the metaphors and symbols of Scripture that had troubled Calvin and Perkins. In his sermons he often uses the ramist method of analyzing by dichotomies, but what stays in the mind are not these structures, but the images he used: the fountain, the stream, the night and darkness giving way to the morning light. And while he would explain the meaning of these symbols in abstract terms, in the course of his sermons, again and again, he returns to the picture he has started with, so that what is left in the listener's (or reader's) mind is the image, enlivened, as it were, by the meaning he has given it. When he describes the loved one as a Dove in the Song of Solomon, for example, Eugenia Delamotte points out that Cotton uses repetition and parallelism to hold the image in the reader's mind so that "the total effect of the passage is not to strip away

---

[78] *Some Treasures Fetched out of the Rubbish* (London: n.p., 1660), p. 21. Subsequent pages in the text.

the metaphors, but to endow them with life."[79] The end result is that the meaning and the image (which often is visual or even tactile and not simply oral) are held together in a way that enhances the impact of the message.

Cotton seems to understand both the inherent power of language and, when it comes to conveying spiritual truth, its limitations. He insisted in *A Treatise of the Covenant of Grace* (1671) that we should not be afraid and "say we have no revelation but the word":

If there were no revelation but the word, there would be no spiritual grace revealed to the soul . . . But there is need of greater light, then [*sic*] the word of itself is able to give; for it is not all the promises in Scripture that at any time wrought any gracious change in any soul.[80]

It is true, he goes on to say, that there is no revelation that is not in accordance with the word. But the working of the Spirit goes beyond the word – this he urged the reader to consider as a "mystery of God." "That neither the word of grace nor all the works of grace, are able to clear up the grace of God unto the soul: it is the Spirit of God that must do it: he must *reveal* the grace of God if ever we see it."

These ruminations were understandably troubling to Cotton's colleagues who were more attuned to Ames's style of theology. During the antinomian debates such sentiments had caused Cotton's colleague Thomas Shepard to write Cotton on behalf of those troubled with things that Cotton had said about "revelations of the spirit." Among his queries was the following: "Whether this revelation of the spirit, is a thing beyond and above the word; and whether tis safe so to say; because the spirit is not separated from the word but in it and is ever according to it."[81] To this Cotton answered:

The word and Revelation of the spirit, I suppose doe as much differ, as letter and spirit. And therefore though I consent to you, that the spirit is not separated from the word, but in it, and ever according to it: yet above, and beyond the letter of the word it reacheth forth comfort, and power to the soule, though not above the sence and Intendment of the Word.[82]

In support for his view Cotton would not only have proposed the theological ground that the working of grace is finally a miracle wrought

---

[79] Eugenia Delamotte, "John Cotton and the Rhetoric of Grace," *Early American Literature* 21 (1986), p. 51. I am dependent here on her discussion of Cotton's imagery.
[80] *A Treatise of the Covenant of Grace,* 3rd edn (London: n.p., 1671), p. 178. His emphasis in the following quote.
[81] "Shepard–Cotton Letters," in Hall (ed.), *Antinomian Controversy,* p. 26.
[82] Hall, *Antinomian Controversy,* p. 30.

on the human soul, but also, a deeper trust in what the symbols and metaphors of Scripture may be allowed to do. They could be trusted, he would say, to strike the heart and the affections in a way that opens them up to this miraculous working. They should be liberated and not only explained.

Cotton in allowing a space in his theology for mystery also, analogously, opened up a place in culture for play. He was more tolerant than his colleagues about diversions – playing cards were not forbidden if not used for gain, music both secular and sacred is allowed, poetry is often praised (indeed he composed poetry himself for special events). A major thrust of his commentary on Ecclesiastes is to argue that we should not forbid the delights that God has allowed.[83] Probably the major legacy of Cotton in America is his work on the *Bay Psalm Book* (1640), considered the first book published in America. The singing of Psalms by the whole congregation during worship was of course the great contribution of Calvin's reformation. Cotton was a leading figure of the group that translated the Psalms into "a plaine and familiar translation of the Psalmes and w[o]rds of David into English metre" (Preface). Later in the preface he says we have a moral duty to sing David's Psalms (and others) because of the extraordinary gifts of the Spirit they represented ("common in those days"), not composing our own but joining together in one voice. The translators he noted sought to stay as close to the original as possible. Beauty and elegance then were not among their goals. "If therefore the verses are not always so smooth and eloquent as some may desire or expect: let them consider that God's altar needs not our polishing."[84]

Nevertheless such singing holds great promise for awakening the soul. For singing Psalms, he says in another place, "holdeth forth as much of Christ externally, as reading of the word, or as the hearing of it read or preached or as falling down upon our knees in prayer."[85] This is because they are accompanied by many gracious effects: they allay passions, scatter temptations, and assuage enmity, showing how much God "delighteth to bless the singing of his holy Psalms with gracious and spiritual affections" (p. 72). It is decidedly not the case then that God forbids the use of our spiritual faculties in thinking about God and our life with him, indeed God has amply provided images on which our soul can feed for its nourishment.

---

[83] Ziff, *Career of John Cotton*, p. 163.
[84] *Bay Psalm Book: The Whole Book of Psalmes Faithfully Translated into English Metre* (Cambridge: Daye, 1640), preface by John Cotton, not paginated.
[85] John Cotton, *Singing of Psalmes: A Gospel Ordinance* (London: M. S. for Hannah Allen, 1647), p. 4. Subsequent pages in the text.

But, in this respect at least, we are not to model God's work. God has provided the stories and images of Psalms to nourish our affections, though he forbids our making any "images or imaginations and inventions for worship" ourselves (p. 30). For these images we erect for our own pleasure; those God sets for his glory.

A PROFILE OF THE PURITAN IMAGINATION

Ames and Cotton are not the only important voices that we might hear, but they provide important clues of the various aspects of the Puritan sensitivities that will become decisive in the visual culture of the New World. Let us then briefly consider the way Puritans would have imagined their world, before we turn in the next chapter to examine the resulting cultural shape these sensitivities tended to take.

The major focus of the spiritual life, and therefore of the life of the imagination, is the life of the mind, or better, in Puritan terms, within the heart. Where Perkins turned his attention to reflection on biblical truth, or the "teaching" of God's character and of his work, Ames developed the notions of the models of "good practice" which could be laid out in diagrammatic form and clearly envisioned in the mind. Indeed it is hard to imagine anything more "visual" than the structure of the *Technometry* as it gives a visible form to the whole of God's truth. For John Cotton, following Sibbes, from the heart are the issues of life. For it is within the imagination (again in our modern sense) that we are to be grasped by our own weakness and sin and be led to turn to Christ who is the fountain of all good things God wishes to pour upon us.

For all three, as for most of their contemporaries, the turn toward the presence of God within was a turning away, not from culture and beauty, so much as from the vanity, suffering and death they saw around them in the world. In the case of the New England colonists, it was a turning from the unkempt wilderness in which God had placed them toward an ordered community. In this respect John Milton captures something of the essence of this imaginative vision in *Paradise Lost*, when the Angel advises Adam and Eve after sending them out of the garden:

> Only add
> Deeds to thy knowledge answerable; add faith,
> Add virtue, patience, temperance; add love,
> By name to some called charity, the soul
> Of all the rest: then wilt thou not be loth

> To leave this Paradise, but shalt possess
> A Paradise within thee happier far.[86]

For within there is to be found the paradise of a mind disciplined by God's word, strengthened by these biblical virtues, but also, in Cotton's case, nourished by cool waters and fresh meats offered by the images of Christ's presence. For all of them in various ways a unique kind of "meditation" was required to nurture this life and gain one's emotional and spiritual balance.

This inward focus, and the resultant meditation it encouraged, became characteristic of Reformed spirituality and influenced the culture it produced in various ways. Barbara Lewalski has pointed out how different this was from an Ignatian type of meditation. In Catholic meditation:

the meditator typically seeks to apply himself to the subject, so that he participates in it; he imagines a scene vividly, as if it were taking place in his presence . . . The typical Protestant procedure is very nearly the reverse: instead of the application of the self to the subject, it calls for the application of the subject to the self – indeed for the subject's location in the self.[87]

This application of the subject underlines the fact that the inward reflection is part of a larger theological movement in which, to the Puritan imagination, God is restructuring lives and communities by the Word. Meditation then is not an escape so much as an inward appropriation of this movement. By this inward motion the believer is not being withdrawn from the world, but rather launched into it.

It is a commonplace that for both Ames and Cotton, the goal of preaching and teaching was to convey the simple truth of God's word in a way that was clear and accessible: what came to be known as the "plain style." In this they continued the tradition of Calvin for whom perspicuity of scriptural truth was to be reflected in the preacher's style. But it would be a mistake to see this impulse as merely a philistine desire to destroy what is "merely" ornamental in the interest of what is literal. Here we recall that the energy behind iconoclasm, as we have argued, was not simply negative but in important senses socially and culturally constructive. There was a sense

---

[86] *Paradise Lost,* XII, 581–7, in *The Complete Poetical Works of John Milton,* ed. Douglas Bush (Boston, Mass.: Houghton Mifflin, 1965), p. 458. Peter Harrison points out how widespread was the notion of the "paradise within" during this time, but argues that this represents "the last gasp of a dying world view" – given the rise of the empirical sciences and their Baconian quest to restore the earth to its pristine condition (*The Bible, Protestantism and the Rise of Natural Science* [Cambridge University Press, 1998], p. 209–11). We will argue that these conceptions did not necessarily compete with each other, rather they could be mutually reinforcing.

[87] Cf. Barbara Lewalski's contention that this issued in a unique Protestant "genre" of literature, the devotional lyric (*Protestant Poetics and the Seventeenth Century Religious Lyric* [Princeton University Press, 1979], p. 149).

in which the old order, which had become, to their thinking, so corrupt and repressive, had to be deconstructed so that something new could be built. Similarly in the experience of John Cotton especially, it became clear that his rejection of the classical style of rhetoric was a deconstruction that reflected his personal rejection of pride and self-seeking, as Cotton Mather put it in his discussion of John Cotton's plain style. The oracles of God "are intended for the conduct of men in the paths of life, and not for *theatrical* ostentations and the Lord needed not any *sin* of ours to maintain his own glory."[88] The point was that preaching was to bring about a conviction of sin and faith, and the means were to be strictly subordinated to these ends. Means that were inherited from the classical tradition, associated as they were with unreformed, and therefore lifeless, churches, were eliminated. But images and stories that Scripture used were exploited in various ways to bring about the needed "pricking" of the heart. And in the development of (especially) the literary culture of the seventeenth century these resources proved extremely fruitful. Indeed it is difficult for a modern person to read Puritan sermons in any number and understand how in fact they exhibit any plainness, beholden as they are to the richness of the biblical world.

But this suggests a positive element of the "plain" tradition: it sought to reorder, or better, to construct a new order. Here we recall Bozeman's helpful description of the Puritan desire to reorder life after the ancient biblical patterns. This was not simply a careless relaxation of effort, nor we might add, merely a removal of ornament to get at some substratum of truth, it was an "act of organized discipline and self-denial."[89] That is to say, putting together life after the biblical patterns, or laying out its truth in the form of an Amesian structure, was an energetic and creative wrestling with life. It was construction and not simply pruning. In the seventeenth century, as we will see in the next chapter, the concept of "artifice" was critical to understanding one's relation to the natural world as well as to the making of art (the "naturalness" of Dutch landscapes cannot be understood apart from this). This we argue correlates with the desire not simply to find order in the world, which indeed was not immediately visible to human eyes, but to construct an order which could be seen and inhabited.

But there could be no question of building an "imaginary" or "ideal" world. For the Puritans the Holy Commonwealth which they were called to build was carefully constructed out of biblical models and with ancient materials. We have noted that the Puritans were, in the words of David Hall, cosmic optimists and this led them to search for order in the events of

---

[88] *Magnalia,* vol. I., p. 256; his emphasis.   [89] *To Live Ancient Lives,* p. 44.

the world. It was because a sovereign God created, redeemed and sustained
the created order that they could set about building a community in the
confidence that they were working with the grain of things – that one
day their work would be approved and vindicated, indeed it would be
"perfected." And the grain of things was the providential direction of God
in all things.

Theodore Bozeman in his study of the Puritan experiment argues that
the dominant metaphor during the first generation of the New England
settlement was an intense desire to "relive" a biblical paradigm, to "live
ancient lives." He stresses their calling was to strenuously enter into the
narrative the bible presents. This he rightly sees as the purpose for the
destruction of the false forms of worship, "to return Christians more completely to the intense, richly imagined world of the biblical primordium."[90]
But he argues that their view of the past obstructs all their eschatological
fervor, and so he argues that millennialism played little role in their project.
Their orientation is toward the past, progress is made through regress and
recovery.[91] But this misconstrues the nature of the narrative, which Puritans believed they were living. It is precisely because the story includes the
future as well as the past that it provided them with a space in which they
could find their own place. And they believed they were living out a part of
that future story in which, as Cotton Mather famously put it, God's glory
was irradiating this barren wilderness. This gave meaning to their lives and
even to their deaths. It allowed them to see death, with which they lived so
incessantly, as firmly rooted in that future which God controlled – indeed
as something which could be memorialized in their art.

Because God directed the course of events, the Puritans could look out
on the world and see "providences" everywhere – in battles, illnesses, even
storms. The world they saw outside corresponded to the one that they
carefully lived through their prayers, readings and meditations – they could
"read it" in the light of Scripture. Just as Lady Margaret Hoby would not
have seen any conflict between the order she constructed in her daily activities and her inner life of prayer, the Puritans would see no conflict between
their Sabbath prayers and weekday sermons and their active building of the
Commonwealth. Though this building reflected a strong faith, for many –
as Keith Sprunger concludes of William Ames – this faith was more activist

---

[90]   Ibid., p. 33.
[91]   Ibid., pp. 218, 230. The weakness of Bozeman's argument in underestimating the centrality of Puritan
       eschatology leads him to see John Cotton as an exception to his thesis.

than pietist.[92] For John Cotton, by contrast, it was the humble openness to grace that was dominant. Because of this, Eugenia Delamotte argues that Cotton developed a rhetoric of grace which liberated his followers from that "nervous incessant activism" so common in New England.[93] Perhaps it is because Ames's followers became dominant, rather than Cotton's, that by the 1690s the spiritual energy seemed to be drained out of the community, and Increase Mather and others were busy writing texts that would restore a lost sacramental piety.[94] The history of these influences does not end here of course; it will continue to shape rationalist and evangelical sensitivities – what came to be called Old Lights and New Lights – in the eighteenth century. But meanwhile they will shape cultural developments of the seventeenth century in distinctive ways, with influences that continue into our own century. It is to an examination of these cultural forms that we turn in the next chapter.

---

[92] This is Sprunger's judgment of Ames (*Learned Doctor,* p. 261), but it is also true of many of his followers in New England.

[93] Delamotte, "John Cotton and the Rhetoric of Grace," p. 58. "Nervous incessant activism" is Michael Walzer's characterization of the Puritan type; see *The Revolution of the Saints: A Study of the Origin of Radical Politics* (Cambridge, Mass.: Harvard University Press, 1965).

[94] David Hall, "Literacy, Religion and the Plain Style," in Fairbanks and Trent (eds.), *New England Begins,* vol. ii, p. 109. On the decline of sacramental piety, see Elmer Holifield, "The Renewal of Sacramental Piety in Colonial New England," *William and Mary Quarterly* 29 (1972), pp. 33–48.

CHAPTER 6

Seventeenth-century visual culture

Sometime toward the end of the seventeenth century Puritan politician and magistrate Samuel Sewall records this experience while traveling:

I lodged at Charlestown, at Mrs. Shepards, who tells me that Mr. Harvard built that house. I lay in the chamber next to the street. As I lay awake past midnight, in my Meditation, I was affected to consider how long ago God made provision for my comfortable lodging that night; seeing that was Mr. Harvards house: and that led to think of Heaven the House not made with hands, which God for many Thousands of years has been storing with the richest furniture (Saints that are from time to time placed there), and that I had some hopes of being entertain'd in that Magnificent Convenient Palace, every way fitted and furnished. These thoughts were very refreshing to me.[1]

Several features of the Puritan imagination appear in Sewall's meditation. The first and most important is the way that the Puritan world was shaped by God's providences, on which one could consistently depend. These were a continual and refreshing subject of reflection, but they had to be constantly appropriated inwardly. Then there is the sense that this world's events are a prelude to what God is planning in the heavenly kingdom toward which life, inexorably, leads the believer. Moreover the events in this life, especially those pleasant providences – and we will see, experiences of beauty in particular – become signs of that other world, types of God's abundant provision which awaits in heaven. There is a sense in which aesthetic language terminates for the Puritans in the description of heaven, and of God's glory there. But it also elides with the language of personal holiness. As Richard Baxter says in a work widely read in New England during this time: "If we can get into the Holy of Holies, and bring thence the Name and Image of God and get it closed up in our hearts, this would

---

[1] *The Diary of Samuel Sewall: 1674–1729*, ed. M. Halsey Thomas (New York: Farrar, Strauss & Giroux, 1973), vol. I, p. 367; entry for January 26, 1696.

enable us to work wonders." Then he says we would speak the pure language of Canaan.[2]

The metaphor that Sewall uses, that of an architect and builder who fashions and furnishes a house, is significant for its use in shaping one's life and thoughts about God and the world. As we have observed, this metaphor of architecture harks back to the work of Calvin's *Institutes*, but beyond this to Scripture itself where believers, with Abraham, wait for a city whose builder and maker is God.[3] Life for Puritan believers was understood in terms of "providences" because it belonged to a larger story that God was shaping. While this was to be inwardly appropriated, by faith, it would also be reflected in the patterns and objects of cultural life.

At the beginning of the seventeenth century, pictures were banned from church walls – such external helps were no longer valued as a means of leading the worshiper to God. Rather through the ministries of teaching and preaching Christians were to be made vigilant over their inner thoughts that should focus on the holiness that God requires. For, at this point in Puritan history, hearing and meditating on the word had become the privileged means by which both the inner and outer world were to be disciplined. But as a critical component of this, the word itself became a constructive influence on the development of culture, including visual culture. The developing visual culture will not only reflect the negative theological principle articulated in the catechisms – that there can be no "likeness or agreement" between God and anything bodily, but positively it will increasingly depend on the actual shape and substance of Scripture itself. Not only did the words of Scripture come to replace images and pictures on the walls of churches, but, as Sewall's diary shows, their cadences and stories came to fill and shape the imagination of the people.

In the last chapter we argued that the theological principles of Calvinism as developed by Perkins, Ames and Cotton led to sensitivities that would prove decisive in the cultural production of the seventeenth century. The theological assumption of God's overpowering grace and human sin was interpreted in a particular way that led to a preoccupation with inward dispositions and feelings, to a determination to see life patterned in terms

---

[2] *Saints Everlasting Rest* (London, 1662), p. 639, quoted in Lowance, *Language of Canaan*, p. 16. We note below that Baxter's work was influential on Puritan reflection on heaven.
[3] Hebrews 11:10. See Catherine Randall's comments on Calvin: "The spatial terms used in the *Institution* sketch the visionary architecture of a redeemed world . . . [But meanwhile] for Calvin, architectural space is not remodeled; sacred and secular space will exist side by side until the invisible church is realized" (*Building Codes*, pp. 33, 37).

of a biblical truth simply seen and explained, and finally to a commitment to live one's life in terms of the narrative of this story. There would be variations in understanding these themes, but all of them will be decisive in some way on the literary and visual culture that is created. In this chapter we turn to a study of the way the visual culture of the century reflected these sensitivities. The major focus will be on New England, but we will note more briefly the influence of these views on the culture of England and Holland, up to 1633 – the year of Ames's death and Cotton's removal to New England.

One must be careful in assessing influences, especially in the case of Holland. The tolerance extended to the various denominations made Holland of the early seventeenth century a religiously diverse place – in some cities, for example, the Catholic population reached 50 percent. Moreover some of what is taken as Calvinist is simply a survival of pre-Reformation traditions associated with groups like the Devotio Moderna, to which we alluded earlier. Still one is hardly mistaken in saying that the general ethos of Dutch culture during this period was strongly influenced by Reformed perspectives. Christian Tümpel argues that after 1759 when Calvinism became the major religion the milieu in which art developed was "largely determined by Calvinism."[4] In any case, we are less interested in seeking specific influences than more general resonances with the theological tradition that we are tracing.

Certainly most people in this period were exposed to Reformed teaching not only in the specific catechizing they received in the English and Dutch Churches, but also in the biblical preaching that they heard in their churches week by week. We have noted repeatedly that the culture formed by the Calvinist Reformation was a preaching culture. This was based on the theological conviction that the preaching of Scripture was the primary medium of God's word. Sermons not only formed the basis of the spiritual life, but made up the substance of the cultural life of most churchgoing people (which is to say most of the population). The expository sermon by a gifted preacher would have been discussed at home, and along with the

---

[4] See Christian Tümpel, "Religious History Painting," in Albert Blankert, *et al.*, *God's Saints and Heroes: Dutch Painting in the Age of Rembrandt* (Washington, DC: National Gallery of Art, 1980), p. 45. This is true notwithstanding the fact individual artists may not have personally aligned themselves with the Reformed Church, or, as in the case of Rembrandt, belonged to more than one group. As A. T. van Deursen notes of Holland's formation: "Most of its leaders were going in the same direction. They based themselves on the model of Calvin" (*Plain Lives in a Golden Age: Popular Culture, Religion and Society in Seventeenth Century Holland,* trans. M. Ultee [Cambridge University Press, 1991], p. 260). The debate is reviewed and alternative views given in Maartin Ultee, "Review Article: The Riches of the Dutch Seventeenth Century," *Seventeenth Century Studies* 3 (1988), pp. 223–42.

regular reading of the bible during the week, it would have formed material for reflection and shaped attitudes toward life and work.[5] But, as Lady Margaret's diary reflects, bible reading also became a central component of domestic culture as well. The Geneva Bible had advised the reader to "diligently keep such order of reading the scriptures" as his work and other duties allow. But "at least twice every day this exercise to be kept . . . The time once appointed hereunto . . . be no [*sic*] otherwise employed."[6] The culture that this preaching and reading produced gradually came to take on the contour of this biblical world. The centrality and influence of biblical themes in all areas of life, Christopher Hill argues, brought about "a cultural revolution of unprecedented proportions."[7]

Before turning to a description of the culture that was produced we address the more general issue of the cultural style lying behind Puritan cultural production. As dramatically illustrated in John Cotton's conversion story, the preaching style that came to be influential was the plain style. William Perkins's work, *The Art of Prophesying*, became the guide for a generation of preachers. The art that Perkins encouraged was to simply read, expound and apply Scripture. The resulting impact depended not on human brilliance but on the power of the Holy Spirit. Early in this treatise he allows that a preacher may well consult philosophers or other learned men in sermon preparation, but when one mounts the pulpit to preach, "he ought in publike to conceale all these from the people and not to make the least ostentation." He goes on to quote the Latin expression: "artis etiam est celare artem [it also a point of art to conceal art]."[8] While much of the "plain style" would be most fully developed in New England, the notion of an "art that conceals art" becomes a major characteristic of art and culture more generally in England and Holland during the early seventeenth century.

That art should be concealed, or hidden, would have been motivated by two quite different factors during this period. The first, which we might call "Nicodemism," resulted from the fact that the arena for Calvinists during the early seventeenth century, whether of the Huguenots in France

---

[5] John Walford, for example, in his study of Dutch landscape artist Jacob van Ruisdael, has shown the role of the Dutch catechism and biblical themes in the development of themes in Ruisdael's art; see *Ruisdael and the Perception of Landscape* (New Haven: Yale University Press, 1991), pp. 19–21 and 33–8.

[6] From the Geneva Bible quoted in Collinson, *Birthpangs of Protestant England*, p. 124.

[7] Christopher Hill, *The English Bible and the Seventeenth Century Revolution* (London: Allen Lane/Penguin, 1993), p. 11.

[8] Perkins, "The Art of Prophesying," in *Workes of the Famous and Worthy Minister William Perkins* (London: John Legat, 1631), vol. II, p. 670. The expression can be traced to Ovid, *Artis amatoriae*, book ii, l, 313, (*c.* BC I), "If art is concealed it succeeds."

or radical Puritans in England, was frequently hostile to any open expression of Calvinist faith. This caused artists and writers to work by indirection, or in code. The most prominent expression of this, touched on earlier, was by Huguenot architects working for the king in France. Catharine Randall points out that even after the Edict of Nantes in 1598, "Calvinist architects would develop hermetic networks of self-protective symbols, requiring a discerning readership to puzzle out their connections."⁹ A major factor in this strategy was the politically hostile situation they faced, but this cultural style was also theologically grounded. Following Calvin these architects saw the "world as a confused hostile space" (p. 136) that had to be reordered according to the scriptural story of redemption – especially as this was laid out in the *Institutes* (p. 27). The architects' royal patron then often represented the hostile arena in which they were called to work. Their drawings and buildings had to fit with the purposes and designs of the patron, while subverting these designs in subtle ways. Their architecture was, in this respect at least, an act of cultural resistance.¹⁰

This cultural strategy deserves further study and may overturn many of the preconceptions about Calvinist influences on art during the early seventeenth century. For example, Menna Prestwich, in a study of Calvinist influence in France, admits that Huguenots Salomon de Brosse and Sebastian Bourdon played a role in the development of French classicism, but then concludes: "although neither de Brosse nor Bourdon wavered in his Calvinism, their styles were uninfluenced by their religion."¹¹ Randall shows that this judgment is clearly mistaken in the case of de Brosse, at least. De Brosse demonstrated his Calvinism in many, albeit subtle, ways. One way, evident in the Protestant Temple at Charenton, lies in the manner de Brosse concealed interior space through the two-tiered columns, as a response to the Edict of Nantes banning outward Protestant monuments.¹² It is known that these Protestants formed a close-knit group congregating in St. Germain, going to church together at Charenton. Moreover, six of the original twenty-four members of the Academy of Painting and Sculpture (founded in 1648)

⁹ *Building Codes*, p. 15. And subsequent pages in the text.
¹⁰ Ironically Calvin had spoken out strongly against the growing movement of "Nicodemists" during his time, arguing – disingenuously one might argue from the safety of Geneva – that this was contrary to the Gospel; see Wendel, *Calvin: Origins and Development*, pp. 47, 82. Though Randall's "hermetic" emphasis has been criticized by architectural historians, indirect communication was certainly more common than modern readers usually notice. We noted that this attitude of indirection characterized the party influenced by Richard Sibbes in England. Christopher Hill notes the common use of shorthand and code by Puritans in England up to 1640 (*The English Bible*, pp. 53–4).
¹¹ Menna Prestwich (ed.), *International Calvinism, 1541–1715* (Oxford: Clarendon, 1985) p. 13.
¹² *Building Codes*, p. 76. See also her references to de Brosse's work, pp. 7, 83.

were Huguenots.[13] Perhaps a closer study of these artists in terms of their need to "conceal" their references to Calvinist themes through code and indirection would give us a fuller picture of this aspect of the Protestant contribution to visual art even in France.

But there was another important motive for Calvinists to conceal their art that is more relevant to the situation in Holland and New England. From a Puritan or Calvinist perspective art always served the higher purpose of teaching or portraying truth that was essential for salvation. Painting in common with other arts had to be "useful." Art was still understood largely as a craft, and its producers considered they were simply playing a modest role in promoting godliness – which may account for the fact that most of the portraits painted in seventeenth-century New England were anonymous.[14] This is not to say that these portraits could not be significant works of art – they often were, but the aesthetic aspect would not have been considered valuable in itself. The situation was different in Holland, with its long tradition of arts and crafts, but even there we will argue the artistry and skill were frequently meant to be unobtrusive and serve other (moral and theological) ends. In this connection it is helpful to recall the impulse behind the iconoclastic temper of Protestantism. Iconoclasm sought to deconstruct the old order and its splendors because these were associated with pride and self-assertion – it was not a rejection of art that led Cotton to reject Renaissance oratory.[15] But the rejection was meant to serve a higher purpose; this pruning and planing was in the service of a new theological vision. In the seventeenth century, especially in Holland, this new vision is informed by Calvin's view of the world as a theater for the glory of God, and salvation is seen as a reordering of a fallen world. When remade, however, it would not necessarily call attention to itself.

---

[13] Prestwich (ed.), *International Calvinism*, pp. 11–12; original membership in the Academy is discussed in Philip Benedict, "Calvinism as a Culture?" in Paul Corby Finney (ed.), *Seeing Beyond the Word: Visual Arts and the Calvinist Tradition* (Grand Rapids, Mich.: Eerdmans, 1999), p. 36 and 36n54. Given that Protestants made up only 5 or 6 percent of the population, the fact they made up a quarter of the original membership of the Academy is surely significant. Prestwich notes that Sebastian Bourdon was among these founding members of the Academy, later becoming its rector (Prestwich [ed.], *International Calvinism*, p. 12).

[14] Ames's treatment of painting typically relegates it to one of the crafts (*Technometry*, par. 149). Gibbs comments on this: Ames's treatment of painting as a mechanical art indicates it "had not yet escaped from the stigma of being associated with manual or corporal labor" (p. 195). But as we have noted, this usefulness was for them an asset, not a liability.

[15] As John Phillips points out, such moral purposes had been behind the rejection of images by earlier humanists as well. Moral qualities were superior to intellectual ones, in their minds, so they had little patience with images "because they appealed to a 'grosser' side of man – ultimately with a human folly grown rampant" (*The Reformation of Images: 1535–1660* [Berkeley: University of California Press, 1975], p. 84).

The world that resulted should appear "natural" – simply a place where one could be at home. As Randall says of Palissy: "Palissy's garden renders literal Calvin's conception of believers as a new Garden of Eden."[16] Art would serve, *ancillae domini*, the goal of this redeeming of human life. So there are deep theological, as well as historical, reasons why art that grows out of this vision should conceal itself.

ENGLISH LITERARY CULTURE

While we cannot give close attention to the literature that has grown out of a Calvinist view of the world, some brief allusions may be illustrative of the developing imagination. Here we note briefly the ways that the English Puritan literature of the seventeenth century reflects the theological vision we have described.[17] Ernest Gilman argues that it is precisely the iconoclastic temper of Protestantism in its collision with Renaissance theory that creates the splendor of the poetry of the English Reformation. For these poets knew "the very imagining power of the mind was tainted by pride and sensuality of fallen humanity and open to the perils of worship misdirected from the creator to the creation," while at the same time they realized that the "word was the bulwark of the spirit against the carnal enticements of the image."[18] Their mistrust of the senses is clear in this Holy Sonnet of John Donne:

> When senses, which thy souldiers are,
> Wee arme against thee and they fight for sinne...
> When plenty, Gods image and seale
> Makes us Idolatrous,
> And love it, not him, whom it should reveale,
> When we are mov'd to seeme religious
> Only to vent wit, Lord deliver us.[19]

But despite this mistrust Donne can draw from the biblical store powerful images that feed the imagination. This was an art that grew from biblical

---

[16] *Building Codes,* p. 55.

[17] We do not speculate as to why these arts flourished, while painting and sculpture did not, indeed, we recognize that one cannot make any claims of simple cause and effect. We seek rather to find resonances, or echoes, between the theological vision and the art produced; see Erwin Panofsky, who noted that each place "developed its own kind of Protestantism and its own kind of art" ("Comments on Art and Reformation," p. 9). Barbara Lewalski distinguishes several poetic styles which Calvinism influenced, but we focus on elements broadly shared by these poets (see *Protestant Poetics,* pp. 217–26).

[18] Gilman, *Iconoclasm and Poetry,* p. 1, and see pp. 5–6. Christopher Hill argues that the biblical influence on literature created "the greatest age of English literature" (*The English Bible,* p. 335).

[19] "A Litanie," xxi, in *John Donne: The Divine Poems,* ed. Helen Gardner (Oxford: Clarendon Press, 1978), p. 23.

roots. As Barbara Lewalski notes, it was not as though these poets intended to be artless. Rather, following the precept of Perkins, they sought an "art whose precepts may be derived, and whose stylistic features may be imitated, from the Scriptures."[20]

These poets also reflected the inner orientation of Puritanism. For the metaphysical poets the focus sooner or later came to rest on the anguish of the human soul. For this is the site of the greatest struggle to embrace God's merciful presence, as George Herbert knew well:

> Sure there is room within our hearts good store;
> For they can lodge transgressions by the score;
> Thousands of toyes dwell there, yet out of door
> They leave thee.[21]

It is in the human heart where the decisive battle is fought, and where God's victory will be achieved or lost, as Donne stresses in this sonnet:

> Battle my heart three person'd God; for, you
> As yet but knocke, breathe, shine and seeke to mend,
> That I may rise, and stand, o'er throw me . . .[22]

There is in this poetry as well the impulse to catalogue and lay out the plain and simple truth for all to see and comprehend that was so evident in Ames's theology and that Perkins celebrated in the *Art of Prophesying*. Puritan poetry frequently reflected this "empirical" temperament. Thomas Traherne in "The Person" begins by reflecting the inclination to pare away decoration:

> Mistake me not, I do not mean to bring
>   New Robes, but to Display the Thing:
> Nor Paint, nor Cloath, nor Crown, nor add a Ray,
> But glorify by taking all away . . .

But this removal is in the service of an "appearance," even a "revelation" of the glory of divine creation (here evident in the human form):

> The Naked Things
>   Are most Sublime and Brightest shew,
>   When they alone are seen:
> Mens hands then Angels Wings
>   Are truer Wealth even here below . . .

---

[20] *Protestant Poetics,* p. 219. She discusses Perkins's instructions for preachers as an important source for this aesthetic disposition.
[21] "Sepulchre," in *Works of George Herbert,* p. 40.
[22] "Holy Sonnets," xx, in *Donne: The Divine Poems,* p. 11.

> Their Worth they then do best reveal,
> When we all Metaphores remove,
>   For Metaphores conceal,
>   And only Vapours prove.

But after these "vapours" have been removed, after the stripping, one can inspect and catalogue the "anatomy" that remains:

> Survey the Skin, cut up the Flesh, the Veins
>   Unfold: The Glory there remains.
> The Muscles, Fibres, Arteries and Bones
> Are better far then Crowns and precious Stones.[23]

Barbara Lewalski describes this poetic strategy as "naming and listing objects and qualities, as if by such naming to evoke their essence."[24] Surely, for Traherne, these anatomical details give their own tribute to God's glory in creating the human image. We note below the way Rembrandt was to develop this theme.

The triumph of this plain style is seen, one might argue, in John Milton's *Paradise Regained*. Here we recall John Cotton's own struggle, as Milton pictures Satan using all the tools of rhetoric to tempt the Savior with the wisdom and learning from the gifted ancients so that "These rules will render thee a king complete/Within thyself, much more with empire joined."[25] The Savior's answer is a brilliant put down of this eloquence:

> Think not but that I know these things, or think
> I know them not; not therefore am I short
> Of knowing what I ought. He who receives
> Light from above, from the Fountain of Light,
> No other doctrine needs, though granted true;
> But these are false, or little else but dreams,
> Conjectures, fancies, built on nothing firm.
>
> (lines 286–92)

By contrast, Scripture "our Law and Story strewed with hymns" is all that we need, "In them is plainest taught and easiest learnt, what makes a nation happy . . . and keeps it so" (lines 334, 361–2).

But what is most characteristic of this body of poetry, with all of its variety, is the tendency to rewrite the narrative of their own lives in terms of the

---

[23] *Thomas Traherne: Poems, Centuries and Three Thanksgivings,* ed. Anne Ridler (London: Oxford University Press, 1966), p. 66.

[24] Lewalski, *Protestant Poetics,* p. 370.

[25] *Paradise Regained,* IV, 283, 284, in *Complete Poetical Works of John Milton,* p. 503; the following lines noted in the text are from p. 505. It stands to reason for those committed to using the "word" as a bulwark against the flesh, temptations of rhetoric would be most compelling.

biblical narrative of sin and salvation – to write themselves into the poetry. William Ames in his *Conscience* identified our process of sanctification with the nailing of Christ on the cross. He wrote: "The nailes whereby in this application sinne is fastened to the cross, are the very same with those whereby Christ was fastened to the cross."[26] John Donne can take this exchange to the biblical extreme:

> Spit in my face ... and pierce my side,
> Buffet, and scoffe, scourge and crucifie mee ...
> They kill'd once an inglorious man, but I
> Crucifie him daily, being now glorified.[27]

George Herbert can celebrate Easter as a personal identification with Christ's death and resurrection in "Easter Wings":

> Lord, who createdst man in wealth and store,
> Though foolishly he lost the same,
> Decaying more and more,
> Till he became
> Most poor;

> With Thee
> O let me rise
> As larks, harmoniously,
> And sing this day thy victories:
> Then shall the fall further the flight in me.[28]

This poem shaped in the form of a pair of wings illustrates the way the visual shaping of words is meant to underline their meaning, in a way analogous to Ames's shaping his theology in the form of a ramist diagram. This provides what Raymond Waddington has called a "visual rhetoric," which may be an attempt to "compensate for the loss of the orator's voice and presence in engaging an unseen audience."[29] Or, from a theological perspective, perhaps these shapes are meant to correspond to and reinforce the presence and structure that words can provide. The aesthetic sensitivities

---

[26] *Conscience with power and cases,* bk II, p. 26.
[27] "Holy Sonnet," vii, in *Donne: The Divine Poems,* p. 9.
[28] "Easter Wings," in *The Works of George Herbert,* p. 43.
[29] "Visual Rhetoric: Chapman and the Extended Poem," *English Literary Renaissance* 13/1 (1983), p. 57. This vestige of visual culture may also be a compensation for a loss of other more embodied forms of culture. Literacy itself encourages certain elements of culture, but it discourages others. Christopher Hill argues that the decline in ballad singing may be associated with the decline of household music making and singing. "Private reading replaced community or family singing ... just as it replaced reading aloud or repetition of sermons by family or group discussion." And it may also have discouraged the biblical drama, even as it encouraged the epic (*The English Bible,* pp. 339, 342).

are not suppressed but displaced, from the visual image to the language, which, to the Puritan mind, paints a truer and more lively picture.

DUTCH SEVENTEENTH-CENTURY ART

By the time William Ames died in Rotterdam in 1633, the influence of the Reformation had been present in Holland for more than a generation. And consistent with Calvinist teaching images had been taken off church walls. In 1631, Pieter Saenredam painted the interior of the famous St. Bavo Church in Haarlem (Figure 18).

In this painting well-dressed worshipers walk amidst columns and barren walls and windows. Before the iconoclasm of 1566 these walls had been covered with murals, and sixty-three altars would have been placed around the nave.[30] But now these spaces were empty leaving room for the narratives portrayed in the regular preaching of Scripture. Pieter Saenredam was raised in a strict Calvinist family and came to specialize in architectural interiors like the one pictured here – he felt there was a special power associated with architectural space, as both a presence and an absence. The space seems to draw the viewer in, but does not draw attention to itself. Indeed the space itself is undefined. Like the meetinghouses in New England, St. Bavo served as both a civic hall and worship space.

Here a group of well-dressed burghers stroll through a space which appears to make no special reference to religion or faith. At least that is what modern observers frequently conclude.[31] But this conclusion would be mistaken, for when one looks more closely, the space of the church is not empty: it is filled with light. The absence of altars and images is replaced by a presence that is symbolized by light. Saenredam gives us a clue to this by the action just to the right of center in the middle distance. There a man points to the only image remaining in the space: a sixteenth-century painting of an architecturally simple church building, probably another church in Haarlem, by Pieter Gerritsz. This is the true image of God's church, the painter is saying, where the word of God is preached and heard. A contemporary minister was quoted as praising St. Bavo's spaciousness for

---

[30] Albert Blankert, introduction to *God's Saints and Heroes*, p. 21. As we will see, not every visual image was removed.

[31] So art critic Christopher Knight can conclude of a 2002 exhibition of Saenredam's paintings in the Getty Museum in Los Angeles: "Saenredam approaches the spiritual subject from a distinctly secular perspective. He emphasizes the art involved in what he sees. Art is what becomes the sacred space contained in this work – sacred because it embodies individual thought and sensibility" (*Los Angeles Times*, April 17, 2002, F5).

Figure 18   Pieter Jansz Saenredam, *St. Bavo in Haarlem*. Panel, 82 × 110 cm.
Philadelphia Museum of Art, Philadelphia, Penn., 1631.

"there one learns his word purely and soundly."[32] With Saenredam a new
art is being created that served not only the Calvinist worldview, but also
the newly emerging Dutch identity.

Scholarly interpretation of seventeenth-century Dutch painting has
struggled with the role of moral and theological influences on the "naturalism" that emerged in Holland during the first third of that century. In
the last generation some scholars have argued the naturalism that developed between 1615 and 1630 reflected a new secularized view of nature and
aesthetics that accompanied a growing empirical tendency. Others have
drawn a strict parallel between their motifs and Calvinist theology and
morals. More recently scholars have seen still other motives – aesthetic,
conventional or descriptive – as playing important roles.[33]

[32] Gary Schwartz and Marten Jan Bok, *Pieter Saenredam: The Painter and his Time* (New York: Abbeville,
1989), p. 66. I owe the reference to light filling the space to Henry Luttikhuizen, private correspondence, October 18, 2002.
[33] A brief survey of the discussion is found in Reindert L. Falkenberg, "Calvinism and the Emergence
of Dutch Seventeenth Century Landscape Art – A Critical Evaluation," in Paul Corby Finney (ed.),
Seeing Beyond the Word: Visual Arts and the Calvinist Tradition (Ground Rapids, Mich.: Eerdmans,
1999), pp. 343–68. But the best comprehensive discussion with contributions from all the major

The actual influence of Calvin's own thinking and writing on art may have been limited. Sergiusz Michalski doubts "whether [Calvin's] brief suggestions for painting landscapes were that much read or conscientiously followed . . . After all, the realist tradition in the Netherlands culminating in the great age of Dutch seventeenth century painting had iconographical and formal antecedents running all the way back through the sixteenth century."[34] But there is a general consensus that, while Calvin's own influence may have been limited, the Calvinism of the dominant Reformed Churches provided a critical component of the environment in which the artists worked, especially in the period leading up to Rembrandt's major works in the 1630s. As Christian Tümpel pointed out, for artists the spirit of the age can be more powerful even than the artist's own religious affiliation. And the dominant spirit of this period was Calvinist.[35]

The influence of this Calvinist vision would have been passed on by the influential Confession of Faith and Catechism of the Netherlands Reformed Churches.[36] The Catechism contains the familiar warning against idolatry: "instead of the one true God, who has revealed Himself in his Word, or beside him, to devise, or have something else on which to place our trust" (Heidelberg, ques. 95). On the question of the use of images in worship the catechism says: "As for creatures, though they may be visibly represented, yet God forbids us to make or have any resemblance of them, in order to worship them or serve God by them" (quest. 97). But the Confession is most notable for its strong emphasis on creation reflecting God's goodness and splendor. In words that directly recall Calvin, Article 2 says: "[The creation] is before our eyes as a most elegant book, wherein all creatures, great and small, are so many characters leading us to contemplate the invisible things of God, namely his eternal power and Godhead."[37] The Catechism speaks

---

parties of the debate is Wayne Franits (ed.), *Looking at Seventeenth Century Dutch Art: Realism Reconsidered* (Cambridge University Press, 1997).

[34] *The Reformation and the Visual Arts*, p. 72.

[35] "Religious History Painting," in Blankert *et al.* (eds.), p. 48. We do not argue that this tradition of painting was specifically shaped by the work of William Ames, rather that his theology articulated themes that would have been well known in the culture and that were featured in the preaching of the time. While at Franeker he was, after all, active in preparing ministers for the Dutch Reformed Church.

[36] *Belijdenis des Geloofs der Gereformeerde Kerken in Nederland*, known as the Belgic Confession; this was the first doctrinal standard of the Dutch Reformed Churches. It was written by Guido de Brès and published in 1561. It was heavily influenced by the French Reformed Confession of 1559, which was written chiefly by John Calvin. The Dutch churches also adopted the Calvinist Heidelberg Catechism almost as soon as it was published in 1563. See Philip Schaff, *The Creeds of Christendom* (Grand Rapids, Mich.: Baker, 1985), vol. III, p. 383ff.

[37] Article 2: "[De wereld] voor onze ogen is als een schoon boek, in het welk alle schepselen, grote en kleine, gelijk als letteren zijn, die ons de onzienlijke dingen Gods geven te aanshowen" (Dutch quoted in Walford, *Ruisdael and the Perception of Landscape*, p. 210n25).

of the fall and subsequent corruption of the earth, but insists that the sustaining providence of God may still be seen. God so governs all creatures "that herbs and grass, rain and drought, fruitful and barren years, food and drink, health and sickness, riches and poverty, yea all things, come not by chance, but by his fatherly hand" (Heidelberg Catechism, ques. 27). These ideas were prominent in Dutch culture during our period and certainly had something to do with the prominent natural motifs of Dutch painting. As Constantijn Huygens, the patron of Rembrandt, would say, "the goodness of God is to be seen in every dune's top."[38]

It is not surprising then that the most dominant characteristic of Dutch art during this period is its "naturalism." This has not always been admired, indeed, when considered in relation to history painting – the highest genre of painting according to neoclassical standards – this characteristic was considered at times something of a liability. Joshua Reynolds on a trip to Holland in 1781, though paying grudging respect to the "naturalness of representation" in the end called it "barren entertainment," since "it is to the eye only that the works of this school are addressed."[39] Presumably this was because it did not appear to promote moral virtues in the way eighteenth-century artists had come to expect. Modern art historians disagreed with this assessment. Eddy de Jongh pointed out that underneath the "barren" appearance of reality was a rich system of symbols and metaphors that revealed much about the seventeenth-century mentality.[40] Building on the iconographic work of Erwin Panofsky, de Jongh gave attention to the symbolic language of Dutch landscapes and interiors, arguing that the symbolic meaning was hidden in the seemingly natural forms.

Inevitably there were those who opposed such symbolic emphases and argued that the realism, the plain contours of the art, had significance in itself. In 1983 Svetlana Alpers characterized Dutch art as an "art of describing." Seventeenth-century Dutch art, she wrote, reflects the emerging empiricism of the century in which "a new authority [is] given to a visual as against a textual form of knowledge."[41] She points to the tendency of Dutch artists to include naturalistic details or to catalogue reality as reflective of the growing empirical temper which she correlated with the contemporary

[38] Quoted in Eddy de Jongh, "Realism and Seeming Realism," in Franits (ed.), *Looking at Seventeenth Century Dutch Art,* p. 26. For a discussion of the spread of these ideas and their prominence across denominational lines see Walford, *Ruisdael and the Perception of Landscape,* pp. 19–21.

[39] Quoted in Svetlana Alpers, *The Art of Describing: Dutch Art in the Seventeenth Century* (University of Chicago Press, 1983), pp. xvii–xviii.

[40] See de Jongh, "Realism and Seeming Realism," in Franits (ed.), pp. 21–56.

[41] *Art of Describing,* p. 8. Subsequent pages in the text. This descriptive art she wants to see as characteristic of northern art, in contrast to the narrative (Albertian) art of Italy, p. xx.

discovery of the microscope. In an important chapter she describes what she calls the mapping impulse evident in Dutch art, pointing out the close relationship between landscape and mapmaking (p. 142). Alpers believes, however, this "art of describing" is only indirectly related to religion: "An appeal to religion as a pervasive moral influence in the society's view of itself and the larger world of nature seems a more fruitful direction to take than to continue to check the art out against the tenets of faith" (p. xxvi).

While Alpers's views have been extremely controversial, especially in Holland, she has clearly put her finger on a critical element of Dutch art. As Samuel van Hoogstraten, the pupil of Rembrandt, notes in his famous *Introduction to the Higher School of the Art of Painting*: "The art of painting is a science (*wetenschap*) of representing all the ideas or images, that the whole visible world contains, and it does so by deceiving the eye with line and color."[42] Calvin would say nature provides a mirror in which we can see God; art, Hoogstraten says, holds up a mirror to nature. But Hoogstraten also underlines the other obvious characteristic of Dutch art during this time: its use of convention, of "artifice." We recall the order that Calvinist thought imposed on Puritan life generally was not a relaxation of classical standards, but a disciplined reordering of life by the word. Similarly we would argue that in the Dutch naturalism of this period there was an artifice that selected and constructed the world according to carefully conceived standards. Lawrence Goedde says of this tendency: "The allusion of reality, the appearance of unmediated, natural experience, can only be achieved by the exercise of self-conscious artistry, however unobtrusive." What looks like "an art without art," is really a careful selection of motifs to achieve a desired end.[43] Alpers then, however helpful her argument, is clearly wrong in connecting this descriptive art too closely with a kind of objectivity that we would associate with empiricism. While there is the tendency to describe or catalogue what is before the eyes, what is drawn (even what is seen!) reflects various conventions and values that artists would have shared. The word *landscape* itself comes from the Dutch *landschap* which was a (probably Frisian) word that was used specifically to describe land recovered from the North Sea.[44] In the terminology of the century it was not simply natural, it was land rescued and made useful.

---

[42] Samuel van Hoogstraten, *Inleyding tot de Hooge Schoole der Schilderkonst: Anders de zichbaere Werelt verdeelt in negen Leerwinkels, uder bestiert eene der Zanggodinnen* (Rotterdam: François van Hoogstraeten, 1678), p. 24. "De schilderkonst is een wetenschap, om alle ideenofte denkbeelden, die de gansche zichbaere natuer kan geven, to verbeelden: en met omtrek en verwe het oog to bedriegen."

[43] Lawrence O. Goedde, "Naturalism as Convention," in Franits (ed.), *Looking at Seventeenth Century Dutch Art*, pp. 143, 142.

[44] Gina Crandell, *Nature Pictorialized: "The View" in Landscape History* (Baltimore, Md.: Johns Hopkins University Press, 1993), pp. 101, 104.

Figure 19   Pieter de Molijn, *Landscape with a Cottage*. Oil on canvas, 37.5 × 55.2 cm. The Metropolitan Museum of Art, New York, 1629.

But, as we have argued with William Ames, these notions – that of describing and cataloguing things and the rigorous reconstruction of reality – are not necessarily in conflict. Consider, for example, the landscape of Pieter de Molijn, *Landscape with a Cottage* from 1629 (Figure 19). When compared with earlier landscapes Molijn represents a breakthrough in portrayal of realistic landscapes. As Ann Jensen Adams puts it, one might think that "something dramatic happened around 1620 in Haarlem . . . as if scales had suddenly and collectively fallen from seventeenth-century Dutch artists' eyes and they could suddenly see and faithfully transcribe the land, in which they found themselves."[45] Indeed this painting and similar ones by Jan van Goyen feature an almost monochrome transcription of land, bushes, trees, aging farmhouses, and weather-worn hillocks. On one level of course this describes the environment around Amsterdam and Haarlem that would have been familiar to the viewers; on another level it selects elements from that environment to which attention should be drawn. At first glance the picture appears to provide a bucolic view of a secure homestead. But closer examination reveals a peaceful parcel of land suspended

[45] Adams, "Competing Communities in the 'Great Bog of Europe': Identity and Seventeenth Century Dutch Landscape Painting," in W. J. T. Mitchell (ed.), *Landscape and Power* (University of Chicago Press, 1994), p. 35.

as it were between the darkness of a kind of grotto below and a darkening sky above. Both these levels are critical to the portrayal of creation during this time.

Clearly Molijn's painting, and much of the landscape of this period, portrayed "pleasant places" that could be enjoyed (and visited) via the imagination from the comfort of home. Dutch burghers could bring into their homes these visual reminders of the pleasant scenes they enjoyed on their walks and holiday outings.[46] But, as is typical in Dutch landscapes, the rural delights were frequently mixed with signals of the darkness that threatened life and, indeed, the land itself. The light could speak of the hope of salvation, but darkness reminded the viewer of the fragility of life and the evil that attended it.

Ann Jensen Adams even goes so far as to connect Molijn's painting specifically with the Dutch concern over the land and the constant threat posed by the North Sea. During the time this painting was made, she points out, a stone's throw from this scene, merchants of Amsterdam and Haarlem were undertaking a massive reclamation project in which more than a hundred square miles of inland lakes and marshes were being drained, increasing the habitable area of the region by one-third.[47] Adams points out how significant issues of land were to the Dutch identity, and the "naturalistic" setting of this dunescape would not have been separated in their minds from issues of land formation and the struggles associated with it. This puts Huygens's comment on God's glory seen in every dune a new setting. For during this time this landscape could not be seen without reflection on the constant need to control the menacing waters through continued communal effort. These landscapes then could "focus communal attention to the taming and control of a potentially threatening enemy."[48]

The land can reflect the glory of God, but it can also image the need to "reclaim" (redeem) it from the enemies that threaten it. Behind this discussion is the important idea of artifice, which we will examine more extensively in connection with New England. Here is an art that describes in great clarity an ordered world, where one can live in safety. But this is also an art that, at the same time, conceals the "art" that lies behind the illusion of security. Its naturalism rests on convention; just as, Calvin said,

---

[46] C. J. Visscher entitled his early seventeenth-century print series "Pleasant Places." I owe this reference to pleasant places to E. John Walford in private correspondence, January 2, 2003.

[47] Adams, "Competing Communities," pp. 48–9. She notes that interestingly no art of the time directly portrayed this giant industrial and commercial project.

[48] Ibid., p. 65.

Figure 20   Hendrick Terbrugghen, *The Incredulity of Thomas*. Oil on panel, 109 × 136 cm. Rijks Museum, Amsterdam, Netherlands, 1626.

the beauty of the world, threatened as it is by sin and corruption, rests on God, the Great Artificer's work of providence and salvation.

So a descriptive even empirical aspect is not in conflict with convention, but neither is it necessarily opposed to an inner personal response to the world. This inward response to the world was widely influential on Dutch art and also clearly reflects its Calvinist orientation. A good example is the painting by Hendrick Terbrugghen, *The Incredulity of Thomas* from 1626 (Figure 20).

Terbrugghen (1588–1629) belonged to the (mostly Catholic) Utrecht school of painters influenced by Carravagio. During this period in Holland the highest prestige was associated with history painting. These paintings achieved prominence especially during the first third of the century while the Protestant influence was strongest,[49] and they featured biblical or

---

[49] Tümpel, "Religious History Painting," in Franits (ed.). He argues that the pre-Rembrandt contribution represented by Pieter Lastman and the Utrecht school raised this art to a visionary level (pp. 46–9).

historical scenes whose purpose was to teach some moral or religious truth. The figures in the picture had to figure prominently, with each being given equal importance in the story that is narrated. For this art to succeed one had to know the story, because the intent of the picture is not simply to record the narrative, but to ask the viewer to identify with the scene. The rising middle class, the burghers, were the major focus for the burgeoning picture market and they have often been accused of wanting paintings that mirrored their bourgeois surroundings. But Albert Blankert disputes this. He argues they wanted history paintings, because, in the Calvinist manner, they understood their lives in terms of biblical scenes and events.[50] But one should be cautious here of isolating and exaggerating the Calvinist influence. As we have noted before, the humble reflection on biblical themes was also a feature of the Devotio Moderna, and, in particular, recalls Thomas à Kempis. Moreover Terbrugghen was influenced by Carravagio, an artist who reflects the values of the Catholic counter-Reformation. Still, the meditative portrayal of this moment surely owes much to the Reformed environment in which the artist worked.

This picture of Terbrugghen's portrays the moment in John's gospel when Thomas has been allowed to put his finger into Christ's wound. For, when he heard that Christ had risen, he said defiantly, "Unless I put my finger into his wound, I will not believe" (John 20:25). In the painting the chiaroscuro influence from Carravagio is evident in the strong contrast between light and dark. The strongest light falls on Christ's side that is held opened for Thomas to see and touch. "Put your finger here in my side," Christ says, "and see my hands" (v. 27). In the gospel there are two kinds of responses represented. The first is represented by Thomas, who, when he touches the wound, can say "My Lord and my God" (v. 28). The second is represented by the figure behind, an unknown disciple looking up into heaven (rather than at the wound in Christ's side that is the center of the picture). Of these Christ says: "Thomas have you believed because your eyes have seen me? Blessed is the one who has not seen and yet believes" (v. 28). The viewer in Terbrugghen's painting is invited to take sides, as it were, with those who have responded in these very different ways.

But that is not the only option open to the viewer. There is a third, unknown person who stands to the right. He looks through his spectacles

---

[50] Introduction, *God's Saints and Heroes*, pp. 22–3. Interestingly they could also understand themselves in terms of mythological scenes that were popular as well. Blankert points out that historical scenes as a percentage of paintings dropped as the century went on. During the decade 1610–19 they made up 46 percent of all pictures; by 1670–79 this had dropped to 16.6 percent, and within these, biblical subjects dropped from 30 percent to just over 11 percent (p. 23).

in a somewhat detached manner, as if to verify what Thomas is doing and the wound that is being displayed. Who is this? Is it the artist? Or is it the one whom the viewer is asked to identify with? The glasses, the attitude of examination, or exploration, recall Alpers's reference to the growing empirical tendencies of the century, and the scientific advances made possible by microscopes and telescopes. It is as though the artist is providing a third alternative to belief and unbelief: a figure displaying a modern suspension of disbelief, while the evidence is being assessed. This figure then provides a third opportunity for identification within the narrative of the story, suggesting a possible tension between the inward vision of faith, and the growing empirical orientation in the seventeenth century.

The master of painting pictures that portray the inner response of the figures is Rembrandt van Rijn (1606–69). In 1634 he painted his own version of *The Incredulity of Thomas* (Figure 21). Here figures crowd around which display a wider variety of responses to the event. But the central figures are again Christ and Thomas, the latter illuminated by a light that seems to radiate from Christ. Thomas here seems to recoil from the experience in a way that illustrates Rembrandt's capacity to focus attention on the psychological moment of the greatest intensity. As two scholars note, "Rembrandt's borrowings are always intended to endow his scenes with the desired dramatic expression and to concentrate the attention of the spectator on the heart of the event."[51] Here there is nothing of the descriptive attention to details, everything is absorbed by the drama of Thomas's discovery. Interestingly Svetlana Alpers acknowledges that Rembrandt is an exception to her thesis that Dutch art features primarily a description of reality. She says, "While the Dutch artists offer us visible texts, Rembrandt insists that it is the Word within and not the surface of the texts that must be valued."[52] For Rembrandt asks the viewer to share in the dramatic moment and take his or her place either with those who, like Thomas, are seeing and believing, or with those on the right, who, though they do not see, believe, or perhaps with those on the far left whose response is more uncertain.

But Rembrandt at times goes further in this press to identify with the story. Like the Puritan poets who may have influenced him, he can actually see himself in terms of the narrative. In 1632 Constantijn approached Rembrandt to do a series of paintings for Frederick Hendrick, the Prince of Orange. Huygens, a devout Calvinist, had been impressed with the work of the young painter and wanted him to do a series of religious scenes that

[51] J. Bolten and Jetteke Bolten-Rempt, *Rembrandt and the Incredulity of Thomas* (Leiden: Aliotta & Manhart, 1981), p. 7.
[52] *Art of Describing*, p. 188, 192.

Figure 21   Rembrandt van Rijn, *Doubting of St. Thomas*. Oil on panel, 53 × 51 cm.
Pushkin Museum of Fine Arts, Moscow, Russia, 1634.

would be placed in the Prince's private quarters. Perhaps he wished to employ Rembrandt so as to counteract some of the criticism that the Prince
preferred art with too many Madonnas.[53]

The first painting he did in 1632 for the series is entitled *The Raising of
the Cross* (Figure 22). Rembrandt clearly takes his inspiration in this (and
others he did for the Prince) from the work of Peter Paul Rubens that had
recently been done in Antwerp. In the great altarpiece, *The Deposition of
Christ* (1612), in a flurry of interacting figures the still bleeding Christ is

[53] See Gary Schwartz, *Rembrandt: His Life, His Paintings* (New York: Viking, 1985), p. 118.

Figure 22   Rembrandt van Rijn, *The Raising of the Cross*. Oil on canvas, 96.2 × 72.2 cm. Alte Pinakothek, Munich, Germany, *c.* 1633.

brought down from the cross. While the motifs are similar and both include self-identification, the tone could not be more different between the
work of these artists, illustrating nicely the contrast between the Counter-
Reformation and the Reformed mentalities. To begin with Rubens's work
towers over the viewer behind the altar (420 cm tall) signaling the importance of the Mass and the real presence of Christ; Rembrandt's work
is less than a fourth the size and is made for private contemplation of the
Prince in his residence. In Rubens the picture is filled with frenzied activity;
Rembrandt's scene evokes a quiet meditation. As Simon Shama puts it, in
Rubens all the figures are in movement as they reach out to touch Jesus,
the real presence, and wrestle him from the cross. In Rembrandt the doers
are replaced by watchers. Rubens's work over the altar speaks of taking and
eating: this is my body; Rembrandt's characters peer out with a sense of
shared guilt in the event they watch.[54]

Though, according to the earliest biographers Rembrandt attached himself to the Mennonites, here – perhaps on instructions from his patron –
he displays Calvinist sensitivities. In the center of the picture note the figure helping to lift the cross, while a man in the back stands and watches.
The man in blue turns out to be a self-portrait of Rembrandt himself. As
Calvin specified, here Rembrandt literally paints himself into the narrative.
Of course it was not unusual for artists to put themselves into the picture:
it was common in the fifteenth century, and in the next century Lucas
Cranach the Elder frequently did it with his religious scenes. But Rembrandt's placement in this picture is unique. Painters put themselves in
the picture, but not, Simon Schama notes, as both artist and instrument of
providence![55] For it turns out that in this picture it is not the figure of Christ,
but Rembrandt himself who provides the fulcrum on which the structure
of the picture turns. In paintings like this and especially in his religious
prints, it has been argued that Rembrandt represents a typical progression
from outward observance to inward witnessing.[56] We have seen that this
represents as well the typical strategy of Puritan metaphysical poetry (especially John Donne and George Herbert), and it could be the resemblance
is not accidental.

The poetry of John Donne was well known in Holland during this time
in part due to the influence of Constantijn Huygens himself. Huygens
himself wrote poetry that echoes themes of the Puritan poets, and he also
translated Donne's poetry into Dutch. Consider the poem entitled "Prayer

---

[54] Simon Schama, *Rembrandt's Eyes* (New York: Knopf, 1999), pp. 291–4.   [55] Ibid.
[56] Mariët Westermann, *Rembrandt* (London: Phaidon Press, 2000), p. 280.

for Holy Communion" which Huygens published in 1642. After noting that the wine and bread could stand for simple commemoration before which our soul stands "untroubled," Huygens says this is not for him:

> Grant me the universal, true, plain, old
> And unsoiled usage of your sacred words.
> Grant one more miracle, my broken God,
> To break at once my body from my soul.
> Rejected stone, who suffered once for me:
> Turn but my stone to flesh, my flesh to stone.[57]

An even closer parallel to Rembrandt's painting may be seen in the work of Amsterdam preacher Jacobus Revius, who in a sonnet published in 1630 wrote what could be a commentary on Rembrandt's *Raising the Cross*:

> 'Tis not the Jews who crucified,
> Nor who betrayed you in the judgment place,
> Nor who, Lord Jesus spat into your face,
> Nor who with buffets struck as you died.

> 'Tis not the soldiers who with brutal fists
> Raised the hammer and raised the nail
> Or the cursed wood on calvary's hill,
> Or drew lots, tossed the dice to win your cloak
> I am the one, oh Lord, who brought you there,
> I am the heavy tree too stout to bear
> I am the rope that reined you in.

> The scourge that flayed you nail and spear,
> The blood soaked crown they made you wear
> 'Twas all for me, alas, 'twas for my sin.[58]

The connection with metaphysical poetry may be even more extensive. Behind Christ's cross there is another figure above Rembrandt who sits on a horse impassively looking out at us. According to standard iconographical analysis – such a figure is common in crucifixion scenes representing the authorities who condemned Jesus to death – he looks at the viewer as though to ask: what do you make of this? But Rembrandt may have intended a deeper meaning with this figure that reflects Huygens's connection to John Donne. The famous poet and preacher had come to preach in Holland just after the Synod of Dort and while there was given a government honor.

---

[57] *A Selection of Poems of Sir Constantijn Huygens (1596–1687): A Parallel Text, Translated with an Introduction* ed. Peter Davidson and Adriaan van der Weel (University of Amsterdam, 1996), p. 113.

[58] Quoted in Westermann, *Rembrandt*, p. 107. She persuasively compares this poem to Rembrandt's own self-portrait in *Raising the Cross*.

By the early 1630s Huygens had translated nineteen of Donne's poems including "Good Friday 1613. Riding Westward."[59] Rembrandt may have had this poem in mind, Gary Schwartz suggests, when painting the figure on horseback. This figure is "riding west" while we look eastward toward the cross. In this poem Donne notes he was "by others hurried every day" so that:

> Pleasure or business, so, our Soules admit
> For their first mover, and are whirld by it.
> Hence is't, that I am carryed towards the West
> This day, when my Soules forme bends toward the East.
> There I should see a Sunne, by rising set,
> And by that setting endlesse day beget;
> But that Christ on this Crosse, did rise and fall,
> Sinne had eternally benighted all.
> Yet dare I'd almost be glad I do not see
> That spectacle of too much weight for me.[60]

Perhaps Rembrandt wanted to add this deeper meaning to a standard iconographical feature. But whether or not one agrees with Schwartz's connection of this painting with Donne's poem, the figure on horseback looking calmly at the viewer does invite response, indeed he becomes the figure addressing the viewer most directly. The man on horseback, along with the stretched body of Christ and the figure holding up the cross (Rembrandt himself), forms the central triangular structure of the painting. On this reading the appeal of the man on horseback cuts through all that would distract the viewer from attending to this greatest of all human dramas – that spectacle of too much weight. This then is an art that narrates the story in a personal and intimate way, intended not for display on church walls, but for the personal chambers of the Prince, to encourage private devotion and reflection on these biblical events. It is not an icon for public worship but it is meant to serve a role in the domestic worship that was so important to Calvinism. Following Calvin, it invited the viewer not only to meditate on Christ's death, but to rethink his or her own life in the light of Christ's call to take up one's cross and become a disciple.

Rembrandt has given a more direct testimony to Calvin's influence in a painting from 1632. Until recently the religious content of this work has

---

[59] See Koos Daley, *The Triple Fool: A Critical Evaluation of Constantijn Huygens' Translations of John Donne* (Nieuwkoop: De Graaf Publishing, 1990). Huygens translated these nineteen poems between 1630 and 1633, "Good Friday. 1613 Riding Westward" among them (p. 95).

[60] "Good Friday, 1613. Riding Westward," in *John Donne: The Divine Poems*, pp. 30–1. See Schwartz, *Rembrandt*, p. 118.

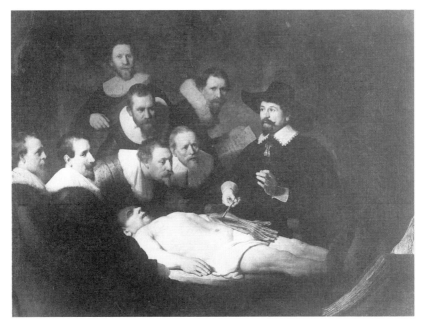

Figure 23   Rembrandt van Rijn, *The Anatomy Lesson of Dr. Nicolaes Tulp*. Oil on canvas, 170 × 217 cm. The Hague, Mauritshuis, The Netherlands, 1632.

been overlooked. In Rembrandt's *The Anatomy Lesson of Dr. Nicolaes Tulp* (Figure 23) rich theological allusions were uncovered two decades ago by William Shupbach.[61]

The painter here records one of the medical lessons the distinguished Dr. Tulp performed for colleagues and medical students. The sessions commonly began with prayer and a statement about the preeminence and dignity of the human person (p. 32). But Dr. Tulp in this painting seems to depart from the usual practice of dissection. In most cases these would have begun with the chest and abdomen; Dr. Tulp begins with the intersection of the finger-flexors, which he seems to hold up for inspection (p. 23). Why begin there? As Thomas Traherne's poem makes clear, though the human body in general testifies to God's creative genius, it was the detailed composition of muscles and bones that was the highest testimony to God's greatness. Shupbach points out that in the seventeenth century it was the

---

[61] William Shupbach, *The Paradox of Rembrandt's Anatomy [Lesson] of Dr. Tulp,* Medical History Supplement 2 (London: Wellcome Institute for the History of Medicine, 1982); pages in the text are to this work.

hand – even the finger-flexors of the hand – in particular that was "one of the preferred organs to demonstrate God's manifestation in the human body" (p. 19).

The theological import of this becomes clear when the iconography of the work is considered – which Shupbach uncovers from contemporary descriptions of the work of Dr. Tulp (p. 33). The symbolic arrangement of the sitters, along with the focus of the lesson itself, point out what for Dr. Tulp was the underlying religious rationale for the anatomy lesson: even in this medical exercise one can come to know oneself and one's God. The knowledge of oneself is nicely symbolized by the topmost man in the triangle of figures who points down to the corpse. Knowing oneself involves not only knowing that one is fearfully and wonderfully made by God, but also that one is mortal. Death comes to everyone. The knowledge of one's God is underlined by Dr. Tulp himself who holds up the flexor-tendons for all to see, and holds out his own hand to underline the point. For Dr. Tulp these speak of the very presence of God. This was memorialized by a poem written in 1639 by Caspar Barlaeus to celebrate a new anatomy theater where Dr. Tulp worked:

> Listener, learn yourself (te disce), and while you
> Proceed through the individual [organs],
> Believe that God is hidden even in the smallest part. (p. 31)

So Rembrandt reiterates in the painting the very structure of Calvin's *Institutes*, which that theologian summarized as knowledge of oneself and knowledge of God (*I*, i, 1).

The central characteristic of Dutch art during this period, whether history painting or landscape, lies in the way the transcript of the external world becomes an emblem of a deeper narrative of God's providential love and care. As we saw in the case of Pieter de Molijn, the pleasant place could be a reminder of both the beauty and grace with which God has endowed the world, and also the darkness and death that constantly threatens. To Dutch artists steeped in a Reformed perspective this was not moralizing, as is sometimes claimed, but a simple description of the character of life in this world. And as the *Anatomy Lesson* shows, the connection between the careful scrutiny of the physical world and the inward reflection on the soul, lies in the presence of God in both.

THE PATTERNS OF NEW ENGLAND LIFE

When John Cotton arrived in New England, the context could not have been more different from the one William Ames had known in Holland.

Rather than a traditional culture with highly developed institutions, Cotton saw a rough wilderness in which civilization was only beginning to emerge. Cotton Mather looking back from the end of the century could sum up the achievements in this way: never was any plantation brought unto such a considerableness, in a

space of time so inconsiderable! An *howling wilderness* in a few years became a *pleasant land,* accommodated with *necessaries* – yea and the *conveniences* of humane life; the *gospel* has carried with it a *fullness of all other blessings.*[62]

However different the contexts, the same theological motives would be at work in New England, as the Puritans sought in biblical fashion to restore creation to its original splendor and build a holy commonwealth. As poet Edward Johnson put it: "This is the place where the Lord will create a new Heaven, and a new Earth in, new Churches, and a new commonwealth together."[63] The passion they brought with them of course, like other Calvinists before them, was grounded on the inward struggle with sin and grace. But externally their lives came to take on patterns that reflected this inner disposition, as they sought to inscribe a particular order both on this external environment and on their homes and communities. The townscape that would emerge reflected the "inscape" of their understanding of salvation. This combined both the elements of an ordered whole as this was described by William Ames, with the inward experience of Cotton's covenant of grace.

Both the order and the lives they sought to live followed, they believed, a biblical model. As in contemporary Holland and England this was a culture that grows out of an intimate familiarity with Scripture, which they read in their homes and heard preached on the Sabbath. As a result it was a highly literate culture – three-fourths of the population could read, which created a publishing industry in Boston that by the end of the seventeenth century was second only to London in the English-speaking world.[64] Reading was the privileged medium of cultural formation. This created a culture more intensive than extensive. It is true that as New Englanders spread out to take possession of the land by their cultivation, they established an unprecedented number of townships within a short span of time. But once settled they stayed put; their perception of the world outside their local "mental maps" was quite narrow. But, David Allen says, "what New Englanders

[62] *Magnalia,* vol. 1, p. 80; his emphasis.
[63] *Johnson's Wonder-Working Providence: 1628–1651,* ed. J. Franklin Jameson (New York: Scribner's Sons, 1910), p. 25.
[64] Jonathan Fairbanks, introduction to Fairbanks and Trent (eds.), *New England Begins,* vol. 1, p. xix; and Kenneth B. Murdock, *Literature and Theology in Colonial New England* (Cambridge, Mass.: Harvard University Press, 1949), pp. 1–10.

lacked in outward expression and understanding they seemed to make up for in inward intensity about the spatial relationships they knew."[65] That is, the lives they set out to compose reflected both Cotton's inward paradise and Ames's cataloguing impulse.

TOWN PLANNING

Externally this was reflected in the way they sought to construct their towns. In the 1630s an anonymous author wrote a treatise entitled *An Essay on Ordering Towns*.[66] This treatise described the way a township is to be laid out in a series of concentric circles. At the center is the Meetinghouse, which, the author comments, is "the centor of the wholl circumferance." Around this houses are arranged, "orderly placed to enjoy the comfortable [*sic*] communion." Outside these is a ring of common fields, with space for larger estates still further out. Beyond these estates are common "swampes and rubbish waest grounds . . . which harbor wolves and . . . noysom beasts and serpents." Finally one reaches the wilderness which may be areas owned by the town but not yet occupied (New England townships included much larger parcels than was common in England, and thus initially more unoccupied land). The ordering of their towns then reflected both their social networks and their central religious convictions about the earth.[67]

This schema also reflects a common seventeenth-century attitude toward nature, which, like human nature, was wild and undisciplined, and needed to be broken. Indeed "nature" would not have had any independent meaning to the New England settler. The world was either "unaltered" or "artificial," that is, either untended (and thus wild) or tended and, through "artifice," made "useful." A piece of land therefore would have been categorized and evaluated along a continuum: waste – land that is not usable; unbroken – land that is potentially usable; land broken, i.e., by the plow; and land that is improved, or properly dressed and tended. Only the last of these would have been properly designated as "culture."[68] Much of this reflects new attitudes toward nature that were articulated by Francis Bacon.[69]

[65] "Vacuum Domicilium: The Social and Cultural Landscape of Seventeenth Century New England," in Fairbanks and Trent (eds.), *New England Begins,* vol. 1, pp. 3–4. "Mental maps" is Allen's term.

[66] Described and quoted in ibid., p. 4.

[67] See Joseph S. Wood, *The New England Village* (Baltimore, Md.: Johns Hopkins University Press, 1997), p. 67. "The Meetinghouse . . . was the dominant feature of the settlement landscape, the focus of community activity" (p. 115).

[68] St. George, "Set thine house in order," pp. 160–1.

[69] Francis Bacon, *Novum organon* (1620), was part of a larger work entitled *The Great Instauration* (or great restoration), in which nature is to be made usable for human advancement. This is discussed at greater length in the next chapter.

But this sense of nature as capable of restoration was also rooted in the narrative that New Englanders would have felt they were living. God had called them to live out their holiness in the New England wilderness. Thus they tended to interpret events in terms of providences, and so they would understand their calling to improve the earth as a spiritual calling. The earth after all was once a garden and could again be made to reflect more clearly the order and beauty of its creator.

Their view of their responsibility toward the creation reflected not only their view of the fallenness of creation and its need for "restoration," but also their typological understanding both of Scripture and of creation. Like Scripture, creation was filled with realities that pointed beyond themselves to God's heavenly kingdom, which was the final goal of both human and natural creation. As their tombstone art will show, they lived and died in keen expectation of God's greater work in the new creation. This led them not only to see their cultivation of the earth as part of God's call, but also to see in the beauties of what was around them a foretaste of heaven itself. Creation was thus the arena in which God's providences could best be seen.

Richard Baxter, who was widely read in New England, urges his readers in the *Saints Everlasting Rest* (1660) to meditate on the things around them, that by this close observation you may be able "to quicken your affections, by comparing the unseen delights of Heaven, with those smaller which you have seen and felt in the flesh."[70] Poet Anne Bradstreet, who was raised in John Cotton's congregation, for example, could celebrate the creature's ability to praise its creator in "Contemplations":

> I heard the merry grasshopper then sing.
> The black-clad cricket bear a second part;
> They kept one tune and played on the same string,
> Seeming to glory in their little art.
> Shall creatures abject thus their voices raise
> And in their kind resound their Maker's praise,
> Whilst I, as mute, can warble forth no higher lays?[71]

[70] IV, 242, 4th ed (London: 1653); quoted in Louis L. Matz, "Foreword" to *The Poems of Edward Taylor,* ed. Donald E. Stanford (New Haven: Yale University Press, 1960), pp. xviii–xxix. At about the same time, the gardener in Oxford, Ralph Austen, could say: "All creatures have a teaching voyce, they read us divinity lectures of divine providence." They can bring us near to the creator: "Climbing up by them, as by steps, or staires til we ascend to the highest good" (*The Spirituall Use of an Orchard* [Oxford: n.p., 1657], preface, third page).

[71] *Works of Anne Bradstreet,* p. 207. For Cotton's impact on Bradstreet, see Elizabeth Wade White, *Anne Bradstreet: The Tenth Muse* (Oxford University Presss, 1971), pp. 76–7. John Walford describes Dutch poems almost identical in style and spirit to Bradstreet's written earlier in the century (*Ruisdael and the Perception of Landscape,* pp. 24–6).

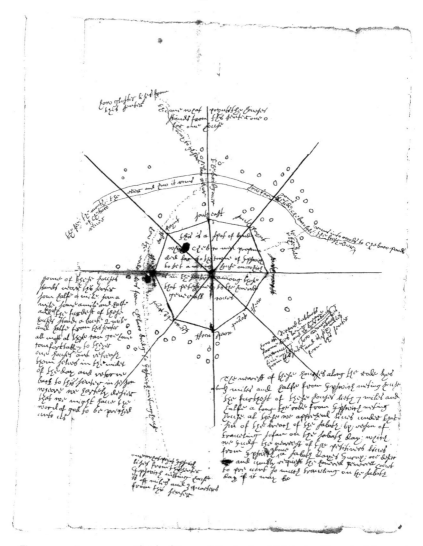

Figure 24   Anonymous, *Sketch of Proposed Site for Ipswich Meeting House,* in *Maps and Plans*, Third Series, v. 1, p. 35, #103. Massachusetts Archives. Boston, Mass., 1667.

But as with the *Technometry* of Ames, the meaning of creation is found not only in the parts, but in the structure by which the parts are related to each other. Here the impulse to reflect their inner orientation in mapping out space becomes clear. The instructions for laying out New England towns, as we saw, prescribed an order that reflected the biblical calling to "restore" creation – create an order that better reflects God's purposes. The center of each town is to be the meetinghouse, as worship is the center of their lives, then houses are to be laid out in a way that promotes community. We know that practical and topographical realities intervened making the ideal structure difficult to achieve, but we do have evidence that the central place of the meetinghouse was a regular factor in planning. In 1667 residents of Ipswich township petitioned the General Court to allow them to build their own meetinghouse closer to their homes. The sketch reproduced (Figure 24) shows the desire to locate their church at an intersection equidistant from most farmhouses (shown by small circles). These residents argued that the journey to the present church required some to travel as much as seven miles and put them "under the sin of the breach of the Sabbath: by reason of traveling so far on the Sabbath day."[72]

An even clearer picture of town structure and the placement of the church is seen in the design of New Haven (Figure 25), which was originally laid out in 1638.[73] The structure seems to clearly to rest on biblical models that were introduced by John Davenport, who was a close follower of John Cotton (and was also influenced by John Preston), and who moved to New Haven in 1637. After they had obtained land by a deed of purchase from the Indians, Davenport composed a Plantation Covenant in which all agreed together that "Scripturs doe holde forth a perfect rule for the directio and governmt [*sic*] of all men in duet[ies]" (p. 141). Following Old Testament precedent, and specifically prophecies from Ezekiel, they divided themselves into tribes who would settle in the eight areas around the tabernacle or meetinghouse. John Archer points out that Davenport in planning the town combines the allegorical and mystical interpretations of the Song of Songs (as Cotton had interpreted it) with the pictorialization of space from Ezekiel. Davenport combines, Archer says, "mystical indwelling and reconstructive pictorialization" (p. 148). Eschatological motives were clearly at work, the people of God were organizing themselves in a way that anticipated the community of heaven. Town planning, as illustrated in the case of New Haven, then becomes an exercise in imaginative projection of the mystical properties of community as they looked forward to the

---

[72] Allen, "Vacuum Domicilium," p. 34.
[73] Though the sketch reproduced is from 1748, it faithfully reflects the earlier plan. For the description of the plan and Davenport's role see John Archer, "Puritan Town Planning in New Haven" *Journal of the Society of Architectural Historians* 34 (1975), pp. 140–9. Subsequent pages in the text. Davenport appears to have been influenced here not only by recently written commentaries on the Song of Songs and Ezekiel, but also by those promoting utopian political and educational reforms (in some cases these people were one and the same).

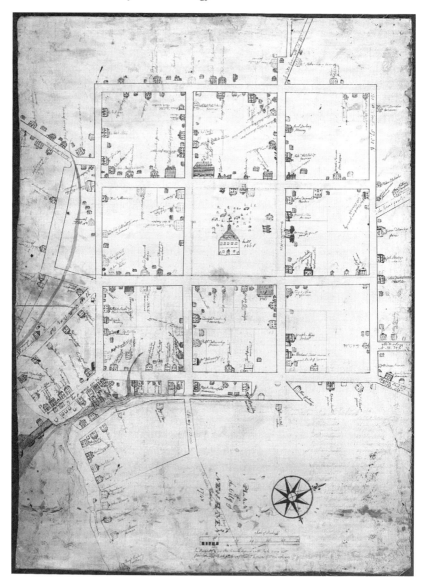

Figure 25   James Wadsworth, *Plan of the City of New Haven Taken in 1748*. Yale Beineke
Library, New Haven, Conn., 1748.

heavenly kingdom – all controlled by a tradition of biblical interpretation then common.

We must be clear that an aesthetic beauty of the whole design would not have been either intended or excluded by those who planned these towns. In their minds higher values would have been at work, such as utility[74] and the promotion of community. Though there is certainly an elegance and dignity in the order that resulted, this sense would have been a "concealed art." In general the values they pursued did not lie in any particular objects of the plan – for example in the meetinghouse constructed and elaborated as a symbol of salvation (as was the medieval cathedral). But rather such symbolism that existed resided in the whole and in the relationships embodied there, and especially in the purposes for which the structure existed – its use. The tendency to good order in Calvin and the structural pattern of Ames has issued in an aesthetic of relationships and coherence, rather than one that featured formal qualities of independent objects.

THE MEETINGHOUSE

The fact outward splendor was not a value in the practice of worship is clear from the development of the meetinghouse itself. The planning and construction of the meetinghouse were the central concern of every community, but, initially at least, there seems not to have been any aesthetic or architectural guidelines.[75] In the beginning, in fact, settlers met under a tree, or in large rooms or parlors of homes (as separatist congregations had frequently done in England). The first building to specifically serve this purpose was built in Boston in 1632–3. Early buildings were simple structures containing a pulpit along one wall and a table in front, and they served for all public meetings of the community – secular and sacred.

Though few sketches or plans survive from this early era, it appears meetinghouses initially simply resembled English houses, rectangular with gabled roofs, or, later, English market halls. Though they were not built for beauty, some clearly were striking, especially when considered in relation to

---

74 For the centrality of the notion of 'usefulness' to the New England man, see Lisa Wilson, *Ye Heart of a Man,* pp. 20–2.
75 See speech of Noah Porter (1882) published in *The New England Meeting House,* Connecticut Tercentenary Commission Publications 18 (New Haven: Yale University Press, 1933), pp. 1–34; Arian Car Donnelly, *The New England Meeting Houses of the Seventeenth Century* (Middlebury, Conn.: Wesleyan University Press, 1968); Peter Benes (ed.), *New England Meeting House and Church* (Boston: Dublin Seminar for New England Folklore, Boston University, 1979). Development of the meetinghouse is from Donnelly.

the whole community. The Puritans could enjoy beauty and color as much
as anyone. Edward Johnson could say when describing Ipswich in 1634:
"Their Houses are many of them very faire built with pleasant Gardens
and Orchards, consisting of about one hundred and forty Families. Their
meeting house is a very good prospect to a great part of the Towne, and
beautifully built."[76] Thus its "prospect" and "construction" could add to
the ordered beauty of the whole, even if it was not sought as an end in itself.
More important were the uses to which it would be put, and its suitability
to these purposes. The common attitude toward these buildings was best
described by separatist Pastor Francis Johnson who ministered in Holland:

> now there is not any one place holy, and peculiarly consecrate [*sic*] to the ministra-
> tions of the Lord's supper, as there was of old for sacrifice onely at Jerusalem. So as
> now therefore a place being a generall circumstance that perteyneth to all actions,
> commodious and necessarie for people to meet in together, and to be kept from
> injurie and unseasonableness of the weather.[77]

In New England unseasonable weather was common and meetinghouses
were notoriously dark and drafty. Samuel Sewall reports that sometimes the
communion bread was frozen on the Lord's table. Ministers preached and
people listened with coats and mittens, while women carried footstools
with live coals to keep their feet warm. Neither heat nor artificial light was
introduced before 1800 and even then the innovations were controversial.[78]

Clearly edification took precedence over comfort in the meetinghouse.
While the dynamic of worship life patterned the whole of life, it was in
Sabbath worship that the whole drama of salvation was reexperienced.
Each week Sabbath services lasting three hours were held in the morning
and the afternoon. Extemporaneous prayer, lasting up to fifteen minutes,
opened the service, followed by Scripture reading, Psalm singing and hour-
long sermons. Preaching of course was the central feature in all services
around which other elements were ranged – singing, more prayers, perhaps
communion or baptism, and finally the blessing.[79]

But contrary to modern stereotypes, neither the space nor the service
were the drab and colorless affairs that we imagine them to be. Not only

[76] *Johnson's Wonder-Working Providence*, p. 96.
[77] Quoted in Donnelly, *New England Meeting Houses*, p. 100. Donnelly notes aptly their purposes were
not negative, to build something ugly, but positive, though carried out with motives more practical
than aesthetic (p. 108).
[78] Jane Nylander, "Toward Comfort and Conformity in New England Meeting Houses: 1750–1850,"
in Peter Benes (ed.), *The New England Meeting House and Church* (Boston, Mass.: Doublin Seminar
for New England Folklore, Boston University Press, 1979), pp. 86, 90.
[79] Charles H. Stowe, "Spiritual Dynamics of Puritan Worship," in Benes (ed.), *New England Meeting
House*, pp. 112–21.

would the service often be lively and joyful – sermons could elicit sighs or crying – but the building itself was probably colored and decorated. Recent research has even confounded the dominant image of the white meeting-house dominating New England villages. Frequently these structures were colored inside and out. Though it is difficult to know with certainty it seems that meetinghouses were colored ("cullered") as early as 1682. Exterior colors ranged from yellow and ochre to parrot green and even red! Yellow seems to have been most common, though orange and blue appeared frequently in Eastern Connecticut. Most interesting is the primitive symbolism associated with blue as the "sky color" – which appeared most often on the New Light meetinghouses. Worshipers in these churches were on their way to heaven.[80]

Pulpits and pews were also decorated – perhaps with tulips or grapevines. There were even reports of cherubim on some pulpits. Pews were similarly carved with natural motifs that reflected a high standard of joinery, in the manner of contemporary furniture for use in homes. A similar set of values were at work in communion vessels which came to be used. While some reflected a high level of silversmithing, they were not made "specially" for church use. Albert Roe and Robert Trent note, "So thoroughgoing was the Puritan commitment to demystifying the two elements of communion that practically any secular vessel was thought appropriate for use in service."[81] The point of these preparations would have been to support the preaching of the Word which was the center of worship. Week by week the families would gather in the meetinghouse, sing Psalms from their *Bay Psalm Book* and hear the Scriptures expounded. It was the richness and beauty of that word preached which captured their imagination. Other elements in the worship environment were clearly secondary, and, initially at least, little thought was given to their making.

HOUSES AND PATTERNED LIVES

Though the meetinghouse would have been, spatially and spiritually, the center of the community, the daily life of Puritans would have centered around work and the home. As Lisa Wilson comments: "Work was the

---

[80] Peter Benes, "Skycolors and Scattered Clouds: The Decorative and Architectural Painting of New England Meeting Houses: 1738–1834," in Benes (ed.), *New England Meeting House,* pp. 51–62.

[81] Robert F. Trent, "The Marblehead Pews," in Benes (ed.), *New England Meeting House,* p. 103; and see p. 63 of Benes, "Skycolors and Scattered Clouds"; Albert S. Roe and Robert F. Trent, "Robert Sanderson and the Founding of the Boston's Silversmith's Trade," in Fairbanks and Trent (eds.), *New England Begins,* vol. III, p. 485.

essence of adult manhood in early New England," because work was the
process by which one made oneself serviceable to God and others, and
transformed wilderness into a pleasant land – an artifact of human industry.
The house stood as the image of both the improvement this implied and the
artifact that resulted, and the structure of the house and grounds reflected
the continuum of land from waste to improvement, that is, from wilderness
to "culture."

The order was reflected in the transition from the back "yard" through
the kitchen garden into the Hall, and the Parlor at the front. The Hall, an
all-purpose room used for cooking in the fireplace, was the center of life.
Here the family shared a common domestic space, gathering for meals at
the large table placed in the center, or sitting in the evening conversing,
reading the bible and having evening prayers. The Parlor, or "Best Room,"
was more the ritual center of the house, with finer furniture, pictures or
portraits, books and the parents' bed. This room was used for entertaining,
courtship, sexual intimacy and even the place where the dead would have
been laid out.[82]

But it is now clear that these houses – like the meetinghouses – were not
the drab places with blank walls that they were previously thought to have
been. The walls of houses might have had maps, and less often pictures
(usually portraits) and a sprinkling of prints. Color played an important
role in the decorative scheme, with color designs frequently added to white-
washed walls and ceilings. Decorative designs were common not only on
walls, but increasingly in the furniture made in New England. In this domestic art the influence of an Anglo-Netherlandish Mannerism became
influential in seventeenth-century New England, which featured a stylized
(i.e. artificial) imitation of forms of nature. The mannerist artist through
these artifices, including even grotesque embellishments of nature, was felt
to be imposing order on the apparent chaos of nature as it existed. This style
was evident in the geometric designs and swirls on furniture, and even in
the "dotting" of walls and ceilings. Interestingly, Robert Trent argues, this
decoration of furniture was itself architecturally inspired. Designs would

---

[82] Robert Blair St. George notes the change in the central metaphor from a great hierarchy to the
"recasting of society as artifact" ("Set thine house in order," pp. 160 and 165–7). Lisa Wilson points
out that though there were "gender and class inequalities" men and women shared the same domestic
space. There were not yet separate spaces or spheres for men and women in the house (*Ye Heart
of a Man*, p. 2; previous quote p. 10). See also Abbott Lowell Cummings, "Notes on Furnishing
the Seventeenth Century House," *Old Time New England* 46/3, serial 163 (1956), pp. 57–67; and
St. George, "Set thine house in order," pp. 168–70; and A. L. Cummings, "Decorative Painters and
House Painting at Massachusetts Bay, 1630–1725," in Ian M. G. Quimby (ed.), *American Painting
to 1776: A Reappraisal* (Charlottesburg: University of Virginia, 1971), pp. 71–8.

often use geometric formulae "to repeat the ground plans, the elevation and the articulation of the rectangular grid." But nothing would have been done freehand which was felt to be too time-consuming and not sufficiently orderly![83]

The moral life of the town was to display a decorum that was coherent with the physical patterning we have described. In 1634 the General Court of Massachusetts forbade lace, gold and ornament on clothes – an ordinance that was broken as soon as it was passed.[84] But within the overall structure of life which is finally meant to reflect a divine order, there were spaces in which life could be lived and enjoyed and elements of visual delight elaborated. What visual art that developed – prints, portraits, furniture design, pewter work and textiles – would focus largely on the home and family. Beyond this enjoyment of popular culture was carefully controlled – recreations were few, gaming was rare in early New England.[85] And even the elements of visual delight were not made to be objects of independent contemplation, they were simply a part of the texture of their domestic lives. Overall the ordered lives they sought to live and impose on their world would have been visibly reflected in the patterns of the developing New England town, even as it was temporally reflected in the schedule of their lives. The "wheel of time" describes the tasks that laid out the ordered year of a yeoman's life, as he sought by useful work to remake the world after the image and purpose of the creator.[86]

SEVENTEENTH-CENTURY PORTRAITS

While painting did not have the prominence of literary work in the Puritan period, it was certainly not suppressed. Indeed every reference I have seen to painting during this period is positive. John Bate could open his well-known work on the *Mysteries of Nature and Art* (1634) by pointing out that Bezalel and Oholiab in Exodus 31 shew, of all the arts, "carving or

---

[83] Cummings, "Notes on Furnishing the Seventeenth Century House," *Old Time New England*, 46/3, Serial 163 (1956) p. 62, notes pictures would have been in the more well-to-do houses. See also on this point and for what follows, Robert F. Trent, "The Concept of Mannerism," in Fairbanks and Trent (eds.), *New England Begins*, vol. III, p. 368. He notes Puritans were clearly aesthetically aware and enjoyed "visual delight"; and Robert Trent, "New England Joinery and Turning before 1700," in Fairbanks and Trent (eds.), *New England Begins*, vol. III, pp. 501–10, esp 504–5.

[84] St. George, "Set thine house in order," p. 185.

[85] Though by the early 1700s playing cards were common even among the clergy; see Catherine Perry Hargrave, "The Playing Cards of Puritan New England," *Old Time New England* 18/4, serial 52 (1928), pp. 167–81.

[86] Fairbanks and Trent (ed.), *New England Begins*, vol. II, p. 325, Figure 27.

drawing to be an especiall gift of God's Spirit."[87] Pictures have clearly been allowed of God, he goes on. So that if the Trinity cannot be drawn, based on ancient practice, other pictures of Christ or other biblical characters could be made for private homes – there is no reason these should be "beaten downe" as Puritans have sometimes done (pp. 12, 13). He even argues that the cross can be used because of its historic place in the Church (pp. 13, 14). Then he proceeds to give a sophisticated guide to drawing the human body, the face, light and shadows, all in the new Mannerist way, even to the proper mixing of gums for colors. We know that this book made its way to New England for it appears in the catalogue of the libraries of both Increase and Cotton Mather. As Jonathan Fairbanks notes: "The book's presence does suggest . . . a favorable artistic climate for the seventeenth century painters in New England as well as an understanding of Mannerist art theories."[88] The following letter of Nathaniel Mather written from Dublin to his brother Increase in March 1684 provides insight into both the situation of the arts and crafts, and the Puritan openness to them:

This I send by Mr. Joseph Allen, son of a godly woman . . . civill and sober, was never taynted with or inclined in the least unto debaucheryes and reigning vices [of] the time and place; onely in this unhappy, that he was bound prentise to an ironmonger, but hath so strong a naturall byass to ingenious handicrafts that hee is thereby mastered and indeed so wholly carryed, that he cannot thryve at buying and selling, but excells in those other things and thence hath acquired good skill in watchmaking, clockmaking, graving, limning that by his own ingenuity and industry chiefly . . . His design in comeing to New England is that he be under a necessity of earning his bread by practicing his skill in one of these things.[89]

Though Joseph Allen might have been welcomed for his skills, his prospects would not have been good in New England during the seventeenth century. Paintings were rare in early New England, though portraits were painted during the first generation of the major religious leaders, and, later, of the leading commercial families.[90] The art that survived has been considered until recently the work of untrained and unsophisticated artists,

[87] *Mysteries of Nature and Art* (London: for Ralph Mab., 1634), p. 1. Subsequent pages in text are to this work.

[88] "Portrait Painting in Seventeenth Century Boston: Its History, Methods and Materials," in Fairbanks and Trent (eds.), *New England Begins*, vol. III, p. 423.

[89] Quoted by Samuel Abott Green, *John Foster: The Earliest American Engraver and First American Printer* (Boston: Massachusetts Historical Society, 1909), pp. 19, 20.

[90] The major studies are Fairbanks, "Portrait Painting in Seventeenth Century Boston"; Lillian B. Miller, "The Puritan Portrait: Its Function in Old and New England," in David D. Hall and David Grayson Allen (eds.), *Seventeenth Century New England* (Boston: Colonial Society of Massachusetts, 1984), pp. 153–84; John Michael Vlach, *Plain Painters: Making Sense of American Folk Art* (Washington, DC: Smithsonian Institution Press, 1988), ch. 4: "The Seventeenth Century: The Freake Limner,"

called "limners" – simple craftsmen, or sign painters, who painted portraits on the side. But there is a growing consensus that the best of this work continued an important tradition of art, called "neomedievalism," that developed in sixteenth-century England, and was transferred to New England (especially) from Norwich.[91] While these portraits clearly failed to use developments in perspective or the psychological techniques of Rembrandt or van Dyck, their styles were intentionally suited to portray higher moral and theological truths by artists who, in some cases, had been trained in England. As we saw with Holbein and Hilliard, portraits in this style combined symbol and allegory to remind the viewer of human mortality and spur them to virtue and abhorrence of vice.

This art of remembrance took on a particular profile in New England. Its characteristic is best represented by poet Edward Johnson's *Wonder-Working Providence: 1628–1651*. In this work Johnson celebrates the great work to which God had called the Puritans in New England, "the place where God will create a new heaven and a new earth."[92] Scattered through this work of providential history are sixty-seven poems celebrating the leaders God had raised up to establish his commonwealth. Johnson's poems are best understood as verbal portraits. We have noticed previously the role that typology plays in the interpretation of Scripture, and in the application of Scripture to the narrative of believers' lives. Here biblical events and characters become types that are reiterated in the lives of New England leaders. Biblical history is made contemporary, as Johnson put it, to "keepe in memory the names of such worthies as Christ made strong for himself."[93] These leaders had begun to die and Johnson took it upon himself by his poetry to fix in memory these whom God had chosen to lead his people in New England, "although sinful dust and ashes":

> Stretch forth thy might, Lord Christ do thou command,
> Their doubled spirit on those left to light:

---

pp. 87–102; and Wayne Craven, *Colonial American Portraiture: The Economic, Religious, Social, Cultural, Scientific and Aesthetic Foundations* (Cambridge University Press, 1986).

[91] The one to first define this style was Strong, *The English Icon*, pp. 13–15. He saw it as more akin to Byzantine art than anything current in Europe. Lillian Miller notes one of the centers of art outside London in the early seventeenth century was Norwich, which also happened to be the heartland of the Puritan rebellion, and, not incidentally, had strong Dutch connections ("Puritan Portrait," p. 161).

[92] *Johnson's Wonder-Working Providence,* p. 25. Subsequent references indicated in the text by *WWP* followed by page number.

[93] *Wonder-Working Providence,* quoted in Jesper Rosenmeier, "To Keep in Memory: The Poetry of Edward Johnson," in Peter White (ed.), *Puritan Poets and Poetics: Seventeenth Century American Poetry in Theory and Practice* (University Park: Penn State University Press, 1985), p. 160; page from Johnson not given.

Forth of their graves call ten times ten again,
That thy dear flocks no damage may sustain.

Can I forget these means that thou hast used,
To quicken up my drowsie drooping soul? (*WWP*, p. 261)

There is a grand perspective to this vision, which reaches back to biblical antecedents – Johnson likens the trip to America to the crossing of the Red Sea – and looks forward to the time when Christ will again call his people from their graves. But his poetry focuses in particular on the present calling of all, to rouse themselves, in the light of this great cloud of witnesses. "Where shall we go, Lord Christ? We turn to thee,/Heal our back slidings, forward press shall we" (p. 261). Johnson's chief means of "stirring up affections" was, Jesper Rosenmeier argues, the "creation of a persona whose voice was simultaneously that of the dead ancestors, of the eternal Christ, and of the living poet."[94]

The theological context for this, which is also that of the Puritan portraits, is clearly provided by John Cotton, and to a lesser extent William Ames, and behind these John Calvin. From Cotton, Johnson gets his typological understanding of history. Johnson was among those embarking for New England, when Cotton preached his famous sermon in 1629, assuring the settlers that God's promises to David accompanied them into the wilderness. And he later sat under his preaching so that he could write of Cotton:

When Christ intends his glorious Kingdome shall
Exalted be on Earth, he Earth doth take,
Even sinfull Man to make his worthies all:
Then praise I Man, no, Christ this Man doth make.
Sage, sober, grave, and learned Cotten [*sic*], thou
Mighty in Scripture, without Booke repeat it,
Anatomise the sence, and shew Man how
Great mysteries in sentence short are seated,
God's word with's word comparing oft unfould
Thy secret truths. (*WWP*, pp. 88, 89)

The sense that a man could, by God's grace, reflect something of Christ's love was also an important theme of the teaching of William Ames. As he wrote in the *Marrow*: "The love of God contained in religion of its own nature produces love toward men, for they are in some sort partakers in the image of God. Therefore we are said to love God in men and men in God."[95] This leads him to write extensively in his *Conscience* on justice which is the

94 "To Keep in Memory," p. 171. 95 *Marrow of Theology*, II, xvi, 8.

virtue by which we are inclined to do our duty to our neighbor. So that the reminder of another person, whether verbal or visual, can come to stand for the love and grace of God himself, calling us to respond in obedience.[96] So portraits, whether visual portraits or Johnson's poetic images, can serve to hold before the reader's imagination the contour of what Christ can do for his people. The portraits, both written and drawn, become symbols of Christ's grace, and moral allegories of the virtue the Puritans were called to pursue.

The portraits we examine must be understood in this context – as other objects in the culture they must be "useful" for improving those who look upon them as well as exhibiting the achievement of particular families. So important is the archival purpose of these artists, that Alexander Eliot can say: "in most cases the documentary value of their work outweighs its aesthetic merit."[97] Consider first this portrait of William Ames, attributed to Willem van der Vliet and painted in 1633 in the last year of Ames's life (Figure 26). This painting displays the values of the Dutch artistic tradition, light and shadows are highlighted and the figure reveals a solid plastic modeling – all in contrast to the tradition that is prominent in New England. But the symbolic details are similar to those that will be done in the new world. The clergyman stands in a symbolic pose, with one hand over his heart – which is given to God.

The other hand holds a glove and paper – speaking of his social standing and education. His face registers a calm dignity and openness which reflects his confidence in God and his moral rectitude.[98]

Something of the same purposes is reflected in the next illustration, a print of Richard Mather (Figure 27). This is the earliest surviving American print and was done, probably in 1670, by John Foster, who was America's first printer and had been a member of Mather's congregation. Mather,

---

[96] Interestingly the only negative reference to the art of portraiture comes from John Wilson, of the orthodox Amesian party. When asked whether he wanted his portrait done, he responded: "What! Such a poor, vile creature as I am! Shall my picture be drawn?" (Miller, "Puritan Portrait," p. 174).

[97] Alexander Eliot, *Three Hundred Years of American Painting* (New York: Time, Inc., 1957), p. 5. Craven argues that Calvin's influence is especially seen in the focus on prosperity, virtue and industry in these portraits, though he overlooks the more properly theological values we stress (*Colonial American Portraiture*, pp. 14–16).

[98] Cf. Calvin's motto was hands holding a heart, with the Latin inscription: "My heart I give thee, freely and sincerely." See Jonathan Fairbanks's comments in the catalogue, *New England Begins,* vol. II, p. 157. Ann Jensen Adams shows that many portraits of this time reflected this calm demeanor as a reflection of "tranquillitas," which in sixteenth- and seventeenth-century literary culture, under the influence of Stoic philosophy, came to be an ideal facial pose ("The Three-Quarter Length Life-Sized Portrait in Seventeenth Century Holland," in Franits [ed.], *Looking at Seventeenth Century Dutch Art*, pp. 168–9).

Figure 26   Willem van der Vliet, *William Ames (1576–1633)*. Oil on white oak panel.
86.1 × 65.5 cm. Harvard University Portrait Collection, Cambridge, Mass., 1633.

who came to New England in 1635, by the 1660s was revered as an example
of the zeal and purity of the original founders – at a time when subsequent
generations were thought to be losing these characteristics. Significantly
done as a woodcut (reprinted several times well into the eighteenth century)
thus making it available to a wide audience, the print probably adorned
walls of New England homes. An icon of holiness, Mather is portrayed in
the scholar's gown the New England pastors wore in place of the vestments
of the Anglican Church. He holds a bible in one hand and the other is
raised as though teaching.

Figure 27   John Foster, *Richard Mather*. Woodcut, Harvard University Houghton
Library, Cambridge, Mass., *c.* 1670.

About the same time Richard Mather's son Increase published a small
biography of his father that serves a purpose that corresponds to Foster's
woodcut.[99] Increase Mather notes "the writing and reading of the lives of
the worthy ones hath been by some accounted amongst the most profitable

[99] *The Life and Death of that Reverend man of God, Richard Mather, Teacher in the Church in Dorchester in
New England* (Cambridge, 1670). Pages in the text are to this work. Interestingly Increase Mather's
name appears nowhere in the text, which purports to be anonymous. See William J. Scheick,
"Anonymity and Art in *The Life and Death of that Reverend man of God Richard Mather*," *American
Literature* 42 (1971), pp. 457–67.

works of men under the sun" (p. 1). This is because it is pleasing to God that
the wonders of Providence "about them should be kept in remembrance"
(p. 2). Because Richard died leaving much undone, it remains for others to
follow in the way of this father in the faith. In this description, the young
Mather notes, you have presented to your view "and for your imitation
in the Lord, the Life of him that was to many of you a Spiritual father"
(p. A2). Like the visual portrait this verbal one was a sign given to promote
what would have been thought to be "real art" to the Puritans: the actual
display of the grace of God toward his servants. These "images" are to urge
the viewer and reader to place their desire in that which transcends this
world: so that seeing the emptiness of life "I should be glad to be removed
hence, where the best that is to be had doth yield so little satisfaction to
my soul, and to be brought into his presence in glory, that there I might
find . . . that satisfying all sufficient contentment in him which under the
sun is not to be enjoyed" (p. 36).

A portrait serving a similar purpose is that of John Davenport, done
by an unknown artist in 1670, the year Davenport died (Figure 28). As
with the Mather print, this painting is more an outline of a person than
a full portrait.[100] He wears again the scholar's gown and puts his hand
over his heart while the other rests on Scripture. Nothing else is visible,
either in the background or on the figure, which serves to highlight the
pleasant and childlike expression of the face. Both Mather and Davenport
are shorthand images, pared down to the essential, which is the truth that
the artist wishes to convey about these figures. These artists produced, in
the words of Alexander Eliot, "flat stylized maps of their sitters," but this
was a reflection of the purpose they set for themselves, rather than simply
their lack of training or aesthetic sense.[101] They intended to document –
to map – the surface as an emblem of spiritual depth.

Recall that for the Puritans the fleshly life was not what mattered –
vulnerable and subject to vanity as it was. Jonathan Fairbanks comments:
"The Puritans were intensely aware of the evanescent nature of the physical
world."[102] The physical likeness and realism would have been beside the

---

[100] The comment is from John Vlach, who notes it serves more "to reinforce a social regime than as
an attempt to capture creatively a person" (*Plain Painters,* p. 92). He attributes the print to John
Foster.
[101] Eliot, *Three Hundred Years,* p. 5, though it is true that these artists were not as highly trained as the
"Freake Limner" we examine below. This is obvious, for example, in the way the face of Davenport
reflects an even light, rather than receding as it is turned away. See catalogue description in *New
England Begins,* vol. ii, pp. 132–3.
[102] "Portrait Painting in Seventeenth Century Boston," p. 417.

Figure 28   Davenport Limner, *Reverend John Davenport (1597–1669/70)*. Oil on canvas,
69.2 × 58.4 cm. Yale University Art Gallery, New Haven, Conn., *c.* 1670.

point, indeed distracting from the major lessons which these images were
designed to teach. Lillian Miller argues tellingly: "All that an individual
conditioned to think in Platonic or Ramean terms required was a simplified
or diagrammatic representation of appearance."[103] The mind conditioned
to reflect on life in certain ways, and shaped by biblical patterns, would fill
in what was missing in the picture.

The way images "signify" has developed consistently in the Reformed
tradition from the time of Calvin. Images are always signs of a deeper truth
that is best laid out in the promises of Scripture, and so they must be read

[103] "Puritan Portrait," p. 171.

Figure 29   Jan van der Spriet, *Reverend Increase Mather*. Oil on canvas, $49\frac{1}{4} \times 40\frac{7}{8}$ inches. Massachusetts Historical Society, Boston, Mass., 1688.

in terms of this deeper understanding. There is a parallel, for example, between this reading of portraits and the reception of the Eucharist in the Calvinist tradition. The elements of the supper, like the images of these holy figures, are pared down. Both are *stripped*, of the accretion of medieval metaphysics on the one hand, and of Renaissance decoration on the other. For Calvin it was the verbal promise that gave meaning to the sign, which, apart from its reception by faith and the working of the Holy Spirit, had no intrinsic value. Similarly the portraits of these mortals are stripped down to the essentials, and have no intrinsic significance apart from the theological context in which they are to be read. They are signs to be received in "faith" along with the word of promise. The faithful read in them images of God's grace and faithfulness.[104]

The next portrait of Increase Mather done in London in 1688 by Jan van der Spriet (Figure 29) provides a more fully developed image, but is driven by similar values. Portraying the pastor of the Second Church in Boston, Mather's portrait is about preaching as well as about the man Increase Mather. Indeed it is painting as an extension of Mather's work as a preacher. While the picture contains significant symbols of status and even wealth – Mather's brass clips, his watch and pin are all given special attention – the center of the picture is Mather's finger pointing to a text in Ecclesiastes, "The Preacher." Indeed the image itself preaches. The scriptural reference emphasizes no doubt the vanity that is the necessary component of learning and life – as of the writing of the books lining the shelves beside him. Mather's wistful expression underlines this scriptural message. Though, in contrast to portraits done in New England, there is a higher degree of resemblance and realism in his clothes and possessions in this painting, these qualities are subordinated to the larger impact the artist wished to portray: the personal identity of the preacher, conveyed through gesture and the cumulative detail of the whole.[105]

The most elaborate of Puritan portraits are clearly those of John and Elizabeth Freake, done in Boston by an anonymous artist – known as the Freake Limner – between 1671 and 1674 (Figures 30 and 31). Like Mather and Davenport, the figures exist in a flat space, against a dark background, focusing the attention on the presence and character of the figures. These paintings were clearly designed to go together as the figures seem to turn toward one another. Though making a straightforward appeal to the viewer, the artist, as John Vlach says, was a "sure-handed and adept painter, fully in control of his abilities who achieved the effect he desired."[106] The portrait of John Freake (Figure 30), a prosperous merchant and attorney in Boston, is

---

[104] I owe the observation of the parallel to the sacrament to E. John Walford, private correspondence, January 2, 2003.
[105] Fairbanks, "Portrait Painting in Seventeenth Century Boston," p. 417.
[106] *Plain Painters,* p. 90. Vlach suggests that similarities to paintings in England suggest the artist may have been trained there (p. 93).

Figure 30   Anonymous, *John Freake*. Oil on canvas, 107.9 × 93.4 cm. Worcester Art
Museum, Worcester, Mass., *c*. 1671.

a visual record not only of his person and character, but also his prosperity.
He fingers his pendant, which in turn serves to call attention to his elaborate
Venetian lace collar; his other hand holds a pair of gloves – all of these
symbols of his status as a gentleman. He looks out at the viewer with
a calm dignity, an example of the Puritan faith that a righteous life was
consistent with prosperity.[107]

---

[107] Ibid., p. 90. Cf. catalogue description in Fairbanks and Trent (eds.), *New England Begins,* vol. III,
pp. 461–2.

Figure 31   Anonymous, *Elizabeth Clarke Freake (Mrs. John Freake) and Baby Mary*. Oil on
canvas, 108 × 93.3 cm. Worcester Art Museum, Worcester, Mass., 1670–74.

Elizabeth Freake holds Baby Mary on her lap (Figure 31), while seated on
an upholstered chair decorated with "Turkey work." As with John Freake,
Mannerist designs are featured on her lace collar and the edges of the baby's
dress. With her head modestly covered she appears serene and confident.
What is most significant in these works is the way strong colors are integrated into a unified design. They are both rich in detail, but provide
only the slightest hint of personality. They are meant to embody values
of family, faith and constancy rather than call attention to themselves as

236   *Reformed theology and visual culture*

individuals. Elizabeth's portrait seems to have been originally painted in 1671, and then repainted in 1674 to include Baby Mary (who was born six months previously). Interestingly the later version includes additional elements indicative of their wealth and standing, displaying the "cataloguing care" of the artist. None of this is given special emphasis; the display of the elaborate textiles and chair is understated. John Vlach sums up the achievement of this artist, which might be said to characterize all the art of this period:

> He was a plain painter who fully understood the cultural style that permeated his society. If art was to be made in New England by concealing art, then he would depict his sitters against a dark ground, subdue their personalities, paint shadows that were not really shadows, and establish perspectives that only hinted at a sense of three dimensions. Early New England paintings thus were works of fine art adapted to the expression of Puritan values, not works of folk art imbued with traditional values.[108]

William Perkins had said that a preacher could read all the philosophy he wanted in preparing for the sermon, but when the listener came to church, all this learning should be invisible. The word alone should be preached and heard. As Richard Mather put it later, he wanted his sermons to be "plain, aiming to shoot his arrows not over his people's heads, but into their hearts and consciences."[109] These divines could as easily have been speaking of the artists that worked in New England as the preachers. For they might have good models, they occasionally studied with the good teachers, but when it came to doing their work they sought out the heart, rather than the display of fancy. They sought the power of presence rather than subtleties of style and wit.

This presentational aesthetic resonates with what we have observed before. We have seen throughout our study that the Protestant impulse to repress various art forms and particular styles – associated as they were in the Reformers' minds with a corrupt order – by no means suppressed altogether their aesthetic sensitivities. If anything the history-shaping character of the biblical narrative with its rich imagery stimulated an imaginative view of the world in which mundane events took on dramatic proportions. One way of putting this is to point out that, even as Puritans were denouncing

---

[108] Vlach, *Plain Painters,* pp. 102–3, and see pp. 96–8. The term "cataloguing care" is from Vlach. The technical description of the x-ray images is found in Fairbanks and Trent (eds.), *New England Begins,* vol. III, pp. 460–1.

[109] *Life and Death of Richard Mather,* p. 31. Increase goes on to say that Richard often repeated "Artis est celare Artem" ([Real] art conceals art).

Figure 32   Anonymous, *Margaret Gibbs*. Oil on canvas, 102.87 × 84.14 cm. Museum of
Fine Arts, Boston, Mass., 1670.

theater, their lives in America had come to take on, in their minds, a decidedly dramatic character.

Another portrait by the Freake Limner provides a visual embodiment
of this sense (Figure 32). Margaret Gibbs's portrait was painted along with
her two brothers in 1670. The painting, like the previous work, emphasizes

overall patterns of design rather than perspective and three-dimensionality. But it is the person that stands out from the space. Little Margaret looks out knowingly at the viewer as she fingers her fan – as if very much aware of the seriousness of life and even of her own importance. Alexander Eliot observes: "The tessellated floor creates a little stage full of order and repose, and Margaret dominates it effortlessly."[110]

For the Puritans images were banished from churches, but in place of such sacred imagery, the whole of life, in its patterns and structures, took on the character of an icon of God's presence. And in the midst of this theater of God's glory, it is the individual person as the special image of God that stands out as the dramatic focus in the narrative of salvation. Of course these believers often failed to accomplish what they set out to do, but their faith in the world to come – itself an act of imaginative construction – kept them hopeful and encouraged them to follow the script. The poets and artists we have surveyed did not shrink from making imaginative and sensuous use of this developing tradition.

Indeed their very failures pointed to the reason that physical images or cultural products could not convey the full weight of God's presence during a person's sojourn on earth. In this both William Ames and John Cotton were agreed. Ames stressed that the sacrament does not lie in its corporeal character but in its use, the way in which it moved a believer toward a better future. Cotton knew that a heart whose desire was misplaced constricted human vision, so biblical images were pressed into service to move the heart toward grace. So, as Michael Clark points out in his discussion of Ames and Cotton, concrete images could not be the basis of meditation, they could only be a point of departure. "They must be there as objects toward which those thoughts are directed by the will's desire." Whereas for both Anglicans and Catholics the image could be used as a step in the process of moving the soul toward God, Protestants more often felt these served to distract rather than direct the mind. So Clark concludes the Puritan process involved "a hermeneutic that was based on the destruction of the image from which it departed."[111] The Puritan conception of the world as a moral arena certainly did not repress all cultural or aesthetic value, as is frequently argued. Rather their settled conviction that the world was

---

[110] Eliot, *Three Hundred Years*, p. 5. Jonathan Fairbanks notes the sophistication and learning reflected in this work; these portraits show "a basic understanding of Renaissance and Mannerist art theory" ("Portraits in Seventeenth Century New England," in Fairbanks and Trent [eds.], *New England Begins*, vol. III, p. 424).

[111] " 'The Crucified Phrase': Sign and Desire in Puritan Semiology," *Early American Literature* 13 (1979), pp. 285, 289. He goes on to argue that this involved "rupturing" the connection which might exist in order to point out the truth that transcends any referential connection (p. 289).

charged with God's purposes allowed them to see objects and events in their life as symbolic instruments. The question then is not the aesthetic validity of their vision, but whether and in what form it could survive amidst the lassitude of later generations. By century's end, this was the question that most concerned them, and which we take up in the following chapter.

CHAPTER 7

Jonathan Edwards: the world as image and shadow

In 1729 Francis Worcester wrote a small book lamenting the decline of spirituality in New England and urging readers toward greater personal holiness. One remedy for the degeneracy Worcester saw around him was to urge people to consider their future state.[1] In their prayer time in dependence on the Holy Spirit he proposed they reflect on the glories of heaven. To illustrate this practice he recalls the ecstatic experiences of Augustine (p. 23) and recounts the testimony of a contemporary who had similar experiences. While meditating in prayer this person "saw" heaven in clearness – though not with bodily eyes since he closed them when he prayed.[2] Sometime in the year 1728 while praying, he had fallen into a trance. This was his testimony: "I seemed to look thro' some darkness and there was a way opened into a glorious place of light. I now seemed to enter into this glorious city, shining exceeding bright. Surely, thought I, this is the New Jerusalem the heavenly city.... How glorious is this place! This is the city of the great king; the streets and walls shining exceeding bright" (p. 27). But above all in this city he desired to see the Lord, "him whom my soul loves . . . I cast my eyes on him shining gloriously being encircled by a multitude of shining ones." When he came to, he was weeping, "my soul seemed uneasy because confined in a house of clay" (p. 28). He beheld the world "as a melancholy place." After some months of such experiences, he notes: "I have such realizing views of unseen and eternal things in my mind, that this world and all the glory thereof appear as things of no value" (p. 29).

[1] *A Bridle for Sinners and a Spur for Saints* (Boston, 1782), though the date of its writing, noted at the end of the book, was 1729 (p. 9). Subsequent pages in the text. This fourth edition was intended for soldiers (see p. 13n), its size (about 4″ × 6″ and only 32 pages in length) made it convenient for carrying in a shirt pocket. Interestingly, extracts of Cotton Mather's little work on "Family Religion" (originally published in 1705) are printed along with Worcester's text, as a running text below Worcester's, beginning on p. 13. Worcester is identified on the title page only as a "Lover of piety and well-wisher to the souls of men," and is not listed in the standard biographical dictionaries, suggesting he was probably a layman.
[2] Accompanying the inward turn of piety we have documented was the innovation of closing one's eyes in prayer.

While not unknown in the previous century, testimonies of such experiences will come to play an increasingly important role in eighteenth-century Puritan spirituality. They find their setting in the growing dismay religious leaders felt at the decline of faith after the pioneer generation – a decline that is marked out by the half-way covenant in 1662, and the trauma associated with Salem witch trials in 1692. These lay testimonies frequently reflect a preoccupation with death and the associated meditation on life's vanity and brevity, and the sense that one must see this life as a pointer and an image of the more real world that lies beyond it. But throughout such testimonies, we become aware of the emergence of a unique voice – reflecting more often the rough accents of the people than the careful vocabulary of the clergy. These meditative practices and the cultural products that resulted will be the central themes of this chapter. These all contributed to the developing imaginative shape of that century's piety, a piety we will argue that is given theological shape in the work of Jonathan Edwards.

THE PEOPLE'S VOICE AND THE VISION OF HEAVEN

By the end of the seventeenth century, the tensions between the two tendencies we traced in William Ames and John Cotton became increasingly evident. On the one hand, as immigration and economic growth changed the face of New England, those concerned with the theological (and moral) precision of Ames found much to lament. As a result, alongside the conversion narrative that Cotton and others encouraged, there arose a new genre of discourse: the Jeremiad.[3] A stream of clergy before him had recited Worcester's complaint: "It is a time of great degeneracy among us: Iniquity abounds, and the love of many is grown cold, strict godliness is laid aside" (p. 18). In 1700, Samuel Willard, Boston minister and vice president of Harvard, preached a famous sermon lamenting the "slight success of the Gospel" during that time. As he looked around him at the turn of the century, he saw little evidence of a genuine transformation of life and morals.[4]

It is significant that Worcester appends extracts from Cotton Mather's little book *Family Religion Excited and Assisted* (1705) to his book on spirituality. Mather's work continues the important focus on family worship that we noted was developing in the seventeenth century. When he speaks of a "form of Godliness" in family practices as a vehicle for the

---

[3] On the rise of this and its significance for forming the American character see Sacvan Bercovitch, *The American Jeremiad* (Madison: University of Wisconsin Press, 1978).

[4] Discussed in Frank Lambert, *Inventing the "Great Awakening"* (Princeton University Press, 1999), pp. 88–9.

power of godliness, he has a very definite understanding of "form." It is to involve particular duties – prayer twice each day, reading of Scripture – which provide a specific routine which will "clothe the mundane in Scripture." As Stephen Foster notes, such forms encouraged believers to enter imaginatively into the truth of the Gospel, simply because they were forced to encounter it at every turn; there was no alternative "picture" by which to make sense of the world.[5] But this monopoly on the imagination was being challenged as the new century dawned.

Samuel Willard's well-known summary of doctrine, *A Compleat Body of Divinity* (1726), is itself a monument to the continuing influence of Ames's all-encompassing vision.[6] This lengthy and precise compendium of doctrine, in the form of a commentary on the Westminster Catechism, would have been found in the libraries of most eighteenth-century clergy. Willard continues Calvin's strong emphasis on the revelatory character of creation. In his discussion of the ninth question of the catechism he notes: "How much of God we have here to contemplate. Every spire of grass sets God before us: upon the Earthly carpet is set the wondrous Glory of God" (p. 118). But when he comes to his discussion of worship this creational glory is allowed no role. For only God determines "positive worship" (p. 612), in which the word preached becomes the instrument of the Spirit (pp. 810, 819). As Ames and others before him, he insists the sacraments only become effectual in their "use," they have no natural "virtue" in them (p. 835). Nor can our bodily nature suggest any physical mediation in worship. Because we humans are spirit, we are naturally suited to be clothed with God who is also a spirit (p. 54).

The emphasis that the catechism (and Calvin before this) placed on the creation as the theater for God's glory had led to the imaginative meditations of Richard Baxter and Anne Bradstreet. But Willard insists, in words that seem to draw the circle ever more tightly around the work of human fancy:

How unsuitable it is to represent the Divine Nature by any corporeal similitude. I mean in Pictures or Images of any visible and bodily substance, and that whether it

---

[5] The family, Mather notes, is "the first society that by the direction of God is produced among the children of men" (*A Bridle for Sinners*, p. 14), thus they should glorify God with daily family worship. "If grace be in the heart can it be long before prayer is in the house?" (p. 16). The phrase "clothe the mundane in Scripture" is from Stephen Foster, "The Godly in Transit: English Popular Protestantism and the Creation of a Puritan Establishment in America," in David D. Hall and David Grayson Allen (eds.), *Seventeenth Century New England* (Boston: Colonial Society of Massachusetts), p. 236.

[6] Samuel Willard, *A Compleat Body of Divinity in Two Hundred and Fifty Expository Lectures on the (Westminster) Assembly's Shorter Catechism* (Boston: Green *et al.*, 1726). This collection of sermons that he preached between 1687 and 1707 reached a staggering 914 folio pages. Subsequent pages in the text are to this work.

be for civility or devotion, i.e. merely as ornamental, or as some pretend, to encrease devout affection in any; how is it possible rightly to shadow a spirit? Who ever was able rightly to decypher the form or shape of a being which is invisible? (p. 54)

God's own creative work and incarnation notwithstanding, we are instructed not to consider possible any such "shadowing" of God who is Spirit. Sunday by Sunday, believers' attention was turned away from the divine patterns Edwards would discover in creation, and instructed in this vast interrelated vision of knowledge – a "compleat" body of what God wanted us to know.

But at the beginning of a new century, such instruction by no means constituted all that people sitting in the pew believed they could know. The ever-present sense of life's vulnerability along with the rich imagery of Scripture combined with ancient streams of tradition and superstition to produce a highly charged vision of life and the world – one that constantly threatened to break out of the forms that the clergy were seeking to enforce. David D. Hall refers to these layers of popular belief as "a loosely bounded set of symbols and motifs that gave significance to rites of passage and life crises, that infused everyday events with the presence of the supernatural."[7] These believers had been taught that they could read and receive the truth of Scripture for themselves, and that they could experience God directly. And many of them did so in ways that confounded the ministers' teaching and, in the First Great Awakening, threatened to break through all the careful boundaries of the clergy. Like Anne Hutchinson before them, some even went so far as to critique ministerial authority. Many of the narratives that are recorded in Worcester (and later in Edwards's "Faithful Narrative" of revival experiences), recall the testimony of Anne Hutchinson during her trial, even, in his unguarded moments, of John Cotton himself.

Perhaps the most poignant moments of such a confrontation came toward the end of the Salem witch trials. During her trial for practicing witchcraft on September 9, 1692, Mary Easty was allowed to address the bench. She spoke haltingly, in plain, even coarse speech:

The Lord above knows my Innocency then and likewise doth now as at the great day will be known to men and Angels – I petition to your honors not for my own life for I know I must die and my appointed time is set. But the Lord He knows it is that if it be possible, that no more innocent blood be shed which undoubtedly cannot be avoyded in the way and course you go in . . . I being confident there

---

[7] *Worlds of Wonder; Days of Judgment; Popular Religious Belief in Early New England* (New York: Knopf, 1989), p. 18. He contrasts this living tradition with the ministers' constructs, which he characterizes as a coherent interlocking whole (p. 66).

is several of them has belied themselves and others as will appear, if not in this world, I am sure in the world to come whither I am going . . . The Lord above who is the Searcher of all hearts know that as I shall answer it at the Tribunal seat that I know not the least thing of witchcraft therefore I cannot I dare not belie my own soule.[8]

Mary Easty was hanged on September 22, 1692, one of the last victims of that sad chapter of Puritan history. But not before she gave this eloquent testimony to her own faith in the reality of God's judgment and the truth of that other world.

In these voices we hear the beginning of a cultural tradition that, for the first time, will stand over against what has been a dominant religious culture. This will be the soil in which popular culture – broadsides, stories and, eventually, the novel – will come to flourish. Here for the first time, in these accounts of lay religious experience, a lay perspective on Puritan life is being validated. These cultures – the clergy and the lay – are not yet separate, they overlap and interact, but this tension provides the starting point of the split between high and low culture that emerges later in the eighteenth century. "By 1800," Peter Burke notes, "in most parts of Europe, the clergy, the nobility, the merchants, the professional men – and their wives – had abandoned popular culture to the lower classes, from whom they were now separated, as never before by profound differences in world view."[9]

Most significant for our purposes, however, is the fact that these experiences, and the culture they encouraged, provided a scope for the development of imaginative constructions that the formal structures discouraged. And, we will argue, Jonathan Edwards will give theological grounding for this experiential religion. In one sense a plain style was still influential – in the construction of knowledge by preaching and catechesis, and in the religious forms which resulted. Edwards could still direct himself to "use as few terms of art as possible" and later rejected "elegance in style" for "unpolished dress."[10] But by this time the plain style no longer dominated New England as it had done in the time of John Cotton. Indeed in a sense it was the very typology and illustrative providences these earlier theologians had endorsed that expanded the figurative discourse of the Puritans. It was this expansive reading of Scripture (and consequently of life) that provided the language for the experiences that were later recounted. This is clearly

---

[8] In Chadwick Hansen, *Witchcraft at Salem* (New York: George Braziller, 1969), pp. 151–2.

[9] Burke, *Popular Culture in Early Modern Europe*, p. 270.

[10] See the discussion in Wallace E. Anderson's introduction to "Images of Divine Things," in Jonathan Edwards, *Typological Writings*, vol. XI of *Works* (New Haven: Yale University Press, 1993), pp. 21–2.

seen, for example, in the biblical resonances of the vision of heaven that opened this chapter.

Life still involved the pursuit of restraint and humility. As John Gatta puts this: "If the poet could not frame language suitable to heaven, he could at least insure its consonance with his own project of self-purification . . . A 'plaine' rhetoric would aptly embody this trait of devoted concentration, warding off pride and blighting the effects of the fall."[11] But within these constraints there was a liberation of language to probe into the heart of things and "see" things for what they were. Though, as we have seen, reading is a dominant metaphor for understanding, this in itself, ironically, allowed "sight" and "vision" to dominate Puritan discourse. Leigh Schmidt notes that the sacramental piety associated with the "Holy Fairs" of Scotland (the heritage of which he argues survives in American revivals) was intensely visual. Sacramental manuals encouraged meditation, even visions, which – much to the chagrin of ministers – occasionally lapsed into the ecstatic.[12]

Consider this instruction of John Willison, a minister in Dundee, to prepare readers for partaking of the sacrament. He asks the reader to recall Christ's death, recounting the kindness of the Lord with doubting Thomas:

O Communicant, can you come to the foot of Christ's cross and see his wounds, and hear such language, and your heart not be affected with love to Christ, and hatred to sin? Can you behold Christ thus cruelly used, nailed to the tree, bleeding and dying in your room? Can you see the heavens turning black, the sun drawing in its head, the earth quaking and the rocks rending at the sufferings of the Son of God, and your heart not quake for sin, that awakened the sword of justice against him as our surety?[13]

Here is a call to meditation that recalls Ignatius' *Spiritual Exercises*. But it is combined with a uniquely Protestant vision of a life that is "experimentally" changed by the experience. Willison encourages believers to keep the mind and thoughts fixed upon the object until their hearts are properly "affected."[14]

---

[11] John Gatta, *Gracious Laughter: The Meditative Wit of Edward Taylor* (Columbia, Mo.: University of Missouri Press, 1989), p. 71.

[12] Schmidt, *Holy Fairs*, pp. 145–6. He goes on to note with respect to ecstatic experiences: "Perhaps at no point was the gap between the mind of the ministers and the piety of the laity more profound" (p. 146). See chapter two, "Visible Gospel," where he notes these events – spoken, sung and enacted – were intensely visual.

[13] John Willison, *Sacramental Meditations and Advices Grounded upon Scripture Texts: Proper for Communicants to Prepare their hearts, Excite their Affections, Quicken their Graces and Enliven their devotions on Sacramental occasions* (London, 1794 [1714]), p. 167.

[14] See the discussion in Leigh, *Holy Fairs*, pp. 138–9. This leads Schmidt to suggest that the revival/sacramental polarity needs rethinking.

But note in particular the connection between vision and sight, between reading and seeing in these experiences. The metaphor of reading goes back to Calvin for whom the glasses of Scripture enable the believer not only to "read" the truth of one's soul, but also to see God's glory in the world. By the end of the seventeenth century this "vision" could be an intensely personal experience that enabled one to "read" creation, even to see through death to what lay on the other side. The reflections that opened this chapter are nothing if not an intensely imaginative projection of what is impossible for actual eyes to see: the very splendor of God and of heaven. By the eighteenth century this is the vision the spectacles of Scripture had made possible.

Perhaps the most important influence on this typological imagination was Richard Baxter's influential treatise, *The Saints Everlasting Rest* (1649/50),[15] which was widely read in New England. In this long work Baxter has two goals. The first is to remind the believer that their true rest is not to be found in this world however delightful it might be, but in heaven which is our true and final "rest." At the same time, secondly, Baxter argues forcefully (especially in the fourth part of the work) that the sensuous experiences of beauty and joy can be pressed into service, as types of the rest for which our souls yearn. Indeed one has to prepare oneself for the meditations on heaven precisely by meditating on, and being affected by, the delights of the world. Here Baxter picks up on a theme in Calvin that had been largely overlooked. Calvin had written:

The Lord had imprinted on [the blessings of this life] . . . marks of divine grace to train them according to the measure of their weakness, they were attracted by its sweetness more than if they had contemplated his grace directly . . . [Thus] the Lord in testifying his benevolence toward believers by present good things, then foreshadowed spiritual happiness by such types and symbol. (II, xi, 3)

So Baxter writes: "What benefit or strength or sweetness canst thou possibly receive by thy meditations on eternity, while thou doest not exercise those Affections, which are the senses of the soul, by which it must receive this sweetness and strength" (Part 4, p. 151). Indeed a major part of Baxter's purpose is to oppose a kind of barren rationalism he saw around him.

---

[15] London: Joseph Caryl: 1649/50. Nine editions appeared in the next twelve years. The pages in the text are from the fourth edition published in 1653. There is good reason to identify Baxter's influence more with the tradition of Cotton than that of Ames and of Thomas Hooker. See the discussion in Louis Matz's foreword to *Poems of Edward Taylor*, pp. xxiii–xxiv. Baxter credits his earliest awakening to reading Richard Sibbes, *A Bruised Reed*, and his most affectionate recommendations to others were works by "that comfortable doctor" (N. H. Keeble, *Richard Baxter: Puritan Man of Letters* [Oxford: Clarendon Press, 1982], pp. 34, 38).

Thinking about, reading about or hearing sermons of heaven, he notes frequently, does not make us heavenly – these are only "necessary helps" (p. 122). The goal is "to get these truths from thy head to thy heart, and that all the sermons which thou hast heard of Heaven . . . be turned into the bloud and spirits of Affection, and thou must feel them revive thee, and warm thee at thy heart" (p. 151). Echoing Calvin's doctrine of God's accommodation, Baxter notes: "God would not have given us either our senses themselves or their usual objects if they might not have been service-able to his own Praise and helps to raise us up to the apprehension of higher things" (p. 217). In ways that recall the medieval uses of vision Baxter urges the believer to make good use of these images. They are meant to lead us to reflect on our true homeland. The images themselves lose nothing of their splendor in this way, rather they are seen more clearly to be an acknowledgment of their source in God. As he says: "All this light that so amazeth, and rejoiceth me is but a Candle lighted from heaven, to lead me thither through this world of darkness" (p. 242).

What we call art, or imagery, could be allowed even encouraged insofar as it reflected this typological connection. Anne Bradstreet, for example, in her "Contemplations," goes out in an autumn evening to see:

> The trees all richly clad, yet void of pride,
> Where gilded o'er by his rich golden head.
> Their leaves and fruits seemed painted, but was [*sic*] true.[16]

Note these trees were as beautiful as something painted, but "true." They were themselves something better than art. This "truth" implies she sees the world as sign or type. But this "seeing as" does not dissolve the creature; it rather enlarges upon it.

> Then on a stately oak I cast mine eye,
> Whose ruffling top the clouds seemed to aspire;
> How long since thou was in thine infancy?[17]

This leads her to reflect on eternity, which scorns the centuries of the oak. But this typological process only underlines the beauty and wonder of the oak; it does not diminish it.[18] This is because biblical narrative (parts of which are recounted in "Contemplations" 11–14) provides both

---

[16] "Contemplations, 1," *Works of Anne Bradstreet*, p. 204. On the typological connections see Robert D. Richardson Jr., "The Puritan Poetry of Anne Bradstreet," in Sacvan Bercovitch (ed.), *The American Puritan Imagination: Essays in Revaluation* (Cambridge University Press, 1974), pp. 114–15.

[17] "Contemplations, 3," in *Works of Anne Bradstreet*, p. 205.

[18] Cf. Richardson, "She does not dismiss the oak to dwell upon eternity" ("Puritan Poetry of Anne Bradstreet," p. 115).

the framework and the language for her imaginative excursions into the world around. Because God indwells this narrative and directs it to its end, the Puritan could look at the natural world and "see" God.

Since the meaning and purpose of this world terminated on the world of heaven, the Puritan notion of beauty was firmly eschatological. Whatever we know of beauty, or of truth, is partial and incomplete. It points beyond itself to the greater beauty and truth of heaven. This is captured nicely in some verse that accompanied a portrait of the poet George Withers (1584–1667):

> What I WAS is passed by;
> What I AM away doth flie;
> What I SHALL BEE none do see;
> Yet in that my Beauties bee.[19]

One of the clearest examples of this typological imagination is found in the poetry of Edward Taylor, surely among the most unusual of the New England clergy. Born in Leicestershire, England in 1642, he came to New England in 1668 where he was given advanced standing at Harvard. Following his graduation in 1671 he became pastor of the church in Westfield, then at the western edge of New England civilization, where he was the pastor and town physician until his death in 1728/9.[20] Though he wrote poetry his whole life, he published nothing during his lifetime, and forbade his heirs from doing so after his death. His work was found in the early 1900s hidden in the binding of books from his library and the first selections were not published until 1937.

Taylor's work then was a concealed art in the most literal sense of the word. But its reticence goes beyond the squirreling of his poems in book bindings; it is evident on every page of his poetry. It is as if he had taken Calvin's admonition that "whatever we think of God is foolishness" (*Inst.* I, ii, 4), and erected on it an entire aesthetic theory. In a sermon he describes this method: "There are Some things whose Excellency is flourisht over with Metaphors. We borrow the Excellency of other things to varnish over their Excellency withall. But Grace excells all Metaphors. The varnish laid upon it doth but darken, and not decorate it: its own Colours are too

---

[19] Quoted in Jonathan Fairbanks, "Portrait Painting in Seventeenth Century Boston," p. 417. Withers was an officer of the party of the Parliament.

[20] See Donald E. Stanford's introduction to *Poems of Edward Taylor*, pp. xxxix–lxii. Most of his poetry was probably written between 1682 and 1717. See also John Gatta, *Gracious Laughter*; and William J. Scheick, "The Jawbone Schema of Edward Taylor's God's Determinations," in Emory Elliott (ed.), *Puritan Influences in American Literature* (Urbana: University of Illinois, 1979), pp. 38–52.

glorious to be made more glorious by any Colour of Secular glory."[21] So the thought of his bringing a suitable gift of eloquence to garnish this grace is ludicrous:

> What, Can I ever tune those Melodies
> Who have no tune at all?
> Not knowing where to stop nor Rise,
> Nor when to Fall.
> To sing thy Praise I am unfit.
> I have not learn'd my Gam-Ut yet.[22]

Or in the "Prologue":

> Lord, can a Crumb of Dust the Earth outweigh?
> Outmatch all mountains, nay the Chrystall sky?

These all, as creations of God, can "trace the Boundless Diety," but what can Taylor himself, this crumb of dust, offer? As he confesses:

> I am this Crumb of Dust which is design'd
> To make my Pen unto they Praise alone,
> And my dull phancy I would gladly grinde
> Unto an Edge on Zions Pretious [*sic*] Stone.
> And Write in Liquid Gold upon thy Name
> My Letters till thy glory forth doth flame.[23]

Such a view of things is of course not "natural." It cannot be read off from the world as it is. Indeed merely depending on the "senses" is a sure way to be misled. The devil "straweth poison" on the things the senses feed upon:

> By some odde straggling thought up poyson flies
> Into the heart; and through the Eares and Eyes.
> Which sick, lies gasping.[24]

This typological vision is based on a clarity that comes only when one's eyes are opened. This in turn is based on a clear inward view of oneself, the proper vision for which necessitates Calvin's "spectacles":

> You want Cleare Spectacles: your eyes are dim:
> Turn inside out: and turn your Eyes within.[25]

---

[21] Edward Taylor, *Christographia*, ed. Norman Grabo (New Haven: Yale University Press, 1962), p. 253.

[22] "The Soul's Admiration Hereupon," from "God's Determinations," in Stanford (ed.), *Poems of Edward Taylor*, p. 457. The "Gam-ut" is a complicated musical scale developed in Italy, from which comes the English word "gamut," meaning the full range.

[23] *Poems of Edward Taylor*, p. 1.   [24] Ibid., p. 406.

[25] Ibid., p. 409. Cf. Sheick's discussion in "Jawbone Schema," pp. 44–50.

The cadences of these scriptural eyeglasses fill every line of Taylor's verse. Towering above this chastened view of himself and his feeble powers is the awesome and sovereign power of God who is able to bring something out of nothing:

> Infinity . . . Which All from Nothing fet [*sic*], from Nothing, All:
> Hath all on nothing set, lets Nothing fall.
> Gave all to nothing Man indeed, whereby
> Through nothing man all might him Glorify.[26]

In many ways Taylor's poetry captures much of the essence of the Puritan imagination. It was nourished on the biblical spirituality and practices of New England, and – one is tempted to say – on nothing else (the only book of poetry found in his large library was Anne Bradstreet's, though there were several works by Richard Baxter). The theology is carefully orthodox and Calvinist – God's power, human depravity (pictured as a maze) and salvation through the death of Christ. Yet within this structure, indeed enabled by this and its biblical framework, he develops an elaborate series of rich, schematic metaphors, of, for example, the soul's coach ride to heaven. As Norman Grabo notes, Taylor's poems "betray [a] quite sophisticated symbolic sense that might be said to be built into Puritan thought through its theology."[27] At the same time, throughout Taylor's work, frequent references to vision and sight, even to color, underline the visual dimension of Puritan piety. As Lynn Maria Haims puts it, Taylor is able to assemble the pieces of a broken creation and, like an abstract artist, make of them a thing of beauty.[28]

Was it, as Haims suggests, the apparently unorthodox forms Taylor gave his orthodox theology that led him to conceal his art? Did he expect that it would have been unwelcome? Everything about his work leads one to believe that it was a very different dynamic that moved him to this reticence. Taylor simply believed his poetic work was, in the end, not that important in the scheme of things. The "art" that was important was the actual impact of "heavens Glory upon the Soul."[29] What was important was the real progress of his parishioners' souls toward heaven, for which he labored throughout

---

[26] *Poems of Edward Taylor*, pp. 387–8.

[27] Norman S. Grabo, "The Veiled Vision: The Role of Aesthetics in Early American Intellectual History," *William and Mary Quarterly* 3rd ser., 19 (1962), p. 500. Grabo goes on to describe the passionate, even erotic character of Taylor's poetry.

[28] Lynn Maria Haims, "The American Puritan Aesthetic: Iconography in Seventeenth Century Poetry and Tombstone Art," Ph.D dissertation, New York University (1981), pp. 165, 197. Taylor uses "a selective mode of expression akin to abstract art" (p. 165).

[29] *Christographia*, ed. Norman Grabo (New Haven: Yale University Press, 1962), p. 253. The sermon goes on: "It's the Angells glory to be gracious. Grace is the glory of Angells. But now Christ is full

his long life. He truly believed that whatever eloquence he was able to achieve would be "unfit within thine Eares to ting."[30] But this did not keep him from enjoying his own reflections on the day when his stammering praise would be suited to its object:

> In Heaven soaring up, I dropt an Eare
>   On Earth: and oh! sweet melody:
> And listening, found it was the Saints who were
>   Encoacht for Heaven that sang for Joy.
>   For in Christs Coach they sweetly sing;
>   As they to Glory ride therein.
> Oh! joyous hearts! Enfir'd with holy Flame!
>   Is speech thus tassled with praise?
> Will not your inward fire of Joy contain;
>   That it in open flames doth blaze?
> For in Christs Coach they sweetly sing;
>   As they to Glory ride therein.[31]

Since the discovery of Edward Taylor's work almost a century ago there has been much lamenting the loss of this treasure for so many years. Though this is a monument of poetic imagination, its recovery points up, ironically, how impoverished our own secularized imagination has become. For it was precisely because Taylor could "imagine" another world in such vivid colors that he was able to shape exquisite metaphors out of the rough stuff of this earthly life. Were he alive, he would lament, not the loss of his work, but our inability to see into and through the world to God and God's world. Whatever the Puritans believed about fancy and imagery, this typological vision, grounded as it was on a vision of creation enlivened by the presence of God, was certainly a work of rich imaginative construction.

DEATH AND TOMBSTONE ART: LIFE AS SHADOW

The Puritans had such a vivid sense of heaven, in part, because their hold on this life seemed so insecure. Much of this uncertainty had to do with the simple facts of demography. Death, especially of the young, was an inescapable part of their daily lives.[32] Indeed death was so common among infants that many deaths went unrecorded – up to 30 percent never survived

---

of all Grace and of all the Glory of Grace. For all the fulness of Grace is in him. He is as I may say, amazingly full of Grace and of all Grace in its fulness."

[30] *Poems of Edward Taylor,* p. 452.

[31] This is from the conclusion of "God's Determinations," in *Poems of Edward Taylor*, pp. 458–9.

[32] I am dependent on David E. Stannard for this background material; see *The Puritan Way of Death: A Study of Religion, Culture and Social Change* (Oxford University Press, 1977), pp. 53–63.

their first year. A quarter of those who did survive would not live to see their tenth birthday.[33] Because of increased mortality from lowered resistance to disease, Puritans dreaded the coming of winter. In late September of 1678, Boston, which in general had a higher mortality rate than surrounding cities, was decimated by an outbreak of smallpox – thirty died on a single day. Increase Mather, among others, took the opportunity to urge the people to cry out to God for help.

But there were also theological motivations behind their uncertain hold on life. Throughout Puritan literature references to a "false hope" of heaven were common. Clergy often pointed out that such false security naturally tends to arise from one's depraved nature. Beyond that, God's providences were "inscrutable" and therefore to presume on God's mercy was surely a sign of overweening pride.[34] But as time went on, the experiences and practices of common people, not always with the endorsement of the clergy, enabled them to come to terms with death in ways that brought them a measure of comfort. The proliferation of tombstone carvings remain one of the clearest evidences of this popular faith.

Practices in connection with death followed no consistent trajectory after the Reformation. Late sixteenth-century practices among Reformed churches, especially in Geneva, often featured elaborate funeral ceremonies. But in early Puritan America burial was to be made as simple as possible. The dead were buried in a white shift after a simple service of Scripture and prayer. After all they believed their lives were in God's hands, and, besides, money spent on elaborate ceremonies could more usefully go to care for the poor. But in the second half of the century, as economic conditions improved, ceremonies grew more elaborate. Gloves were sent out to friends on the day of the funeral, costly rings were sometimes given to all in attendance – resulting in total costs that could amount to 20 percent of the estate![35] Beginning in the 1650s gravestones began to be carved that symbolized their faith in the life of heaven.

The imagery on graves seems to have been influenced by broadsides and emblem books.[36] Already in the sixteenth century printed broadsides

---

[33] Stannard argues that this motivated parents to keep some emotional distance from their children, not wanting to form strong attachments that would result in a painful sense of loss, should they die (*Puritan Way of Death*, p. 57). Haims notes that Edward Taylor lost five of eight children from his first wife and only one in six survived from his second ("American Puritan Aesthetic," p. 60).

[34] See Stannard and literature cited there, *Puritan Way of Death*, pp. 74–89.

[35] Ibid., pp. 101–2 and 112–13.

[36] An early comprehensive study is Allan I. Ludwig, *Graven Images: New England Stonecarving and Its Symbols 1650–1815* (Middleton: Wesleyan University Press, 1966); and see Haims, "American Puritan Aesthetic," ch. 2, "Stone Icons."

celebrating the life of the deceased persons had become common. Like contemporary death announcements in Europe these were posted on walls and given out to friends. A broadside from about 1668 celebrates the life of the religious and virtuous Mrs. Lydia Minot (Figure 33). This woodcut was probably printed in Cambridge, Massachusetts by Samuel Green. It provides an opportunity not only to indicate the significance of this person – a faithful wife and mother of five who died during the birth of her sixth child, but more importantly to express her faith in her eternal life with God. For the people who read it, it would have served the dual purpose of reminding them of the certainty of their own death (underlined by the phrase "remember death" carved on the freize across the top), and also inspiring them by the testimony of her life and her assurance of being with God:

> When Breath expir'd, my Life came flowing in;
> My Soul reviv'd, made free from th'death of Sin.
> New Light, new Love, new Joy me now do fill.

These anonymous verses, though they must have been composed quickly, show a remarkable facility with poetic language. The symbolism in the freize – the hourglass speaking of the passing of life's days, and the skeleton with a sickle symbolizing death – reiterates the message that is expressed in verse below.

The interaction of verse and images was characteristic of the influential emblem books published in the seventeenth century. The most famous by Francis Quarles, first published in 1639, paired visual images with Scripture (and classical) passages and verse.[37] The passage in Philippians 3:19 and the verse printed on the right-hand page speak of the human inclination to treasure things (Figure 34). As the Philippians passage says, there are those who make a god of their belly, "their minds [are] set on earthly things." The verse printed below the passage points out how attached to earthly splendor the child tends to be – the sparkle of trinkets is the only thing that can keep its attention. These themes are elaborated in the images on the left-hand page, with a view of the heavenly realm above and the child with cupid (symbolizing earthly love) below. Together these say: as the child is attracted to earthly pleasures so will the man – something that is reiterated in the Latin inscription below the picture. The image then does not simply illustrate the verse, but adds something of its own, so that the full message of the emblem is to be found in the word and the image together. One has

---

[37] Francis Quarles, *Emblems: With the Hieroglyphicks: All the Cuts being newly illustrated* (London: for M. Gillyflower, 1696), illustrated in figure thirty four from pp. 92–3.

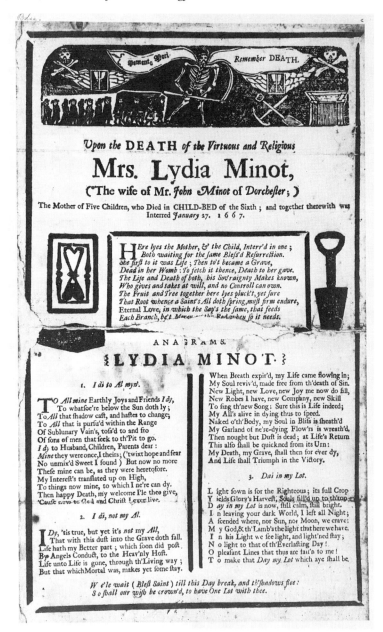

Figure 33   Samuel Green, *Funeral Broadside: Mrs. Lydia Minot.* Massachusetts Historical Society, Boston, Mass., 1668.

to put together the passage, the image and the verse to fully comprehend the emblem. Each element makes its contribution to the impact. As we will see these emblems will appear on the grave carvings, and there, too, the image will bring something to the interpretation of the piece. This symbolism is consistent with the use of imagery we have been tracing. The image has a role to play, but not independently of the word. The word and image together display the truth that God has placed in the order of things, just as the sign and promise together give meaning to the sacrament. As Barbara Lewalski points out, Protestants believed these emblems were a discovered symbolism rather than a constructed one. The meaning they conveyed, Protestants were convinced, lay in the order of things that God had made – in the world as a mirror of God. They are "grounded in the divine order of things rather than simply in the conceits of human wit – that is, as symbol or allegories found, not made."[38]

These broadsides and the emblem books would have been familiar to the carvers who began to work in the 1650s and 1660s. This headstone of Joseph Tapping, attributed to the anonymous Charlestown Stonecutter, displays the typical forms of the carved tombstone (Figure 35). On the top is a double-scrolled Mannerist pediment, which is meant to represent a doorway between death and the new life of heaven. In the pediment an hourglass sits on the winged skull, symbolic of the soul flying to heaven, accompanied by the Latin inscription "Fugit Hora," "The hour flies" – also repeated in the archway on the lower right. The juxtaposing of a skull with the wings (of angels?) results in a catachrestic image – death being almost literally "swallowed up in victory"(1 Cor. 15:54). Stars and foliage fill out the decoration on the top. Below, between the epitaph and Latin mottoes, appears the first known example from a seventeenth-century emblem book on a New England tombstone.[39] The image represents time, pictured as an old man staying the hand of Death, pictured as a skeleton, as Death seeks to snuff out the candle of life. Father Time is pictured with two of his attributes, the hourglass and the scythe.

Notably missing on these carvings is any symbolism that could be interpreted as strictly biblical. The "civil" imagery, however, is clearly meant to present in other (covert?) ways the same truth that is found in Scripture.[40] At the same time, there seems to be a tolerance for what would be called secular images, as long as they are used to speak of truths that are found

---

[38] *Protestant Poetics*, p. 185.   [39] Fairbanks and Trent (eds.), *New England Begins,* vol. II, p. 318.

[40] Haims believes this was to avoid censures of the clergy against a violation of the Second Commandment ("American Puritan Aesthetic," pp. 54, 105).

Figure 34 Francis Quarles, *Emblemes*. Huntington Library Museum, San Marino, Calif., 1696.

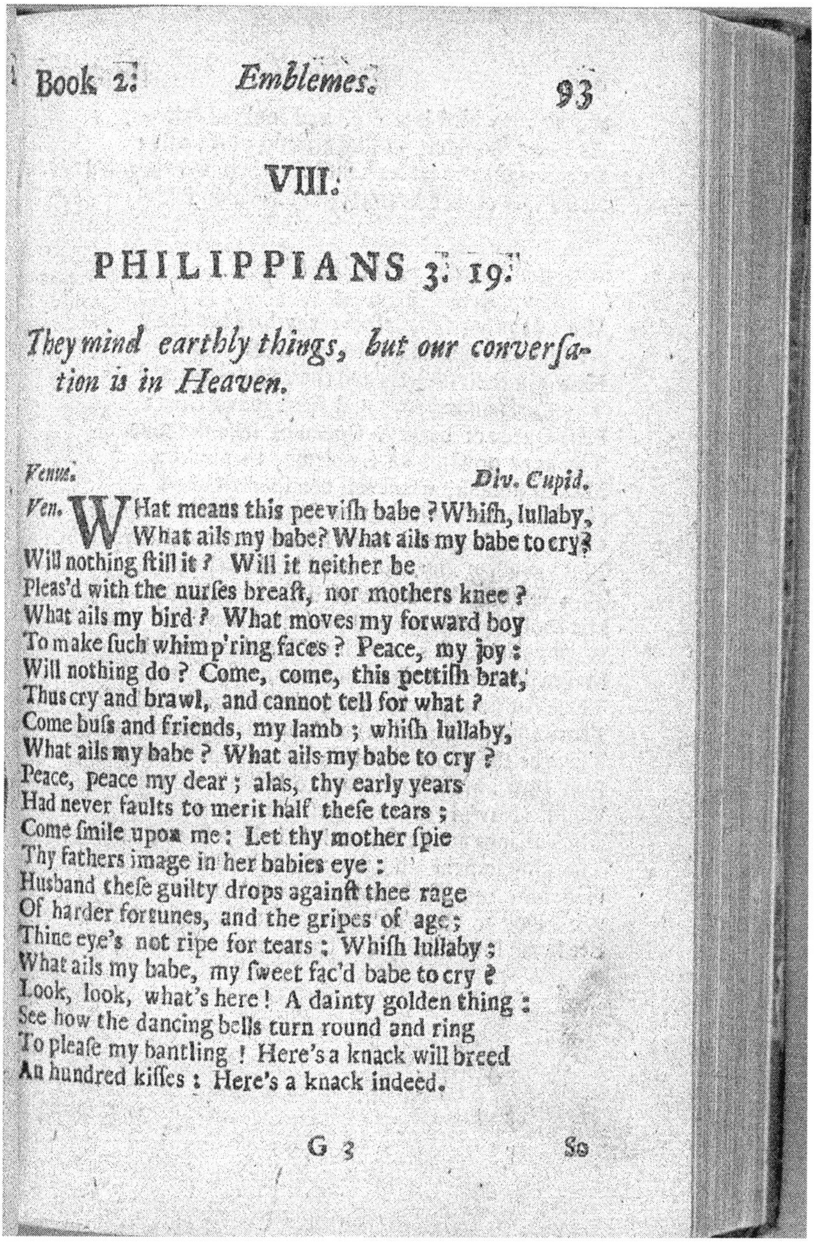

Book 2. *Emblemes.* 93

VIII.

PHILIPPIANS 3. 19.

They mind earthly things, but our conversation is in Heaven.

Venus.   *Div. Cupid.*

Ven. WHat means this peevish babe? Whish, lullaby,
What ails my babe? What ails my babe to cry?
Will nothing still it? Will it neither be
Pleas'd with the nurses breast, nor mothers knee?
What ails my bird? What moves my forward boy
To make such whimp'ring faces? Peace, my joy:
Will nothing do? Come, come, this pettish brat,
Thus cry and brawl, and cannot tell for what?
Come buss and friends, my lamb; whish lullaby,
What ails my babe? What ails my babe to cry?
Peace, peace my dear; alas, thy early years
Had never faults to merit half these tears;
Come smile upon me: Let thy mother spie
Thy fathers image in her babies eye:
Husband these guilty drops against thee rage
Of harder fortunes, and the gripes of age;
Thine eye's not ripe for tears: Whish lullaby:
What ails my babe, my sweet fac'd babe to cry?
Look, look, what's here! A dainty golden thing:
See how the dancing bells turn round and ring
To please my bantling! Here's a knack will breed
An hundred kisses: Here's a knack indeed.

G 3   So

Figure 34   (*continued*)

Figure 35   Charlestown Stonecutter, *Joseph Tapping Headstone*. American Antiquarian
Society, Worcester, Mass., 1678.

in the Scripture. The Puritans of this period did not look down on imagery, even on traditional and classical references in images, but their use of these was strictly disciplined by the word which, in one way or another, accompanied the images.

   The response of the clergy was typically ambivalent toward such display. For their part they used funerals increasingly as an opportunity to call people back to the faith of an earlier generation. That ministers were not uniformly hostile is to be seen in the tombstone of John Foster, the famous Boston printer who died at age 33 in 1681 (Figure 36).

Figure 36   Anonymous, *John Foster's Headstone.* American Antiquarian Society,
Worcester, Mass., 1681.

Foster had allocated twenty or thirty shillings in his will for a set of handsome gravestones.[41] When hearing that his friend Foster was dying, Increase Mather composed a greeting in Latin which appears immediately beneath the date and reads: "Living thou studiest the stars; dying, mayest thou, Foster, I pray, mount above the skies and learn to measure the highest heaven." Foster though only 33 had not only become a successful printer who established the first press in Boston, but he was known also as an astronomer and publisher of almanacs. Upon receiving Mather's verse Foster composed (in Latin) a response which appears after Mather's couplet (see their initials carved to the left): "I measure it and it's mine; the Lord Jesus has bought it for me; now I am held to pay aught for it but thanks."

Some of the same symbolism is evident in this carving as in the Tapping headstone. Again the Quarles emblem is repeated of Father Time staying the hand of death. Together these determine how long a person has under the sun, which is personified above these figures. In addition, along the

[41] Fairbanks and Trent (eds.), *New England Begins,* vol. II, p. 318. It was common for both a headstone and a footstone to be carved. See Robert St. Clair's discussion of this in pp. 318 and 319, for this paragraph.

sides and bottom, decorative serpentine circles fill the space. While the headstone speaks of the certainty of death, the plain footstone refers to Foster's life with its simple epitaph: "Skill was his cash," which is a reference to Ovid (skill here translating the Latin "ars" which can mean either skill or art).

Lynn Maria Haims, in her study, distinguishes between a Boston tradition of stone carvings that featured sinister skulls and emphasized the terror of death, and the more auspicious Essex tradition, which portrayed the soul in heaven. The Huntington Stone (Figure 37) displays the influence of this latter tradition. This stone, attributed to Benjamin Collins, displays no skull or other reminder of the brevity of life and the certainty of death. Rather it projects the soul into heaven, anticipating "what it would be like to see God."[42] Especially interesting in this tradition is the focus on the eyes wide open, speaking of the time when faith becomes sight and the believer will "see God as he is" (1 Cor. 13:12). This recalls Increase Mather's reference to things invisible to "bodily eyes" in his *Meditations on Death* (1707):

[Faith] . . . makes them [i.e. saints] see the Reality and Excellency of things that are Invisible . . . To faith invisible things are as real as those that are visible . . . Things belonging to the Invisible world, things that are of an Heavenly nature, and that are not seen with Bodily Eyes, Faith gives substance to them: It makes them Real.[43]

One might almost say that these images together constitute little more than an expression of confidence in the face of death. Their theological reference is muted – though it is present in subtle ways. This subtlety may reflect not only their reticence to display their faith in actual images, but the fact that the tradition of Christian iconography has been specifically given up by the Reformers. But as we have seen frequently the theological references are implicit, even if they are not immediately visible. The expression of faith is found, for example, in Foster's response to Increase Mather's tribute (who himself makes only oblique reference to faith): "The Lord Jesus has bought it for me." The testimony of the faith of this lay artist remains; but its meaning apparently does little to inspire the art in which it is set. Was it because death was too theologically sensitive? Or was it because death was only a doorway to that other better life, it was not significant enough? Was it after all only a shadow?

[42] Haims, "American Puritan Aesthetic," pp. 33, 50. She argues that by this projection into the future the artist was protected from committing an idolatrous act. On the influence of the Essex tradition on these stones in Connecticut, see Ludwig, *Graven Images*, p. 380.

[43] *Meditations on Death* (1707); quoted in Haims, "American Puritan Aesthetic," p. 49.

Figure 37   Attributed to Benjamin Collins, *Joshua Huntington Stone.* Connecticut
Historical Society, Hartford, Conn., 1745.

CREATION AS IMAGE OF THE DIVINE

The most acceptable place to look for Puritan images of faith is the created
order. This was briefly discussed in the last chapter in connection with
Dutch art and town planning, but here we will elaborate the growing

significance of the restoration of nature for the Puritans. As we have noted, Reformation thought was permeated with a millennial sense: God was bringing about a restoration of the Gospel, which was destined to spread its light throughout the world. This led to a general sense of expectation that runs throughout, for example, Foxe's martyrology. While the exact shape of the millennial kingdom was subject to a wide variety of interpretations, a constant underlying theme was the call for human efforts to reverse the effects of the curse – to restore the earth to its edenic purity.[44]

John Winthrop, when listing the reasons that justified the Puritan settlement in New England, notes first the call to carry the Gospel to the whole world, in spite of the sorry state of European churches. But he goes on to say: "The whole earth is the Lord's garden and he hath given it to the sonnes of men with a general commission to replenish the earth and subdue it" (Gen. 1:28). How then could they allow this continent to lie waste without suitable "improvement"?[45]

In the *New Organon* (1620) Francis Bacon had given classic expression to the common view that creation was to be made useful for human life. There he argued famously that "The true and lawful goal of the sciences is . . . that human life be endowed with new discoveries and powers." In his essay "On gardens" (1625) he opines that since God first planted a garden, gardening for the human person "is the purest of Humane Pleasures."[46] Indeed for the Puritans gardening was itself a means of reversing the curse, done not only in the light of heaven but more specifically of Eden. But its purpose was not so much to provide delight as to be a "useful knowledge" which was to serve for the benefit of people. This (very Baconian) idea is another example of the fact that for the Puritans the useful arts took precedence over "art" that served no other purpose than giving pleasure. The human calling on earth was to make creation useful and thence enable it to glorify God in the way that God intended. When Ames and others placed painting with the manual arts, it should not be seen as a demotion

---

[44] Though the theme of restoring the garden was common even in the Middle Ages, the Protestants developed the notion in unique ways. See on this general topic, Charles Webster, *The Great Instauration: Science, Medicine and Reform: 1626–1660* (New York: Holmes & Meier, 1975); and Harrison, *The Bible, Protestantism and the Rise of Natural Science*.

[45] *Winthrop Papers* (Boston: Massachusetts Historical Society, 1931), vol. II, p. 139.

[46] Though this name is the most commonly used for Bacon's work, the first section and overall title of the work actually was "The Great Instauration," which indicated his sense that a renewal of both learning and the resulting control of nature was underway. See *Selected Writings of Francis Bacon*, intro. and notes by Hugh G. Dick (New York: Random House/Modern Library, 1955), p. 499; "Of Gardens," p. 118. Bacon goes on to give his plan for planning and planting an "elegant and civil" garden. Charles Webster notes that Bacon's philosophy "was assimilated into the general religious worldview of the Protestants" (*The Great Instauration*, p. 335). Bacon of course was developing themes that were implicit in Calvin and the other reformers.

of art to something mean and lowly. For the Puritans this meant that it could be taken up into the larger calling of making creation, that had been so seriously defaced in the Fall, into the theater of God's glory.

For the Puritans spiritual and physical health were intricately intertwined. So the outward mastery could be understood as related to an inward renewal. It is a mistake then to see this focus on the control of nature as a gradually dawning modernism in which an outward (and increasingly secular) mastery of nature is replacing an inward and spiritual orientation.[47] The Puritans firmly believed that God speaks through the creation *and* through the word of Scripture in its impact on the heart. Though these (inward and outward) callings were occasionally in tension, they could be seen as a part of the larger work of God. Charles Webster argues that this theological impulse to remake the earth lay behind the founding of the Royal Society in 1662 and behind the rise of empirical science in Britain more generally. Interestingly he underlines the idea of intellectual organization so central to Ames's thought, as a critical influence in the organization of these scientific meetings.[48] Peter Harrison shows that this same ordering impulse lay behind many of the most prominent gardens in the seventeenth century (when, he notes, most of the encyclopedic gardens of Europe were designed). "The geometric formality of the seventeenth century garden . . . bore witness to the god-like capacity of the gardener to bring order out of chaos."[49]

But at the same time the external work of ordering a fallen nature mirrored the work of sanctification in which human lives are ordered in Christ-like godliness. For as George Herbert put this in his poem "Paradise":

> I blesse thee, Lord, because I GROW
> Among thy Trees, which in a ROW
> To Thee both fruit and order OW.
>
> What open force, or hidden CHARM
> Can blast my fruit, or bring HARM,
> While the inclosure is Thine ARM.[50]

---

[47] This is the argument of Peter Harrison. He acknowledges that references to the "paradise within" continue to be common in this period, but believes that these are "the last gasp of a dying world view" which will give way to a modern and empirical understanding of the place of humanity in nature (*The Bible, Protestantism and the Rise of Natural Science*, pp. 209–11).

[48] He argues that this is behind "both . . . the initiation of the 1645 meetings and . . . the process of institutionalization that occurred between 1660 and 1663" (*The Great Instauration*, p. 99).

[49] *The Bible, Protestantism and the Rise of Natural Science*, pp. 237–8.

[50] *Works of George Herbert*, pp. 132–3. The notion of "inclosure" was considered the principal means of ordering a garden (see John Worlidge's work below) and also recalled the enclosed garden, coming from Song of Solomon, which became a prominent symbol of edenic purity in medieval art.

Several important treatises written during this time trade on this vital connection between the spiritual and the material worlds, and therefore the connection between the inner and the outer calling of the Christian. Ralph A. Austen, an Oxford don, wrote a *Treatise on Fruit Trees* in 1657, which was bound together with *The Spirituall Use of an Orchard, or Garden of Fruit Trees set forth in divers similitudes between natural and spiritual Fruit Trees.*[51] The frontispiece features a figure of a square garden with paths leading to a fountain in the center. Around the side is the verse from Song of Solomon (4:12): "A garden enclosed is my sister." The first treatise is simply a detailed description of the husbandry of trees. In the preface preceding the second book, *The Spirituall Use of an Orchard,* Austen quoted Bacon's famous reference to the two books of God: "God hath two great Books which we ought to study, his word and his works: the one discovers his will, the other his power." Noting the world is a great library, Austen gives a new, and very Protestant twist to Gregory's "bible of the illiterate." The creatures are to be studied as books, Austen insists, "so those who cannot read a line in any Printed book, may read good lessons in the book of the creatures." Citing Romans 1:20 Austen notes: "All creatures have a teaching voyce, they read us divinity lectures of divine Providence." We must use them to bring us near the creature. "Climbing up by them, as by steps, or stairs til we ascend to the highest good."[52]

In the text which follows in Book II Austen goes on to draw the likeness between the physical husbandman and God. As the gardener prunes his trees so we may understand God's work in the trials of the current church (p. 41). Too many leaves without fruit is likened to legalism; nourishment coming up through the roots is compared to the grace Christ gives to the believer (p. 201). Throughout there is the emphasis on the connection between the outer and inner. The gardener does not concern himself only with the outer form but seeks to make the "inward form be good, so the trees have good natures and properties, bringing forth good fruits" (p. 191). In the end, however, the external gives way to the internal: the external

---

[51] *A Treatise on Fruit Trees* (Oxford: Henri Hall for Thomas Robinson, 1657).

[52] *A Treatise on Fruit Trees/The Spirituall Use of an Orchard,* preface to the latter (unpaginated), second and third pages. The subsequent pages in the text are to this (second) work. It is this way of thinking about creation that Peter Harrison overlooks when he says: "Natural objects were regarded as having been designed for their use rather than their meaning: creatures were not symbols to be read, but objects to be used or investigated for potential application" (*The Bible, Protestantism and the Rise of Natural Science,* p. 203). The Protestants of this time saw no tension between believing both in their use and in their meaning.

unity of churches, Austen says, is far less important than the inward unity of worship.

John Worlidge was one of the most widely consulted agricultural theorists of the seventeenth century. In 1669 he published his *Systema Agriculturae* in which the frontispiece displays the essence of his agricultural theory.[53] He explains the frontispiece in this way (Figure 38):

> First cast your eye upon a Rustick Seat,
> Built strong and plain, yet well contrived and neat . . .
> A pleasant garden from high windes and cold
> Defended (by a spreading fruitful wall
> With rows of lime and fir trees straight and tall).
> Full fraught with necessary flowers and fruits . . .[54]

The idea as he explains further in the preface is that the proper ordering of the land not only will issue in the most bounty, but will correlate with a healthy spirit. "This country life improves and exercises the most noble and excellent parts of our intellects."

The order of nature "improved" is portrayed in this picture: the kitchen gardens around the house give way to fertile fields, then forests where animals are at home. This comes from a careful and difficult working, and, more particularly, a proper structuring of the land. Much of his "Systema" concerns the proper "inclosing" of the land. Enclosure, he says, "is the most principal way of improvement."[55] For enclosure ensures both a just distribution of property and appropriate space for useful improvements and employment. Worlidge belonged to those theorists who believed that all social problems could be solved by a proper maintenance of the land. The problem, they believed, was not scarcity of land but the failure to properly use what was available. Marshes and brackish fen needed to be drained; barren land had to be appropriately fertilized. If this were done there would be land aplenty for the poor and wars would no longer be fought – and not incidentally people would not feel the need to migrate to the New World![56]

---

[53] See Worlidge, *Systema Agriculturae: The Mystery of Husbandry Discovered and Layd Open* (London: T. Johnson for Samuel Speed, 1669).

[54] Ibid., from the explanation of the frontispiece.   [55] Ibid., p. 10.

[56] See the description of these theorists in Fairbanks and Trent (eds.), *New England Begins*, vol. II, pp. 188, 190. Robert St. George points out that a conservative mentality often thwarted the plans of these forward-thinking theorists, both in England and New England. Their description of the moral value of working the land, to their minds, provided grounds for limiting franchise to those who owned and worked the land.

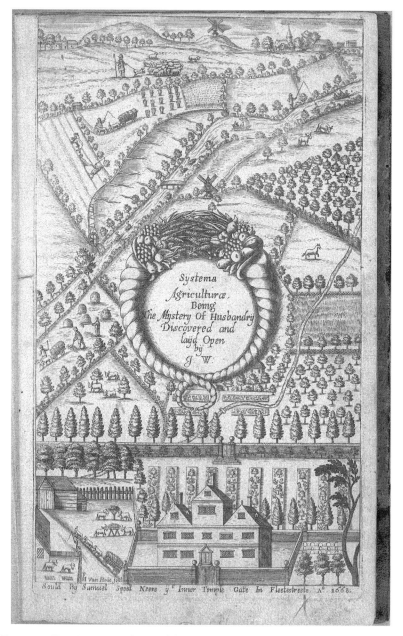

Figure 38   Frontispiece, in John Worlidge, *Systema Agriculturae: The Mystery of Husbandry Discovered*. London: Printed by T. Johnson for S. Speed, 1669. Huntington Library Museum, San Marino, Calif., 1669.

Soon the design that Worlidge called for made its way to New England and was evident in the structure of the gardens there. Indeed as Winthrop wrote it was in part the prospect of remaking Eden that drew the settlers to Massachusetts originally. And as they began clearing and planting fields they worked to structure the land as they believed God had intended at the beginning. As we saw in the last chapter the concentric circles of woodlot, orchards and kitchen gardens surrounding the towns with the meetinghouse in the center were meant to reflect a biblical ordering of things. Originally utility was the chief consideration; gardens were to produce food, clothing and herbs (i.e., medicines). The design was also for convenience with square patches defined by narrow paths in the medieval fashion. But by 1700 some gardens began to be planted for pleasure. But even then virtue and beauty were best displayed in a garden that was "useful" – the more elaborate estates and gardens never caught on in colonial America.[57] But this all reflected, for the Puritans, the larger order of a renewed earth of which the fruitful garden was emblematic.

Perhaps the most influential writer in the new world on this spiritual context of gardening was John Flavell, a conformist minister in Devon who published *Husbandry Spiritualized*, in 1669.[58] The frontispiece (Figure 39) features an emblem, which is explained in the verse. These earthly things repay meditation, they "imply more than at first glance you see." Their art is hidden. It is only the shadows you see: "Would you see the Things, She couches [*sic*] under them." In the Epistle Dedicatory Flavell recalls Calvin's notion of creation as a mirror, noting: "It has been long since observed, that the world below is a Glass, to discover the world above." Seculum est speculum, he says. Inanimate objects have a language in a metaphorical sense (as, he notes, Psalm 19 tells us), they together add their voice to creation's praise of God. Therefore it is an excellent "art" to discourse on Birds and Beasts, but only if we use such discourse to spiritual ends and not only natural ones. Though, Flavell concedes, the revelation of God in Scripture is still the superior voice.[59]

Flavell begins his book by noting that we are God's husbandry (1 Cor. 3:9), purchased by God (p. 3) to bring forth fruit (p. 6). As in husbandry, so spiritually barrenness is a shame (p. 12). As with husbandry, so in religion

---

[57] See Alan Emmet, *So Fine a Prospect: Historic New England Gardens* (Hannover, N.H. and London: University Press of New England, 1996), pp. xi–xv; and cf. Diane Kostal McGuire, *Gardens of America: Three Centuries of Design* (Charlottesville, Va.: Thomasson-Grant, 1989), p. 9.

[58] John Flavell, *Husbandry Spiritualized: or, The Heavenly Use of Earthly Things. Consisting of Many Pleasant Observations, Pertinent Applications, and serious Reflections, and each Chapter concluded with a Divine and Suitable Poem* (London: Robert Boulter, 1669; also published in Boston, 1669).

[59] Epistle Dedicatory, nonpaginated, and subsequent pages in the text.

Figure 39 Frontispiece, in John Flavel, *Husbandry Spiritualized: Or, the Heavenly Use of Earthly Things*. Boston, New-England: Reprinted by John Allen for Nicholas Boone, 1709. Huntington Library Museum, San Marino, Calif., 1669.

there is much do, "Tis the highest honour of a creature to be active and useful for its God" (p. 25). Just as the plowmen sings and whistles we should rouse our delight in the divine call to godliness (pp. 34–5). Withal, the processes of planting, watering and harvest are likened to the course of spiritual growth whereby we seek to reap our harvest of Christ's presence in heaven (*passim*, p. 155). Poems are scattered through the text, along with occasional meditations on birds, beasts and trees. But though the call to careful labor on the land is the dominant message – Flavell after all does give good advice on husbandry – the harvest of life transcends a proper ordering of land. Just as Anne Bradstreet does not dismiss the oak to dwell on eternity, so Flavell does not dismiss the art of husbandry to grasp the true harvest in heaven. Rather he argues *a fortiori*, since this work is so important, how much more attention should we give to our spiritual harvest. Would that we would care for our place in heaven, he notes, as much as we are concerned with deeds to our earthly land (p. 226).

 The art that such care implies is not to be despised, but its real meaning does not lie on the surface: it is coded, visible only to those who wear the proper spectacles. These alone are able to see that God's creatures and the responsibility for their care are a part of a larger narrative, and that believers find their place, indeed their very identity, in working out this narrative of redemption and restoration throughout the warp and woof of their lives.

CLERICAL STRUGGLES WITH THE MIRROR OF NATURE

Both ministers and their parishioners struggled to keep the balance: not to lose the spiritual in the mundane, nor to absorb the creature into the spiritual. The project of the New England Puritans was to remake the world after the image of the world to come. But by the beginning of the eighteenth century, as we have noted, that project was in crisis. And this crisis threatened to upset the proper balance between the inward and outward call – for many the earthly calling faded before the promise of heaven, for others it claimed the whole of their attention. This tension surely provides some of the spark that would light the awakening of the 1730s. Ironically the awakening itself would open up new ways in which God and the world could be imagined, possibilities that were given theological grounding in the thinking of the revival's greatest apologete, Jonathan Edwards. Before turning to his thinking we review three older contemporaries of Edwards who give us some sense of contemporary reflection on the Christian uses of the creation, and the mental shape this took.

In 1727 Cotton Mather is inspired by Flavell's work to write his own attempt at spiritual husbandry, *Agricola*.[60] Writing a year before his death, Mather is not sanguine about the spiritual condition of his people. Unlike Flavell he does not really write about husbandry at all, but, as he says, he will use the language of husbandry as a vehicle for his spiritual concerns. As the pastors of Boston note in their recommendation, in a country that subsists mostly on husbandry, "to spiritualize the common actions of life and make religious improvement of worldly affairs, is an holy and happy art."[61] As we plow our fields to break up the hard earth, Mather notes, so we break our hard hearts by repentance. This, like plowing, is a difficult work. But keep at it: "The harvest will repay you; heaven will make amends for all" (p. 16). Then comes sowing, which is the word of God entering our hearts, which brings forth grain like itself (p. 25). In an extended commentary on the parable of the sower, Mather speaks of all the things that keep the seed

---

[60] Cotton Mather, *Agricola, or The Religious Husbandman: The Intentions of Religion served in the Language of Husbandry* (Boston: T. Fleet for D. Henchman, 1727).

[61] Recommendations of the united pastors of Boston in preface, *Agricola,* preface nonpaginated. Subsequent pages in the text are to this work.

from germinating. But if you hear with affection it will grow. And "while you conform to the word of God your savior, you shall be sure to possess the things of this world so far as you have any occasion for them" (p. 72). Then he speaks of the withholding of rain, which is God's judgment on the believer; of the grass, which is ready for the mower (which is death); and finally of the flourishing orchard, which is the life of godliness that brings forth good fruit. In the poem closing the section on the grass ready for the mower Mather sounds the theme of the vulnerability of life. That I stand at all is an action of thy wondrous grace, O God. But I await the scythe. "I see the Mower: He's on the road," Mather testifies (p. 151). Only by committing himself to the savior can he gather the courage to say in the final stanza:

> Now welcome sithe: Come, do thy worst;
>   Strike; thou canst do no more
> But fit me to be lodg'd I trust,
>   In my God's blessed Floor. (p. 152)

This was published in 1727. Though it was probably written before the famous earthquake of that year, its tone of the judgment due New England, which ministers had been sounding for more than a generation, was the backdrop against which that event was to be interpreted. On the night of October 29, 1727 there was a flash of light, horrid rumbling and a shaking felt throughout New England. People gathered on the streets certain that God's judgment had indeed fallen upon them. More than any other single event this began the series of revivals that are called the First Great Awakening in America. Fasts were spontaneously called across the land and people flocked to the churches.[62] The earthquake became itself, like Mather's planting and sowing and harvesting, an emblem that served to draw the attention of New England to God's rule.

Samuel Wigglesworth, a contemporary minister, seeks to take the created order with more seriousness than Mather. Like Baxter and Bradstreet before him, he seeks to see in the world actual images of grace, rather than simply ciphers by which grace can be explained. The work of this minister is also associated with the famous earthquake. Two weeks before that event Wigglesworth had addressed a society of young men at Ipswich on the

---

[62] See the description of these events and their significance for the revival in Harry S. Stout, *The New England Soul: Preaching and Religious Culture in Colonial New England* (Oxford University Press, 1986), pp. 177–8. Cf. Lambert's comment on the significance of the event (*Inventing the "Great Awakening,"* p. 64).

Pleasures of Religion.[63] His work was to persuade these eager young people that God affirmed yet transcended all that they legitimately longed for in this world. He began by noting: "The desire of enjoying God is natural to Men" (p. i). Moreover, God's ways are the ways of Pleasantness and that God invites us to "drink in the river of his pleasures" (p. iii). All people naturally desire the good, and this, Wigglesworth argues, is really a desire to enjoy God. But in our present state we are not able to decide what is really good and what is evil. Echoing Calvin he notes that our affections are captivated by honor, pleasure and profit. "The general inclination of youth is to have their swing [*sic*] in pleasures" (p. 2). So, he says, persuade them that true pleasures reside in godliness, and they are almost persuaded to become Christians.

But Wigglesworth's point is not so much that godliness replaces earthly pleasures as that it adds to, or fulfills, these (p. 4). Godliness enables one to enjoy what he has because he is able to look above secondary causes and see God as the true ground of what is good. In a way that anticipates Edwards he says: "The Godly Man enjoys ravishing discoveries of the divine excellencies: and his Redeemers all sufficiency, Beauty and Goodness" (pp. 6, 7). Beyond the goods of this life, the Christian can feast on the delightful prospect of the heavenly Canaan: "The beatific vision of the blessed trinity will afford men unutterable pleasures" (p. 7). But again these future pleasures are not meant to supplant, or in marxist fashion, to dull our present sensitivities, they rather "sweeten" them. After all religious pleasures are more real than any other (p. 13), and more lasting (p. 14). Therefore "Religious pleasures are absolutely necessary to sweeten all the other Ingredients of your Felicity" (p. 28). So "learn to realize the brevity of life" (p. 34). Let your soul seek to fly, on eagles' wings, to the Father's house. "Woundrous will be the pleasures flowing from having your conversation in heaven: It will heighten all your joys and allay all your sorrows" (p. 34).

The spiritual dimension that is to be found in earthly pleasures, as one might expect, does not lie on the surface. When these pleasures are sought on their own terms, they disintegrate, Wigglesworth would say. But when seen in a larger perspective their joys are seen as, more than pointers, tokens of a greater joy.

A few years later Isaac Watts, minister and musician in England widely read and revered in America, writes in a similar vein to stir up a lethargic people to true godliness. His *Humble Attempt toward the Revival of Practical*

---

[63] Wigglesworth, *The Pleasures of Religion: A Sermon Preached to a Society of Young Men at Ipswich, About a Fortnight Before the Earthquake* (Boston: For T. Hancock, 1728). Pages in the text are to this work.

Religion addresses "the decay of vital religion in the hearts and lives of men."[64] But his take on the role of the creature is significantly different from that of Wigglesworth. Watts is not able to give the creature any significant role in the Christian's imagination. Studies of logic, math and geometry are useful. Even some geography and *belles-lettres*, while ornamental rather than necessary, may profit. But none of this, he insists, should distract us from our central goal: pursuit of God (pp. 15, 22). Preachers should strive not for elegance but for clarity. They should not ask, what fine things, or powerful words, can I say, but how can I "say most usefully to those who hear for the instruction of their minds" what I want to say (p. 25). The reason for this is clear to Watts: to see Grace, you must "lay human nature low" (p. 32). A focus on the Gospel diminishes the luster of the creature (p. 39). True we should use a lively language to encourage virtue and piety (p. 44), but we should take care that we not add "fancies of Men to our divine Religion" (p. 62). True enough, fancy and imagination can be harnessed to the appeal to reason. "In your Representation of Things to the reason and understanding of men it would sometimes be of special Advantage to have some power over the Fancy and Imagination: This would help us to paint our themes in their proper colours, whether of the alluring or forbidding kind" (pp. 70–1).[65] But the use of imagination is strategic, not substantial; it is simply a good thing to use this power, so often exploited by the tempter, for God and salvation, "to kindle the soul to zeal in the holy warfare" (p. 77). But it will not, in itself, help us see in the creature an "image" of God.

In a later book, *The Doctrine of the Passions Explained and Improved*, Watts develops the implications of this for our emotional attachments.[66] Bring your loves often to account before the bar of reason and Scripture, he advises (p. 134). Think of the uncertainty even of the highest good, "bear not an immortal fondness to perishing comforts" (p. 135). If you feel yourself entangled in excessive love, reflect on the faults and temporality of the object. Above all, he urges, practice a voluntary self-denial: "Set a guard upon your eyes and ears, upon your senses and your thoughts, and avoid everything that would bring to your mind the object of your immoderate love" (p. 136). Unlike the Puritan instruction to order life according to

---

[64] *An Humble Attempt toward the Revival of Practical Religion among Christians, and Particularly the Protestant Dissenters, by a Serious Address to Ministers and People in some Occasional Discourses* (London: for E. Matthews, 1631), pp. i–ii. Subsequent pages in the text.

[65] Though in contrast to Wigglesworth, he argues that this aspect of inviting qualities is not enough without a similar focus on evil (p. 71).

[66] *Doctrine of the Passions Explained and Improved* (New York: Shepard Kollock, 1795). Pages in the text are from this work.

God's desires, Watts is content to advise the Christian to simply keep loose to all attachments beneath God and heaven. This advice is based on deep theological convictions about the nature of the person as spirit. As he says: "Consider that the fewer the strong affections, and the less engagements of the heart you have to mortal creatures, the easier will it be to leave this world, and enter into the world of spirits" (p. 138). The world cannot bear symbolic weight, not only because it is fallen, it would seem, but simply because it is finite and material.

These sentiments of Watts's came to influence generations of Protestants by means of his hymns. So central are these to later Christian experience that it is important to give some attention to them here. We have seen previously that singing in Puritan worship had focused almost entirely on the singing of Psalms, especially from the *Bay Psalm Book* (1640), which had been one of the first books published in America. One of the fruits of the awakening, much to the consternation of the conservative Old Lights, would be the practice of singing "hymns" as well as the Psalms. A key figure here was James Davenport, grandson of John Davenport of New Haven, who encouraged the singing of hymns by those awakened, not only in church but along the streets and roads *en route* to meetings.[67] Some of the hymns were written by Davenport himself, but the best known, and most enduring, were written by Isaac Watts.

In the standard edition of his hymns Watts notes that singing is the nearest we reach to life in the New Jerusalem.[68] But despite its value, it is most troubled, Watts notes, in our churches – it is "most unhappily managed" (p. iii). So Watts set out in his songs, he tells us, to copy the "most frequent tempers and changes of our spiritual conditions of our life" (p. vi). He confesses he was tempted by "gay and flowery expression that gratified the fancy," that too often "the bright images . . . prevailed above the fire of divine affection," but in the end he hoped "devotion dictated the song" (p. ix). Modern Christians, used to singing Watts's "Joy to the World" or "I sing the Mighty Power of God that made the mountains rise," would be surprised at the strong suspicion of earthly value so evident in many

---

[67] See Alan Heimert and Perry Miller (eds.), *The Great Awakening: Documents Illustrating the Crisis and Its Consequences* (Indianapolis: Bobbs-Merrill, 1967), pp. 201–2. Davenport was a controversial figure, accused of reviving antinomianism, but his introduction of hymn singing, according to these scholars, "represented the revolution in hymnology that was to be among the enduring consequences of the Awakening" (p. 202).

[68] *Hymns and Spiritual Songs in Three Books* (Boston: Mein & Fleming, 1769), pp. i–ii. The seventh (1719) edition seemed to have become the standard, as it added 150 new hymns to the previous editions and reached 340 pages and some 500 hymns. The three books comprised hymns collected from Scriptures; composed on Divine Subjects; and prepared for the Lord's Supper. That edition was frequently reprinted; I am citing the twenty-second edition, pages in the text.

of Watts's original hymns. In Book II of his Hymns, for example, there is a section entitled "Parting with carnal joys," in which this verse is typical:

> My soul forsake her vain delight,
> And bids the world farewell,
> Base as the dirt beneath my feet
> And mischievous as hell. (Bk II, no. x, p. 112)

Or this testimony:

> I send the joys of earth away,
> Away ye tempters of the mind.
> False as the smooth deceitful sea,
> And empty as the whistling wind. (Bk II, no. xi, p. 113)

Like Taylor before him, Watts's verses feature prominently the joys of heaven toward which the soul turns, as a brightness which darkens even the best that earth has to offer:

> God from on high invites us home,
> But we march heedless on,
> And ever hast'ning to the tomb,
> Stoop downward as we run. (Bk. II, no. xxxii, p. 129)

As spirits we are not made for earth. "There is nothing round this spacious earth," Watts writes, "that suits my large desire" (p. 112). The soul's life with God has taken over the affections. While the earth may continue to reflect God's glory, it is an evanescent reflection that we cannot capture – like Calvin's bolt of lightning that shines on our pathway and then is gone, plunging us again into darkness.

JONATHAN EDWARDS AND THE VISIBILITY OF GOD

Though their names are often associated in reflections on the Great Awakening, in one sense Watts and Edwards are not singing from the same hymnbook. For Edwards places great significance on the human perception of beauty in creation. Previously, deliberation on creation and the ordering of that creation, especially in people like Watts and Mather, took its impetus, not from a larger theological vision of things, but from the more constricted concerns of evangelical piety – exacerbated in many cases by the apparent decline in godliness they saw around them. Edwards by contrast is able to find a harmony between the creature and the creator, and thus suggest a healthier way of understanding beauty and imagination, precisely because he worked out of a careful, and highly original theological framework. This enabled him to connect the believer's perception of beauty and the creature directly to the presence and activity of God. Unfortunately, partly because Edwards did not always follow up his best insights in his more popular writings, and partly because some of his most original thinking was not published until the twentieth century, his insights did not have the influence on subsequent Protestant reflection on the arts and imagination that they might have had. But in his best moments he suggests a way out of the dichotomies that had bedeviled the Protestant imagination up to his time.[69]

Scholarly study of Edwards has usually grounded his originality on the influence of John Locke's empiricism and of the Enlightenment more generally. But recently this dependence on Locke has been shown to be a mistake, or at least an exaggeration – Locke's influence can be seen in the working out of his thinking but not in its grounding. Norman Fiering argues the major influence on Edwards initially was not Locke, but the continental rationalists, especially Nicolas Malebranche.[70] From these Edwards received his emphasis on divine concurrence, on teleology as the ultimate level of explanation, and his neo-Platonic typological system. By making highly original use of these materials, Edwards was able to provide a theological framework for the mental world that he inherited from his Puritan ancestors, especially William Ames. One might put it this way: Ames's vision of knowledge as an interrelated map of knowledge, in Edwards, becomes a system of dynamic, related impulses that are grounded in the triune life of God.[71] This grounding gave him scope for a broader and more lively view of "affections" which in many ways recalls another of his ancestors, John Cotton.[72] In many respects then Edwards represents a kind of culmination of Puritan thinking on the imagination – but a culmination that did not serve as an impetus for cultural creativity.

[69] The most authoritative commentary on Edwards's work is to be found in the introduction and notes to the Yale University Press edition of his works, which will be noted as *Works,* with volume number and date. The bibliography on Edwards has become immense. I have been especially helped by James Carse, *Jonathan Edwards and the Visibility of God* (New York: Charles Scribner & Sons 1967); Sang Hyun Lee, *The Philosophical Theology of Jonathan Edwards* (Princeton University Press, 1988); Terrence Erdt, *Jonathan Edwards: Art and the Sense of the Heart* (Amherst: University of Massachusetts Press, 1980); the essays collected in Nathan O. Hatch and Harry S. Stout (eds.), *Jonathan Edwards and the American Experience* (New York: Oxford University Press, 1988); and Amy Plantinga Pauw, *The Supreme Harmony of All: The Trinitarian Theology of Jonathan Edwards* (Grand Rapids, Mich.: Eerdmans, 2002).

[70] See Fiering, "The Rationalist Foundation to Edwards's Metaphysics," in Hatch and Stout (eds.), *Jonathan Edwards and the American Experience,* pp. 78–88.

[71] See ibid. Like William Ames, Edwards believed "the task of scientia, or sytematic knowledge is to reconstruct the world mentally in accordance with the archetypes." Only then will the human mind be a true image of God (Fiering, "The Rationalist Foundation," p. 85).

[72] Janice Knight argues in her epilogue: "One might argue that on almost every important issue Edwards gave new voice to the principles of the Cambridge faith" of Cotton and Sibbes (*Orthodoxies in Massachusetts,* p. 199).

His theological influences were the usual Puritan sources, Calvin and Perkins, but like Cotton, his theology also grew from the observance of the working of grace in creation and in believers' lives. Indeed it is often the testimony, of people and of creation, that he seeks to measure in his theological reflection. For our purposes we will describe briefly this theological grounding and then the view of beauty that resulted, before turning to explore several exemplary works and assessing their significance for our project. Perhaps Edwards's most important contribution to theology was the replacement of traditional substance metaphysics with a more relational and dynamic conception of reality. This enabled Edwards to portray the Puritan understanding of typology in a radically new way. Reality for Edwards is a network of dispositional powers, or as Edwards liked to say, "habits." He defined habits as patterns according to which existences are caused by God. As Edwards writes in *The Mind*:

That which truly is the substance of all bodies is the infinitely exact and precise and perfectible stable idea in God's mind, together with his stable will that the same shall gradually be communicated to us, and to other minds, according to certain fixed and exact established methods and laws.

This led him to propose the strikingly modern idea that material solidity is not something fixed, but an activity of resistance, ultimately dependent on God himself.[73]

As Edwards's quote makes clear, the purpose of the patterns that God has established (and which Christ, as God's idea of himself, upholds) is that they might be communicated to human minds. Communication is a central theme in Edwards's thought. It is more than the passing on of ideas, it is the actual sharing of God's nature. Another way of putting this is to say that it is part of God's nature as love to desire that the divine fulness be extended and reproduced. In creation and the continuing communication of the divine presence through the Holy Spirit in creation, God realizes this desire. As Lee explains this "created existence . . . is the spatio-temporal repetition of God's inner trinitarian fulness."[74] Central to this vision is Edwards's conviction that the basic characteristic of this fulness, manifest as a dynamic network of dispositions, is beauty. Beauty is what this order, properly comprehended, looks like. And this for Edwards is particularly related to the Holy Spirit. "It was more especially the Holy Spirit's work

---

[73] See Sang Hyun Lee, *Philosophical Theology*, pp. 30, 47, 50, 52. The quote from *The Mind* is from *Scientific and Philosophical Writings*, vol. VI of *Works*, ed. Wallace Anderson (New Haven: Yale University Press, 1980), p. 344.

[74] *Philosophical Theology*, p. 173. As Christ is the true image of God, the Holy Spirit is the "eternal and complete repetitions of the Father's actuality" (p. 189).

to bring the world to its beauty and perfection out of the chaos, for the beauty of the world is a communication of God's beauty."[75]

The excellencies of creation, which reflect God's inner reality, are of two kinds: primary and secondary beauty.[76] The former relates to the spiritual "consent," that is love, between perceiving beings, the latter is the resonance (since these cannot "consent") between material elements of creation. Another way of putting this is to say that external things can communicate God's beauty because they are ultimately rooted in God. Believers can perceive this because their eyes have been opened; unregenerate persons can experience the secondary beauty, but are blind to this primary beauty – they do not consent to its being in God. As Edwards says in *The Mind*: "The highest excellency . . . must be the consent of spirits to one another . . . in their mutual love one to another, and the sweet harmony between the various parts of the universe is only an image of mutual love."[77] This establishes the basis by which the world can be seen to actually image God's glory in a positive sense, embodying in its own creaturely way the beauty that resides supremely in the triune God.

Though at times the distinction between the higher and lower being seems to be grounded in the moral differences between the regenerate and unregenerate, for Edwards this is also grounded in reality: the material reality is subordinated to the moral and spiritual world. For just before his description of mutual consent he writes: "As nothing else has a proper being but spirits, and as bodies are but the shadow of being, therefore the consent of bodies to one another, and the harmony that is among them, is but a shadow of excellency." This leads him to propose that this lower, or secondary, kind of love (i.e. consent) "may be odious, because it hinders or is contrary to a higher or more general. Even a lower proportion is often a deformity, because it is contrary to a more general proportion."[78] Edwards is clear that since the excellencies of God's habits are indeed *communicated* to the creatures and not just reflected (shadowed) there, so the beauty that comes to expression there has integrity, in this sense it is not "lower." But if the material creation is itself an expression of God's inner excellency, especially as this is celebrated in Christ's human existence, why must only

[75] *The "Miscellanies,"* ed. Thomas Schafer, vol. XIII of *Works* (New Haven: Yale University Press, 1994), p. 384.
[76] See the discussion in Lee, *Philosophical Theology*, pp. 83–4.
[77] *The Mind,* vol. VI of *Works*, pp. 337–8.
[78] Ibid., p. 337. Cf. in *Miscellanies*, "It's agreeable to God's wisdom that it should be so, that the inferior and shadowy parts of his excellent, spiritual and divine, to represent the things that immediately concern himself and the highest part of his work. Spiritual things are the crown and glory . . . of all other works" (*Works*, vol. XIII, pp. 434–5).

spirit have proper being? Edwards was not always consistent in disparaging the lower as "odious," but this tendency, as we will see, was to have important consequences.

The communication of God's beauty to the created order leads to the view that the material reality corresponds to or speaks of the spiritual realm. This typological understanding of created reality as a dynamic nexus that expresses God's own excellencies runs as a constant theme through Edwards. As a result of this dynamic relationship, the perception of God never departs from the perception of sensible things. This is seen especially in his *Images of Divine Things*.[79] Recalling John Flavell (whom he cites, p. 108), he notes in creation "things of the world are ordered [and] designed to shadow forth spiritual things" (p. 53). The comprehensive descriptions of reality and their common reference to God and his purposes recall Ames's great interconnected map of reality. The natural nurture of sun and rain represents our spiritual nurturing by the Holy Spirit. The likeness between lower creatures and persons he calls a "type" or "analogy" (pp. 53, 56). Moreover these worlds are divided into two parts. "The material world and all things pertaining to it, is by the Creator wholly subordinated to the spiritual and moral world" (p. 61). Accordingly not all things reflect equally the divine excellencies. Christ's representations, for example, are not simple illustrations but "evidences of the truth of what he says" (p. 57). These are more "lively" images, others are more "faint" (p. 114). Among the more lively images of course is the human person. As Caesar stamps his image on his coins, so God's image is stamped on human hearts, which are God's peculiar treasure (p. 99). Finally even the millennial direction of history comes to expression in various images and shadows. The telescope and other discoveries surely presage "the great increase of knowledge of heavenly things that shall be in the approaching glorious times of the Christian church" (p. 101).

Significantly, for Edwards the medium of our appropriation of this higher reality are what he calls the "affections." The affections represent the apprehension of the heart – what Puritans frequently termed "experimental knowledge" – though Edwards expresses this in terms inclusive of emotions. Edwards stresses that the primary alteration at conversion is in the affections, the heart is made sensible (it consents) to God's excellencies. Edwards inherited the reigning suspicions toward the imagination, as we will see, but he was emphatic that the imagination could be useful in

---

[79] *Images of Divine Things*, from *Typological Writings*, ed. Wallace E. Anderson and Mason I. Lowance Jr., with David Watters, vol. XI of *Works* (1993); pages in the text.

portraying in lively pictures either of heaven or of hell, that could move sinners to repentance. This function, Terrence Erdt has argued, provides the ground for a new aesthetic. The purpose of this aesthetic, Erdt notes, "was to provoke affections, to draw out emotions that would be felt in hell – or heaven – in a vastly greater degree."[80] Calvin had allowed that paintings and music could give pleasure, but they were useless in teaching. Edwards, like Baxter, goes further than Calvin in insisting that the affections can be pressed into service to draw people to God. In their own way they can "teach."

Bringing together the dimensions of reality surely demands an imaginative leap, a putting together, a seeing together widely diverse entities. This construction we will see, is an important result of Edwards's theology of creation and views of art. To discover what Edwards has to say specifically about the role of the imagination in living the Christian life, we look in particular to his writings that deal with the revival. We do this for two reasons. First, more than any other event of that century, the awakening replayed the controversies about God's presence and activity that we saw in the antinomian debate of the previous century, and that are critical for developing a theology of culture. In a fallen world, how does a sinful person claim to "see" God's intervention? How is this intervention drawn? And with what implications for culture and society? Secondly these events mark the place where lay perceptions of God become most explicit. The Great Awakening was the place where Edwards's theory of the higher and lower beauty hit up against a reality with ragged edges, one that was soon the subject of much controversy.

The spiritual stirrings of revival, after some initial outbreaks in late 1727, came to life especially in Edwards's own church in 1734–5. After the arrival of George Whitefield (in October 1740), in the early 1740s the revivals spread throughout New England and beyond. These events soon attracted severe criticism. A major contrary voice was that of Charles Chauncy (1705–87), minister in Boston. In general Chauncy and other heirs of William Ames focused on the reformation of life and morals and were disgusted at the outbursts of emotion – which they immediately associated with the antinomian outbreaks of the previous century. In 1742 Chauncy wrote a letter to George Wishart in Edinburgh, warning him of the excesses he saw, and which, he supposed, would surely follow Whitefield back to Scotland.[81] He wanted to correct what he was sure had been exaggerated

---

[80] Erdt, *Jonathan Edwards*, p. 71.
[81] *A Letter from a Gentleman in Boston to Mr. George Wishart Concerning the State of Religion in New England* (Edinburgh, 1742/Clarendon Historical Society's Reprints, 1883), pages in the text. While

accounts of the "glorious work of grace" in America (p. 73). Whitefield, he notes, has been received as "an angel of God" though ministers have been more cautious. But, Chauncy says, the evangelist has chiefly aroused the passions of many (especially the women!). These shriek and cry out until the whole congregation is affected (p. 75). Some perhaps were helped by these evangelists, but "the town in general was not much mended in those things wherein a Reformation was greatly needed" (p. 75). What was especially influential, Chauncy complained, was Whitefield's doctrine of inward feeling leading to commotion and, alas, lay preaching (p. 76). Never was there such a spirit of enthusiasm in the land, all of which boiled down, Chauncy believed, to a commotion in the passions (which he feared would lead to Quakerism and infidelity, p. 81).[82]

Edwards surely had such "Old Light" criticism in mind when he wrote his accounts of the revival, but he had his own scruples to deal with. He and his New Light colleagues felt the emphasis on "preparation" of these traditionalists amounted to a latent Arminianism. The results of Edwards's reflections on the revivals are the major treatises describing the awakening, his *Faithful Narrative* (appearing in several editions, first published in 1737), the *Distinguishing Marks* (given as a lecture at Yale in 1741), *Some Thoughts Concerning Revival* (1742), and finally his mature thinking on these matters in *The Religious Affections* (1746). In general of course there is substantial overlap between the opponents of revivals and those in the tradition of Ames, as there is between those who support the revival and John Cotton, but there is also a clear divergence as well. Part of Edwards's struggle reflected the fact that his own grandfather, Solomon Stoddard (1643–1729), whose church he took over after the latter's death, was influential among the former group.[83]

Early in his ministry Edwards had been particularly concerned, as he wrote in 1749, for persons who come to church "and pretend to own the covenant, freely to declare to their neighbors, [in spite of the fact] they have no imagination that they have any true faith in Christ, or love to him."[84] Accordingly when stirrings began in his church in Northampton

---

the pamphlet is anonymous, it has clearly been presumed to be by Chauncy. See C. C. Goen in Edwards, *The Great Awakening*, vol. IV of *Works* (New Haven: Yale University Press, 1972), p. 473n.

[82] The next year he wrote a longer tract along similar lines against Edwards's *Religious Affections* after having traveled through the region seeking evidence for the excesses he lamented (see Goen, *Works*, vol. IV, pp. 80–1).

[83] For Edwards's relationship with the ministry (and followers) of Stoddard, see Goen's introduction in *Works*, vol. IV, pp. 14–16. He notes, "Stoddardism marked a major break with the experiential tradition, and indeed with the whole congregational way" (p. 16). Interestingly one who strongly resisted this "drift" was Edward Taylor at Westfield.

[84] Quoted in Goen's introducton to *Works*, vol. IV, p. 14.

during 1734, Edwards was gratified, endowing the revivals with a sense of millennial meaning. It is not unlikely, he says later, that this work of the Spirit "is the dawning, or at least a prelude of that glorious work of God . . . which . . . shall renew the world of mankind."[85] Interestingly Edwards in one place laments that such an outbreak of revival had been quenched in New England one hundred years previously, thus explicitly linking these awakenings, in his own mind, to those preceding the antinomian controversy.[86]

Particularly significant for our purposes are Edwards's reflections on the impact of these events on people's imagination. In his *Faithful Narrative*, Edwards describes persons touched by God as moved by a "sense of the glory and divine perfections" until their natures "sink under it."[87] He notes that some have experienced a significant impact on their "imaginations": "Under the power of spiritual discoveries, they have had livelily [*sic*] impressed ideas of Christ shedding blood for sinners, his blood running from his veins, and of Christ in his glory in heaven" (*FN* 107). Though, he quickly notes, they are taught not to lay great weight on such things! Others have "nothing of any such imaginations" (*FN* 108). With an eye on his critics, he emphasizes that it is not the opinion of any of us "that any weight is to be laid on anything seen with bodily eyes" (*FN* 188).

What is perhaps most interesting in this particular document is Edwards's attempt to engage in a kind of qualitative analysis of experiences he has seen and heard about. In these accounts it is the people's (even the child's!) voice, rather than the ministers', that emerges as definitive. For he acknowledges that "There is no one thing that I know of, that God has made such a means of promoting his work amongst us, as the news of others' conversion" (*FN* 176) – news that even ministers are sometimes not able to judge accurately. For "Conversion is a great and glorious work of God's power, at once changing the heart and infusing life into the dead soul" (*FN* 177) – like seed pushing its way up through a dry and barren soil, as he put it. It is the practice moreover "of the people to converse freely with one another of their spiritual experiences" (*FN* 190, though many, he acknowledges, are disgusted by this!). Many converts recount a "delightful manifestation . . . of the grace of God," or "a glorious brightness suddenly shining upon a person" (*FN* 171, 177). He goes on to recount the experience of Abigail Hutchinson

---

[85] *Works,* vol. IV, p. 353.
[86] In Edwards's preface to *Religious Affections,* vol. II of *Works* (1957), p. 87.
[87] *Works,* vol. IV, p. 105. Hereafter references to these works cited in the text as *Faithful Narrative* (*FN*), *Distinguishing Marks* (*DM*), *Some Thoughts* (*ST*) or *Religious Affections* (*RA*) followed by the page number.

who "had many extraordinary discoveries of the glory of God and Christ" (*FN* 194), to the extent that she felt she would collapse under the weight of this glory. She "often expressed a sense of the glory of God appearing in trees, and growth of the fields . . . and other works of God's hands" (*FN* 195). Then he describes the experience of 4-year-old Phebe Bartlett who was so greatly affected by her brother's conversion (at age 12) that she began to go off by herself to pray five or six times a day expressing her great concern for the souls of others (*FN* 199–205).

Though Edwards can summarize these experiences in terms of Christ being made "the object of the mind" (*FN* 171), he acknowledges that at times he is frankly puzzled by what he hears and sees: "I have not been able well to satisfy myself, whether their imaginary ideas have been more than could naturally arise in their spiritual sense of things" (*FN* 189). This puzzlement results from his determination to maintain the distinction between the spiritual and the imaginary, that is between the primary and the secondary beauty. Stress is to be placed on the inner and not the outward glory. And the work of imagination is clearly relegated to the latter, while the work of God's regenerating Spirit is connected to the former.

In the *Distinguishing Marks* he insists that the commotion that results is not a sign of the working of the Spirit, though "many that are the subjects of it, have great impressions on their imaginations" (*DM* 235). But in themselves, while these are not "distinguishing marks," neither do they invalidate these experiences. Here he goes further to admit that "such is our nature that we can't think of things invisible without a degree of imagination" and that "the more engaged the mind is, and the more intense the contemplation and affection, still the more lively and strong will the imaginary idea ordinarily be" (*DM* 236). Consistent with the faculty psychology of his day he goes on to stipulate that this faculty (i.e., Imagination) "is really subservient and helpful to the other faculties of the mind, when a proper use is made of it"(*DM* 236). Thus the overbearing exercise of the former can "disturb their exercise." Since ecstasy and transport are "natural" at such times (especially among the ignorant!), he sees "no manner of need of bringing in the help of the devil into the account that we give of these things" (*DM* 237). Human nature accounts for it well enough. It is not surprising that the brain is "so taken off from impressions made on the organs of external sense, and wholly employed in a train of pleasing and delightful imaginations" (*DM* 237).

This recognition of the natural God-given nature of these capacities is undermined by his insistence that these are "accidental" (*DM* 238), *always* mixed, he says elsewhere, with the "natural and carnal": "The beam of light (i.e., grace), as it comes from the fountain of light upon our hearts, is pure, but as it is reflected thence, it is mixed" (*ST* 459). This mixture arises from "the constitution of the body" (*ST* 461). But once again it is not clear that this is a distortion of human experience caused by sin, or an inevitable by-produce of the bodily existence. While at times he implies that the problem is the corruption due to sin, at other times Edwards says, in Platonic fashion, that, since nothing has a proper being but spirit, it is inherent in the nature of body as a lesser being. The experiences of Christians thus include "layers" that must be discarded, "like a thick smoke that hinders all the shining of the fire" (*ST* 461). This is due to the corrupt nature, he says, immediately qualifying this: "though it be not always so" (*ST* 461). At the end of the day these experiences are "chaff" not "wheat," they often increase while the spiritual part decreases (*ST* 467).

The mature expression of his thinking in *Religious Affections* (1746) does much to clarify his thinking but does not eliminate this ambiguity. This treatise is designed as a careful response to the critics of the revivals on the one hand, and a powerful explication of proper "spiritual affections" as joy in Christ and love for him, on the other. He acknowledges, as he has done previously, that, depending on their temperaments, many are affected in their imaginations in their experiences with God, even admitting that affections and imaginations can act reciprocally on one another until one "loses possession of himself" (*RA* 157). But he insists again that external ideas in themselves, inasmuch as they are bodily and not necessarily grounded in a Spiritual vision, have nothing which is spiritual or divine in them (*RA* 213–14). The affections, for example, that one has looking at images in the Catholic Church (though the way of receiving the idea "may not be so bad"), "if built primarily on such imaginations, [are not] any better than the affections raised in the ignorant people, by the sight of those images, which oftentimes are very great" (*RA* 214). The problem with them is that they remain external and therefore Satan can surely manipulate them (*RA* 215). Though our minds are frequently struck by such images, he says further on ("such is the nature of man"), there is nothing of the nature of knowledge or instruction in them. Truly spiritual and gracious affections are not raised in this way (*RA* 267).

Though he does not locate this strictly with "sight" as Calvin had done, Edwards continues Calvin's emphasis that it is in imagination or fantasy where the devil particularly chooses to form delusions. In fact:

'Tis very much to be doubted whether the devil can come at the soul of man, at all to affect it, or to excite any thought or motion, or produce any affect whatsoever in it, any other way, than the phantasy; which is that power of the soul, by which it receives, and is the subject of the species, or ideas of outward and sensible things. (*RA* 288)[88]

But why is this necessarily so? Cannot the devil also act on the reason, or through the will? Are these not also fallen in the same way as the imagination? No, Edwards seems to say, because the imagination cannot in the nature of the case deal with the proper being of things as they are rooted in God. Only when a believer sees the beauty of a tree as rooted in God is the being of that tree fully realized, not otherwise. Only then does the tree have ultimate reference.[89]

To put it in the best light, Edwards's views contain a highly original formulation that carries forward the best insights of Calvin and the tradition he represents. One could suggest that Edwards proposes an iconoclastic dismantling of the control of a fallen sensible imagination, so that it can be replaced with an – equally sensible – apprehension of divine beauty.

As he says: "When the true beauty and amiableness of the holiness or true moral good that is in divine things, is discovered to the soul, it, as it were, opens a new world to its view. This shows the glory of all the perfections of God, and of everything appertaining to the divine being" (*RA* 273). Notice that this spiritual sensitivity includes a new human perception of beauty that is grounded in God.[90] This includes seeing the beauty of God in both creation and in providence. This dismantling and rebuilding, moreover, is clearly based on the dynamic and relational view of God's trinitarian being. The believer literally sees things in nature the unbeliever cannot see, however moved that person may be by outward physical beauty.

At the same time Edwards often is unable to capture the full implications of this insight. The weakness lies in the discontinuity that he poses between these two sensitivities, a discontinuity that in the end appears as often metaphysical as it is moral and spiritual. The "general tendency" of the

---

[88] On the following page Edwards quotes approvingly Anthony Burgess's comment that the imagination is the place where the devil most often appears, and also François Turrentine who argues that only God can deal directly with reason, while angels and demons can only act mediately upon the human soul through the imagination.

[89] I owe this insight to Sang Lee from personal conversation. Professor Lee points out that this means Edwards is ultimately an objective idealist; see also *Philosophical Theology,* pp. 53–67.

[90] Significantly for Edwards, the "affections" in this instance have become a part of the knowing process. As he says, "This new spiritual sense is not a new faculty of understanding, but it is a new foundation laid in the nature of the soul, for a new kind of exercises of the same faculty" (*Religious Affections,* p. 206). William Wainwright points out this is a new element of cognition the mechanism of which is benevolence toward being, which is ultimately grounded in God (*Reason and the Heart: A Prolegomenon to a Critique of Passional Reason* [Ithaca, N.Y.: Cornell University Press, 1995], pp. 26–7).

sensible imagination is "to draw men off from the Word of God, and to cause 'em to reject the gospel and to establish unbelief and atheism" (*RA* 309), even if occasionally it can be used to draw men to the truth. This is because Edwards finally opposes the external and internal realms. However grand the ideas, if they are external, they are of no value.

As these external ideas have nothing divine or spiritual in their nature, and nothing but what natural men, without any new principles, are capable; so there is nothing in their nature which requires that peculiar, inimitable and unparalleled exercise of the gracious power of God. (*RA* 215)

But is there nothing in their nature, as part of God's good created order, that allows them to communicate the peculiar power of God? As Amy Plantinga Pauw notes, despite the fact that communicating God's goodness to the creature is the end for which creation was made, Edwards's idealist and rationalist impulses result in a "drastic truncation of the moral and theological significance of the creaturely world within Edwards' thought."[91]

Despite its many merits, the problem may lie in Edwards's theological formulation, and not only in his philosophical framework. On the one hand Edwards is resolutely trinitarian: he stresses appropriately Christ's mediatorship in creation even as he insists on the Spirit's role in bringing order out of chaos. He says:

The glorifying of God's moral perfections, is the special end of all of God's hands. By this sense of the moral beauty of divine things, is understood the sufficiency of Christ as a mediator: for it is only by the discovery of the beauty of the moral perfection of Christ, that the believer is let into the knowledge of the excellency of his person . . . and it is only by the knowledge of the excellency of Christ's person . . . [that the believer] sees the beauty of holiness, or true moral good, sees the greatest and most important thing in the world, which is the fulness of all things, without which all the world is empty, no better than nothing, yea, worse than nothing. (*RA* 273–4)

The dispositional ontology of Edwards that grounds this, we have noted, has the advantage of exchanging the static categories of substance metaphysics for the more dynamic vision of a world created for the communication and extension of God's glory. Moreover it is through the imagination of the person as she discovers these excellencies, and imagines the world in this new way, that God communicates this glory.[92]

---

[91] Pauw, *The Supreme Harmony of All*, p. 131–2. She goes on to say that "reprobate humanity fails to receive these gifts of Christ and the Spirit; thus they fail to participate in God's end for creation" (p. 133).

[92] See Lee, *Philosophical Theology*, p. 168. "The imagination . . . is the instrument through which God continues his creative activity."

While this opens vast opportunities for exploring creativity theologically, the dynamic and relational character of Edwards's metaphysics, grounded as it is in idealism, has its weakness as well. Its dynamism, and the stress on the imagination as the means of discerning God's creativity, when connected with Edwards's spiritualist metaphysic tends to reduce reality and the divine–human relation to a spiritual entity. Calvin could say of God's goodness: "because it is bestowed indiscriminately upon pious and impious, it is rightly counted among natural gifts." And: "It is no wonder then, that the knowledge of all that is most excellent in human life is said to be communicated to us through the Spirit of God . . . [Since God] fills, moves, and quickens all things by the power of the same Spirit, and does so according to the character that he bestowed upon each kind by the law of creation" (ii, ii, 14 and 16). For Edwards, while God's beauty can be glimpsed by the unbeliever in the richly interrelated creation, this can only be at one remove. Ultimately the believer and unbeliever can develop no common aesthetic discourse. Beauty, grounded as it is in God, can only be seen by eyes opened to the divine presence – it is connected finally with God's special grace, not with his general presence. As Michael M. McClymond concludes: "Only the regenerate perceive the divine excellency, and the unregenerate remain wholly insensitive to it." Though, as McClymond notes, Edwards was not entirely satisfied with this radical discontinuity holding that "religious experience is not the nullification of ordinary sense experience but rather its fulfillment."[93]

This radical dependence on God is both the strength and the weakness of Edwards's aesthetic. On the one hand he gave a powerful and influential expression to the affections as capable, by the illumination of the Spirit, of grasping the beauty of God's presence. This language of the heart, taken out of its theological context, certainly played a role in the development of eighteenth-century aesthetics, especially in the work of Ralph Waldo Emerson. But his properly theological influence did not serve to encourage creativity and a broader cultural vision.[94] For though he proposed a powerful theological aesthetic, he proposed no cultural forms in which this aesthetic could come to expression. It was never clear whether the fault of creation is its fallenness or its finitude. As a result it seems that no material

---

[93] Michael M. McClymond, "Spiritual Perception in Jonathan Edwards," *Journal of Religion* 77 (1997), pp. 213–14.

[94] Erdt, *Jonathan Edwards*, pp. 79–84. He argues that Edwards's influence on the arts was greater than usually thought because it was indirect (p. 82). Though Edwards's influence on the political developments may have been considerable, as Alan Heimert argued famously in *Religion and the American Mind from the Great Awakening to the Revolution* (Cambridge: Harvard University Press, 1966).

form in itself was of sufficient "being" to hold the consent to Being, and that spirits alone are able to express and that the Holy Spirit makes alive. But perhaps this way of putting things is not entirely fair. Perhaps one should say that Edwards, like Reformed Protestants before him, ultimately allowed no form for his aesthetics except human life itself. This impulse is both its limitation and its opportunity, it expresses both the genius and the limitation of Protestant aesthetics.

POSTSCRIPT: WHAT WAS THE LEGACY OF PROTESTANT AESTHETICS?

Whether Edwards appreciated it or not, the life of his time had considerable aesthetic, or at least theatrical, qualities. The experience of the Great Awakening for a people without the rich popular culture that would develop in the next century must have provided ample doses of drama and spectacle. Whitefield's preaching had all the qualities of a performance; the awakenings themselves have been described as a "visible Gospel."[95] These events were powerful "ritual" events that lifted people out of their everyday lives and transformed their world. This is certainly the testimony of Nathan Cole, a Connecticut farmer working in his field when he received word that Whitefield was preaching nearby. He dropped his farming tools and ran with his wife "as if we were fleeing for our lives." This is what he saw:

It was like a steady stream of horses and their riders scarcely a horse more than his length behind another, all of a lather and foam with sweat, their breath rolling out of their nostrils . . . Every horse seemed to go with all his might to carry his rider to hear news from heaven for the saving of souls. It made me tremble to see the sight, how the world was in a struggle. The banks over the river lookt black with people and horses all along the twelve miles I see no man at work in his field but all seemed to be gone.[96]

The ferry on the river, the horses, people, everything seemed to be struggling for life. As for Whitefield, he "looked as if he was clothed with authority from the Great God, and a sweet solemnity sat upon his brow, and my hearing him preach gave me a warm heart wound. By God's blessing, my old

---

[95] See Schmidt, *Holy Fairs,* ch. 2, "Visible Gospel." However exaggerated Ann Kibbey's conclusions may be, her point that Calvin and the Puritans had collapsed the distinction between art and life is sound (*The Interpretation of Material Shapes in Puritanism* [Cambridge: Cambridge University Press, 1986], p. 48).

[96] Nathan Cole, "Spiritual Travels," in Heimert and Miller (eds.), *The Great Awakening,* pp. 185–6.

foundation was broken up, and I saw that my righteousness would not save me."[97] Clearly it was the performance and drama of the events along with the preaching that caused Cole to see his world change before his very eyes – the sign of the event was joined to the promise of the word. The struggle of horses, boats and people became a metaphor for the struggle within his soul. More than this it became the stuff of a popular dramatic interlude in the daily lives of these people. It made God and the ways of God visible and accessible. In one sense these events were consistent with the theology of grace developed by Cotton and his colleagues. But in other ways this expression of experiential religion had an impact on the developing culture that even these theologians could not have envisioned. For in ways not unlike the images and pilgrimages of the Middle Ages, these practices provided a visible and experimental component to religion. They opened an arena in which people's experience mattered and their faith and culture were affirmed. Such experiences, and the retelling of them, prepared the ground for, indeed in many ways they inaugurated, the development of a truly popular culture in America.

Meanwhile the development of elite culture little by little cut its ties with this theological vision and its imaginative reordering of life. Four paintings stretching from 1691 to 1788 give shape to these changing allegiances and show a progressive emancipation from the culture-forming vision of Calvin. The first of these is the famous "self-portrait" of Captain Thomas Smith (Figure 40).

Thomas Smith was active as an artist and mariner in the 1680s in Boston, though little else is known of his life. From the inventory of his will (dated 1688, though he died in 1691) we learn that he was a wealthy man.[98] But from the picture we learn a great deal about both the man and his faith. Its style is advanced for the time reflecting a change from a flat picture plain to a more Baroque sense of modeling.[99] In many respects this picture represents an image of America's view of itself as it neared the end of the seventeenth century. On the one hand, it was growing more and more prosperous. Smith wears an expensive collar of Milan lace, he gazes self-confidently out at the viewer. In the window picture at the upper left is an image of a sea battle, speaking of his life as a sea captain, a successful man of the world.

---

[97] Ibid., p. 186.
[98] There is a record that he painted an "effigy" of William Ames per order of the corporation of Harvard College; see Fairbanks and Trent (eds.), *New England Begins,* vol. III, p. 474.
[99] See the technical description in Roger B. Stein, "Thomas Smith's Self-Portrait: Image/Text as Artifact," *Art Journal* 44 (1984), pp. 317–18.

Figure 40   Captain Thomas Smith, *Self Portrait*. Oil on canvas, 62.9 cm × 60.4 cm.
Worcester Art Museum, Worcester, Mass., 1680.

Yet on the other hand the sea battle adds an unsettling element. The small picture portrays a battle, perhaps a naval battle on the Barbary Coast of Africa – the English and Dutch flags are visible and the fortification is Islamic. Perhaps it recalls a victory over unbelievers, but it may as well recall a defeat. In any case it certainly speaks of the human struggles of life in a fallen world, the warfare the Christian wages against evil. All this is explained by the poem which is pointedly placed under the skull at the bottom left of the picture.[100] The skull, a dominant *memento mori*

---

[100]   Stein's excellent discussion of this picture argues that this is the "central organizing element" of the composition ("Thomas Smith's Self-Portrait," p. 317).

appearing often on gravestones, contrasts sharply with the energy of the
small picture above it. Smith's right hand rests on the skull as if to remind
us that the success and the vigorous assertion of the world and life that
appears elsewhere in the picture is to be tempered by the reminder of the
vulnerability of life. This is expressed vividly in the poem which seems
almost to be coming out of the mouth of the skull:

> Why why should I the World be minding
> Therein a world of evils finding
> Then farwell World: Farwell thy Jarres
> Thy Joies thy Toies thy wiles thy Warrs
> Truth Sounds Retreat: I am not sorye
> The Eternal drawes to him my heart
> By Faith (which can thy Force subvert)
> To crowne me (after Grace) with Glory. T.S.

As in an emblem, the verbal structure and the visual images interact to
complete the meaning of the whole. These both together suggest that other
world which to Smith's imagination is more real than this, and, in the last
lines, draws him – like Edward Taylor's coach – up to heaven. The lesser
glory is exchanged for the greater; the visible pleasures of this world (in the
Puritan view not to be despised) are replaced by the more solid ones, the
"glory," of the next. Smith sees himself not simply in terms of what he has
been able to accomplish and experience in this life, but in the light of what,
as a "figura Christi," he will see in the next.[101]

By the beginning of the eighteenth century, painting was firmly established as an important art, both in England and America. In 1715 Jonathan
Richardson published his influential *Theory of Painting*.[102] Though some
still consider painting a low art, Richardson notes, it is bounty from heaven
which we should esteem highly. This is because it provides another language,
portraying a thing clearly and without ambiguity (p. 2). The artist, he says
later, should thus go directly to his point and "tell his story with all possible
simplicity" (p. 34). Richardson's focus on the language of painting and on
narrative underlines the fact that writing is still the dominant metaphor
for art – he even suggests the artist write out the story first to get it right
(p. 37). "Since [painting] is a sort of writing it ought to be clearly legible"
(p. 40). Portraits then can portray not only the person but "the character
of virtues" – they can improve nature. The goal is to paint so that people

---

[101] Ibid., p. 324.
[102] *The Works of Jonathan Richardson. Corrected and prepared by his son Mr. J. Richardson* (London: T.
Davies, 1773), pages in the text.

Figure 41   John Smibert, *Dean Berkeley and His Entourage (The Bermuda Group)*. Oil on canvas, 176.5 × 236.2 cm. Yale Library Museum, New Haven, Conn., 1729–31.

may be excited to imitate good actions (p. 8). In this way "a kind of new world may be formed in the imagination, consisting, as this, of people of all degrees and characters, only heightened and improved" (p. 94). Note that art can both please and teach. Its moral calling is intact, but its theological grounding is less clear.

By the time the next painting is done, much has changed in Colonial America. John Smibert, often considered the Father of American painting, painted this group portrait of "*The Bermuda Group*" (Figure 41) some-time between 1729 and 1731.[103] Smibert had been academically trained in Europe and arrived in Boston in 1728, where he established a shop which sold artists' materials and at the same time displayed his important collection of European prints. This painting, the first group portrait done in America, captures something both of the high ideals and the faded dreams that characterized this period of American history. During the early 1720s George (later Bishop) Berkeley had become deeply discouraged about the

[103] See Richard Henry Saunders III, "John Smibert: Anglo-American Portrait Painter," Ph.D dissertation, Yale University (1979), p. 148.

spiritual state of Britain and of Europe more generally. It was to America that he looked as the hope for a future spiritual renewal. As he put it famously in his poem entitled "America":

> Westward the Course of Empire takes its Way;
> The four first Acts already past,
> A fifth shall close the Drama with the Day;
> Time's noblest Offspring is the last.[104]

He became convinced that his best contribution to the realization of this final act was to move to Bermuda and there establish a training school to train pastors of good morals for the churches of the western world. Bermuda was chosen as a place equidistant from many of the settlements of the New World. In a twist that recalls John Cotton's advice to the settlers leaving for New England one hundred years previously, Berkeley insisted that "a number of young American savages" should be trained at this college alongside "the English youth of our plantations." The former he believed, properly trained, would "become the fittest missionaries for spreading religion."[105] Throughout the 1720s Berkeley gave himself to seeking support and planning for the project. He gave careful attention to the proposed layout of the town, and to details of the proposed curriculum of the college. Artist John Smibert was chosen to accompany Berkeley and teach art and architecture in the proposed college. Arts were no mere frill to Berkeley's mind. As he wrote in 1721, echoing Philip Sidney a century and a half before, "Those noble arts of architecture, sculpture and painting, do not only adorn the public but have also an influence on the minds and manners of men, filling them with great ideas and spiriting them up to an emulation of worthy actions."[106]

Berkeley therefore brought Smibert with him when he came to America to await the final charter and support needed to settle in Bermuda. While waiting Smibert painted portraits – of Berkeley and others, and this group portrait of the "Bermuda Group." Here Smibert places Berkeley and his project in the grandest possible context. Intentionally recalling the *School of Athens* 1510–11 by Raphael in the Papal Apartments in Rome, Smibert

---

[104] Quoted in A. A. Luce, *The Life of George Berkeley Bishop of Cloyne* (New York: Thomas Nelson & Sons, 1949), p. 96. For what follows I am dependent on Luce and also on Edwin S. Gaustad, *George Berkeley in America* (New Haven: Yale University Press, 1979), pp. 25–51. In his proposal of 1724, Berkeley had expressed his dream to "rescue historic Christianity, to purify and preserve Western civilization" (Gaustad, *George Berkeley in America*, p. 50).

[105] Gaustad, *George Berkeley in America*, p. 25. Luce notes the proliferation of Anglican missionary movements during this period (*Life of George Berkeley*, p. 95).

[106] *George Berkeley in America*, p. 69.

wants to say that here is the new enlightened philosopher who wants to shine the light of his wisdom throughout the New World. To the right the Bishop stands speaking, his right hand resting on a book,[107] while his family – his wife holds his son Henry, with her companion to her right – sits beside him. Seated at the front, and dominating the picture, is John Wainwright, a supporter of Berkeley, who commissioned the piece and considered accompanying Berkeley to America (though in the end he did not). He sits expectantly with pen in hand ready to take down what Berkeley is about to say. Behind are Richard Dalton and John James and to the far left Smibert himself, all members of the proposed expedition. The group sits in a classic portico, with a fertile view of land and trees visible just to the left of center of the picture, balanced in the composition by the open book waiting to be written upon, below. America was the place where the purity of the divine religion, Berkeley believed, would "in due time have a great effect,"[108] and this group would be God's instrument to this end.

In the event a number of factors doomed the project of Berkeley – it was too far from the mainland, too difficult to supply, and too expensive – in spite of the fact that the charter was finally granted and the project approved by parliament. In 1731 Berkeley finally gave up and returned to England. By this time Smibert was busy painting members of the Boston elite (many of them members of the Old South Church which Smibert had joined). He married Mary Williams in 1731 and, after Berkeley left, opened his "Color Shop" in Boston. The painting of the "Bermuda Group" however remains a kind of cultural metaphor for America. It speaks of a genuine desire for a missionary outreach, and an establishment of a truly righteous kingdom, the same motivations that had motivated the settlers in the 1620s. But it was also an image of faded dreams. The picture was never claimed by Wainwright, who apparently did not wish to be reminded of the failed project (nor perhaps of the money he lost in supporting it). But, ironically, the painting hung for years in Smibert's shop and influenced many of the first generation of American artists. They were influenced by the academic quality of Smibert's work; they probably no longer resonated with the Berkeleyan dreams which produced it.

One artist who was clearly influenced by Smibert and his "Bermuda Group" was Robert Feke (1707–52). Feke was born in Oyster Bay, Long

---

[107] Symbolizing the fact that some of Berkeley's most important philosophical works were written while he was in America (Richard H. Saunders and Ellen G. Miles, *American Colonial Portraits: 1700–1776* [Washington, DC: Smithsonian Institution, 1987], p. 120).

[108] *George Berkeley in America*, p. 50.

Figure 42   Robert Feke, *Tench Francis*. Oil on canvas, 39 × 49 inches. New York
Metropolitan Museum of Art, New York, 1746.

Island, his father a pastor in a Baptist church, a faith which he followed
throughout his life.[109] His encounter with Smibert was critical to his

[109] See Frank W. Bayley, *Five Colonial Artists of New England* (Boston: privately printed, 1929); and
Henry W. Foote, *Life and Work of Robert Feke* (Cambridge, Mass.: Harvard University Press,
1930).

development for, apart from this influence, Feke was completely self-taught. One can see Smibert's influence in this portrait of Tench Francis painted in 1746 (Figure 42). Francis had emigrated to Maryland in 1710 and later moved to Philadelphia where he became attorney general of the colony. After retirement he lived on a large farm in New Jersey until his death in 1758. Feke places Francis out in the landscape, probably, of his farm.[110] The vertical edges of the coat form a pyramidal structure which leads up to Francis's face. Feke's portraits are characterized by their marvelously fresh and closely observed style. Though the structure and setting is similar to Smibert, the character seems more accessible, less mysterious. Here the landscape does not consist merely of symbolic elements added in a corner or behind the figure, but it is the dominant setting for the work. This natural setting adds its own decorative quality to the composition as a whole, much like the poetry did in Thomas Smith's picture. Only in this picture the "language" which the landscape speaks is the serenity and nobility of the figure in front of it, not a message of the struggle for God's glory. His stance and the gleaming sword at his side speak of Francis's exalted position, a statement which is reiterated by his placement in the setting. The work is visually well constructed even if the colors lack the modeling of Smibert and the setting is less classical in character. Whether he knew of it or not he followed the advice on portrait painting that was expressed by a well-known eighteenth-century writer on "Decorum" in painting portraits, Jonathan Richardson: "Each character must have an attitude and dress; the ornaments and background proper to it: every part of the portrait and all about it, must be expressive of the man, and have a resemblance as well as the features of the face."[111]

Like most of his contemporaries Feke was still a strong Christian, but he had not been taught to see that its demands made any difference for his painting. Meanwhile his work does reflect developments of mid-eighteenth-century America – the rise of Deism, the evolution of a stable social structure and an elite colonial culture. This was the same time that traditional meetinghouses were giving way to more elaborate and imposing church structures influenced by English architecture.[112] American artistic styles continued to reflect their European sources even at one remove, but the

---

[110] See R. Peter Mooz, "Robert Feke: The Philadelphia Story," in Ian Quimby (ed.), *American Painting to 1776: A Reappraisal* (Charlottesburg: University of Virginia, 1971) p. 189.

[111] Richardson was writing in 1715; quoted in Mooz, "Robert Feke," p. 192.

[112] Mooz sees the contemporary influences on Feke evident in comparing Feke's work with that of Smibert ("Robert Feke," p. 191). Cf. Harry Stout's comments on the changing style of meetinghouses (*The New England Soul*, p. 176).

correlation between the people's faith and their images was being lost. While Feke's portraits retain an American directness and even a puritan simplicity, unlike a century earlier, there is no theological consensus that comes to expression in the forms and structures of his art.

Where this is leading can be seen in the work of Charles Willson Peale (1741–1827), perhaps the best-known artist of his generation (Figure 43). In 1788 Peale painted William Smith (1728–1814), a Scotch Irish Presbyterian who moved to Baltimore around 1760 and made a fortune as a wheat merchant during the Revolutionary war.[113] Though he was a well-known figure there were those who doubted his wealth was entirely legitimate. In January of 1789, just after Smith had been elected to the first United States Congress, a popular broadside appeared which said in part: "Mr. Smith has distilled RICHES from the tears of the POOR; and grown FAT upon their curses." It was signed "Antismithites" (p. 588). The previous year he had asked Peale to paint him and his grandson at his country retreat. In apparent violation of Richardson's specifications for portrait painting, Smith wanted no reference to his life as a merchant included, no symbols of the dignity of his position in society. He simply wanted to be shown in the midst of the "simple" life of his country retreat. Peale portrays the farm in the background as self-sufficient, "a visual ode to the benefits of rural retirement" (p. 595). All the symbols depicted reiterate this theme: the peach, the branch, the book on gardening, and a pruning knife. The chair is even a well-known garden chair, imported from England (p. 601)!

But perhaps Peale is following Richardson's advice after all. For Brandon Fortune points out that the books on the table beside Smith were by popular writers who celebrated Virgil's praise of the rural life, urging the landowner to drink the pure pleasures of rural life (pp. 602, 605). The house and landscape then are "attributes" which Smith wished to display. He wanted to show a suspicious world that he was indeed a man of honest character who lived on the land and whose honest labors had been crowned with the success of possessing such property – a small, tidy, and self-sufficient farm. Peale's portrayal contains values that had now become traditional in America; it is neat, elegant and yet plain. Such an image could capture the truly good life, one lived without ostentation or excess.

Smith's portrait is a metaphor for America in the late eighteenth century. To be a farmer was to be an honest citizen, one contributing to the good of the emerging nation and of one's neighbors. A worker of the land is

---

[113] Brandon Brame Fortune, "'From the World Escaped': Peale's Portrait of William Smith and his Grandson," *Eighteenth Century Studies* 25/4 (1992), p. 588–90. Subsequent pages in the text.

Figure 43   Charles Willson Peale, *William Smith and His Grandson*. Oil on canvas, $51\frac{1}{4} \times 40\frac{3}{8}$ inches. Virginia Museum of Fine Arts, Richmond, Va., 1788.

the truest American, even an emblem of America itself. A few years earlier John Adams had toured some English gardens with Thomas Jefferson. According to the account of this visit he liked best William Shenstone's "The Leasowes" because he said it was "the simplest and plainest, but the most rural of all." Virtues and beauty he believed were seen in a useful landscape. All the more elaborate estates were "mere ostentations of vanity." He confided to his friend that he hoped riding parks, pleasure grounds, or ornamental farms never caught on in America. For there "nature has done greater Things and furnished nobler Materials."[114]

Beauty is to be found in the useful landscape, and so newly wealthy landowners were eager to claim the high moral ground represented by their rural estates. But notice how far we have come from the "Spiritual Husbandry" of John Flavell, and the utopian social structures of John Worlidge. There the root metaphor is a redemptive drive to restore creation to its edenic purity, and a typological impulse to see through creation to the other better world. Now the honesty of the rural living itself purifies, it has become a kind of this-worldly converting ordinance. The intense theological vision has faded, but it has left behind a residue of values, and a distinct aesthetic impulse – a longing for purity, simplicity and elegance. These values are seen in the artwork that we have reviewed, especially in Feke and Peale. But they are seen even more in the life that people like Adams and Smith sought to live. These continued to put themselves into the narrative. They sought to live out a dramatic narrative, now of goodness and simplicity. The more solid world to which Thomas Smith looked forward in heaven, for William Smith one hundred years later on, has been transferred to his rural retreat. There the struggles of life as a merchant have been left behind for the purity and simplicity of the land.

One might argue that to the degree that the vision of the heavenly kingdom that motivated previous generations of Puritans took exclusive and visible shape in a life well lived or in the things that furnished or "pictured" that life, to that extent the imagination withered. This is true even if, ironically, the art produced was of higher quality and more important. The tradition stretching from Calvin to Edwards had mustered valuable theological resources embracing a compelling vision of a world sustained and endowed by the grace and glory of God. But by mid-century this vision was fading. As a result, after Edwards this world grew increasingly opaque; one could no longer see through it to God's world, or better, see that world in this one. For it takes a great imaginative leap to see the city "whose

---

[114] Quoted in Emmet, *So Fine a Prospect*, p. 3.

builder and maker is God." Yet, our study suggests, when enjoying and building this world can feed off the imaginative grasp of the next, when the goodness of this world can be refracted into images and sacraments of that world, having an integrity that rests on the triune presence of God, then the imagination has ample room to flourish.

Epilogue

When Ralph Waldo Emerson rose to give his famous divinity school address at Harvard on July 15, 1838 there is no doubt that he considered himself to be striking a blow on behalf of spontaneity and a direct access to God over against the dead dogmatism that he saw around him.[1] He certainly would not have put it in the terms we have developed, but in this respect he was surely standing with John Cotton over against the descendants of William Ames. But though the aim is similar and the rich natural – even biblical – imagery resonates with those earlier Puritan preachers, it is their imagination and not their faith that animates this heir. Emerson is persuaded the Puritan "creed is passing away, and none arises in its room . . . It has lost its grasp on the affection of the good, and the fear of the bad" (p. 88). Now it is not the person of Christ who is the fountain of this grace – Emerson rejects this "noxious exaggeration about the *person* of Jesus. The soul knows no persons" (p. 82, his emphasis) – it is rather the soul opened to the Moral Nature, which is God himself. The gospel is still sought within, though it is the soul and not God that liberates; and reading is still the dominant trope. As he puts it: "In the soul, then, let the redemption be sought. In one soul, in your soul, there are resources for the world. Wherever a man comes, there comes revelation . . . When a man comes, all books are legible, all things transparent" (p. 89). And the world is still a mirror, but no longer of God's glory. Emerson looks for those, he says in the concluding lines of this address, who "shall see the world to be the mirror of the soul" (p. 93).

Though Emerson's heritage is clearly rooted in the tradition we have examined, there are many questions that remain about the cultural impact of the Protestant imagination, especially in its Reformed variety. More attention needs to be paid to the connections between the theological

[1] See *The Collected Works of Ralph Waldo Emerson*, general editor, Alfred R. Ferguson, intro. and notes by Robert E. Spiller (Cambridge: Harvard University Press, 1971), vol. I, pp. 76–93. Pages in the text are to this work.

propositions and the cultural strategies that emerged. We hope at least to have demonstrated that these connections can no longer be ignored. Similarly more work needs to be done in exploring the faith motivations and the cultural strategies of Huguenot, Reformed, or Puritan artists during this period. We need to find out more about the way art objects and prints were actually received and how they functioned in people's lives, especially in relation to other cultural products. In these areas as in others, there is more work to be done. Moreover further developments after our period could well throw fresh light on, or even raise questions about, the suggestions we have made.

Nevertheless in these concluding comments we will seek to sketch out dimensions of an imagination that is uniquely Protestant and Reformed. In each of these areas there will obviously be both continuities and discontinuities with the medieval traditions, just as there will be similarities with views of, for example, Lutheran or Catholic painters. But we argue that, taken as a whole, these broad tendencies, if not unique, at least are typical of developing Protestant attitudes toward the arts. Our comments will suggest not only general tendencies but evidence for these Protestant impulses later in the tradition.

ICONOCLASM: PULLING DOWN STRONGHOLDS

A major aspect of the temperament we have traced is what might broadly be called "iconoclastic." Obviously the motives for iconoclasm were complex and the suspicions that irrupted in the sixteenth century had a long history in the Church. But the inclination to question, and, if necessary, dismantle idolatrous imagery and associated ideas, became a recognizable constituent of the Protestant attitude to both art and culture. Contrary to what is often thought, this disposition does not belittle the importance of imagery, but rather recognizes all too clearly its power and importance. As Thomas Matthews says of patristic images: "Images are dangerous. Images, no matter how discretely chosen, come freighted with conscious or subliminal memories; no matter how limited their projected use, they burn indelible outlines into the mind... Images not only express conviction, they alter feelings, and end up justifying convictions. Eventually they invite worship."[2] The age-old arguments for and against images are, as David Freedberg has shown, two sides of the same coin. The arguments all range

[2] *The Clash of the Gods: A Reinterpretation of Early Christian Art* (Princeton: Princeton University Press, 1993), p. 11. So, he notes, one cannot write a history of the early Church without including a history of images. One could make a similar argument for the Reformation.

around the possibility that images "provide a channel for the more suscep-tible sense of sight, so that the mind can ascend to that which it otherwise could not grasp; the awareness throughout of the possibility – and the danger – of the fusion of image and prototype."[3] The Protestant suspicion toward images and the external mediation of grace connects with the an-cient apophatic tradition in the Church. Since God is separate from the world, and those created in the divine image have their eyesight so severely damaged, one must treat all human constructions of God with suspicion.

If one accepts this view of things, Calvin's scruples would have been more realistic than Luther's tolerance. For Calvin understood that in a sinful world patterns and practices often coalesce into particular images, and if health is to be restored, these images must not only be denounced but they must also be destroyed. For the reformers knew that much more was at stake than cultural products alone. The reformers, we have argued, were not worried so much about art as about the health and development of a social order in which individuals and families could flourish. Calvin went so far as to suggest such a world offered a better "mirror" of God. But they also knew that the accepted mental prejudices often stood in the way of such reform and reconstruction. A major unnoticed by-product of the dominant images underlying cultural values is the way they authorize and reinforce the world-as-taken-for-granted. Calvin is often accused of enforcing dictatorial practices in setting up Geneva. But his belief in the power and transcendence of God not only kept him from thinking any human construction, whether an image or social structure, could embody perfectly values of the kingdom of God, but more importantly it provided leverage whereby corrupt practices and injustices could be addressed and when necessary overturned. The presence of this holy God, speaking to the Church through the Word and the Spirit, exercised a continual critique of the status quo.

What is equally clear is that iconoclastic practices were not a form of social control exercised by the elite. If anything Calvin, and especially Luther, had more scruples about these destructive practices than the people themselves. Rather iconoclasm was an impulse that spread among the people, one of the first popular movements of the early modern period. The people did not need the theological arguments about image and prototype to join the crowds tearing down the images. Having passed their time (and spent their money) on the pilgrimages and penitential practices, once enlightened, they were eager to remove the proliferating altars and images, frequently

---

[3] Freedberg, *The Power of Images*, p. 406. This was especially recognized, he notes, by defenders of images.

from their own churches. Their instinctive response, we have argued, was a kind of social repentance.

But repentance is for the sake of sanctification. As we have noted frequently the iconoclastic temperament was understood not merely as critique and deconstruction, but as an essential component of the positive work of reforming people and society. Because of their power and importance images associated with idolatrous practices and a corrupt social order had not only to be denounced, they had to be destroyed. Just as persons needed, in biblical terms, to repent, that is turn around and go in a new direction, so iconoclasm, from one point of view, was a social "turning around." The destruction was not an end in itself, but a necessary prelude to the construction of something different which was intended to fill the spaces that were left. Iconoclasm as an underlying attitude allowed Puritans to have the world without grasping it. The world could be valued, even celebrated as in the work of the Dutch landscapes or the poetic images of Anne Bradstreet, without losing sight of its brokenness or the need to struggle against the darkness it contained.

In art and literature in particular this positive role of "iconoclasm" has yet to be fully appreciated. Scottish poet Robert Crawford, for example, has pointed out that iconoclasm has been an important impulse to creativity, especially in the development of modern art and poetry. He argues: "Iconoclasm has appealed to aspects of the romantic and modernist imagination, whether in the poetry of Byron or in Mendelssohn's Reformation Symphony, just as it was relished by successive generations of modernist artists."[4] Crawford goes on to suggest iconoclasm may be an interpretive key to understanding, for example, T. S. Eliot's early poetry. Eliot, who had roots in Puritan New England, makes generous use in these poems of the tropes of darkness, absence and barrenness. In the first section of *The Waste Land* (1922), for example, one finds these lines:

> What are the roots that clutch, what branches grow
> Out of this stony rubbish? Son of man,
> You cannot say, or guess, for you know only
> A heap of *broken images*, where the sun beats,
> And the dead tree gives no shelter, the cricket no relief,
> And the dry stone no sound of water.[5]

---

[4] Robert Crawford, "Presbyterianism and Imagination in Modern Scotland," in T. M. Devine (ed.), *Scotland's Shame: Bigotry and Sectarianism in Modern Scotland* (Edinburgh and London: Mainstream Publications, 2000), p. 189. Over against a Catholic focus on plenitude and presence, Crawford suggests, a component of a Protestant aesthetic might well be absence (p. 190).

[5] *T. S. Eliot: Selected Poems* (New York: Harcourt, Brace & World, 1930), p. 51; emphasis added.

Writing during the emptiness of the post-war "roaring twenties," did Eliot feel the intuitive need to deconstruct a world that had lost its way?

It is well known that Protestant countries have nourished principles of political revolution, but it is possible these impulses had influence beyond these areas. Why, for example, did the Cubists in an anticlerical France during the first decades of the 1900s feel the oppression of a world whose dreams were fading, and respond by instinctively dismantling their subjects as a means to constructing a fresh vision of the world? Art-historical studies of this period provide intriguing hints. Werner Haftmann in his discussion of Analytic Cubism notes Braque and Picasso arrived in 1909 at "an analytic dissection of the object. They began by separating the facets of an object, by spreading them out, and by blending them with the forms of other objects . . . [Among those who joined the movement was] Marcel Duchamp, whose brilliant and anarchic mind had recognized that Analytical Cubism, with its fragmentation of object, reflected the psychology of modern man whom technology has alienated from the world of things."[6] Of course there were other sources for such cultural critique but it may be that the Protestant iconoclastic impulse, perhaps mediated through Jansenist influences in the late eighteenth-century Catholic revival, was among them.

LOOKING INWARD

A second tendency in the developing Reformed imagination has been the encouragement to look within oneself to discover and reflect on the presence of God. Since the external forms of piety were forbidden, believers, raised on the catechism and exposed to the weekly preaching of Scripture, inevitably turned inward to shape their images of God. It is one of the ironies that we have traced, that in rejecting the visual mediation of spiritual power prominent in the Middle Ages – in turning away from the great imaginative works of earlier artists – the Protestants were forced to develop their own "imaginations" as the template within which the new spiritual world was to be constructed and perceived. Though we have not traced these connections, there is clearly a relationship here with the subjective aesthetics that would develop with Alexander Baumgarten and John Locke.[7]

---

[6] Werner Haftmann, *Painting in the Twentieth Century*, trans. Ralph Manheim (London: Lund Humphries, 1965), vol. I, pp. 99, 101. Notice the connection between dissection and reordering.

[7] See Monroe C. Beardsley, *Aesthetics from Classical Greek to the Present* (New York: Macmillan Press, 1966), pp. 156–60 and 173–7. Beardsley notes that Baumgarten was consciously seeking to develop an aesthetic that corresponded to the clear and distinct ideas of Descartes.

More specifically this inward turn has three components important to the Protestant imagination. First was the encouragement to "imagine" God and heaven by drawing pictures, as it were, in the mind. Our argument was that this inward turn was double-edged. On the one hand, persistent icono-clastic worries led to a mental structuring that was at times aniconic; on the other hand the dependence on the rich narratives and images of the scrip-tural world encouraged the development of what might be called a richly furnished, biblical imagination. The first tendency was best exemplified by William Ames. Based on the logic of Peter Ramus, Ames believed that it was possible to imagine a mental picture of the world that corresponded more accurately than previous logics to the way things really are. God has so ordered things, these writers believed, that the human mind can imagine and draw a map that accurately reflects this order. But whereas the medieval map of reality was crowded with images and accompanied by the music of the spheres, this map replaced the images with abstract dichotomous patterns, a practice Frances Yates called an "iconoclasm" of the mind.

As we have noticed frequently, while this tendency militated against certain cultural forms, it encouraged others. In particular it clearly took a step in the direction of a mathematical structuring of reality that was to bear such important fruit in the developing scientific worldview. Surely Descartes was influenced by these tendencies in developing his notion of clear and distinct ideas on the basis of a mathematical model. More recently Ramus's dichotomous logic may find some resonance in the processes of the modern computer.[8] The persistent danger of course was that this (highly conventional) picture of the world, since it was assumed to accurately reflect the world as God made it, could exercise unnoticed and sometimes oppressive control. As W. J. T. Mitchell says of this artificial perspective of the world:

The effect of this invention was nothing less than to convince an entire civilization that it possessed an infallible method of representation, a system for the automatic and mechanical production of truths about the material and mental world. The best index to the hegemony of artificial perspective is the way it denies its own artificiality and lays claim to being a "natural" representation of the "way things look", or . . . "the way things really are".[9]

[8] See Peter Drucker on the knowledge revolution: "Software is the reorganization of traditional work, based on centuries of experience, through the application of knowledge and especially of system-atic logical analysis. The key is not electronics; it is cognitive science" ("Beyond the Information Revolution," *Atlantic Monthly,* October 1999, p. 57).

[9] He traces the development of this picture back to Alberti in 1435, but Ramus and Ames are certainly working on the same project (W. J. T. Mitchell, *Iconology: Image, Text, Ideology* [University of Chicago Press, 1986], p. 37).

The new idolatries to which this can lead can be seen by reading any of the many modern critiques of technology.[10]

The second tendency we traced in the development of this inward turn was the emerging cultural patterns that reflected the rich language of biblical images and stories. John Cotton and Jonathan Edwards, among others, reflected an openness to seeing God in the world, and indeed, on the basis of this openness, nurtured what Milton had called the "paradise within." They too believed that God had so made the world that the human mind could imagine God's reality, especially as this, later, came to expression in anticipating the joys of heaven. But they allowed the imagery of Scripture, in which they were immersed week after week, to work on their minds and imagination. This enabled them to see the world as filled with signs and "types" of the spiritual world. Lying behind this development was a struggle over the use of Scripture that we have touched on only indirectly. Calvin of course had proposed the more narrow view that only what Scripture specifically commanded should be allowed in worship and Christian living – although he was less restrictive in this regard than some of his followers. While most of the theologians we have reviewed would have endorsed Calvin's view, among some there were deeper influences at work. Over time the influence of biblical patterns and cadences began to exercise its own spell, especially over the followers of Richard Sibbes who have been called the Cambridge Brethren. These allowed Scripture to determine more fundamental structures of their thinking, which in turn released fresh creative energies.

One example we have described of these influences was the development of portraiture. More work needs to be done on the relation between the Reformation and the concurrent flowering of portraiture. Renaissance humanism surely played a role here as well, but even this had its religious dimension. What is clearly mistaken is to understand this simply as a secular development – at least in those areas influenced by Calvinism theological motives were at work. The reformers consistently emphasized the human person as the proper image of God, and the necessity of paying appropriate tribute to this image rather than wasting resources on material images. But an additional element must surely relate to this inward turn we are emphasizing here. Portraits, especially of spiritual leaders, embodied a call to remembrance of what Puritans might call the "real art" of God: God's spiritual gifts of grace in his servants. Portraits ought to be seen then as actual images of God's grace. But they also should be understood as allegories of

---

[10] See, for example, Jacques Ellul, *La Technique* (Paris, 1971).

virtue. Seeing these images the viewer is moved to desire the godliness that is expressed in the faces (and the various symbolic associations) of these people of God. Since the fleshly life of these people, like the fleshly life of Christ, was not important to the Puritans, it was the inward beauty of the soul they sought to highlight by the demeanor, dress and accompanying objects. But as we observed frequently, the goal of capturing a spiritual reality did not diminish the personal presence of the figure drawn, quite the reverse. One often comes away from the experience of these portraits with an enhanced sense of the sitter's presence. Indeed one might say puritan portraits reflect an aesthetic of presence. Just as the glories of this world, while vulnerable and evanescent, are not undermined by their grounding in God or their role as types of the heavenly world, so the physical image of the person, while reflective of deeper values, is not deprecated.

But there is a third dimension of puritan interiority that shaped its aesthetic: its simplicity. What is frequently referred to as the "plain style" of puritan aesthetics we would argue is a component of the inward turn of the imagination. We noted that the desire to live simple lives ordered according to the Word of God, was not a careless relaxation of effort, nor was it simply a paring away of useless ornament to reach some rock bottom reality. It was an imaginative struggle with life in order to reach and explore some of the depth and mystery that God's presence provided. The quiet and plainness of puritan worship, of the structure of their lives, even of their communities, was a disciplined attempt to embody values that transcended this world. What their lives and culture lacked in extensive elaboration, they gained in intensive depth. This recent description of a camp meeting by Lionel Basney captures these values beautifully:

We stood, sang, knelt, prayed in the tabernacle on late July nights and waited there together. In their prayer caps and wide garish ties, these people had made a cultural triumph by paying attention first of all to other things. They had built according to an ideal of plainness – light, dark, the wooden roof, the grove. What the plainness meant was: the intention to *be plain*, with yourself and others; directness of purpose, the long establishment of languages in which spiritual things could be spoken of directly, plainly, in which spiritual business could be done. I would go back and sit there again, if I could – if the tabernacle had not been torn down and the people gone elsewhere – and absorb the preacher's words, the songs, watch the night and the rain wait on the threshold, smell the dense unflowered sweetness of the northern woods. I know the place for what it was: Immanuel's ground.[11]

---

[11] Lionel Basney, "Immanuel's Ground," *The American Scholar* 68/3 (Summer 1999), 119; emphasis is Basney's.

This description of a worship and lifestyle both embodies and refers to the beauty that is associated with a pared-down focus on purity of life and of style. This devotion to purity is perhaps the most important characteristic of the Calvinist imagination for it embodies so much besides – God's distance and nearness, the longing for holiness and the focus on the joy of the present.

We have traced some of the impact of this plain style on Dutch and puritan art, especially in the sense of the simplicity and naturalness of life. But the influence of this Reformed impulse toward purity may also have had more of an impact on the development of modern art than has been recognized. Professor A. Sedlemeyer has argued that the development of abstract art owes a debt to this Calvinist longing for purity. He argues: "We can see this from the fact that 'pure' abstract art found especially fertile soil in Holland and the United States. There the Old Testament prohibition of images were referred to in defense of abstract art."[12]

REMAKING THE WORLD

A third general tendency that we have traced in the developing Protestant imagination is the longing to see the world remade, restored to its edenic purity. In Calvin's instructions on art we noted two parallel admonitions. First he stressed that one should follow the natural order, for there one can glimpse – and record – the glory of God. Secondly, this is not a move to detach painting (or indeed any description of the natural order) from God and religion, but rather to extend God's purposes throughout that order, thus extending the call of religion to all of God's creation. Accordingly since the time of Calvin it has been the hallmark of art in countries dominated by a Reformed influence to feature, in addition to the portraits we discussed above, landscape and careful descriptions of the order of nature. This was seen clearly in the development of the landscape and still life traditions in Holland and it appears to have been influential in the development of the American Hudson River school of painters.[13]

We have noted that the inward and outward tendencies have not been without their tensions in this tradition, coming to a head in the differences we described between Ames and Cotton. But in general the Reformed view

---

[12] A. Sedlemeyer, *Die Revolution der Modernen Kunst* (Hamburg, 1955), p. 100; quoted in Michalski, *The Reformation and the Visual Arts*, pp. 167–8.
[13] See Gene Veith, *Painters of Faith: The Spiritual Landscape in Nineteenth Century America* (Washington, DC: Regnery, 2001).

is that the integration of these realms follows from the presence of God in both. Salvation, for Calvin and his followers, is never simply a matter of the inner life, but finds its larger context and purpose in the reordering of the whole of life. Recall Calvin's treatment of the cross that we discussed above. For Calvin the cross did not simply reflect the ancient transaction of Christ's work on the cross, though that is certainly not denied. Rather the cross becomes a symbolic reality of what the life of faith looks like in a fallen order. We are to take our cross with us, Calvin says, out into the world, into our everyday life. For it is there in the world that the narrative of God's redemption has been and will be worked out until Christ returns from heaven to set up his eternal kingdom. And it is this narrative that gives the believer's life its meaning and its particular contour. Thus everyday life, the life of ordinary persons, is given a new dignity in the Protestant view that will eventually work to overthrow the traditional hierarchies of art. Vincent van Gogh's treatment of an old pair of shoes, or a poor family eating potatoes is surely working at the far end of this tendency to dignify ordinary life. Indeed we have seen indications that this impulse may have had something to do with the rise of popular culture more generally. Here is an area where further work is called for.

We have spoken frequently of the impulse to order reality, which grows out of the mental structuring and that follows both from Calvin's admonition to "sound investigation" and from ramist logic. This led to the desire to carefully record and describe the glories of God's good creation. If creation is a theater, or mirror, of God's glory one could do no better than study diligently the splendors God has placed there. This led to what has been called a mapping or cataloguing impulse that is characteristic of William Ames's theology and of sixteenth-century Dutch art. This tendency, we suggested, may have been one of the stepping stones that led to the development of scientific method, but it has also produced a unique kind of art. The beauty of truth that we discussed briefly in connection with George Herbert has its counterparts in art that develops, among other places, in nineteenth-century Scotland. Robert Crawford notes that some of Scotland's best poets, such as Edwin Muir, Carlyle and Edwin Morgan, "find a kind of imaginative poetry within (sometimes recondite) factual, historiographical, or scientific material."[14] This could also be a description of the novels of Robert Louis

---

[14] "Presbyterianism and Imagination," p. 192. Crawford argues this emphasis on lucidity and order comes from the Protestant emphasis on direct access to the word and knowledge may have influenced the development of popular education.

Stevenson, who demonstrates what one scholar has called a "documentary imagination."[15]

While the ordering impulse that is common in this tradition certainly had an impact on developing notions of "encyclopedia," there is a larger theological framework in which this order must be placed. As our discussion of painter Pieter de Molijn suggests, behind the natural appearance of the Dutch landscapes lies the conviction that the existing world is vulnerable to various destructive forces. Like the land around Haarlem that was saved from the North Sea, the world must be reclaimed. This view of a world that is broken is a parable of the Calvinist view of a world marred by sin and redeemed by the work of Christ. This gives art a particular calling: while celebrating the world's glory, it must call attention to its need of redemption. Abraham Kuyper, in his discussion of Calvinism and art more than a hundred years ago, described the calling of Reformed art in this way: "If you confess that the world once *was* beautiful, but by the curse has become *undone*, and by a final catastrophe is to pass to its full state of glory, excelling even the beautiful of paradise, then art has the mystical task of reminding us in its productions of the beautiful that was lost and of anticipating its perfect coming luster. This . . . is the Calvinist confession."[16]

Another way of putting this is to say that Protestant art is linked to a particular narrative shape, which frames its way of looking at the world. The portrait cannot be understood apart from this narrative order, but neither can landscape or, indeed, genre painting. Though persons and objects may be isolated from this story for special scrutiny, their meaning, even their aesthetic impact, will not be seen in isolation. So to the aesthetic of presence we add an aesthetic of relationships, in which the beauty or meaning lies not in the object or objects by themselves, but in the pattern by which they are ordered. And in the Puritan and Reformed view the order is a typological order that is defined by the redemptive activities of God in creation.

This brings us finally to several unanswered questions. If the order of things is only understood in terms of the redemptive story that, in the Reformed view, informs and shapes history, then can only those whose eyes have been Spiritually opened truly perceive its reality? We have noted that frequently Protestant artists were forced, whether by political circumstance

---

[15] Professor Barry Menikoff, in personal conversation. He believes this reflects in part Stevenson's Presbyterian religious context.

[16] Abraham Kuyper, *Lectures on Calvinism* (Grand Rapids, Mich.: Eerdmans, 1931 [1898]), p. 155; emphasis his.

or by theological inclination, to work by code and indirection. In Cotton
there is recognition of the power of images but only in a carefully controlled
(biblical) setting, as though their inspiration alone made them powerful.
Edwards seems to go even further in his assertion that beauty really can only
reveal God when one's eyes have been opened by the Spirit to understand
the grounding of all things in God. The believer, we noted, appears to see
a different tree than the unbeliever. Calvin, while acknowledging the role
that the Spirit plays in our perception, seems to have a more robust appreciation for the role of the Spirit in the broader (unredeemed) culture, that
is grounded in God's creative work. God, Calvin says after his discussion
of how much we owe to the gifts of unredeemed people, "fills, moves and
quickens all things by the power of the same Spirit, and does so according to the character that he bestowed upon each kind by the law of creation" (ii, ii, 16). Whether one can proceed from assertions like this to construct a kind of aesthetics of natural revelation, or whether such attempts,
for the believer in this tradition, are finally doomed to failure remains
unclear.

Evidence for this ambiguity lies in the later development of the tradition.
While the revivalist heirs of the Puritans will continue to insist on the need
for new birth to properly perceive the beauty of God, most nineteenth-
century persons demurred. Under the influence of the Romantic movement, the "eye of faith" lost its particular theological content, and became
part of the subjective process of viewing and appreciating works of art.
Novelist Nathaniel Hawthorne captures nicely this development in *The
Marble Faun* (1860). As he describes the response of Hilda – a child of the
Puritans – to the art of Rome he says:

A picture, however admirable the painter's art, and wonderful his power requires of the spectator a surrender of himself, in due proportion with the miracle which has been wrought. Let the canvas glow as it may, you must look with
the eye of faith, or its highest excellence escapes you. There is always the necessity of helping out the painter's art with your own resources of sensibility and
imagination.[17]

The eye of faith has now become the "resources of sensibility and imagination." Moreover it can be shared by those outside of the household of
faith, indeed as Emerson insists, by any whose soul has been opened to the
beauty that is everywhere.[18] This dispersion of beauty over all of life finds

[17] *The Marble Faun, or the Romance of Monte Beni* (New York: Airmont Publishing Co., 1966 [1860]),
p. 229.
[18] Interestingly, Emerson accepts Edwards's notion of primary and secondary beauty. The first is the
simple perception of natural forms; the second is the spiritual element "essential to its perfection."

a later expression in the work of George Santayana, who has been called the last Puritan. We are naturally disposed, Santayana believed, to "operate aesthetically over the whole face of life." As he says in the *Sense of Beauty*: "Whenever the golden thread of pleasure enters the web of things which our intelligence is always busily spinning, it lends to the visible world that mysterious and subtle charm which we call beauty."[19]

A second question that remains from our discussion is the continuing debate over the priority of word over image. It is a commonplace that the Reformed tradition has bequeathed to the developing modern world a bias for the word over image, and of the ear over the eye. In recent years this priority has been seriously challenged, and popular culture, so long under Protestant sway, seems to give the image pride of place – much to the chagrin of those nurtured on the culture of the word. Clearly we are in the midst of a revolution in the relationship between word and image, a fact that will call for further comment presently. Culture critics like Neil Postman have recently decried the loss of verbal literacy in the rising sea of images. Postman has recognized the Faustian bargain that characterizes the modern age. "Literacy gives us an analytical delayed response in perceiving the world, which is good for pursuits such as science or engineering. But we do lose some part of the cerebral development of the sense, the sensorium."[20] But our study has shown that matters are not as simple as this. Imaginative writing, contrary to Ramus's wishes, cannot be kept from flights of fancy and the irruption of metaphor – as we have seen in Puritan sermons and diaries. For it is these images that invite the reader – and not just the unlearned ones – into conversation with the matter under discussion. Indeed the best writing inevitably sketches inviting images of the world, just as the best visual images lay out parameters of meaning. Image and thought cannot long survive without each other, as the Reformed tradition itself gives (sometimes unwilling) testimony.[21] In this respect we pay tribute to what the tradition fostered – an inward enriched imaging connected to and feeding off a delight in the ordered (and reordered) creation of God,

---

This latter beauty however is open to every rational creature. "It is his, if he will" ("Nature" [1836], in *Collected Works*, vol. I, pp. 13, 15).

[19] George Santayana, *The Sense of Beauty*, ed. William G. Hozberger and Herman J. Saatkamp Jr. (Cambridge Mass.: MIT Press, 1988 [1896]), pp. xxvii and 37.

[20] Though overall he believes the triumph of literacy to be a good thing. His protagonist in this debate, Camille Paglia, disagrees ("She Wants her TV! He Wants his Book!" *Harper's Magazine* 285 [May 1991], p. 47). See also Jacques Ellul, *The Humiliation of the Word* (Grand Rapids, Mich.: Eerdmans, 1985). For an opposing view see Mitchell Stephens, *The Rise of the Image and the Fall of the Word* (Oxford University Press, 1998).

[21] This interrelationship is developed by Ruth Finnegan, *Literacy and Orality: Studies in the Technology of Communication* (Oxford: Basil Blackwell, 1988).

but not necessarily to what it excluded. Why cannot images be consciously and critically pressed into service not only for a functional remaking of the world, but for the delight and celebration that characterizes worship at its best? Why must the ancient connection between beauty and worship, so amply evident in the Old Testament itself, be severed?

But the final question is both a tribute to the imagination we have sketched and a nagging question. The disposition toward popular involvement in worship and art early on became a critical component of the emerging Protestant consciousness. We noted that from the first acts of iconoclasm through the revivals of the first great awakening, the people were responding to what they heard as the voice of God. In the worship that emerged, art was dispersed through the congregation in congregational singing, and, in the dignifying and ordering of the ordinary, through the whole of life. This of course reflects deeper theological themes – justification by faith, the perspicuity of Scripture, and even new polycentric views of the Trinity, as these were disseminated through preaching and catechism.[22] All of this was important and was to have deep consequences for the later development of popular culture. But it may also reflect a weakness in the developing heritage: is there a leaching out of the depth and mystery of creation, especially of its transcendent meaning? Is there the tendency to stress more the transactional than the substantial in the application of Christology (reduced to the benefits of his work) and even of the Trinity (constituting more a model than a constituent ground)?

Whatever the judgment on these issues, the lasting contribution of this developing imagination is the placement of aesthetics and art in the midst of life. For as a modern commentator on this tradition notes:

The aesthetic can never be realized in its fullness without these other elements (making up the whole life), and the other elements only get their artistic meaning because they are brought together in an artistic way . . . The norms of art are in fact basically no different from the norms for the whole of life. Art belongs to human life, is part of it and obeys the same rules.[23]

Though written a generation ago, contemporary discussions of art and life bear continuing witness to the relevance of this way of looking at the world.

Our final word then must be addressed to contemporary pastors and believers who have inherited many of the values this study has explored.

---

[22] For the latter see Miroslav Volf, *After Our Likeness: The Church as the Image of the Trinity* (Grand Rapids, Mich.: Eerdmans, 1998). He shows this from the views of congregational theologian John Smyth.

[23] Hans R. Rookmaaker, *Modern Art and the Death of a Culture* (Downers Grove, Ill.: InterVarsity Press, 1970), pp. 232, 236.

They often find themselves alternatively troubled and stimulated by the rise of visual culture around them. The temptation is either to adopt or reject, in either case uncritically, communication styles they see around them. Painted images, banners and video clips certainly may have their place in the worship of those raised on television and MTV. But there is still much to be gained by a careful reflection on what this tradition gained from their rereading of Scripture and their careful application of that to their lives and communities. There is no reason why the values that we have outlined in this epilogue cannot be used to develop a faithful discrimination and redemption of cultural values in general, and the rise of visual culture in particular. Indeed it should be possible to see in these values the possibility not simply of learning from the culture, but of shaping it in God-honoring ways.

Select bibliography

PRIMARY SOURCES

Ames, William. *De conscientia et eius jure vel casibus: libri quinque* Amsterdam: n.p., 1630; English translation: *Conscience with power and cases thereof: Five Books* London: n.p., 1639.

A Fresh Suit Against Human Ceremonies in God's Worship. [Amsterdam]: n.p., 1633.

The Marrow of Theology. Trans. and intro. John D. Eusden. Boston, Mass.: Pilgrim Press, 1968 [1627].

Reply to Dr. Mortons Defence of three nocent Ceremonies, viz. The Surplice, Crosse in Baptisme and Kneeling at the receiving of the sacramental elements of bread and wine [Amsterdam]: n.p., 1622.

Technometry. Trans. and intro. Lee W. Gibbs. Philadelphia: University of Pennsylvania, 1979 [1633].

Aquinas, Thomas. *Summa theologicae.* Trans. Fathers of the English Dominican Province. Revised by Daniel J. Sullivan. Vol. 1. Chicago: Encyclopedia Britannica, Inc., 1952.

Augustine. *The Literal Meaning of Genesis.* Trans. John H. Taylor. New York: Newman Press, 1982.

On Christian Doctrine. Trans. D. W. Robertson. New York: Library of Liberal Arts, 1958.

Austen, Ralph. *The Spirituall Use of an Orchard.* Oxford: n.p., 1657.

A Treatise on Fruit Trees. Oxford: Henri Hall for Thomas Robinson, 1657.

Bacon, Francis. *The Great Instauration.* In *Selected Writings of Francis Bacon.* Intro. and notes by Hugh G. Dick. New York: Random House/Modern Library, 1955.

"On Gardens." In *Selected Writings of Francis Bacon.* Intro. and notes by Hugh G. Dick. New York: Random House/Modern Library, 1955.

Bale, John. *The Image of Both Churches.* London: Richard Fugge, 1548.

Bate, John. *Mysteries of Nature and Art.* London: for Ralph Mab., 1634.

Baxter, Richard. *The Saints Everlasting Rest.* London: Joseph Caryl, 1949/50.

Bede's Ecclesiastical History. Ed. Bertram Colgrave and R. A. B. Mynors. Oxford: Clarendon Press, 1969.

Bernard of Clairvaux, Saint. *Apologia*. In *"Things of Greater Importance": Bernard of Clairvaux's Apologia and Medieval Attitudes toward Art*. Trans. Conrad Rudolph. Philadelphia: University of Pennsylvania, 1990.

"On the Song of Songs," Sermon 20. 6. In *The Works of Bernard of Clairvaux*. Trans. Kilian Walsh. Spencer, Mass.: Cistercian Publications, 1971.

Bernard, Richard. *Contemplative Pictures with wholesome Precepts*. London: William Hall for William Welfie, 1610.

Bradstreet, Anne. *The Works of Anne Bradstreet*. Ed. Jeannine Hensley. Cambridge, Mass.: Harvard University Press, 1967.

Bucer, Martin. *A Treatise Declaring and Showing . . . that Pictures and other Images are not to be Suffered in the Temples and Churches of Christian Men*. Trans. W. Marshall. London: W. Marshall, 1535.

Calvin, John. "Acts of the Council of Trent with the Antidote." In *Tracts Relating to the Reformation*, vol. III. Ed. Henry Beveridge. Edinburgh: Calvin Translation Society, 1851.

Commentary on Genesis: Commentaries on the First Book of Moses Called Genesis. Trans. John King. Edinburgh: Calvin Translation Society, 1847.

Epistle of Paul the Apostle to the Galatians, Ephesians, and Colossians: Calvin's New Testament Commentaries. Ed. and trans. T. H. L. Parker. Grand Rapids, Mich.: Eerdmans, 1965.

The Form of Prayers and Ministrations of the Sacraments, used in the English Congregation at Geneva: And approved by the famous and godly learned man John Calvin. Geneva: John Crespin, 1556.

"Geneva Catechism." In *Theological Treatises*. Ed. J. K. S. Reid. London: SCM Press, 1954.

Institutes. Trans. Ford Battles. Ed. John McNeill. Philadelphia: Westminster Press, 1960.

"An Inventory of Relics" In *Tracts Relating to the Reformation*, vol. I. Ed. Henry Beveridge. Edinburgh: Calvin Translation Society, 1844.

Tracts and Treatises on the Reformation of the Church. Ed. Henry Beveridge. Edinburgh: Oliver & Boyd, 1958.

Caus, Salomon de. *La Perspective avec La Raison des ombres et miroirs*. London: Norbon, 1612.

Chauncy, Charles. *A Letter from a Gentleman in Boston to Mr. George Wishart Concerning the State of Religion in New England*. Edinburgh, 1742/Clarendon Historical Society's Reprints, 1883.

Cole, Nathan. "Spiritual Travels." In Alan Heimert and Perry Miller (eds.). *The Great Awakening: Documents Illustrating the Crisis and its Consequences*. New York: Bobs-Merrill, 1967.

Cotton, John. *Bay Psalm Book: The Whole Book of Psalmes Faithfully Translated into English Metre*. Cambridge: Daye, 1640.

Christ the Fountaine of Life; Sundry Choyce Sermons . . . of First John. London: Robert Ibbitson, 1651.

God's Promise to his Plantation. London: William Jones, 1630.

Gospel Conversion: Discovering whether any gracious condition or qualification are wrought in the soule before faith in Christ; How the assurance of a man's salvation is to be evidenced. The Manner of the Soul's Closing with Christ. London: J. Dawson, 1646.

The Pouring out of the Seven Vials or an Exposition of Chapter Sixteen of Revelation with an application of it to our time. London: for R. S., 1642.

Singing of Psalmes: A Gospel Ordinance. London: M. S. for Hannah Allen, 1647.

Some Treasures Fetched out of the Rubbish. London: n.p., 1660.

A Treatise of the Covenant of Grace. 3rd edn. London: n.p., 1671.

The Way of Life or God's way and course, in bringing the soule into keeping it and carrying it on in the ways of peace and life. London: By M. F. for L. Fawne and S. Gellibrand, 1641.

The Way of the Churches of Christ in New England. London: By Matthew Simmons, 1645.

Cranmer, Thomas. *Catechismus: That is to say a short Introduction into Christian Religion.* London: W. Lynne, 1548.

Dante Alighieri. *Divine Comedy.* Trans. John Ciardi. New York: Norton, 1961.

Donne, John. *The Divine Poems.* Ed. Helen Gardner. Oxford: Clarendon Press, 1978.

Dionysius the Areopagite. *The Mystical Theology.* Trans. C. E. Rolt. New York: SPCK, 1920.

Edwards, Jonathan. *The Great Awakening.* Ed. C. C. Goen. *Works of Jonathan Edwards*, vol. IV. New Haven: Yale University Press, 1972.

The "Miscellanies." Ed. Thomas A. Schafer. *Works of Jonathan Edwards*, vol. XIII. New Haven: Yale University Press, 1994.

The Religious Affections. Ed. John E. Smith. *Works of Jonathan Edwards*, vol. II. New Haven: Yale University Press, 1959.

Scientific and Philosophical Writings. Ed. Wallace E. Anderson. *Works of Jonathan Edwards*, vol. VI. New Haven: Yale University Press, 1980.

Typological Writings. Ed. Wallace Anderson and Mason L. Lowance, Jr. with David Watters. *Works of Jonathan Edwards*, vol. XI. New Haven: Yale University Press, 1993.

Emerson, Ralph Waldo. *The Collected Works of Ralph Waldo Emerson*, vol. I. Gen. ed. Alfred R. Ferguson. Intro. and notes, Robert E. Spillar. Cambridge, Mass.: Harvard University Press, 1971.

Farel, Guillaume. *Du vray usage de la croix.* Geneva: Imprimerie de Jules-Guillaume Fick, new edn, 1865 [1530].

Flavell, John. *Husbandry Spiritualized: or, The Heavenly Use of Earthly Things: Consisting of Many Pleasant Observations, Pertinent Applications, and serious Reflections, and each Chapter concluded with a Divine and Suitable Poem.* London: Robert Boulter, 1669.

Gregory the Great. *Selected Epistles of Gregory the Great.* Trans. James Barmby. In *A Select Library of Nicene and Post-Nicene Fathers of the Christian Church*, vol. XIII. Series 2. Grand Rapids, Mich.: Eerdmans, 1979.

Guigo I. *Meditations of Guigo, Prior of Charterhouse*. Milwaukee, Wisc.: Marquette University Press: 1951.

Hawthorne, Nathaniel. *The Marble Faun, or the Romance of Monte Beni*. New York: Airmont Publishing Co., 1966 [1860].

Herbert, George. *The Works of George Herbert in Prose and Verse*. Ed. H. E. Hutchinson. Oxford: Clarendon Press, 1941.

Hilliard, Nicholas. *The Art of Limning: A New Edition of a Treatise concerning the Art of Limning*. Transcription by Arthur F. Kinney. Boston, Mass.: Northeastern University Press, 1983.

Hoby, Lady Margaret. *Diary of Lady Margaret Hoby (1599–1605)*. Ed. Dorothy M. Meads. London: Routledge & Sons, 1930.

Hoogstraten, Samuel van. *Inleyding tot de Hooge Schoole der Schilderkonst: Anders de zichbaere Werelt verdeelt in regen Leerwinkels, uder bestiert eene der Zanggodinnen*. Rotterdam: François van Hoogstraeten, 1678.

Hume, David. *An Enquiry concerning Human Understanding*. Ed. Tom L. Beauchamp. Oxford: Clarendon Press, 2000.

A Treatise of Human Nature. Ed. L. A. Selby-Bigge. Oxford: Clarendon, 1981.

Huygens, Constantijn. *A Selection of Poems of Sir Constantijn Huygens (1596–1687): A Parallel Text, Translated with an Introduction*. Trans. and ed. Peter Davidson and Adriaan van der Weel. University of Amsterdam, 1996.

John of Damascus, St. "First Apology against Those who attack the Divine Images." In *On the Divine Images: Three Apologies against those who attack Divine Images*. Trans. David Anderson. Crestwood, N.Y.: St. Vladimir's Seminary Press, 1980.

Johnson, Edward. *Johnson's Wonder-Working Providence: 1628–1651*. Ed. J. Franklin Jameson. New York: Scribner's Sons, 1910.

Kant, Immanuel. *Critique of the Power of Judgment*. Ed. Paul Guyer. Cambridge University Press, 2000.

Kempis, Thomas à. *Of the Imitation of Christ*. Trans. Abbot Justin McCann. New York: Mentor Books, 1957.

Lovell, Thomas. *A Dialogue Between Custom and Vertie concerning the use and abuse of Dauncing and Minstrelry*. London: John Allde, 1581.

Loyola, Ignatius. *The Spiritual Exercises of Ignatius on the Crucifixion*. Trans. Anthony Mottola. Garden City, N.Y.: Image/Doubleday, 1964.

Luther, Martin. *Lectures on Romans*. Ed. and trans. Wilhelm Pauck. Philadelphia: Westminster Press, 1961.

Luther's Works, vol. xxvi. Ed. J. Pelikan. St. Louis: Concordia, 1963.

Luther's Works, vol. xl. Ed. Conrad Bergendoff. Philadelphia: Muhlenberg Press (Fortress), 1958.

Luther's Works, vol. li. Ed. John Doberstein. Philadelphia: Muhlenberg Press (Fortress), 1957.

Mather, Cotton. *Agricola, or The Religious Husbandman: The Intentions of Religion served in the Language of Husbandry*. Boston: T. Fleet for D. Henchman, 1727.

Magnalia Christi Americana: The Ecclesiastica History of New England, vol. i. Hartford, Conn.: Silas Andrus & Son 1855 [1702].

Mather, Increase. *The Life and Death of that Reverend Man of God, Richard Mather, Teacher in the Church in Dorchester in New England.* Cambridge, 1670.

Milton, John. *Paradise Lost.* In *The Complete Poetical Works of John Milton.* Ed. Douglas Bush. Boston, Mass.: Houghton Mifflin, 1962.

  Paradise Regained, In *Milton: Poems and Selected Prose.* Ed. Marjorie Hope Nicolson. Boston, Mass.: Houghton-Mifflin, 1965.

More, Thomas. *Thomas More's English Works* (1557). Ed. W. E. Campbell. London: Eyre & Spottiswoode, 1927.

Palissy, Bernard. *Les Oeuvres de Bernard Palissy*, vol. 1. Ed. P. Fillon. Niort: Clouzot Librairie, 1888.

Perkins, William. "The Art of Prophesying." In *Workes of the Famous and Worthy Minister William Perkins,* vol. 11. London: John Legat, 1931.

  A Reformed Catholike: Or, a Declaration shewing how neere we may come to the present church of Rome in sundrie points of religion and wherein we must forever depart. Cambridge: Lohn Legat, Printer to the University of Cambridge, 1598.

  A Treatise of Man's Imagination: Shewing his natural evill thoughts; his want of good thoughts; the way to reform them. Cambridge: John Legat, 1607.

  A Warning against the Idolatrie of the Last Times: And an instruction touching Religion and Divine Worship. Cambridge: John Legat, at the University of Cambridge, 1601.

Plato. *The Republic.* Ed. Francis Cornford. Oxford University Press, 1945.

Quarles, Francis. *Emblems: With the Hieroglyphicks: All the Cuts being newly illustrated.* London: for M. Gillyflower, 1696.

Ramus, Peter. *The Logik of the Most Excellent Philosopher P. Ramus Martyr.* Trans. M. Poll and M. Hamlini. London: Thomas Vantrolier, 1581.

Richardson, Jonathan. *The Works of Jonathan Richardson. Corrected and prepared by his son Mr. J. Richardson.* London: T. Davies, 1773.

Schaff, Philip. *The Creeds of Christendom*, vol. 111. Grand Rapids, Mich.: Baker, 1985.

Schroeder, H. J. *Canons and Decrees of the Council of Trent.* St. Louis: Herder, 1941.

Sewall, Samuel. *The Diary of Samuel Sewall.* Ed. M. Halsey Thomas. New York: Farrar, Strauss & Giroux, 1973.

Sibbes, Richard. "The Soul's Conflict with itself." In *The Complete Works of Richard Sibbes*, vol. 1. Ed. Alexander B. Grosart. Edinburgh: James Nichol, 1862.

Sidney, Philip. *A Defence of Poetry: In Miscellaneous Prose of Sir Philip Sidney.* Ed. Katherine Duncan-Jones and Jan van Dorsten. Oxford: Clarendon Press, 1973.

Stubbes, Phillip. *The Anatomie of Abuses, a briefe summarie of notable vices and Imperfections, as now raigne in many Christian Countries of the World.* London: Richard Jones, 1583.

Taylor, Edward. *Christographia.* Ed. Norman Grabo. New Haven: Yale University Press, 1962.

  The Poems of Edward Taylor. Ed. Donald E. Stanford. New Haven: Yale University Press, 1960.

Traheme, Thomas. *Poems, Centuries and Three Thanksgivings*, Ed. Anne Ridler. London: Oxford University Press, 1966.

Watts, Isaac. *Doctrine of the Passions Explained and Improved*. New York: Shepard Kollock, 1795.

An Humble Attempt toward the Revival of Practical Religion among Christians, and Particularly the Protestant Dissenters, by a Serious Address to Ministers and People in some Occasional Discourses. London: for E. Matthews, 1631.

Hymns and Spiritual Songs in Three Books. Boston: Mein & Fleming 1769 [1719].

Wigglesworth, Samuel. *The Pleasures of Religion: A Sermon Preached to a Society of Young Men at Ipswich, About a Fortnight Before the Earthquake*. Boston: n.p., 1728.

Willard, Samuel. *A Compleat Body of Divinity in Two Hundred and Fifty Expository Lectures on the Assembly's Shorter Catechism*. Boston: Green *et al.*, 1726.

Willison, John. *Sacramental Meditations and Advices Grounded upon Scripture Texts: Proper for Communicants to Prepare their hearts, Excite their Affections, Quicken their Graces and Enliven their devotions on Sacramental occasions*. London: n.p., 1794 [1714].

Worcester, Francis. *A Bridle for Sinners and a Spur for Saints*. Boston: n.p., 1782 [1729].

Wordsworth, William. *The Prelude*. Ed. J. C. Maxwell. New Haven: Yale Unversity Press, 1971.

Worlidge, John. *Systema Agriculturae: The Mystery of Husbandry Discovered and Layd Open*. London: T. Johnson for Samuel Speed, 1669.

Zwingli, Ulrich. *An Account of the Faith*. Trans. Thomas Cotsford. Geneva: n.p., 1555.

Commentary on True and False Religion. Ed. Samuel M. Jackson and Clarence N. Heller. Durham: Labyrinth Press, 1981.

SECONDARY WORKS

Adams, Ann Jensen. "Competing Communities in the 'Great Bog of Europe': Identity and Seventeenth Century Dutch Landscape Painting." In W. J. T. Mitchell (ed.). *Landscape and Power*. University of Chicago Press, 1994.

"The Three-Quarter Length Life-Sized Portrait in Seventeenth Century Holland." In Wayne Franits (ed.). *Looking at Seventeenth Century Dutch Art: Realism Reconsidered*. Cambridge University Press, 1997.

Ahlstrom, Sydney. *A Religious History of the American People*. New Haven: Yale University Press, 1972.

Allen, David. "Vacuum Domicilium: The Social and Cultural Landscape of Seventeenth Century New England." In Jonathan L. Fairbanks and Robert F. Trent (eds.). *New England Begins: The Seventeenth Century*, vol. 1. Boston, Mass.: Museum of Fine Arts, 1982.

Alpers, Svetlana. *The Art of Describing: Dutch Art in the Seventeenth Century*. University of Chicago Press, 1983.

Archer, John. "Puritan Town Planning in New Haven." *Journal of the Society of Architectural Historians* 34 (1975), pp. 140–9.

Aston, Margaret. *England's Iconoclasts*, vol. 1. Oxford: Clarendon Press, 1988.

    Faith and Fire: Popular and Unpopular Religion 1350–1600. London: Hambledon Press, 1993.

    Lollards and Reformers: Images and Literacy in Late Medieval Religion. London: Hambledon Press, 1984.

Auerbach, Erich. *Mimesis: The Representation of Reality in Western Literature*. Princeton University Press, 1953.

Auksi, P. "Simplicity and Silence: The Influence of Scripture on the Aesthetic Thought of the Major Reformers." *Journal of Religious History* 10/4 (1978/9), pp. 341–64.

Bainton, Roland. *Here I Stand: A Life of Martin Luther*. New York: Abingdon-Cokesbury, 1957.

Basney, Lionel. "Immanuel's Ground." *The American Scholar* 68/3 (Summer 1999), pp. 109–19.

Bätschmann, Oskar and Grienen, Pascal. *Hans Holbein*. London: Reaktion Books, 1997.

Baxandall, Michael. *The Limewood Sculptors of Renaissance Germany*. New Haven: Yale University Press, 1980.

Bayley, Frank W. *Five Colonial Artists of New England*. Boston, Mass.: privately printed, 1929.

Beardsley, Monroe C. *Aesthetics from Classical Greek to the Present*. New York: Macmillan Press, 1966.

Belting, Hans. *Image and Likeness: A History of the Image before the Era of Art*. Ed. and trans. Edmund Jephcott. Chicago: University of Chicago Press, 1994.

Benedict, Philip. "Calvinism as a Culture?" In Paul Corby Finney (ed.). *Seeing Beyond the Word: Visual Arts and the Calvinist Tradition*. Grand Rapids, Mich.: Eerdmans, 1999.

Benes, Peter (ed.). *The New England Meeting House and Church*. Boston, Mass.: Dublin Seminar for New England Folklore, Boston University Press, 1979.

Bercovitch, Sacvan. *The American Jeremiad*. Madison: University of Wisconsin Press, 1978.

Binski, Paul. "Art and Architecture." In *The New Cambridge Medieval History*, vol. v. Cambridge University Press, 1999.

Blankert, Albert *et al.* (eds.). *God's Saints and Heroes: Dutch Painting in the Age of Rembrandt*. Washington, DC: National Gallery of Art, 1980.

Blunt, Anthony. *Artistic Theory in Italy*. Oxford University Press, 1962.

Bolten, J. and Bolten-Rempt, Jetteke. *Rembrandt and the Incredulity of Thomas*. Leiden: Aliotta & Manhart, 1981.

Bossy, John. *Christianity in the West 1400–1700*. Oxford University Press, 1985.

Bousma, William J. *Calvin: A Sixteenth Century Portrait*. Oxford University Press, 1988.

Bozeman, Theodore Dwight. *To Live Ancient Lives: The Primitivist Dimension in Puritanism*. Chapel Hill: University of North Carolina Press, 1988.

Brown, Peter. *The Cult of the Saints: Its Rise and Function in Latin Christianity*. University of Chicago Press, 1981.

Burke, Peter. *Popular Culture in Early Modern Europe*. New York University Press, 1978; rev. edn, 1994.

Varieties of Cultural History. Ithaca, N.Y.: Cornell University Press, 1997.

Caldwell, Patricia. *The Puritan Conversion Narrative: The Beginnings of American Expression*. Cambridge University Press, 1983.

Cameron, Euan (ed.). *Early Modern Europe: An Oxford History*. Oxford University Press, 1999.

Camille, Michael. "Seeing and Reading: Some Visual Implications of Medieval Literacy and Illiteracy." *Art History* 8 (1985), pp. 26–49.

The Gothic Idol: Ideology and Image-Making in Medieval Art. Cambridge University Press, 1989.

Carse, James. *Jonathan Edwards and the Visibility of God*. New York: Charles Scribner & Sons, 1967.

Christensen, Carl C. *Art and the Reformation in Germany*. Athens, Ohio: Ohio University Press, 1979.

Clark, Michael. "'The Crucified Phrase': Sign and Desire in Puritan Semiology." *Early American Literature* 13 (1979), pp. 278–93.

Coakley, Sarah (ed.). *Religion and the Body*. Cambridge University Press, 2000.

Collinson, Patrick. *The Birthpangs of Protestant England: Religion and Cultural Change in the Sixteenth and Seventeenth Century*. New York: St. Martin's Press, 1988.

"Elizabethan and Jacobean Puritanism as Forms of Popular Culture." In Christopher Dursten and Jacqueline Eales (eds.). *The Culture of English Puritanism*. New York: St. Martin's Press, 1996.

Cook, Nicholas. *Music, Imagination and Culture*. Oxford University Press, 1990.

Cooper, David J. C. "The Theology of Image in Eastern Orthodoxy and John Calvin." *Scottish Journal of Theology* 35 (1982), pp. 219–41.

Cowie, Murray and Cowie, Marian. "Geiler von Kaisersberg and Abuses in 15th C. Strasbourg." *Studies in Philology* 58 (1961), pp. 483–95.

Crandell, Gina. *Nature Pictorialized: "The View" in Landscape History*. Baltimore, Md.: Johns Hopkins University Press, 1993.

Craven, Wayne. *Colonial American Portraiture: The Economic, Religious, Social, Cultural, Scientific and Aesthetic Foundations*. Cambridge University Press, 1986.

Crawford, Robert. "Presbyterianism and Imagination in Modern Scotland." In T. M. Devine (ed.). *Scotland's Shame: Bigotry and Sectarianism in Modern Scotland*. Edinburgh: Mainstream Publications, 2000.

Crew, Phyllis Mack. *Calvinist Preaching and Iconoclasm in the Netherlands, 1544–1569*. Cambridge University Press, 1978.

Crockett, Brian. "'Holy Cozenage' and the Renaissance Cult of the Ear." *Sixteenth Century Journal* 24/1 (1993), pp. 47–65.

Crow, Thomas. *The Intelligence of Art*. Chapel Hill: University of North Carolina Press, 1999.

Cummings, Abbott Lowell. "Notes on Furnishing the Seventeenth Century House." *Old Time New England* 46/3, serial no. 163 (1956), pp. 57–67.

Daley, Koos. *The Triple Fool: A Critical Evaluation of Constantijn Huygens' Translations of John Donne*. Nieuwkoop: De Graaf Publishing, 1990.

Daly, Robert. *God's Altar: The World and the Flesh in Puritan Poetry*. Berkeley: University of California Press, 1978.

Danner, Dan. *Pilgrimage to Puritanism: History and Theology of the Marian Exiles at Geneva: 1555–1560*. New York: Peter Lang, 1999.

Davidson, Clifford and Nichols, Ann, eds. *Iconoclasm vs. Art and Drama.* Early Drama, Art and Music Series II. Kalamazoo, Mich.: Western Michigan University Press, 1989.

De Jongh, Eddy. "Realism and Seeming Realism." In Wayne Franits (ed.). *Looking at Seventeenth Century Dutch Art: Realism Reconsidered*. Cambridge University Press, 1997.

Delamotte, Eugenia. "John Cotton and the Rhetoric of Grace." *Early American Literature* 21 (1986), pp. 49–66.

Deursen, A. T. van. *Plain Lives in a Golden Age: Popular Culture, Religion and Society in Seventeenth Century Holland*. Trans. M. Ultee. Cambridge University Press, 1991.

Dever, Mark E. *Richard Sibbes: Puritanism and Calvinism in Late Elizabethan and Early Stuart England*. Macon, Ga.: Mercer University Press, 2000.

Diebold William J. *Word and Image: An Introduction to Early Medieval Art*. Boulder: Westview, 2000.

Diehl, Huston. "Into the Maze of Self: The Protestant Transformation of the Image of the Labyrinth." *Journal of Medieval and Renaissance Studies* 16/2 (1986), pp. 281–301.

Dillenberger, John. *Images and Relics: Theological Perceptions and Visual Images in Sixteenth Century Europe*. Oxford University Press, 1999.

Donnelly, Arian Car. *The New England Meeting Houses of the Seventeenth Century*. Middlebury, Conn.: Wesleyan University Press, 1968.

Douglass, E. Jane. *Justification in Late Medieval Preaching: A Study of John Geiler of Kaisersberg*. Leiden: E. J. Brill, 1966.

Doumergue, Emile. *Iconographie calvinienne*. Lausanne: Georges Bridal, 1909.

Dowey, Edward A. *The Knowledge of God in Calvin's Theology*. New York: Columbia University Press, 1952.

Drucker, Peter. "Beyond the Information Revolutions." *Atlantic Monthly*, October 1999.

Drury, John. *Painting the Word: Christian Pictures and their Meaning*. New Haven: Yale University Press, 1999.

Duffy, Eamon. *The Stripping of the Altars: Traditional Religion in England. C.1400–1580*. New Haven: Yale University Press: 1992.

Durston, Christopher and Eales, Jacqueline (eds.). *The Culture of English Puritanism, 1560–1700*. New York: St. Martin's, 1996.

Ebeling, G. *Luther: An Introduction to His Thought*. Trans. R. A. Wilson. Philadelphia: Fortress Press, 1970.

Eco, Umberto. *Art and Beauty in the Middle Ages*. Trans. Hugh Bredin. New Haven: Yale University Press, 1986.

Eire, Carlos. *War Against the Idols: The Reformation of Worship from Erasmus to Calvin*. Cambridge University Press, 1986.

Eliot, Alexander. *Three Hundred Years of American Painting*. New York: Time, Inc., 1957.

Eliot, T. S. *Selected Essays: 1917–1932*. London: Faber & Faber, 1932.

Selected Poems. New York: Harcourt, Brace & World, 1930.

Emerson, Everett H. *John Cotton*. New York: Twayne Publishing, 1965.

Emmet, Alan. *So Fine a Prospect: Historic New England Gardens*. Hannover, N.H. and London: University Press of New England, 1996.

Erdt, Terrence. *Jonathan Edwards: Art and the Sense of the Heart*. Amherst: University of Massachusetts Press, 1980.

Fairbanks, Jonathan L. "Portrait Painting in Seventeenth Century Boston: Its History, Methods and Materials." In Jonathan L. Fairbanks and Robert F. Trent (eds.). *New England Begins: The Seventeenth Century*, vol. III. Boston, Mass.: Museum of Fine Arts, 1982.

Fairbanks, Jonathan L. and Trent, Robert F. (eds.). *New England Begins: The Seventeenth Century*, vols. I–III. Boston, Mass.: Museum of Fine Arts, 1982.

Falkenberg, Reindert L. "Calvinism and the Emergence of Dutch Seventeenth Century Landscape Art – A Critical Evaluation." In Paul Corby Finney (ed.). *Seeing Beyond the Word: Visual Arts and the Calvinist Tradition*. Grand Rapids, Mich.: Eerdmans, 1999.

Farrow, Douglas. "Between the Rock and a Hard Place: In Support of (something like) a Reformed View of the Eucharist." *International Journal of Systematic Theology* 3/2 (2001), pp. 167–86.

Febvre, Lucien and Martin, Henri-Jean. *The Coming of the Book: The Impact of Printing 1450–1800*. Ed. and trans. David Gerard. Atlantic Highlands, N.J.: Humanities Press, 1958; London: Verso, 1990.

Fiering, Norman S. "The Rationalist Foundation to Edwards's Metaphysics." In Nathan O. Hatch and Harry S. Stout (eds.). *Jonathan Edwards and the American Experience*. New York: Oxford University Press, 1988. Pp. 78–85.

"Will and Intellect in the New England Mind." *William and Mary Quarterly* 29 (1972), pp. 515–58.

Finnegan, H. Ruth. *Literacy and Orality: Studies in the Technology of Communication*. Oxford: Basil Blackwell, 1988.

Finney, Corbin Scott (ed.). *Seeing Beyond the Word: Visual Arts and the Calvinist Tradition*. Grand Rapids, Mich.: Eerdmans, 1999.

Fletcher, Richard. *The Barbarian Conversion: From Paganism to Christianity*. New York: Henry Holt, 1997.

Foote, Henry W. *Life and Work of Robert Feke*. Cambridge, Mass.: Harvard University Press, 1930.

Forstman, H. Jackson. *Word and Spirit: Calvin's Doctrine of Biblical Authority*. Palo Alto, Calif.: Stanford University Press, 1962.

Fortune, Brandon Frame. "'From the World Escaped': Peale's Portrait of William Smith and his Grandson." *Eighteenth Century Studies* 25/4 (1992), pp. 588–608.

Foster, Stephen. "The Godly in Transit: English Popular Protestantism and the Creation of a Puritan Establishment in America." In David D. Hall and David Grayson Allen (eds.). *Seventeenth Century New England*. Boston, Mass.: Colonial Society of Massachusetts, 1984.

Franits, Wayne (ed.). *Looking at Seventeenth Century Dutch Art: Realism Reconsidered*. Cambridge University Press, 1997.

Freedberg, David. "Johannus Molanus on Provocative Paintings." *Journal of the Warburg and Courtauld Institutes* 34 (1971), pp. 229–45.

   The Power of Images: Studies in the History and Theory of Response. University of Chicago Press, 1989.

Frost, R. N. "Richard Sibbes' Theology of Grace and the Division of English Reformed Theology." Ph.D dissertation, London University, 1996.

Garside, Charles. *Zwingli and the Arts*. New Haven: Yale University Press, 1966.

Gatta, John. *Gracious Laughter: The Meditative Wit of Edward Taylor*. Columbia, Mo.: University of Missouri Press, 1989.

Gaustad, Edwin S. *George Berkeley in America*. New Haven: Yale University Press, 1979.

Gero, Stephen. "Byzantine Iconoclasm and the Failure of a Medieval Reformation." In Joseph Gutmann (ed.). *The Image and the Word*. Missoula, Mont.: Scholars Press, 1977.

Gerrish, B. A. *Grace and Gratitude: The Eucharistic Theology of John Calvin*. Minneapolis: Augsburg Fortress, 1993.

Gilbert, Neal W. *Renaissance Concepts of Method*. New York: Columbia University Press, 1960.

Gilman, Ernest B. *Iconoclasm and Poetry in the English Reformation*. University of Chicago, 1986.

Goedde, Lawrence O. "Naturalism as Convention." In Wayne Franits (ed.). *Looking at Seventeenth Century Dutch Art: Realism Reconsidered*. Cambridge University Press, 1997.

Goring, Jeremy. *Godly Exercises or the Devil's Dance? Puritanism and Popular Culture in Pre-Civil War England*. Friends of Dr. Williams Lecture, 37 (1983). London: Dr. Williams Trust.

Grabo, Norman S. "The Veiled Vision: The Role of Aesthetics in Early American Intellectual History." *William and Mary Quarterly* 3rd ser., 19 (1962), pp. 493–510.

Graham, Fred. *Constructive Revolutionary: John Calvin and his Socio-economic Impact*. Richmond, Va.: John Knox Press, 1971.

Graves, Pamela. "Social Space in the English Medieval Parish Church." *Economy and Society* 18 (1989), pp. 297–322.

Greeley, Andrew. *The Catholic Imagination*. Berkeley: University of California Press, 2000.

Green, Garrett. *Imagining God: Theology and the Religious Imagination*. Grand Rapids, Mich.: Eerdmans, 1989.

Green, Samuel Abbott, *John Foster: The Earliest American Engraver and First American Printer*. Boston: Massachusetts Historical Society, 1909.

Gutman, Joseph (ed.). *The Image and the Word*. Missoula, Mont.: Scholars Press, 1977.

Hadot, Pierre. *Philosophy as a Way of Life: Spiritual Exercises from Socrates to Foucault*. Ed. and trans. Michael Chase. University of Chicago Press, 1995.

Haftmann, Werner. *Painting in the Twentieth Century*. 2 vols. Trans. Ralph Manheim. London: Lund Humphries, 1965.

Haims, Lynn Maria. "The American Puritan Aesthetic: Iconography in Seventeenth Century Poetry and Tombstone Art." Ph.D Dissertation, New York University, 1981.

Hall, David D. "Literacy, Religion and the Plain Style." In Fairbanks and Trent (eds.). *New England Begins*, vol. ii. Boston, Mass.: Museum of Fine Arts, 1982.

   "A Reader's Guide to the New England Mind and the Seventeenth Century." *American Quarterly* 34 (1982), pp. 32–6.

   "Towards a History of Popular Religion in Early New England." *William and Mary Quarterly* 3rd ser., 41 (1984), pp. 49–55.

   Worlds of Wonder, Days of Judgment: Popular Religious Belief in Early New England. New York: Knopf, 1989.

Hall, David D. (ed.). *The Antinomian Controversy, 1636–1638: A Documentary History*. 2nd edn. Chapel Hill: Duke University Press, 1990.

Hall, David D. and Allen, David Grayson (eds.). *Seventeenth Century New England*. Boston: Colonial Society of Massachusetts, 1984.

Haller, William. *The Elect Nation: The Meaning and Relevance of Foxe's Book of Martyrs*. New York: Harper & Row, 1963.

Hamon, Leo (ed.). *Un Siècle et demi d'histoire Protestante: Théodore de Bèze et les Protestant sujets du roi*. Paris: Edition de la Maison de la Science de L'Homme, 1989.

Hansen, Chadwick. *Witchcraft at Salem*. New York: George Braziller, 1969.

Haraszti, Zoltan. *The Enigma of the Bay Psalm Book*. Chicago: Chicago University Press, 1956.

Harbison, Craig. *Jan van Eyck: The Play of Realism*. London: Reaktion, 1991.

   "Some Artistic Anticipations of Theological Thought." *Art Quarterly* n.s. 2 (1979), pp. 67–89.

Harbison, Craig (ed.). *Symbols in Transformation: Iconographic Themes at the Time of the Reformation: An Exhibition in Memory of Erwin Panofsky*. The Art Museum of Princeton University, 1969.

Hargrave, Catherine Perry. "The Playing Cards of Puritan New England." *Old Time New England* 18 (1928), pp. 167–81.

Harrison, Peter. *The Bible, Protestantism and the Rise of Natural Science*. Cambridge University Press, 1998.

Hatch, Nathan O. and Stout, Harry S. (eds.). *Jonathan Edwards and the American Experience*. New York: Oxford University Press, 1988.

Heimert, Alan. *Religion and the American Mind from the Great Awakening to the Revolution*. Cambridge University Press, 1966.

Heimert, Alan and Miller, Perry (eds.). *The Great Awakening: Documents Illustrating the Crisis and Its Consequences*. Indianapolis: Bobs-Merrill, 1967.

Hill, Christopher. *The English Bible and the Seventeenth Century Revolution*. London: Allen Lane/Penguin, 1993.
   Society and Puritanism in Pre-revolutionary England. London: Secker & Warburg, 1964.

Holifield, Elmer. "The Renewal of Sacramental Piety in Colonial New England." *William and Mary Quarterly* 29 (1972), pp. 33–48.

Hooykaas, R. *Humanisme, science et réforme: Pierre de la Ramée*. Leyden: E. J. Brill, 1958.

Huizinga, Johan. *The Waning of the Middle Ages: A Study of the Forms of Life, Thought and Art in France and the Netherlands in the Fourteenth and Fifteenth Centuries*. London: Edward Arnold, 1927 [1924].

Hunter, G. K. "Shakespeare and the Church." In John M. Mucciolo (ed.). *Shakespeare's Universe: Renaissance Ideas and Conventions: Essays in Honor of W. R. Elton*. Aldershot, England: Scolar Press, 1996.

Hyma, Albert. *The Christian Renaissance: A History of the "Devotio Moderna."* 2nd edn. Hamden, Conn.: Archon Books, 1965,

Ingram, Martin. *Church Courts, Sex and Marriage in England, 1570–1640*. Cambridge University Press, 1987.

Keeble, N. H. *Richard Baxter: Puritan Man of Letters*. Oxford: Clarendon Press, 1982.

Kibbey, Ann. *The Interpretation of Material Shapes in Puritanism*. Cambridge University Press, 1986.

Kieckhefer, Richard. "Major Currents in Late Medieval Devotion." In Jill Raitt (ed.). *Christian Spirituality: High Middle Ages and Reformation*. New York: Crossroads, 1987.

King, John N. *English Reformation Literature: The Tudor Origins of the Protestant Tradition*. Princeton University Press, 1982.

Knight, Janice. *Orthodoxies in Massachusetts: Rereading American Puritanism*. Cambridge, Mass.: Harvard University Press, 1994.

Kuyper, Abraham. *Lectures on Calvinism*. Grand Rapids, Mich.: Eerdmans, 1931 [1898].

Lambert, Frank. *Inventing the "Great Awakening."* Princeton University Press, 1999.

Landau, David and Parshall, Peter. *The Renaissance Print: 1470–1550*. New Haven: Yale University Press, 1994.

Lee, Sang Hyun. *The Philosophical Theology of Jonathan Edwards*. Princeton University Press, 1988.

Lesnick, Laniel. "Civic Preaching in the Early Renaissance." In Timothy Verdon and John Henderson (eds.). *Christianity and the Renaissance: Image and Religious Imagination in the Quattrocento*. Syracuse University Press, 1990.

Lewalski, Barbara. *Protestant Poetics and the Seventeenth Century Religious Lyric*. Princeton University Press, 1979.

Lewis, Gillian. "Calvinism and Geneva: 1541–1608, in the Time of Calvin and of Beza." In Menna Prestwich (ed.). *International Calvinism: 1541–1715.* Oxford: Clarendon, 1985.

Lovejoy, Arthur. *The Great Chain of Being.* Cambridge, Mass.: Harvard University Press, 1936.

Lowance, Mason I. *The Language of Canaan: Metaphor and Symbol in New England from the Puritans to Transcendentalists.* Cambridge, Mass.: Harvard University Press, 1980.

Luce, A. A. *The Life of George Berkeley Bishop of Cloyne.* New York: Thomas Nelson & Sons, 1949.

Ludwig, Allan I. *Graven Images: New England Stonecarving and Its Symbols 1650–1815.* Middleton: Wesleyan University Press, 1966.

Luxon, Thomas H. "Calvin and Bunyan on Words and Image: Is there a Text in Interpreter's House?" *English Literary Renaissance* 18 (1988), pp. 441–51.

McAdoo, H. R. *Protestant Poetics and the Seventeenth Century Religious Lyric.* Princeton University Press, 1979.

McClymond, Michael M. "Spiritual Perception in Jonathan Edwards." *Journal of Religion* 77 (1997).

MacCulloch, Diarmaid. *Thomas Cranmer: A Life.* New Haven: Yale University Press, 1996.

MacGregor, Neil, with Langmuir, Erika. *Seeing Salvation: Images of Christ in Art.* New Haven: Yale University Press, 2000.

McGuire, Diane Kostal. *Gardens of America: Three Centuries of Design.* Charlottesville, Va.: Thomasson-Grant, 1989.

McKim, Donald K. *Ramism in William Perkins' Theology.* New York: Peter Lang, 1987.

McNeill, John. *The History and Character of Calvinism.* Rev. edn. Oxford University Press, 1967.

Mâle, Emile. *L'Art religieux du XIIIe siècle en France: étude sur l'iconographie du Moyen Age et sur ses sources d'inspiration.* Paris, Librairie Armand Colin, 1925. Revised version translated as *The Gothic Image: Religious Art in the Thirteenth Century.* London: Collins, 1961.

Marsden, George. "Perry Miller's Rehabilitation of the Puritans: A Critique." *Church History* 39 (1970), pp. 91–105.

Marsden, Peter V. "Religious Americans and the Arts in the 1990s." In Alberta Arthurs and Glenn Wallech (eds.). *Crossroads: Art and Religion in American Life.* New York: The New Press, 2001.

Matheson, Peter. *The Imaginative World of the Reformation.* Minneapolis: Fortress Press, 2001.

Matthews, Thomas. *The Clash of the Gods: A Reinterpretation of Early Christian Art.* Princeton University Press, 1993.

Mazorati, Gerald. "Plate it as it Lies" (interview with Julian Schnabel). *Art News* 85/4 (April 1985), pp. 63–9.

Michalski, Sergiusz. *The Reformation and the Visual Arts: The Protestant Image Question in Western and Eastern Europe.* New York/London: Routledge, 1993.

Miles, Margaret. *Image as Insight: Visual Understanding in Western Christianity and Secular Culture*. Boston, Mass.: Beacon, 1985.

Miller, Lillian B. "The Puritan Portrait: Its Function in Old and New England." In David D. Hall and David Grayson Allen (eds.). *Seventeenth Century New England*. Boston: Colonial Society of Massachusetts, 1984.

Miller, Perry. *The New England Mind: The Seventeenth Century, and Orthodoxy in Massachusetts, 1630–1650*. Gloucester, Mass.: Peter Smith, 1965 [1933].

  Orthodoxy in Massachusetts, 1630–1650. Gloucester, Mass.: Peter Smith, 1965 [1933].

Mitchell, W. J. T. *Iconology: Image, Text, Ideology*. University of Chicago Press, 1986.

Moeller, Pamela Ann. *Calvin's Doxology: Worship in the 1559 Institutes with a view to Contemporary Worship Renewal*. Allison Park, Penn.: Pickwick Publications, 1997.

Monter, E. William. *Calvin's Geneva*. New York: John Wiley & Sons, 1967.

Mooz, R. Peter. "Robert Feke: The Philadelphia Story." In Ian Quimby (ed.). *American Painting to 1776: A Reappraisal*. Charlottesburg: University of Virginia, 1971.

Moxey, Keith. *Peasants, Warriors and Wives: Popular Imagery in the Reformation*. Chicago University Press, 1989.

Muller, Richard. "In the Light of Orthodoxy: The 'Method and Disposition' of Calvin's Institution from the Perspective of Calvin's Late Sixteenth Century Editors." *Sixteenth Century Journal* 28/4 (1997), pp. 1204–17.

  The Unaccommodated Calvin: Studies in the Foundation of a Theological Tradition. New York: Oxford University Press, 2000.

Murdock, Kenneth B. *Literature and Theology in Colonial New England*. Cambridge, Mass.: Harvard University Press, 1949.

Naef, Henri. *Les Origines de la réforme à Genéve*. Geneva: Julien, 1936.

O'Connell, Michael. "The Idolatrous Eye." *English Literary History* 52 (1985), pp. 279–307.

O'Daly, Gerard. *Augustine's Philosophy of Mind*. Berkeley: University of California Press, 1987.

Ong, Walter. *Orality and Literacy: The Technologizing of the Word*. London: Methuen, 1982.

  Peter Ramus, Method and the Decay of Dialogue: From the Art of Discourse to the Art of Reason. Cambridge, Mass.: Harvard University Press, 1958.

Ozment, Steven. *The Age of Reform 1250–1550: An Intellectual and Religious History of Late Medieval and Reformation Europe*. New Haven: Yale University Press, 1980.

  The Reformation in the Cities. New Haven: Yale University Press, 1975.

Paglia, Camille and Postman, Neil. "She Wants her TV! He Wants his Book!" A Conversation between Camille Paglia and Neil Postman. *Harpers Magazine* 285 (May 1991), pp. 44–55.

Panofsky, Erwin. "Comments on Art and the Reformation." In Craig Harbison (ed.). *Symbols in Transformation: Iconographic Themes at the Time of the Reformation: An Exhibition of Prints.* The Art Musuem of Princeton University, 1969.

Early Netherlandish Art. Vol. 1. New York: Harper & Row, 1971.

Parker, T. H. L. *The Doctrine of the Knowledge of God: A Study in Calvin's Theology.* Grand Rapids, Mich.: Eerdmans, 1959 [1952].

Pauw, Amy Plantinga. *The Supreme Harmony of All: The Trinitarian Theology of Jonathan Edwards.* Grand Rapids, Mich.: Eerdmans, 2002.

Phillips, John. *The Reformation of Images: 1535–1660.* Berkeley: University of California Press, 1975.

Pitkin, Barbara. *What Pure Eyes Could See: Calvin's Doctrine of Faith in its Exegetical Context.* Oxford University Press, 1999.

Porter, Noah. *The New England Meeting House.* (Speech delivered 1882.) Connecticut Tercentenary Committee Publications 18. New Haven: Yale University Press, 1933.

Prestwich, Menna (ed.). *International Calvinism: 1541–1715.* Oxford: Clarendon, 1985.

Quimby, Ian M. G. (ed.). *American Painting to 1776: A Reappraisal.* Charlottesburg: University of Virginia, 1971.

Raitt, Jill (ed.). *Christian Spirituality: High Middle Ages and Reformation.* New York: Crossroads, 1987.

Randall (Coats), Catherine. *Building Codes: The Aesthetics of Calvinism in Early Modern Europe.* Philadelphia: University of Pennsylvania, 1999.

"Structuring Protestant Scriptural Space in Sixteenth Century Catholic France." *Sixteenth Century Journal* 25/2 (1994), pp. 341–53.

Rees, A. L. and Borzello, Frances. *The New Art History.* London: Camden Press, 1986.

Reid, W. Stanford. "The Battle Hymns of the Lord: Calvinist Psalmody of the Sixteenth Century." *Sixteenth Century Essays and Studies* 2 (1971), pp. 38–53.

Reiss, Jonathan. *The Renaissance Anti-Christ.* Princeton University Press, 1995.

Reynolds, Graham. *British Portrait Minaitures.* Cambridge University Press, 1988.

Richardson, Robert D., Jr. "The Puritan Poetry of Anne Bradstreet." In Sacvan Bercovitch (ed.). *The American Puritan Imagination: Essays in Revaluation.* Cambridge University Press, 1974.

Ringbom, Sixten. *Icon to Narrative: The Rise of the Dramatic Close-up in Fifteenth Century Devotional Painting.* Acta Academiae Aboensis, Series A 31/1. Abo, Finland: Abo Academi, 1965.

Roe, Albert S. and Trent, Robert F. "Robert Sanderson and the Founding of the Boston's Silversmith's Trade." In Jonathan L. Fairbanks and Robert F. Trent (eds.). *New England Begins: The Seventeenth Century,* vol. iii. Boston, Mass.: Museum of Fine Arts, 1982.

Rookmaaker, Hans R. *Modern Art and the Death of a Culture.* Downers Grove, Ill.: InterVarsity Press, 1970.

Rosenmeier, Jesper. "To Keep in Memory: The Poetry of Edward Johnson." In Peter White (ed.). *Puritan Poets and Poetics: Seventeenth Century American*

Poetry in Theory and Practice. University Park, Penn.: Penn State University, 1985.

Rosenthal, Bernard. *Salem Story: Reading the Witch Trial of 1692*. Cambridge University Press, 1993.

Rowlands, Alison. "The Conditions of Life for the Masses." In Euan Cameron (ed.). *Early Modern Europe: An Oxford History*. Oxford University Press, 1999.

Ruben, Miri. *Corpus Christi: The Eucharist in Late Medieval Culture*. Cambridge University Press, 1991.

St. George, Robert Blair. "Decorative Painters and House Painting at Massachusetts Bay, 1630–1725." In Ian Quimby (ed.). *American Painting to 1776: A Reappraisal*. Charlottesburg: University of Virginia, 1971.

"'Set Thine House in Order': The Domestication of the Yeomanry in Seventeenth Century New England." In Jonathan L. Fairbanks and Robert F. Trent (eds.). *New England Begins: The Seventeenth Century*, vol. II. Boston, Mass.: Museum of Fine Arts, 1982.

Santayana, George. *The Sense of Beauty*. Ed. William G. Hozberger and Herman J. Saatkamp, Jr. Cambridge, Mass.: MIT Press, 1988 [1896].

Saunders, Richard Henry, III. "John Smibert: Anglo-American Portrait Painter." Ph.D Dissertation, Yale University, 1979.

Saunders, Richard H. and Miles, Ellen G. *American Colonial Portraits: 1700–1776*. Washington, DC: Smithsonian Institution, 1987.

Schama, Simon. *Rembrandt's Eyes*. New York: Knopf, 1999.

Scheick, William J. "Anonymity and Art in *The Life and Death of that Reverend man of God Richard Mather*." *American Literature* 42 (1971), pp. 457–67.

"The Jawbone Schema of Edward Taylor's God's Determinations." In Emory Elliott (ed.). *Puritan Influences in American Literature*. Urbana: University of Illinois, 1979.

Schmidt, Leigh E. *Holy Fairs: Scottish Communions and American Revivals in the Early Modern Period*. Princeton University Press, 1989.

Schreiner, Susan. *The Theatre of his Glory: Nature and the Natural Order in the Thought of John Calvin*. Grand Rapids, Mich.: Baker, 1991.

Schwartz, Gary. *Rembrandt: His Life, His Paintings*. New York: Viking, 1985.

Schwartz, Gary and Bok, Marten Jan. *Pieter Saenredam: The Painter and his Time*. New York: Abbeville, 1989.

Scribner, Robert W. *For the Sake of the Simple Folk: Popular Propaganda for the German Reformation*. Cambridge University Press, 1981.

Shupbach, William. *The Paradox of Rembrandt's Anatomy [Lesson] of Dr. Tulp*. Medical History Supplement 2. London: Wellcome Instiude for the History of Medicine, 1982.

Smith, Lacey Baldwin, "'Christ What a Fright!': The Tudor Portrait as Icon." *Journal of Interdisciplinary Studies* 4/1 (Summer 1973), pp. 119–27.

Spinks, Bryan. *Two Faces of Elizabethan Anglican Theology: Sacraments and Salvation in the Thought of William Perkins and Richard Hooker.* Lanham, Md. and London: Scarecrow Press, 1999.

Sprunger, Keith. *The Learned Doctor William Ames: Dutch Backgrounds of English and American Puritanism.* Urbana: University of Illinois, 1972.

Stannard, David E. *The Puritan Way of Death: A Study of Religion, Culture and Social Change.* Oxford University Press, 1977.

Stein, Roger B. "Thomas Smith's Self-Portrait: Image/Text as Artifact." *Art Journal* 44 (1984), pp. 317–27.

Steinmetz, David. *Calvin in Context.* Oxford University Press, 1995.

Stephens, Mitchell. *The Rise of the Image and the Decline of the Word.* Oxford University Press, 1998.

Stephens, W. P. *The Theology of Huldrych Zwingli.* Oxford: Clarendon Press, 1986.

Stout, Harry S. *The New England Soul: Preaching and Religious Culture in Colonial New England.* Oxford University Press, 1986.

Strachan, James. *Early Bible Illustrations: A Short Study Based on some Fifteenth and Early Sixteenth Century Printed Texts.* Cambridge University Press, 1957.

Strong, Roy. *The English Icon: Elizabethan and Jacobean Portraiture.* New York: Pantheon, 1969.

Tawney, R. H. *Religion and the Rise of Capitalism.* New York: Harcourt, Brace & Company, 1962 [1959].

Taylor, Charles. *Sources of the Self: The Making of the Modern Identity.* Cambridge, Mass.: Harvard University Press, 1989.

Trent, Robert F. "The Concept of Mannerism." In Jonathan L. Fairbanks and Robert F. Trent (eds.). *New England Begins: The Seventeenth Century*, vol. III. Boston, Mass.: Museum of Fine Arts, 1982.

   "New England Joinery and Turning before 1700." In Jonathan L. Fairbanks and Robert F. Trent (eds.). *New England Begins: The Seventeenth Century*, vol. III. Boston Mass.: Museum of Fine Arts, 1982.

Tugwell, Simon. "The Spirituality of the Dominicans." In Jill Raitt (ed.). *Christian Spirituality: High Middle Ages and Reformation.* New York: Crossroads, 1987.

Tümpel, Christian. "Religious History Painting." In Albert Blankert *et al. God's Saints and Heroes: Dutch Painting in the Age of Rembrandt.* Washington, DC: National Gallery of Art, 1980.

Turner, Victor. "Are there Universals of Performance in Myth, Ritual and Drama?" In Richard Schechner and Willa Appel (eds.). *By Means of Performance: Intercultural Studies of Theatre and Ritual.* Cambridge University Press, 1990.

Ugolnik, Anthony. "The Libri Carolini: Antecedents of Reformation Iconoclasms." In Clifford Davidson and Ann Nichols (eds.). *Iconoclasm vs. Art and Drama.* Early Drama and Music Series. Kalamazoo: Western Michigan University Press, 1989.

Ultee, Maarin. "Review Article: The Riches of the Dutch Seventeenth Century." *Seventeenth Century Studies* 3 (1988), pp. 223–42.

Veith, Gene. *Painters of Faith: The Spiritual Landscape in Nineteenth Century America*. Washington, DC: Regnery, 2001.

Venchez, André. "The Church and the Laity." In *The New Cambridge Medieval History*. Cambridge University Press, 1999.

Verdon, Timothy and Henderson, John (eds.). *Christianity and the Renaissance: Image and Religious Imagination in the Quattrocento*. Syracuse University Press, 1990.

Vlach, John Michael. *Plain Painters: Making Sense of American Folk Art*. Washington, DC: Smithsonian Institution Press, 1988.

Volf, Miroslav. *After our Likeness: The Church as the Image of the Trinity*. Grand Rapids, Mich.: Eerdmans, 1998.

Waddington, Raymond. "Visual Rhetoric: Chapman and the Extended Poem." *English Literary Renaissance* 13/1 (1983), pp. 36–57.

Wainwright, William. *Reason and the Heart: A Prolegomenon to a Critique of Passional Reason*. Ithaca, N.Y.: Cornell University Press, 1995.

Walford, John. *Ruisdael and the Perception of Landscape*. New Haven: Yale University Press, 1991.

Walzer, Michael. *The Revolution of the Saints: A Study of the Origin of Radical Politics*. Cambridge, Mass.: Harvard University Press, 1965.

Wandel, Lee Palmer. "Envisioning God: Image and Liturgy in Reformation Zurich." *Sixteenth Century Journal* 24/1 (1993), pp. 21–40.

   Voracious Idols and Violent Hands: Iconoclasm in Reformation Zurich, Strasbourg, and Basel. Cambridge University Press, 1995.

Warner, Malcolm (ed.). *Great British Paintings from American Collections: Holbein to Hockney*. Catalogue of the Exhibit at the Yale Center of British Art and the Huntington Library. New Haven: Yale University Press, 2001.

Warnock, Mary. *Imagination*. Berkeley: University of California Press, 1976.

Watson, Philip. *Let God be God: An Interpretation of the Theology of Martin Luther*. Philadelphia: Fortress, 1947.

Watt, Tessa. *Cheap Print and Popular Piety: 1550–1640*. Cambridge University Press, 1991.

Weber, Max. *The Protestant Ethic and the Spirit of Capitalism*. Trans. Stephen Kalberg. Hardcover edn. London: Fitzroy Dearborn, 2001 [1905].

Webster, Charles. *The Great Instauration: Science, Medicine and Reform: 1626–1660*. New York: Holmes & Meier, 1975.

Wells-Cole, Anthony. *Art and Decoration in Elizabethan and Jacobean England: The Influence of Continental Prints, 1558–1625*. New Haven: Yale University Press, 1997.

Wencelius, Léon. *L'Esthétique de Calvin*. Paris: Société d'Edition "Les Belles Lettres", n.d. [1937].

Wendel, François. *Calvin: The Origins and Development of his Religious Thought*. Trans. Philip Mairet. London: Collins, 1963 [1950].

Westermann, Mariët. *Rembrandt*. London: Phaidon Press, 2000.

White, Elizabeth Wade. *Anne Bradstreet: The Tenth Muse*. Oxford University Press, 1971.

Wieck, Roger S. *Painted Prayers: The Book of Hours in Medieval and Renaissance Art*. New York: George Brasiller and The Pierpoint Morgan Library, 1997.

Wiley, Basil. *The Seventeenth Century Background: Studies in the Thought of the Age in Relation to Poetry and Religion*. London: Chatto & Windus, 1949.

Willis-Watkins, David. *The Second Commandment and Church Reform: The Colloquy of St.Germaine-en-Laye of 1562*. Studies in Reformed Theology and History 2, no. 2. Princeton Theological Seminary, 1994.

Wilson, Derek, *Hans Holbein: Portrait of an Unknown Man*. London: Weidenfeld & Nicolson, 1996.

Wilson, Lisa. *Ye Heart of a Man: The Domestic Life of Men in Colonial New England*. New Haven: Yale University Press, 1999.

Wood, Joseph S. *The New England Village*. Baltimore, Md.: Johns Hopkins University Press, 1997.

Yates, Frances. *The Art of Memory*. University of Chicago Press, 1966.

Ziff, Larzer. *The Career of John Cotton: Puritanism and the American Experience*. Princeton University Press, 1962.

Index